RICHARD

JO

NEUHAUS

RICHARD JOHN NEUHAUS

A LIFE IN THE PUBLIC SQUARE

RANDY BOYAGODA

IMAGE
NEW YORK

Published in the United States by Image,
an imprint of the Crown Publishing Group,
a division of Random House LLC,
a Penguin Random House Company, New York.
www.crownpublishing.com

Library of Congress Cataloging-in-Publication Data
Boyagoda, Randy, 1976–
Richard John Neuhaus : a life in the public square /
Randy Boyagoda. –First Edition.
pages cm
Includes bibliographical references.
1. Neuhaus, Richard John. 2. Catholics–United States–
Biography. I. Title. BX4705.N426B69 2015
282.092–dc23
[B] 2014034028

ISBN 978-0-307-95396-4
eBook ISBN 978-0-307-95397-1

Printed in the United States of America

Jacket photograph: © *St. Petersburg Times*/ZUMAPRESS.com/Jonathan Wiggs

10 9 8 7 6 5 4 3 2 1

First Edition

For Anna, Mira, Olive, Ever, and Imogen,

my first and best things

"We have to see that the priest as *priest* is a public person, that he is a political person."

—Richard John Neuhaus, 1967

Contents

Preface

There was smoke and ash and great singing in the church that night in 1967. The pews were filled with left-wing radicals and their marijuana and cigarettes. They had come over from Manhattan to a broken-down corner of Brooklyn, along with some television cameras and reporters, for "A Service of Conscience and Hope," an event that yoked prayer and protest over the grave injustice of the U.S. war effort in Vietnam. During its signal moment, some two hundred young men solemnly walked to the altar bearing their draft cards, which they deposited in a bowl. This was their symbolic and efficacious means of refusing to join the American war machine: following the service, the cards would be sent on to the Justice Department. The young men walked forward amid much sixties-era atmospherics, but the church was far from silent. The long-haired people on the scored wooden benches were singing with everything they had, but this time, they were not running through one of their standard angry protest chants, or cooing the latest soft-melt folk paean to peace. They were singing "America the Beautiful," following the deep-voiced man of God presiding over the service, thirty-one-year-old Richard John Neuhaus.

He was the pastor at St. John the Evangelist, the thriving

Lutheran church hosting the event; he was also one of the founders of a leading antiwar group, Clergy and Laity Concerned About Vietnam, and a fast-rising intellectual and activist on the American Left. But this trajectory would never be finally or fully his trajectory. The song he wanted his fellow antiwar activists to sing at St. John the Evangelist indicated as much: as he would later recount, his suggestion was met with silence, even shock. Asking this particular gathering to sing that particular song was basically like asking Billy Graham and Bob Hope to sing Communist anthems at an Honor America rally. Neuhaus, however, was convinced prayer and protest could be joined to patriotism; in fact, at difficult and fraught times in American public life, they had to be, whether to rescue love of country from war-making scoundrels and other ugly conservatives, or to remind myopic pacifists and other sweet, dreamy liberals that they were citizens called by God and by history to love and help redeem their troubled nation, not hate it and abandon it to its hateful elements. And so this was why, as far as he was concerned, nothing less than "America the Beautiful" had to sound forth in the church while all the young men said no to what their country was doing in Vietnam. Pastor Neuhaus preached to the hazy protestors in the hazy pews that the song did not describe the United States as it was. He told them it described the United States they all hoped for, the nation they hoped would come into existence because of the very acts of conscientious objection that they were committing together in the church that night. Provocative, contrarian, challenging, persuasive—Neuhaus won them over. What came of it, as New York TV news audiences and newspaper readers learned the next day, and he would observe in one of his many books, "was the lustiest and most heartfelt rendition of 'America the Beautiful' I have ever heard."

Almost thirty years later, amid all the cheering and applause, it was everything Father Richard John Neuhaus could do to stop his admiring audience from belting out songs like "America the Beautiful." He was in Washington to speak at the annual "Road to Victory" convention in September 1994, two months before the midterm elections. The event was sponsored by the Christian Coalition, a political operation dedicated to securing conservative Christian voters for the Republican Party by persuading them to put their electoral trust in the GOP. The three thousand in attendance were certainly open to the proposition: as far as many conservative Christians in America were concerned, their beloved and God-blessed nation was now run by godless, decadent liberals and, unsurprisingly, going to hell. Public schools taught lefty nonsense and anti-American garbage in place of sound values and strong traditions; popular culture was a sex-encrusted cesspool; you could abort your unborn child and claim it as a constitutional right more easily than you could quote the Bible at a public meeting or put up a crèche at city hall. Something had to be done about all of this—namely, get the right kind of people elected to public office—and if you were a delegate at a Christian Coalition conference, the right kind of people were Republicans. The coming election, however, would not be easy; the attendees needed encouragement, even blessings, for their effort to turn out fellow churchgoers on Election Day. And who better to do it than the author of the national bestseller *The Naked Public Square: Religion and Democracy in America*? Who better than Father Richard John Neuhaus to praise and inspire the God- and GOP-loving crowd?

He did not deliver the goods they might have been expecting. Instead, he warned his audience, "We can confuse our Christian hope with political success"; furthermore, "there is a danger that we confuse our political policy judgments with the judgments of God." And the crowd went wild! It went wild to his dismay, as he would observe in one of his magazine columns. Here he was, challenging his listeners to recognize that the call of faith could not be collapsed into an election campaign, that the dictates of the Bible were far greater than any party platform, and yet they were not really listening to his words; they were merely enthusiastically responding to his presence. After all, this was the famously fearsome Father Neuhaus, culture warrior extraordinaire, neoconservative Catholic priest and editor in chief of *First Things* magazine, the heroic and hilarious blade-sharp scourge of silly and soft liberals inside the churches and most everywhere else. But as much as Neuhaus enjoyed the stab-and-spike vitalities of professional opinion-making—and indeed, he enjoyed these—carrying out his vocation as a priest was more important than burnishing his profile as a punchy public intellectual. That was why, that September 1994 day in Washington, he challenged his convention audience to put not their trust in princes, Republican or otherwise. Following his remarks, one of his listeners approached him, someone who had, in fact, heard what Neuhaus had said, and was upset by it. As Neuhaus recalled, the man was holding back tears as he confronted the very priest and commentator whose writings had inspired him to become involved, as a Christian, in political activity, the same priest and commentator who was now telling him to take great care as a Christian involved in politics.

Reflecting on the doubly confused experience of religion in American life that he witnessed and was part of—a convention hall full of Christian Republicans untroubled, indeed energized, by the seemingly mutual supports of their faith and their party affiliation, and one man so suddenly troubled that he wondered if anything could be done in politics as a Christian—Neuhaus wrote, "Christian political engagement is an endlessly difficult subject. Our Lord said to render to Caesar what is Caesar's and to God what is God's, but he did not accommodate us by spelling out the details. Over two thousand years, Christians have again and again thought they got the mix just right, only to have it blow up in their faces—and, not so incidentally, in the faces of others. We're always having to go back to the drawing board, which is to say, to first things. Even when, especially when, we are most intensely engaged in the battle, first things must be kept first in mind. It is not easy but it is imperative. It profits us nothing if we win all the political battles while losing our own souls."

Richard John Neuhaus' life and work attests to the endless difficulties, battles, and necessarily imperfect victories of Christian political engagement in modern American culture and politics, whether as a leading clergyman of the American Left in the 1960s and 1970s, or as the most prominent clergyman of the American Right from the 1980s through to his death, in 2009. If Neuhaus always understood himself, foremost, as a man of God, he was regarded by colleagues, collaborators, critics, friends, congregations, parishes, and the national media as a theologian, an intellectual, an activist, an ecumenist, a writer, an editor, a cultural commentator, a political pundit, a political candidate, a policy expert, a religious journalist, a religious leader, a spiritual director, a spiritual father, a teacher, a pastor, and a priest. This multiplicity corresponds to the array of efforts Neuhaus made, over decades, and in any number of contexts, to bring Judeo-Christian concepts of human dignity, worth, and purpose to bear on every dimension of American public life—meaning, the nation's leading sacred and secular institutions, its political, legislative, and judicial deliberations, its intellectual milieus and media landscape. For all that he attempted and accomplished, Neuhaus was admired and scorned, closely followed and intensely opposed, and never but taken seriously.

His efforts led to the founding and running of many coalitions, institutes, and magazines, and also to the writing and preaching of hundreds of thousands of words that variously turned on his core insights and governing beliefs about modern religious experience and about American public life itself: That the United States is an incorrigibly if confusedly religious nation. That democracy is the political system that best corresponds to man's God-given rights and responsibilities for himself and others. That politics is a function of culture, and culture is ultimately a function of religion. That the most important question about religion and politics is not whether religion has a role to play in politics and in broader public life, but instead, what that role ought to be. That the Catholic Church is the fullest substantiation of the church that Christ founded upon the earth before his death and resurrection, and therefore the church Neuhaus was called to join and to serve. That the Catholic Church is likewise the world's singularly indispensable source of moral authority, guidance, and wisdom, for the right ordering of global affairs and of late Western civilization. That every Christian is first and always a citizen of what Augustine called the heavenly and eternal City of God, and that this citizenship informs how he lives in this fallen, mortal world, the City of Man. That God is not indifferent to the American Experiment. That upon his death, Neuhaus expected to meet God as an American and expected he would be asked to give an account of how he had lived out, and lived up to, the prophet Isaiah's hope and promise, that "the word shall not return void."

Indeed, Neuhaus measured his life and work against this biblical dictum for the better part of his seventy-three years, from his Canadian boyhood through his schooling in Nebraska and Texas and St. Louis, and onward from there to his life as a Lutheran pastor in Brooklyn and a Catholic priest in New York. The results of his efforts, by earthly standards at least, are attested to by the religious conversions and vocational realizations he brought about through his personal friendships and public witness, and by the outsized figures of Christian example and cultural-historical influence to whom he was compared upon his death—John Henry Newman, G. K. Chesterton, C. S. Lewis, Reinhold Niebuhr, John Courtney Murray, Fulton Sheen, Orestes Brownson, Ralph Waldo Emerson, even Jonathan Edwards. And while a case could be made for any one of these comparisons, none finally captures fully what were Richard John Neuhaus' distinctive and often controversial contributions to the ongoing story of conflict and renewal in postwar American culture and politics, and likewise to the greater story of conflict and renewal in post-Reformation Western Christianity. What follows is an effort to establish and explore these contributions.

Late nights at his apartment on East 19th Street in lower Manhattan, after dinner and evening prayer, Neuhaus liked to sit and hold forth, his Roman collar loosed, an old plaid shirt keeping him warm, a Baccarat cigar in one hand and a glass of Old Weller bourbon in the other, his eyes twinkling and his mouth set to that lifelong wry grin. Bach would be playing on the stereo and his dog, whether Sammy or his successor, Sammy II, would be sleeping by the fireplace, and when Neuhaus was finally done with his authoritative statements on this and that and everything else that was right and wrong about America and Christianity; when he had stopped telling great old stories of his Canadian boyhood and his hell-raising days as a young man; when he had finished recounting his cherished times on the march with Martin Luther King and his meeting in the Oval Office with this president and dining in the papal apartment with that pope, Richard John Neuhaus would turn his attention to the very first of first things. He would tell his friends that all his life, he wanted to do something beautiful for God.

This is the story of all that he tried, all that he did.

Part I

FROM SMALL-TOWN CANADA TO CONCORDIA SEMINARY, 1936–1960

"He was two ax handles and a block of chewing tobacco ahead of us, eh?"

Donald Stressman, boyhood friend

CHAPTER ONE

A Pastor's Son, Born and Baptized on "the Canadian Frontier"

The pastor took bricks from the stove and wrapped them in newspaper. Through the sudden steam that clouded his wire-rimmed spectacles, he saw his daughter watching him. She was dressed in her Sunday best. She looked grateful. The hot bricks were for her, she knew, as were the bearskin rugs he would wrap around her legs for the journey ahead. Soon, father and daughter would exit the parsonage through the rear door into the snow-filled backyard where, this morning at least, there were no hungry, desperate men offering to split wood for a little food. Instead, there waited only the horse and cutter that Clemens Neuhaus rented on Sundays, in the winter months of his 1930s life and work as a Lutheran pastor leading two congregations in the Ottawa Valley. He used the cutter to trek up to a mission church that sat some ten miles northeast of St. John's Lutheran Church of Pembroke, Ontario, his main congregation. He'd answered a call and come here in 1933, then aged thirty-three, moving his young family from a congregation some two hundred miles farther to the north, in Sudbury. In either place, they were far from what once was home—Illinois in Clem's case, Arkansas for his wife, Ella. The Neuhaus family had been glad to leave the deep far north of Sudbury, where they had lived overtop a sugar factory that sat cheek-by-jowl beside the church that had been the young pastor's first major assignment after he'd married. His second assignment, to St. John's Pembroke as it was locally known, was to lead a congregation that was part of a lumber town located along the dark, wide Ottawa River. Like small towns across North America in the 1930s, Pembroke was struggling with the hardships of the Great Depression.[1]

Lutheran settlers from north Germany had first migrated to this verdant fold of central Canada in the middle of the nineteenth century. Strong in their faith but isolated, they were "spiritually-hungry," as one historian describes them, and were intermittently served through the latter half of the 1800s by a succession of missionary-pastors who ministered to their scattered small settlements by horseback. These men came first from Germany, and then from Lutheran seminaries in the United States that were connected to various synods, or ecclesial governing councils, the basic units of organization in Lutheranism. These were self-organized around a complicated set of geographic, ethnic, and doctrinal factors, often in opposition to one another. Over time, these Lutherans of the Ottawa Valley became identified and organized as part of the Canada Synod, which was served predominantly by pastors from the powerful and conservative Missouri Synod. Founded in 1847, it was to be a new "Zion on the Mississippi," according to its leading pastor, C. F. Walther, who vowed that this council would be a "true church," preaching and teaching in fidelity to the sixteenth-century founding statements of Lutheranism itself. Such a promise would have been appealing to Lutherans in the Ottawa Valley; throughout their early history, concerns and controversies over the perceived orthodoxy of various pastors—as determined by the strength and purity of their commitments to the Lutheran Confessions contained in the Book of Concord (1580), a series of declarations on belief and doctrine devised principally by Martin Luther and Philippe Melanchthon—were of a piece with the intensity of the people's faith.[2]

The Ottawa Valley Lutherans first practiced this faith in services that were held in a little log cabin owned by a cabinetmaker and in assorted private homes, until these places proved insufficient for the growing number of Lutherans living in and around the town of Pembroke—which, in addition to being ninety minutes from Canada's capital city, Ottawa, was itself a regional center of some significance owing to its robust lumber industry. By 1891, a strong enough community of believers had been established in the town that a Lutheran congregation was founded and a rudimentary church built. Forty years later, in 1933, after four pastors had come and gone through a time of great growth for the congregation, growth dramatized by the 1920 erection of a grand new church that could boast of the tallest steeple in town, Clemens Neuhaus took charge. He led them in a glorious celebration that first year, of the 450th anniversary of Martin Luther's birth, and went on to serve for almost three decades, longer than any pastor before him, while living next door with his wife, Ella, at 357 Miller Street, in a simple red brick eight-room pastorage where, on $81 a month, they raised their eight children.[3]

By mid-April, 1936, Ella was a month away from giving birth to the seventh of these children, a son who would be called Richard John thanks to a naming contest secretly handicapped by her husband. Not that she likely had much time to consider any naming possibilities herself. Ella was, as ever in those years, busy taking care of the children. In this latest case, while almost to term, she was already occupied with infant twin boys and with their rambunctious trio of older brothers. The best help Ella's nine-year-old daughter could afford her on a cold Sunday in April was to accompany Clem on his Sunday visit to the mission church and, in Ella's absence, fulfill the important duties of the pastor's wife: to ask after the new babies in the congregation; to console those who had lately lost loved ones; to commiserate about the weather and the tough times for the many out of work; to agree that the choir was once more both solemn and beautiful; and also to agree that the pastor's sermon had indeed been another good one, strong and sound, *echt* Missouri, *echt*

Lutheran. And so to offer this great help to her mother was why the little girl, who was named Mildred and called Mim, was waiting in the Neuhaus kitchen on this cold Sunday morning, watching as her father heated and wrapped up the bricks he would place beneath her feet for the cold journey ahead.

Ready to depart, Clem strode down the hall to bid Ella good-bye. As was her way whenever the day allowed for it, she was seated in the front parlor, reading to the children. Clem sternly commanded the older boys to mind their mother. He had reason to do so; as usual, Fred, Joe, and Clem Jr. weren't sitting still so much as readying for the latest round of horseplay once their father left. But he informed them he would hear word of their behavior once he returned home later that Sunday, when he would gather the family together after a roast chicken dinner—while Clem carved, he made the children laugh with a decidedly Lutheran kind of levity, calling the chicken's tail end "the Pope's nose"—for devotional readings, a hymn, and evening prayer. Turning away from the bigger boys, who knew their father readily backed up his words with a stick, and just before leaving the parlor, Clem looked in on his and Ella's youngest children, Tom and George, twin boys born the year before Richard John. They lay quiet in their bassinets. Clem showed then that rare tenderness and warm, wide smile that newborn life inspired in him. Recalling his sacred duties and practical plans to fulfill them, he put on his heavy coat and his massive fur hat, gathered up the hot bricks and his pastor's kit, and walked out the back door with Mim. They climbed into the cutter, Clem took up the reins, the horse stamped, and they set off in the bright cold weather. Before they were out of town, Clem began going over the different family names and particular family situations of the congregants whom Mim was responsible for knowing and asking after in place of her mother. They rode along a Sunday-quiet country road surrounded by banks of snow through which you could see, now and then, timeworn parts of simple wooden fences marking off farmers' steads. Great snowcapped evergreens and leaf-barren trees edged in frost surrounded them as they made their way to the waiting congregation.[4]

Almost forty years later, perhaps inspired more by his father's memories of these days circulating through the wintry heart of the Ottawa Valley than by his own small-town childhood, Richard John Neuhaus would evoke a boyhood spent on the "Canadian frontier" in one of his earliest books, *In Defense of People* (1971). This evocation was, as these usually would be for Neuhaus, less sentimental than pointed, less romantic than strategic. In conjuring up an image of the "Canadian frontier," Neuhaus compared roughing it in the wilds of 1930s rural Canada with rough living in 1960s New York City. He made this rather strange but autobiographical comparison to defend the dignity of life in New York from critics of its urban blight. This was an urban blight that, for Neuhaus, never obscured the wonders and promise of life in the city where he lived for almost fifty years, first as a Lutheran pastor and then as a Roman Catholic priest, a city that was, for him, after growing up in Pembroke and then living and studying and discerning and pursuing his vocation to God and man in small-town Nebraska, rural Texas, and St. Louis, nothing less than "the prolepsis of the New Jerusalem."[5]

But back in 1936, a month before Richard John Neuhaus was born, his father would not have been thinking about New York City—never mind imagining that any son of his would grow up to defend the place as all-but-heaven-on-earth in an array of books and magazines, no less become a Catholic priest, among the most prominent and influential in America! No, while riding along the cold, hard road to his mission church, his daughter bundled up beside him against the cold weather persisting past Easter and into springtime, Clem would have been thinking and, no doubt, also praying more immediately about the readings and the Gospel for that morning's service, and about the sermon he was to give thereafter. This was the second Sunday of Easter, and, with the fullness of life and faith that Clemens Neuhaus had received and created as a pastor and a family man, he may have been thinking and praying especially on the last line of the fifth chapter of the Acts of the Apostles: "And daily in the temple, and in every house, they ceased not to teach and preach Jesus Christ." This was a standard Lutheran Eastertime selection, and in describing the joyful efforts of Christ's earliest disciples, the line captures the very efforts that Clem had robustly taken up as his every day's work and his lifelong vocation, at church and home both.

This was work and a vocation that his son Richard would eventually take on and make his own. "I have often thought the life I have lived is in very large part his," Neuhaus wrote in a 1994 essay, puckishly and pointedly entitled "Like Father, Like Son, Almost." And through the many lines of continuity and also discontinuity that emerged and endured between Richard and Clemens, and between all that Richard sought to be and become and all that Clemens Neuhaus taught and embodied, there came a remarkable, controversial, and decisively Christian life in the American public square.[6]

This was a life informed significantly by Neuhaus' growing up as a pastor's son in a small town in which that Lutheran pastor commanded so much authority that he was called "Pope Neuhaus" out of respect, admiration, and not a little fear. Clemens didn't mind this; in fact, he once lent a book to one of his congregants with "C. Pope" inscribed on the inside cover. As a nickname, "Pope Neuhaus" was both theologically loaded and highly ironic when fitted to a Lutheran pastor emerging from a confession that had a decidedly anti-papal bent: *Lehre und Wehre,* the Missouri Synod's main theological journal, ran articles in the early twentieth century emphasizing that "everything truly Lutheran condemns the pope and everything papistic" while also demonizing the pope himself: "The 'old man' . . . looks as if a whole flock of devils had taken possession of him. He smiles so antagonistically, so repulsively, so diabolically." In light of this virulence, it's more ironic still, in retrospect, that a Lutheran pastor formed by such a strongly anti-Catholic Protestantism would raise a son who would become a Catholic priest so passionately and enthusiastically committed to Rome and the papacy, friends and foes alike would describe him as sometimes seeming "more Catholic than the pope." Clem's own papal moniker came from his seminary days in Springfield, Illinois, as Neuhaus himself noted elsewhere in that same 1994 essay, where he also admitted to being "endlessly fascinated by my parents' stories about 'the olden days,' meaning mainly the mid-1920s to the mid-1930s, the decade before my birth." To underscore this fascination, Neuhaus then quoted a wonder-tinged meditation from the early twentieth-century English writer Llewelyn Powys: "The years lived by our father before he begot us have upon them a wonder that cannot be easily matched. . . . In some dim way we share in those adventures of this mortal who not so long ago moved over the face of the earth like a god called to us out of the deep."[7]

It is no great surprise that Clemens Neuhaus inspired such outsized notions on the part of his children. More than six feet tall, he weighed well over two hundred pounds by the time his seventh child came around. His contemporaries and congregants alike remember his sizeable presence; one in-law describes him in nearmythic terms, recalling how he "could walk up to a stranger, grasp him by the belt, and twist him over his head with one arm." He made much of his size, himself. Many years after he had had to visit his mission church in a rented horse and cutter in the winter, and, in summer months, by a bicycle (which was displayed at the church for years thereafter as much to signal the congregation's humble history as it was to prove Clem Neuhaus' gravity-defiance), he drove a succession of small cars—a Baby Austin, then an Anglia, and eventually a Volkswagen Beetle. When he was asked by congregants and fellow pastors how a man of his size could get into such small cars, his grinning response was always "I don't get into it. I wear it." Not that he was always a grinning giant. Indeed, one of his Pembroke nieces recalls a Saturday morning confirmation class in the 1940s where another of the children "gave him attitude, and he bolted off the stage over a table and he had to weigh at least 230 pounds and he said 'Out! Out!'" Decades later, this same niece could still shudder and laugh and shake her head in wonder at the recollection: an angered Pastor Neuhaus moving at top speed was as terrifying to witness from up close as it was amazing, because of the velocity that this massive man could generate when he had to, and he had to, in this case, because he perceived a show of disrespect to his holy office and teaching.[8]

Clemens Neuhaus had been, at first, reluctant about a life in ministry. He was born in Steelville, Illinois, in 1900. His father, Fritz, was a contractor, and his mother, Clara, was a milliner. He enjoyed a comfortable upbringing. His family's deeper ancestry was made up of German immigrants who had settled in the Lutheran stronghold that developed across the midwestern states through the nineteenth century, and it included a Union soldier and also, if quietly at the time, a Jewish line. In fact, family lore has it that Clemens' Hanover-born grandmother, Maria, was initially denied a Christian burial because she was Jewish, even though her 1927 obituary reports that she "was a faithful member of the St. Mark's Lutheran Church, and died in firm faith in her Savior." By the same family lore, the initial denial of burial was reportedly overturned after her grieving husband threatened to burn down the church if he couldn't "await the last trumpet side by side" in the earth with his beloved wife, as one of their great-grandchildren describes the widower's demands in an informal family history.[9]

A man of less volatile bearing and dramatic religiosity than his grandfather, who was in fact more inclined to hunting, boxing, tennis, and baseball than ministry, Clem wasn't naturally drawn to religious life. But his parents desperately wanted him to become a pastor. He acquiesced, enrolling in a Lutheran seminary in Springfield, Illinois. This led to his spending the better part of his seminarian vicarage year, 1923–24, assigned to a Missouri Synod church in Crockett's Bluff, Arkansas. This town sits some eighty miles southeast of Little Rock by way of Stuttgart, which was founded in the late nineteenth century by a Lutheran minister and populated with

German immigrants. In time, some of them went farther along, to the little town set up on the banks of the White River that Clem Neuhaus reached in 1923. He spent that year living at the home of the local superintendent of schools, C. F. Prange, who had a free bedroom because his daughter Ella was away teaching every week. When she would come home for weekends, the seminarian-boarder slept elsewhere. But this petite and demure young woman was on Clem's mind throughout his vicarage year in Crockett's Bluff. As he morosely but dutifully reported in his diary, he proposed to her twice and was rebuffed both times.[10]

But Clem wasn't so easily discouraged. After leaving Arkansas to return for his final year of seminary in September 1925, he wrote her many letters—letters that went unanswered. Meanwhile, Ella had left Crockett's Bluff as well; she'd moved out to California to be with her sister, who was expecting a baby. While there, she worked part-time in the library at UCLA. Throughout Ella's year in California, letters kept coming from Clem, and then, more starkly, a one-line postcard: "Your man would appreciate letters at this address." This must have been a gamble: there was no clear evidence yet that he was, in fact, her man. Indeed, when her father died in April 1926, she didn't even write Clem with that news, though she knew how fond Clem had been of him. Instead, she took a train home for the funeral, only to be met at the station by Clemens Neuhaus. One of Ella's brothers had informed him. After the funeral, as Ella was preparing to return to California, Clem made his case in person. No sweet words alone would do; Ella was a practical-minded young woman: she insisted she wouldn't consider marrying him unless he accepted a call first.

Whether providentially or tactically or both, upon graduating from seminary that June, Clem accepted a call to a church in Russellville, Arkansas, a town north of Little Rock. Right away, he made plans to see Ella, inviting her to visit with him in a neutral location—the home of a pastor friend of his in the town of Waldenburg, which was near Stuttgart, where Ella was then living with a friend. (She hadn't gone back to California, after all.) Ella agreed to the visit, but didn't know what to expect. She packed a dress for the journey, just in case she ended up married. She did, faster than either she or even long-smitten Clem could have imagined. He met her at the station and said, "We have to get married because Frank and Crystal just got company and they don't have enough bedrooms." And so fifteen minutes later, Ella wed Clem in Frank and Crystal's garden. She didn't even change her dress.[11]

Their wedding portrait captures the make-do beginnings of their life together. Chambered in lush southern foliage, the background trees all but blocking out the dusk-hour light while plants and bushes encircle them, the young couple pose for the photographer. Clem, who weighed 185 pounds to Ella's 85 on their wedding day, towers beside her in a white dress shirt rolled up at the sleeves, dark trousers, and a black bow-tie that looks almost comically small against the broad expanse of his frame. He is excessively clean-shaven; the razor line extends into his side-parted brown hair well above his big ears, drawing that much more attention to their flappy, turned-out shape. He is not staring at the camera but instead down at Ella, while fidgeting with the leafy tail end of a shrub. Beside him, she looks very small, very slight. She is wearing a light-colored short-sleeved dress hemmed a few hand-lengths below her knees. Her shoes are flat and plain, ideal for a long journey, if not for a wedding. Indeed, but for a bit of frill around the collar of her dress, Ella is dressed simply. She looks directly into the camera. She wears her brown hair in a close-crop, as she always would. She's smiling, sort of. If Clem looks nervous but intent in their wedding portrait, Ella seems calmer but also enigmatic. For the rest of her life, whether when her children were arguing about how much longer Clem had to live before the cancer claimed him, or when her son Richard was scolding her for hanging up on the President of the United States while Richard was napping, or when a crowd of academic and religious worthies were laughing at a sweet sharp joke she'd just made at Richard's expense, Ella would often show the world an inscrutable face. She didn't say much beyond what needed to be said, and in the meantime, becoming in 1926 a pastor's wife and thereafter mother to six sons and two daughters, moving from Arkansas to northern Canada to less northern Canada as her husband's ministerial work developed and finally found the right fit at St. John's Pembroke, Ella just kept doing what needed to be done—what God and family life were calling her to be and do.

On May 14, 1936, she gave birth to a sixth son. Clem went to visit Ella and the new baby, who were lying in at a maternity home in town. He brought along Mim and two of his older boys, Fred and Joe. On the way, the children argued over what to name their new baby brother. Fred insisted he should be called Burton Arnold, in honor of a friend of his from the congregation whose claim to fame was his skill as an ice-skater—no small source of acclaim in small-town Canada. But Clem signaled to Mim that he wasn't much taken with that name. He preferred her suggestion instead. After looking in on Ella and meeting the new baby, they returned home. Gathering the children together in the kitchen, Clem instructed them to commit their picks to scraps of paper. He gave Fred a larger piece than the others, so he would know which one read "Burton Arnold." Clem placed all of these scraps in a bowl and asked Mim to pick the winning name. He took her hand and guided it right to the scrap that read "Richard John." Nineteen days later, Pastor Clemens Neuhaus baptized his new son, cleansing him of original sin and claiming him for God and His Church.

And even though this was the seventh baptism in nine years for the Neuhaus family, and even though the pastor father would have no doubt been officiating at the baptism of many other children in those days, Richard John's was especially memorable. He grew up hearing stories about it, and he would write about the event decades later, with his distinctive combination of wry wit and theological seriousness: "For many years I've been responding to evangelical friends who want to know when I was born again or, as it is commonly put, when I became a Christian," he wrote in a 2000 issue of his magazine *First Things.* "'I don't remember it at all,' I say, 'but I know precisely the time and place. It was at 357 Miller St., Pembroke, Ontario, on Sunday June 2, 1936 twelve [*sic*] days after birth I was born again in the sacrament of Holy Baptism." And even though it was sitting right next door, no baptismal font was involved in the administering of this sacrament. Instead, Richard John Neuhaus was "born again in the sacrament of Holy Baptism" in the family kitchen, over the sink. On police orders, the Neuhaus family wasn't allowed outside. The day and hour baby Richard John became a Christian, the rest of the Neuhaus kids were quarantined with the measles.[12]

CHAPTER TWO

Pembroke's Most Patriotic Pastor, and Its Youngest and Most Newsworthy

Richard John Neuhaus generated his first media coverage when he was about five years old. Decades before he began appearing on a regular basis in the *New York Times* and the *Wall Street Journal,* he made it into the *Pembroke Bulletin.* Fittingly, he made news by "playing church," according to his then most reliable congregant, his three-year-old baby sister, Johanna. While his older brothers were off playing ice hockey and also war—such were the times that the Neuhaus kids always had to play German soldiers battling the Irish-, French-, and Scottish-stock Allied boys from up and down Miller Street—little "Dickie" pretended he was a pastor. This was his favorite boyhood game, so much so that Clem and Ella had to set some ground rules. After a couple of embarrassing incidents, Dickie wasn't allowed to drag the rocker from the living room into the front hall and set it up before the stairs: this was part of the house's public space, and with all the people passing through to see Pastor Neuhaus every day, it wouldn't do for them to walk in and be greeted by his five-year-old son perched partway up the stairs, preaching from on high overtop the kid-rigged pulpit of a rocking chair's ribbed back.

If Dickie wanted to preach, and he could convince Johanna and her doll to listen, then he could do his best for God and Church in the kitchen, declaiming from inside one chair stacked upside down on top of another. Out of a greater concern for orthodoxy than for keeping up appearances around the pastorage, his parents also forbade him from performing baptisms or giving out Communion in play. This instilled a sense of the seriousness and solemnity of the sacraments in Neuhaus from the earliest possible age. But Clem and Ella could also see that little Dickie had enthusiastic and harmless interests in ministry. They told him weddings and funerals were fine. And so he married off Johanna to his Catholic buddy Tommy Spooner, from across the street. He also performed many, many funerals—for stray bees from the apiary beside the pastorage, for barn mice, pet turtles, whatever fallen little things the neighborhood kids brought to him for a final benediction. There were times the Neuhaus family backyard was all but filled with little graves. In tending to the cows and chickens and vegetable patch that he maintained to make ends meet in those days, big Clem had to step carefully lest he crush one of the many child-made crosses.

As frequent as playing church was for Dickie Neuhaus, his boyhood ministry only became newsworthy one day in 1941 or so, when, before the assembled children of Miller Street, he solemnly performed the marriage of Buck and Minnie, two neighborhood dogs. Minnie wore a veil courtesy of Ella Neuhaus' curtains. That this occasion made it into the *Pembroke Bulletin* tells us two important things about the early world of Richard John Neuhaus. First, that its defining culture was charmingly small town: Pembroke was the kind of place where an innocent amusement like a dog wedding performed by the five-year-old son of a well-known local pastor was welcome. Second, that a story like this was especially welcome just then; it afforded a moment's respite from the grave and tragic news otherwise dominating newspaper pages in Pembroke and around the world in the early 1940s.[1]

World War II posed particular challenges for the predominantly ethnic German congregation of St. John's Pembroke. Twenty-five years earlier, during World War I, its pastor could only speak

German; before coming to Canada, he had fought under Bismarck in the Franco-Prussian War, and had a bullet wound scar in his leg to prove it. Aside from this martial portion of the pastor's biography, the local authorities were more concerned with assessing the congregation's loyalty to the British Empire—so much so that observers were stationed at the back of the church during services to monitor the proceedings for signs of sedition during the Great War. Taking over at St. John's in 1933, Clemens Neuhaus would have known about this recent history of suspicion; its implications would have only intensified as he followed the news of growing unrest and then conflict that was emerging in Europe throughout the 1930s. Partway through 1939, Germany had already invaded Czechoslovakia and was maneuvering to take Poland; Franco's fascist forces were victorious in the Spanish Civil War; Great Britain and its allies, colonies, and dominions—including Canada—were now facing an all but inevitable war. It was around then that Clem received a call from a congregation in North Dakota: here was a chance at once for the family to return to its beloved native country and to avoid the immediate prospect of living in a nation already at war. Clem refused the call. He applied for Canadian citizenship instead. If he was going to be a leader in this community, he wanted his congregants to know he was with them fully, not just on Sunday mornings.

This decision came to bear on the evening of September 3, 1939. Clem was upstairs in the parsonage, listening to the radio, which broadcast British Prime Minister Neville Chamberlain's declaration of war against Adolf Hitler and his militaristic and expansionist Germany: "His action shows convincingly that there is no chance of expecting that this man will ever give up his practice of using force to gain his will. He can only be stopped by force. . . . I know that you will all play your part with calmness and courage." Clem switched off the radio and went downstairs, immediately resolved to play his part. "Either German goes, or I go," he declared to Ella, and thereafter to members of the congregation—who, to his surprise, rather readily agreed to suspend all German-language services at the church for the duration of the war. This was a show of patriotism that was as symbolic as it was pragmatic. Now, in every sense of the word, the people of St. John's and the people of Pembroke would be able to understand exactly how loyal this congregation was to the Allied war effort.

Indeed, putting aside German for English was only Clem's first step. Setting a pattern that his son would follow vigorously, Clemens Neuhaus' deciding to get behind something meant he got out in front. He organized a Red Cross branch at St. John's and authorized a regular slate of special collections for the armed forces generally and, as such demands came forward, for more particular and tragic needs, like money to purchase an artificial leg for a congregant wounded while fighting overseas. Just as these new demands emerged, the pastor's salary was raised, and after twenty years, the church interior was refurbished and the congregation's debt substantially paid down. Coming at the far end of a hard decade, such unexpectedly strong finances were thanks largely to an again-thriving local economy. Pembroke owed much of this renewal to its proximity to the major military base in Petawawa that became a hub of activity during World War II and was also, for central Canada, the last major military base west of Halifax from whence troops would be shipped overseas to see action in the European theater. Petawawa also happened to be home to Clem's mission church, which was made up of a community of Missouri Synod Lutherans that was not yet large enough to have a dedicated pastor, and in the meantime were ministered to by the pastor of the nearest major congregation, in this case St. John's, Pembroke. The war effort intensified his already-strong bond with that community and created a new one involving the young men passing through for training and transit, and also their families and his own.[2]

Beginning in 1941, the Neuhaus family rented bedrooms to a succession of in-transit soldiers and their loved ones. Clem and Ella moved Mim and Johanna into one room and sent all the boys up into the attic. Husband and wife slept on a pullout couch in the dining room. The vacated bedrooms went to young military families, who each had a hot plate to make meals. The entire household—which by now included Dorothy Prange, a relative of Ella's who had come up from Texas to help out with the children—shared a single bathroom. From Clem's vantage point, this was all to the good: it meant small but steady income that, in spite of his recent raise, was certainly needed to help maintain a family of many children, most of them growing boys; the brood could go through sixteen quarts of milk a day. More importantly, welcoming soldiers into the family home was a clear and lived-out statement of just how complete a commitment Pastor Neuhaus had made to the war effort—preaching in English, sleeping in the dining room. Indeed, on May 14, 1941, while Ella hosted a birthday party for Dickie and his friends behind front-room windows that were covered in heavy blankets as part of a government-ordered rehearsal for an enemy bombing raid, Clem was working on a conference paper for the Ontario District Pastoral Conference of the Missouri Synod. In it, he argued forcefully against a government proposal to establish state-funded—and state-determined—religious education in public schools. Clem regarded this as an ill-conceived effort to encourage wartime patriotism among young people that could inadvertently lead to the establishment of a state religion (Erastianism) at the expense of religious freedom, the very freedom that had inspired generations of immigrants to leave Europe, with its sectarian conflicts and Erastian arrangements, for North America.

In more immediate terms, the proposal would fail in its main purpose because, Clem argued provocatively, its success depended on the efforts of clergymen who were questionable in their own patriotism, whether they were "rabid pacifists" running liberal churches or conservatives who "taught a shallow, supercilious, hysterical brand of patriotism [that swings] too far to the opposite extreme." Anticipating the rhetorical self-positioning that his son would rely on throughout his own career as a polemicist, Clem advocated for his own kind of patriotism as "true patriotism" by exposing the dangers of the extremist alternatives to his left and right both. Richard John Neuhaus himself acknowledged some of what father and son shared, many years later, in writing about Clem's wartime conference paper which, within the admittedly small orbit of the Missouri Synod's Ontario public policy circles, was widely circulated and admired at the time: "This son cannot read it without entertaining a question about how it is that arguments are transmitted from one generation to another. . . . Certainly Dad and I had not discussed these matters in any detail . . . and yet I discover more than fifty years later that—with a smidgen of difference here and there—his arguments are mine."[3]

This generous, contemplative cast of mind owed something to retrospection and historical distance. More immediately, as young Richard Neuhaus grew older, there would emerge far more than a smidgen of difference between himself and his father, and many, many arguments, owing, ironically, to their shared penchants for stubbornness and dispute. At dramatically different scales and scopes, they also both regarded journalism as part of their ministerial vocations. During World War II, Clem published *Odds and Ends,* a "newsy little paper" intended for members of the congregation who were fighting overseas. It offered easy humor about local Pembroke characters and endearing anecdotes about the misadventures of the Neuhaus kids, alongside spirit-lifting remarks about military promotions and prayers for speedy recoveries, not to mention then cornball, now off-color jokes—"The three gals from China who are not yet married: Tu-young-tu, Tu-dumb-tu, No-yen-tu." Clem intended these mimeographed sheets to serve as a lifeline of sorts for homesick soldiers whom he still regarded, despite their distance, as his pastoral responsibility. Affection and encouragements aside, this meant he wanted to make sure they kept vital their own Christian responsibilities, even in the midst of the fighting. In one issue, Clem swiftly transitioned from church news to easy nostalgia to doctrinal instruction by describing a Confirmation Day held at St. John's and then asking his overseas readers to recall the vows they themselves had made. He listed these and then made a sympathetic but demanding connection between a sacred event no doubt distant-seeming for his soldier audience and the events more immediately and dangerously before them:

> *Many of you had only a short time to prove your loyalty to your church and to take an active part in the work of that church, and then you were thrown out into a world which seemed new and different to you. The sound of our church-bells, inviting men to hear, pray, praise, give thanks and to partake of the Lord's Supper cannot reach many of you in the distant places where you now are. . . . [Nevertheless] it is our fervent hope that by God's Grace you have been kept loyal to that God with Whom you have been made acquainted, and it is our sincere prayer that God might keep His Holy Spirit in your hearts to help, guide and direct you so that you may be kept faithful to that promise in the future.*

The demands of war did not cancel the demands of faith for the fighting boys of St. John's Pembroke. Their pastor prayed for them, raised money for them, and tried to make them laugh, but he also maintained his—and God's—expectations of them, in clear and moving language. And if that weren't enough to recall the boys to the true source of their best selves, the front page of *Odds and Ends* featured a picture of St. John's itself, captioned with a command: "REMEMBER THIS PLACE!"[4]

Clem's robust support of the war against Nazi Germany put him years ahead of his Missouri Synod colleagues in the United States. As one Lutheran historian notes, "The Missouri Synod's official organ, the *Lutheran Witness,* withheld criticism of Hitler and the Nazis for several years. Between 1934 and 1939, the *Witness* carried articles that reflected [in one later critic's estimation] 'starry-eyed approval of the Nazi regime' and silence regarding the persecution of the Jews." And even after the United States entered the war, and other American Lutheran bodies, working together under the auspices of the National Lutheran Council, offered an array of ministerial and relief-focused support—some patriotically focused, others transcending conflict lines to succor the universal injured—Missouri held back. Symptomatically, this was less out of any lingering ethnic sympathies for the Hitler-led fatherland than out of theological and ecclesial concerns over the dread prospect of unionism: intentional collaboration with other churches despite differences in doctrine and worship, whether substantive or perceived, depending on the rigor and rigidity of the Missourian making the assessment.[5]

Clem Neuhaus was no supporter of unionism, to be sure, but during the fighting his patriotic church work was so quickly decided on and discerned, applied and locally focused, that the prospect limiting his U.S. coreligionists' commitments posed no challenge for him. Indeed, the Neuhaus family was so thoroughly committed to the Allied cause that even while the older boys gamely played German soldiers around the neighborhood, at home they reveled in war games waged from the more immediately felt home side. During the winter months of World War II, they liked to drip water onto the scalding hot surface of the family's wood-burning stove and then, over the resulting hiss and steamy smoke, boom out "Boooooombs over Germany! Boooooombs over Germany!", no doubt inspired by CBC Radio reports of the B-17 flying fortresses' many missions across the English Channel in the early 1940s. Small as he was then, Dickie was likely more of a witness than a participant in these homespun bombing runs, and he likely understood little of what was so consuming the world around him. Still, he couldn't help but notice its more exceptional and dramatic manifestations—the little star that appeared one day in the window of a neighboring home to signal a son lost in battle; that time the big blue sky suddenly turned white and fluttery with propaganda papers dropped from a military plane passing over Pembroke.[6]

Aside from the war's various influences on his family's daily life and his father's pastoral efforts, and beyond his admittedly peculiar if suggestive zest for playing church—"He was always presiding, he was always the minister," recalled Johanna decades later—Richard John Neuhaus' 1940s childhood, as part of a big family in a small town, was a combination of the idyllic and the straitened. A rhubarb patch grew down a hill near the house; in summer months, Ella would give each of the children a little jar of sugar, and they could dip rhubarb stalks in it and chew away the lazy afternoons. In the evenings, when Clem wasn't reading to the family from *Egermeier's Bible Stories,* Ella could be easily persuaded to sing dirges and recite folk poems for the younger children, like the centuries-old "Poor Babes in the Woods." At the end of each recitation, Dickie and Johanna would silently study each other's face to see if the other was crying too and then, in perfect concert, turn to their mother and excitedly plead, "Do it again! Do it again!" Decades later, recalling these days, an abashed Johanna could not account for why she and her brother so enjoyed these studied occasions for crying, beyond the focused attention it afforded them from Ella in an otherwise very busy household. Instead, a retrospective Johanna noted other experiences like this one, which involved not just shoebox coffins and laments for butterflies and honeybees. Whenever they could get away with it, on certain appointed days—identified by Clem's stern warning that there was to be no playing outside the house for the following hours—the two would sneak onto the porch, lie down, and press their eyes into the drain holes bored into its wooden planks. There and then, brimming with competitive tears inspired by complete strangers, brother and sister would follow the gathering and dispersal of mourners below at St. John's where their father was presiding over funerals.

Babes in the woods, bugs in the backyard, congregants in coffins—death seems to have been an early fascination for Richard John Neuhaus. He would, in fact, take a lifelong interest in its irreducible fact and great mystery. Early days aside, this interest was punctuated by a formative if also terrifying turn in the 1960s, as a young chaplain ministering to deathbed patients at a New York hospital full of Dantean suffering but also wisdom and dignity; and by his own near-death experience in 1993 because of a cancerous colon that was discovered almost too late. This was an experience that inspired the piercing formulations that open his 2002 book *As I Lay Dying:* "We are born to die. Not that death is the purpose of our being born, but we are born toward death, and in each of our lives the work of dying is already under way. . . . Death is the warp and woof of our existence in the ordinary, the quotidian, the way things are. It is the horizon against which we get up in the morning and go to bed at night, and the next morning we awake to find the horizon one day closer."[7] This reckoning with death was always, for Neuhaus, more invested with a higher realism than driven by any romantic morbidity: in dying upon the cross and rising to new life, Christ defeated death once and for all, for all. Though it would not dispel fears and worries about his own condition or that of others confronted with mortal situations, Neuhaus was firm in this conviction from his earliest remembering. Christ's crucifixion and resurrection meant death itself was the necessary disintegration that made possible the greater, the greatest possible, unity, which he voiced every night, his whole life, in the popular child's bedtime prayer inspired by a twelfth-century prayer: "Now I lay me down to sleep/I pray thee, Lord, my soul to keep/If I should die before I wake,/I pray thee, Lord, my soul to take." Little Dickie would have prayed these words alongside his older brothers as a child, before their going to sleep in the shared attic bedroom in the 1940s.[8]

They gained a particularly intense meaning for him one summer night in 1943. Earlier that day, he'd attended the congregation's annual mission festival, held up at Petawawa. A popular feature of the festival was the presence of a guest pastor, who was usually selected because of his oratorical power. No one at St. John's liked to say it outright at the time—indeed, almost forty years after he died, elderly congregants were still hesitant to admit this, such was their respect for Clemens Neuhaus—but preaching with passion and fire for the Gospel wasn't exactly his gift as a pastor. And so the congregation would happily trek up to the fields around the little white mission church and, sitting on logs, listen to a lively visitor who could hold the crowd for sermons that lasted an hour or longer and often focused on an evangelical dimension of the Church's mission in the world. In this particular instance, an American preacher paused partway through his preaching and for a full minute stared intently and silently at his wristwatch, then looked up and, as Neuhaus later recalled the experience, "tossed his head, threw out his arm, and pointing directly at me in the third row, announced 'In the last one minute, thirty-seven thousand lost souls have gone to eternal damnation without a saving knowledge of their Lord and Savior Jesus Christ!' "

This was, Neuhaus acknowledged in his meditation on Christ's last words from the cross, *Death on a Friday Afternoon,* "the first theological crisis of my life." He spent the rest of the sermon trying to calculate how many souls were headed to hell in the time they'd all been sitting there, while struggling at the same time to understand why no one else seemed to be as shocked and worried as he was: "Everybody else [was] taking the news so calmly. Mrs. Appler was straightening the bow in her daughter's hair, and Mr. Radke was actually smiling as he nodded approval at the preacher's words. Hadn't they heard what he said?"[9]

Neuhaus clearly had, and the preacher's words stayed within him thereafter, as Johanna recalls. Following the service, they retired to a little schoolhouse. Helping out as the pastor's children would be expected to, they cleared pine needles from the benches so others could sit more comfortably. Their chore done, Johanna wanted to go outside, but she couldn't, not yet. Her brother was still fixated on the preacher's words. How could they go off and play, how could anyone do anything, how could his father go fishing with the pastor after the festival, with so many thousands dying and falling into eternal perdition every single minute? "Well if that's true," he declared to his sister, "then why aren't we doing something about it?" Aged seven, there was only so much he could do, but the experience of souls at risk of being lost forever, and the Church's capacity, indeed mission, for preventing this stayed with him, as he wrote elsewhere in *Death on a Cross:* "Since then, I have come to understand the mission of the Church—and what we call the 'missions'—in a very different way, yet in a way not untouched by that electrifying sense of urgency that so gripped me on a Sunday afternoon in Petawawa."[10]

The following autumn, Dick encountered a different source of fear: the Catholic nuns he and Johanna had to visit whenever there were too many crops and maybe not enough cash around 357 Miller Street. Converting the church's garage into a makeshift little barn, Clem kept a cow (named Millie, to his eldest daughter Mildred's great horror) and chickens (teaching the children the birds and the bees by caponizing the birds in front of them). He sold the excess milk and eggs around the neighborhood by enlisting the older children as his delivery team and outfitting their bicycles with baskets and honey pails that brimmed with whatever the family couldn't use. He also maintained a thriving garden and converted Johanna's baby buggy into a mobile vegetable stand. He sent her and Dickie out in tandem. Clem was a shrewd man—he knew his market, and he knew just how charming a sight it would be to watch a little boy and girl push a baby buggy full of corn and tomatoes up your front walk, but he also knew charm wasn't enough for his customers: he made sure he had the best prices in town. And for the most part, the children were glad to be part of the operation. Describing the key factor of her brother's 1940s success as a vegetable hawker in Pembroke just as much as she could have been describing his later successes as an activist and public intellectual in New York and Washington and Rome, Johanna observes that "Richard was very good at knocking on everybody's door." Almost everybody, as it turns out: on Pembroke Street stood a great brick building set back from the street behind an imposing wrought-iron fence. Within lived the Sisters of Charity, a Catholic order founded in Montreal in the eighteenth century and commonly called the Grey Nuns, who had come to Pembroke in 1926 to teach and minister to the sick. A fast-talking salesman everywhere else, Dickie refused even to enter the Grey Nuns' gate. He always persuaded an unhappy Johanna to knock on the door, and when the invariably sweet sisters came out and beckoned for him to bring the vegetables closer, he refused again. Instead, they swooshed out to the street in their habits and bought some tomatoes and bid farewell to nervous Johanna and wary Dickie. And then, at last, the Lutheran pastor's youngest children escaped down Pembroke Street, having survived another close encounter with the Catholics.[11]

Indeed, in those days, and largely owing to their father's stated views rather than his habit of amiably hunting every deer season with a local monsignor, the Neuhaus children grew up presuming that Catholics were simply "terrible," in Johanna's recollection. It's not surprising, then, that they were nervous to approach a convent, even if—children being children—it's equally unsurprising that they didn't think much of religious differences in playing with the many, many Catholic kids of Polish, French, and Irish backgrounds who lived along Miller Street. Dickie spent a lot of time in particular with the Spooner family across the street—one of his most infamous childhood exploits happened on their front porch, when he helped persuade Johanna to swing off the side of the house with a rope tied around her neck as part of a "Tarzan and Jane" game, which resulted in her choking and blacking out until someone intervened before she choked to death. She had to wear a scarf around her neck for the summer to hide the rope burn. Near-lethal antics aside, Neuhaus' time with the Spooners had an unexpectedly formative effect on his faith life. In a 2002 essay titled "How I Became the Catholic I Was" and again in his 2006 book *Catholic Matters,* Neuhaus anchored his firm conviction that his was a lifelong receptivity, indeed inclination, toward Roman Catholicism in his early friendship with Tommy Spooner and his brothers (rather than in his dealings with the grim, tomato-eating Grey Nuns of Pembroke Street).

From the earliest age, Neuhaus wrote, he felt a greater sense of shared experience with the Spooner boys, who attended St. Columbkille's while he went to St. John's, because for Catholics and Lutherans both, "our being saved was something God did through

His Church; it was a given, a gift" manifested in the sacraments and liturgy, while salvation for their evangelical buddy Dougy Cahill depended "upon feelings or spiritual experience." Indeed, Neuhaus remembers being moved to more than just comparative identifications between Lutherans and Catholics as both "ecclesial Christians": "I am sure that I as a boy thought—not very seriously, certainly not obsessively—but I thought about being a Catholic. It seemed that, of all the good things we had, they had more. Catholicism was more." Could little Dickie Neuhaus really discern this much ecclesial longing as a boy? Or was this more of a predictable back-formation for an ardent Lutheran turned ardent Catholic, who, in this same article and elsewhere, declared, "I became a Catholic in order to become more fully what I was and who I was as a Lutheran." Leaving aside, for now, the historical-cultural contexts and ecclesiology and theology that formed the basis for this crucial and controversial claim, Richard John Neuhaus grew up in World War II–era small-town Canada the Lutheran son of a Lutheran pastor who loved playing at pastor. Sure, he almost hanged his sister, and once he stuffed her beloved doll full of cow manure, but otherwise he was a good and obedient little boy. Beyond conducting the occasional dog wedding, he didn't make much of an impression on others. This would soon change.[12]

CHAPTER THREE

An "Uneducable" Little Lutheran Professor Enlists in a Grand Cause

"Dumb brutes and irrational hogs": this was Martin Luther's 1529 assessment of the unformed Christians and, worse still, poorly formed Christians that he was then encountering in the villages surrounding Wittenberg. With his wife and six children, Luther was living in the former cloister of an order of Augustinian monks, on the campus of the University of Wittenberg, where he was teaching theology and developing some of the foundational documents of what soon became the fuller Protestant Reformation. Having fought against the elite figures in European religious and political life in preceding years, Luther now confronted a more quotidian situation: the sorry, widespread state of instruction in the faith among ordinary believers, which, in his assessment, owed mostly to the failings of local bishops and pastors and also parents in their respective offices as teachers of doctrine. Because of these failings, Luther contended, believers had gained a terrible freedom from Christian teachings, and, he added caustically, they "abuse it like experts." In other words, this was far from the renewed and reformed Christianity he had called for with his 1517 *Ninety-Five Theses,* nor was it what he had striven to make possible through years of volatile debates and clashes with Pope Leo X and his bishops and theologians in Rome and Saxony, or thanks to his 1521 excommunication, or his subsequent branding at the Diet of Worms as not just a heretic but (in the words of the papal nuncio who wrote the culminating edict against him) as a "'devil' who had 'assumed the likeness of a monk,' [who] had gathered his whole accursed doctrine into one 'stinking puddle'" and was committed to preaching "'insurrection, schism, war, death, robbery and incendiarism.'" Convicted as a satanic fugitive from sacred and secular justice under the combined power and jurisdictions of the pope and the Holy Roman emperor (Charles V himself presided over the Diet of Worms), Martin Luther was leading a life under constant threat of arrest, demonization, and even death in the 1520s—and all this had been tried and risked and accomplished and suffered to make possible the free-thinking, dumb, and irrational approach to the faith that he was noticing among the children and common folk of Wittenberg?[1]

Identifying what he saw as a great doctrinal need, Luther set about creating catechisms that could form Christians into the God-fearing, God-knowing, God-loving people they were called to be. The first book, initially called *The Shorter Catechism* and known thereafter as *Luther's Small Catechism,* was written for bishops, pastors, and parents charged with forming children and ordinary folk. Its preface laid out, in the pungent language earlier quoted, the immediate necessity of such a manual, while its main parts were simple, pedagogic commentaries and directives on the Ten Commandments, the Apostles' Creed, the Lord's Prayer, and the sacraments of baptism, confession, Communion, and daily prayers, to which were appended scripturally based definitions of the duties and responsibilities of all members of a society in their overlapping ecclesial, secular, and family situations. Indeed, one of Luther's primary themes throughout the document is the necessity of obedience for any good and holy Christian life, as manifested in one's relationships with God, with His "Christian Church upon the earth," with the Church's bishops, pastors, and preachers, and with civil authorities and also one's own parents. Rhetorically and practically, Luther imagines the work of formation as proceeding in familial terms; the instruction that prefaces every element of the catechism sets forth how it should be communicated: "As the head of the family should teach it in a simple way to his household."

For centuries, as Lutheranism has spread from Saxony around the world, to places as far-flung as Sri Lanka and the Ottawa Valley, Lutherans have learned the *Small Catechism* at home and in their churches, where it forms the basis of the multiyear classes children take in preparation for their confirmation at age fourteen. Naturally, Richard John Neuhaus also prepared for his confirmation this way and, with his siblings and friends from church, was taught by his father around the dinner table and in the parlor afterward every night and, more formally, once a week next door in the basement of St. John's. But years before he finished taking his father's Saturday morning catechism class, Neuhaus was teaching it himself. And to the kids gathered in the church basement, who were used to Pastor Neuhaus' dry if not droning methods—relieved on occasion by sudden great leaps across tables and, more happily, by ending class early and surprising everyone by taking the kids to watch one of their fellow catechumens play in a big hockey game—young Dick, aged ten in 1946, was a relief that Saturday morning he showed up in place of his father, who had been unexpectedly called out elsewhere.

Clem had asked his ten-year-old son to run the class instead of one of the older children who'd already taken it and been confirmed. He clearly had good reason for doing so. "He was impressive, he was a professor at that point," remembers Donny Stressman, a friend of Neuhaus' from his Pembroke days, who matter-of-factly rated his buddy turned fill-in teacher "three, four times better than Pastor Neuhaus." Given the gravity of catechetical formation, and Clem's own gravitas about all matters related to his ministry, it seems shocking that he'd allow a ten-year-old to teach such important matters of faith, no less to children two and three and four years older than he was, but obviously Clem Neuhaus could tell his church-playing son possessed an extraordinary intelligence that matched his extraordinary interest in ministry from an early age. Clem wasn't alone in discerning and drawing on this. Donny, for instance, wasn't surprised at all that the pastor sent his young son in his place; as this lifelong Pembroke resident later recalled, "He was two ax handles and a block of chewing tobacco ahead of us, eh?"[2]

But Clem and the Saturday morning catechism class aside, not everyone shared this assessment of Richard John Neuhaus as a boy. His very first teacher declared him "uneducable," and his parents pulled him out of school after this early, failed effort. A member of the congregation who was himself a teacher, away from work on sick leave, volunteered to teach young Dick the following year. Thereafter, Neuhaus returned to school and thrived, quickly skipping a grade and outpacing his twin brothers Tom and George, eighteen months ahead of him but in the same classes. Eventually, he won a province-wide medal for academic excellence. Thanks to a generous and timely helping of situational amnesia, his very first teacher approached him at the awards ceremony and declared, "Oh Dickie! I always knew you'd go far!" Neuhaus reveled in recalling this teacher's hypocritical praise for the rest of his life, which he occasionally appraised with a salty dismissal: "The bitch!" But he went there one too many times when he ran through the story at a *First Things* magazine board meeting in New York, in the early 1990s. Having no doubt heard it more than enough by that point, his longtime personal assistant Davida Goldman sighed in a perfect stage whisper, "Let it go, Richard, let it go."[3]

That he wouldn't, aside from reasons owing to the reliably amusing anecdote it afforded him, and the playful ribbing it encouraged from his colleagues and friends, is not surprising. Throughout his boyhood, Neuhaus' personal experiences were consistently exceptional, if not always positively so. Aside from his involvements at school and church, Neuhaus was often a boy set apart from others because he was more drawn to reading than roughhousing. Unsurprisingly, years later, neighbors could still recall his elevated prose and mature bearing in his discoursing with parents rather than just running off to play with their kids. And he dressed rather snappily as well—pictures of him in his boyhood and early adolescence have him wearing crisp white shirts and dressy trousers and polished brogues. He didn't look like a typical boy growing up in a 1940s Canadian lumber town. And he wasn't very good at acting like one, either. During winters, his older brothers brought him along to the pond hockey games they daily played on a stretch of river located down the hill from the Neuhaus end of Miller Street. They tried him at forward and defense, but he couldn't skate well enough to keep up with the other boys. In the time-honored solution to such problems, they appointed him goalie. They stuck him in front of a makeshift net marked out by snow-filled tin cans. He was hopeless in net, too. Finally, they made him referee, which may have suited him better, but it didn't work for the other boys. Finally, he was relegated to spectator status and had to watch his brothers rush along the ice, chasing the puck with their friends, while Johanna, his very own baby sister, played goalie because she was better than nothing, and better than Dickie too.[4]

Neuhaus' limited talents in these respects were well known and, with the needling cruelty that children can sometimes display to one another, exploited. Johanna recalls a summer day of races where someone came up with the great idea of making Dickie run against his little sister. This was quietly very mean—everyone knew Johanna was very fast, and certainly much faster than her big brother. Johanna hesitated, but Dick had to rise to the challenge—sure, he would race. Before a cheering, crowing crowd, they sprinted along Miller Street. He lost. Years later, Johanna sobbed in telling the story because of how badly she felt, embarrassing him like that. With more retrospective relief than enduring sadness, George and Tom, Neuhaus' twin older brothers, both recalled another time young Dick tried to prove something by rising to a challenge beyond his ken. In the late 1940s, Ella left Pembroke for Arkansas to spend the summer with her relatives, whom she hadn't seen in some time, though the more immediate motive seems to have been her desire for a much needed break from the daily intensities of family and church life at 357 Miller Street. In her absence, Clem was fully in charge of the kids just as he was fully in charge of St. John's. Naturally, he expected the older ones to look after the younger ones, let them tag along on outings and so on. This obligation turned near-tragic the day young Dick followed his older brothers down to the great Ottawa River, which in those days was lined with Pembroke's lumber mills. Logs would travel through the water, and the local boys liked to watch the lumbermen run the booms, straightening out the logs shuttling down the river.

Of course they couldn't just watch. Ignoring dire warnings from various elders, Pembroke boys ran the booms too, whenever they could get away with it. Dick only tried once, when he was about twelve. His brothers and their friends came upon a load of logs being shipped downstream to a lumberyard. There were hundreds of them, covering the glittering water all the way across to the deep green Quebec woods on the far side of the river. George and Tom and their friends dared one another to a race along the logs, and Dick decided he was going to beat them all. There would be no more jokes about lost races and hockey failures. He charged onto the wet, fast-moving logs and after three or four steps slipped, fell, and disappeared. The logs immediately closed around him. After almost too long, they heard splashing and sputtering gasps for air. Dick surfaced, and the older boys made their way across the rolling logs to reach him. He was hanging on with one hand and wiping the cold water from his thin pale face with the other. He looked up at them, six tough teenagers suddenly full of concern and relief. But he was fine. He was, in fact, triumphant. "Well, I showed you, didn't I!"[5]

Neuhaus enjoyed less complicated success elsewhere in his life during the last few years he would spend at home, while throughout the 1940s, his older siblings left Canada for the United States to attend Lutheran preparatory schools, enlist in the armed forces, and, in Mim's case, marry and settle in Seward, Nebraska (where, in turn, she would play host to her younger siblings while they attended school nearby, Dickie included). Winning academic medals in Pembroke wasn't enough for him. Attending the local high school, he became a noted prankster, organizing the kids in the class into various exploits like laughing wildly at his signal in an English class on the concept of comedy: he made a point of signaling that they laugh at the exact wrong times. When, eventually, the beleaguered teacher realized what was happening, and who was making it happen, she declared, "Neuhaus, you were the problem, overall." Actually, he regarded himself more as a solution to problems at Pembroke Collegiate. In another class, he interrupted the teacher in the middle of a lesson by telling her that she was getting it all wrong. Not knowing the kind of young man she was dealing with, she sarcastically invited him to teach the class if he was so certain she wasn't teaching it properly. So Neuhaus got up from his desk, walked to the front of the room, and began teaching the class. And after a few moments, the dumbfounded teacher actually sat down at an empty desk and listened along with everyone else.[6]

Neuhaus' public performances owe only in part to his wanting to prove himself in arenas where he was an assured and obvious champion; they owe more accurately to his insatiable intellectual interests and equally insatiable need to display and apply these, whether as authoritative dictates, or in relentless arguments, or more creatively and entrepreneurially, as when he founded his first periodical, at the age of nine, the *News of Miller Street.* Using a hectograph device to make copies, which involved rubbing sheets of paper against a gelatin imprint—or, more accurately, directing Johanna to do this while he supervised—he distributed the rag throughout the neighborhood. It was full of his musings, of local gossip that he picked up, and, more scandalously, included select excerpts from his big sister Mim's diary, which he'd found after she left home for Nebraska. Recalling this childhood venture into journalism many years later, he rated it "a really first-class neighborhood newspaper . . . for Pembroke, Ontario," and then acknowledged, with playful self-regard, "From early on . . . I assumed people would be, or should be, interested in what I had to say." Indeed, neighbors, catechists, students, and teachers alike were interested, but aside from assorted brainy, bratty exploits around town, the defining elements of his personality and relationships with others really took form at home—through reading and daydreaming, and through emulating and fighting with his father, who could easily appreciate and praise his other sons because of the premium he openly placed on athleticism and sporting success. This wasn't possible with Dickie.[7]

His formative reading and daydreaming mostly happened in the family attic, which he made his own by the late 1940s, with his brothers going off to America and no more military families to board in the second-floor bedrooms. To this day, you can read the words "To Dick Neuhaus's Abode," complete with an "→" written in black ink and spidery cursive on the wall of the landing leading up to the room where, while all the other children of Miller Street were playing outside, Dick read and played and dreamt large. He decorated the place with pictures cut from different magazines of the day. Ironically, for someone who became a zealous advocate for American democracy, the three images dominating the walls were large portraits of Queen Victoria, King George, and Queen Elizabeth I. Early monarchal affections aside, Neuhaus would remember this place, and those days, fondly, for the rest of his life. In a passage of Proustian intensity from early in *As I Lay Dying*, he evoked

> *the attic bedroom in Pembroke, Ontario . . . where the rain ricocheted off the tin roof, and I could see from the bed my empire of toy trains extending across the entire floor. Six engines, switches galore, and passenger cars with leather seats and little interior lights—the gift of an uncle who, he said, looted it from the castle of Hermann Göring during the occupation of Germany. That attic bedroom was the space of magic. . . . I have not forgotten it, and never will. That is where I read* Black Beauty *and* Ben Hur *and Captain Marvel comics without end. That is where I dreamed about going off to school, about doing important things in a world bigger than my attic could imagine.*[8]

Consuming boys' adventure books and butcher print comic books alone didn't inspire these ambitions. At twelve, in 1948, Neuhaus also read the spiritual reflections of O. P. Kretzmann, a prominent Lutheran pastor, intellectual, and academic who was then president of Valparaiso University in Indiana. This work helped inspire a willing, even ardent Neuhaus to discern his own vocation for life in religious and, more accurately, ecclesial terms, as he would later acknowledge, in quoting Kretzmann directly: "He wrote, as I now recall it, 'In this would my life be fulfilled, if by it I had lighted one candle at the shrine of Holy Mother Church.' A bit on the sentimental side one might now think," the grown-up Neuhaus allowed, "but then," in the rain-ricocheting solitude of his attic abode, "my heart burned within me. This was the great thing, to be enlisted in a grand cause, and the Church was that grand cause."

Clem Neuhaus helped this along by having Dick teach his confirmation class on occasion. And while he might not have seen it this way, he also helped this along by arguing with his son as he entered his teenage years. Family and friends alike recall a familiar image in the Neuhaus home in the late 1940s and early 1950s: Clem and Dick seated at the dining room table, long after a meal had finished, still in the midst of a heated argument. Dick didn't follow his older brothers' example here, either: they tended to avoid confrontation by agreeing right away when Clem laid down a command (like being late for a date so they could join the family in evening prayers), or they just left the room before something got started. Not Dick; he seemed to relish these chances to dispute his father on a point of doctrine or church practice. This seems to have been as much because he wanted to understand the logic informing the matter as because he wanted to prove to his father his excellence in an area of Clem's life certainly more important than sports. He also simply enjoyed a chance to argue for the sake of arguing, something that wasn't possible for him with his indifferent siblings, his less cerebral friends, or his cowed teachers. Bright and bold, he was growing restless and had energies to burn, and his father offered a natural, if naturally difficult, focus. A cousin and frequent lunchtime guest of the family in those days suggests why the arguments went on for so long: "One of them had to be right, and it usually had to be Uncle Clem, but Dick didn't tolerate that and so he'd come back and address it again," and again, and again. The son wasn't content to accept the simple, authoritative explanations that Clem was used to giving—"As the head of the family should teach it in a simple way to his household," instructed Luther in the *Small Catechism.* And the father wasn't used to someone resisting his arguments. Neither man, in other words, was used to anyone questioning him on his claims, except, of course, the other.

This tense dynamic between them persisted for years. Indeed, when Johanna came home to be married in 1961, Richard came as well, to officiate, traveling from his very first church assignment, a small Lutheran congregation in upstate New York. Afterward, when Johanna and her husband Jerry were ready to depart, they looked in on Clem and Richard. They were, as usual, in the dining room, arguing. Johanna and Jerry tried to interrupt them to say good-bye, but neither man paid the newlyweds any attention, so they shrugged and left. By the early 1960s, Clem and Richard likely would have been arguing about religion's place in American life, about the Christian Church and U.S. politics, about the Missouri Synod and Civil Rights, about whether blacks were the cursed sons of Ham or fellow Christians subject to a grave national injustice. Father and son, old pastor and young pastor, they were at odds, and they were both convinced they were on the right side of things, the Church's side, God's side of things. Richard might have argued, no doubt to no avail, that his father's ideas were outdated because he hadn't lived in America for more than thirty years, whereas Richard had been there for a decade of dramatic and ongoing events. These were events that, by then, he was engaging as a pastor, an intellectual, and also, to his father's greater discomfort, as an activist, a combination he pursued then and for the rest of his life that owed much to the significant vocational and intellectual maturity he'd achieved since leaving his small-town Canadian childhood behind in the early 1950s. That was when he left Pembroke, and St. John's Pembroke, and 357 Miller Street, for Nebraska, Texas, St. Louis, New York, and Rome. And so began Richard John Neuhaus' great adventure and lifelong mission: to make something of himself in America, but not for his own sake. No, he wanted to be "enlisted in a grand cause," and there was none grander than working for the salvation of souls, and for the healing of broken, sinful times.

CHAPTER FOUR

Boarding School Days: Prayer and Mischief Without Ceasing

They entered the poolroom that Saturday evening as boarding school boys will—elbowing into one another, calling back and forth with challenges and ribbing and exaggerated boasts. They also traded in the typical rumor-mongering and theatrical complaints of young people living far away from home, come the cold season: would the dining hall serve turkey on Thanksgiving? And judging from what they'd been fed so far, would this be a blessing or a curse? Were the upperclassmen just joking around, or were they actually serious about the freshmen being forced to run through a snowball gauntlet after the first winter storm? Did anybody know anybody willing to make a beer run for some underage men in need? Did the women of the college really have the authority to declare a Sadie Hawkins dance, and did you really have to go if one of them asked you? And most important, just when were they going to turn on the heat around here?

Maybe this Saturday's student preacher would know something about some of these questions—after all, the brainy, big-talking guy from Canada moved around campus like he knew something about everything. He might have been bluffing; now and then, in the middle of another of his boastful stories or authoritative judgments, he might squint or grin or cock one of his jaunty eyebrows, like he knew that you knew there could sometimes be as much bluster behind his points as there was brains. And so sometimes, he was just waiting for you to call bullshit on him—like he actually wanted you to, because the only thing Richard John Neuhaus would always enjoy as much as a captive audience for his unchallenged pronouncements was a captive audience for when he waged and won an argument.

Few tried him, at least during his first year away from home. In November 1951, Neuhaus was living at a Lutheran boarding school on the plains of Nebraska. The great-rooted trees around the austere buildings were bare and black-branched, and the school greens were edged in frost, as were the windowpanes through which Neuhaus and the other dormitory students of Seward College looked out early each day when they woke for breakfast and morning chapel and their day's studies. Saturdays, at least, weren't as regimented as the other six days at Concordia Seward, a Lutheran teachers' college founded in 1894 in a small town some twenty-five miles northwest of Lincoln. But beyond the sorts of ritual relaxation and planned mischief students get into on their free days at boarding schools everywhere—sports, pranks, beer runs—Concordia Seward distinguished itself by one further element (and a leavening element at that): the students themselves organized a Saturday prayer service that took place in the pool room of Miessner Hall, one of the older college buildings, in which Neuhaus and others also had their dorm rooms. The service featured devotional hymns, accompanied by a piano that one of the boys was always up for playing, and a combination of scriptural readings, psalms, and brief meditations cribbed from the writings of various Lutheran pastors and theologians, arranged and recommended by a Missouri Synod publication called *Portals of Prayer.*

One occasional element of these Saturday services, if somebody was willing to try it, was a homily crafted and delivered by a member of the student body—the residential portion of which was exclusively male and Lutheran, and sent there by Missouri families and congregations from the upper Midwest for pre-seminary studies or for teacher training. Many students were PKs—preacher's kids—and their parents, Clem and Ella included, enjoyed a pastor's discount when it came to paying tuition. This particular Saturday in November 1951, the homilist's theme was the set of joyful duties to be taken up by Christians in light of the dynamic relationship that Lutheranism proposed between Law and Gospel; the scriptural through-line came from St. Paul's First Letter to the Thessalonians; the preacher was fifteen-year-old Dick Neuhaus.[1]

This wasn't his first out-of-the-ordinary effort at Concordia Seward. Nominating himself to work as an investigative journalist for the school paper upon arriving, he wrote a self-styled exposé of the bread-making practices in the cafeteria: didn't anyone else care that they were baking two thousand loaves a week? (Apparently not, he realized afterward.) His faculty advisor was amused that most of their check-in sessions were devoted to Neuhaus' offering ideas and proposals for improvement around the school, rather than to his taking any advice. At the conclusion of one such meeting, he asked his student the question that most every other person who ever tried to advise Richard John Neuhaus would eventually ask, already knowing the answer: "Just which one of us is the advisor here, and which one of us is the advisee?" In short, Dick Neuhaus wasn't like his older brothers who had come through the school—good at sports, good enough at school, regular guys—and he certainly seemed to have little in common with his brother-in-law Lou Schwich, a popular and energetic young phys ed teacher and coach. He occasionally brought Dick home for dinner with his wife, Mim, Dick's big sister. Dick would observe the domestic chaos of their growing family—many young children either playing, crying, or playing *and* crying—with a bemused passivity while set up in the middle of the Schwich living room, gumming on the tobacco pipe he began sporting in his boarding school days.

Years later, Mim Schwich would joke with her little brother that his early visits to her houseful of children were formative experiences for him in his lifelong commitment to celibacy. Mim and Richard could, at a distance, laugh at this shared memory with ease: it may have been one of the very few memories of Neuhaus' otherwise tumultuous year at a Missouri Synod boarding school in Nebraska that afforded a common smile. Not that his time there wasn't memorable for others. Indeed, almost forty years later, one of Neuhaus' schooldays friends, Leroy Vogel, who also went on to become a Lutheran pastor, wrote him to express thanks for delivering a Saturday night homily when they were both fifteen years old and living far from home, a homily that both taught and inspired him so profoundly that decades later he could quote at length from Neuhaus' remarks.[2]

For Neuhaus himself, the Seward occasion was a step up from the rocking chair pulpit and baby sister congregation of his Pembroke preaching days. Instead, here was an entire dormitory of his fellow students, arranged around a drafty recreation room while he presided from the head of the pool table, taking St. Paul's charge to the Thessalonians—"Pray without ceasing" (1 Thessalonians 5:17)—as his departure point for a charge to his fellow young Lutherans over how they should pursue thriving Christian lives lived out in fidelity to Law and Gospel. This pairing in Lutheran theology dated back to the Reformation's origins, when, in sixteenth-century disputes with Jacobus Latomus, a Flemish theologian loyal to Rome, Luther held that every Christian is *simul justus et peccator:* simultaneously righteous by virtue of his faith in the Gospel, in Christ's redemptive triumph over sin; and sinful because of his failings before God's Law, as set forth in the Decalogue and also expressed in the imperatives of just secular rulers. In other words, man is always already found sinful under Divine judgment but has been redeemed by Christ: as such, faith alone, *sola fidei,* rather than faith expressed through works or in works, was for Luther the soundest and truest possible grounds for the human person's relationship to his Creator and Redeemer. This being the case, what more could anyone do but "pray without ceasing," as St. Paul counseled the Thessalonians and Dick Neuhaus charged his dorm buddies to do?[3]

The problem was, however, what did this actually mean for

the Christian in his daily life? For Leroy Vogel and no doubt many other Seward boys listening to what might have been Richard John Neuhaus' first public homily, the basic challenge of "any Scriptural passage that sounded imperative" was what this demanded by logical extension: after all, this was a Divine "word of law and was to be taken quite literally," and so, in this particular case, Vogel acknowledged, "to pray without ceasing meant just that, and I was a total failure, unworthy to enter God's presence." Neuhaus' homily, however, transformed what felt like an impossibly heavy sentence of Law into the great good news of the Gospel: "You set those words in an entirely different light," Vogel told Neuhaus with gratitude and admiration in his 1990 letter. This setting was both practical in its quotidian terms—Neuhaus preached that to pray without ceasing meant, among many things, "crossing the busy street without being run over and then pausing on the other side and saying 'Thank you, God' "—and practical in the higher terms of theology: in his meditation on Paul, Neuhaus invited his fellow young Christians gathered around the pool table to recognize and rejoice in an imperative that was not a Law impossible to follow but instead "ultimately God's own gift, an attitude of a renewed heart and mind that made of one's life a constant rejoicing in what he Had done for us in Christ Jesus."

Neuhaus' intellectual facility in discussing Law and Gospel, his confidence in interpreting it in its relationship to both Scripture and the believer's daily life, no doubt owed much to his growing up in Clem Neuhaus' household—as pastor's son, as pastor's occasional stand-in at catechism class, and as pastor's more than occasional debating partner. Its currency and effect at Seward, where he was known as the "campus brain," owed to Neuhaus' standing out as a bold, convicted, and comparatively sophisticated student preacher residing at a school that, by Vogel's frank accounting, back then "did not offer an array of professors known for their homiletical abilities or their acumen for Law/Gospel distinctions." And indeed, setting a pattern that would hold for the rest of his life as a demanding example to others, Neuhaus' "eloquently proclaiming" and "declaiming in front of the population of an entire dormitory," instead of mumbling out a familiar reading from a staid prayer book like most boys did for the Saturday service, was profoundly formative for Vogel. He credited Neuhaus not just with expanding his lived-out understanding of Law and Gospel at a maturing point in his faith life, but also with embodying, if in still embryonic form, the figure of a joyfully convicted pastor and preacher so well that Vogel decided he would try for this too.[4]

Theological insight, vocational example, stories about Coach Schwich's life at home—what else could Richard John Neuhaus possibly offer his fellow students at Seward that would eventually earn him status as the campus "kingpin"? He could offer them the bold promise of success in the boarding school boys' universal and eternal crusades for booze and girls' underwear. He fulfilled these promises only too well, which in turn made possible and necessary a punitive fall and then a redemptive turn during his year at Seward—while also making possible a self-consciously scandalous anecdote that could be recounted, for years afterward, to shock and amuse audiences who wouldn't immediately associate beer runs and panty raids with the teenage life of a neoconservative Catholic priest. In a 2002 television interview occasioned by the publication of *As I Lay Dying,* Neuhaus offered a potted autobiography in which he noted that after leaving small-town Canada at fourteen, his first American destination, Concordia Seward, did not work out as planned. And why was that? Because, he said with that crooked grin that always signaled Richard John Neuhaus' wry bemusement, the school authorities "didn't tell me that you weren't supposed to have panty raids on a girls' dormitory or beer parties in the dormitory, and so forth."[5]

Panty raids were a sudden epidemic on American college campuses in the early 1950s, as *Time* magazine, among many others, reported: "Night after night from coast to coast last week college boys leaped and howled like Comanches under the windows of squealing coeds; by week's end, despite arrests, expulsions, editorial blasts, and the best efforts of police riot squads—a few of whom even used tear gas—pantie [*sic*] raiders had made night hideous at 52 different colleges and universities." At Concordia Seward, Neuhaus led the bold and hysterical charge seemingly more than once, no doubt fueled by the beer he also obtained for his fellow students. Eventually, though, he took things too far: he led a panty raid one night in the middle of the Concordia Seward a cappella choir's annual springtime tour of the far Western states. Upon returning to campus after working up the kind of ruckus that was generating news stories and raising alarm across the nation, never mind risking what would have been the outsized public scandal of Lutheran choirboys stealing the underwear of Lutheran choirgirls in some Sun Valley motel, Neuhaus was austerely disciplined. He was placed under "room arrest" in his dorm a few floors above his onetime pool table pulpit. By his later accounting, this extended period of detention—for several weeks, he was allowed to leave only for meals and classes—would prove spiritually scouring, then revelatory, and finally life-changing.[6]

"One day, a young teacher came by to check on my spiritual well-being," Neuhaus recounted in *Catholic Matters* (2006) in describing how "in high school I had what evangelical Protestant friends call a 'born-again experience.'" But as we know from his writing about the born-anew moment that was his kitchen sink baptism, Neuhaus rejected this primary feature of evangelical Christianity's understanding of the human person's victorious turn toward God, but this dorm-room encounter nevertheless retained a decisive significance for him along these lines—so much so that, he wrote, "I can recall the details with remarkable vividness as I write this so many years later. What [the teacher] said was unremarkable. I had undoubtedly heard it a thousand times before. But now I heard it as if for the first time: 'God is very disappointed with what you did, for He thinks so highly of you. But, because He loves you so much, He forgives you and will help you to be better.'" Hearing these words as he had never heard or felt them before, Neuhaus broke down. He sobbed and repented of his sins and resolved "from that day on to live to please God who loved me so."

Of course, as he immediately acknowledged in writing about this experience, "the resolution has been broken times beyond remembering" since then, but this did not cancel that first moment of recognition, which extended, as Neuhaus recalls, from a moment into days: "Maybe for a week after that encounter, I lived in an ecstatic state of the experienced immediacy of God's presence such as I have not known since. To this day, as I recall them, I draw on the experience of those days. To this day I am grateful for those days. In the years that followed I would, from time to time, try to re-create them, to experience again what I experienced then. It never worked." Trying to account for their singular richness and describe their lifelong tracery of spiritual longing and vocational direction, Neuhaus turned to "the words T. S. Eliot gives the martyred Thomas Becket in his *Murder in the Cathedral:* 'I have had a tremor of bliss, a wink of heaven, a whisper/And I would no longer be denied; all things/Proceed to a joyful consummation.' Ah yes, I thought, that is it. And I have thought so ever since."[7]

We might wonder why it was that a detention-serving preacher's son with competing streaks for mischief, self-aggrandizement, and love for God would have this insight while stuck in a Lutheran college dorm room on the Great Plains of Nebraska. And we might also wonder why it was that years later, as a nationally prominent Catholic priest and public intellectual, he would invest this much significance in such a distant, indeed minor-seeming event, no less make it the centerpiece of a book chapter titled "Becoming the Catholic I Was." But such wondering finds only partial answer in the explanatory powers of the psychological for the event itself, and in the rhetorical currency of its subsequent rendering. Instead, it seems more generous and illuminating, in terms of understanding the whole person of Richard John Neuhaus, to accept and understand the event as Neuhaus himself did—as would be necessary again when Neuhaus, near death from cancer in 1993, had an even more dramatic and direct encounter with the Divine. Which is to say, with a frank acknowledgment of the unexpectedness of the event matched to a spirit of humility and openness to God's sudden, suddenly affecting presence in one's life. Here was an intimately felt imperative to "pray without ceasing," and indeed the spiritual ecstasies of Neuhaus' dorm room detention time occasioned an interior turn that proved lasting and memorable thereafter.

But most immediately, these moments made him something of a self-righteous pietist—pietism representing a disorderedly enthusiastic, undisciplined approach to the spiritual life by Missouri Synod standards, standards that were themselves anchored in Luther's own battles against what he polemically called the *Schwarmgeister*.[8] If not so fanatical as this early group of pietists, for a period immediately after his dorm room Damascus moment Neuhaus was similarly "contemptuous of the ritual and sacramental formalities of what I [then] viewed as a spiritually comatose Lutheranism," as he later acknowledged. Though obviously distant from his adult ministry and limited in its particular purchase on that ministry, this pietistic reaction against the ritual and sacramental represents a notable discontinuity in Richard John Neuhaus' life. From childhood through to his final days, he maintained a robust, even at times reactionary commitment to hierarchical and traditional forms of prayer and worship, set over and against the more free-form and individualistic. Indeed, he would certainly have associated the latter with an ungainly combination of the emotive and the rebellious, having experienced just this combination in a variety of contexts during his rocky and formative school year in Seward, Nebraska: preacher and panty raider, beer king and campus brain, detention ward and Damascene beloved of God.[9]

He was not, however, exactly beloved by the school authorities at Concordia Seward. The principal wrote his parents at the end of the school year to inform them that Richard had been "asked not to come back." Surprisingly, at least to the other Neuhaus children, Clem and Ella weren't particularly upset about this, perhaps because they weren't entirely surprised. Or perhaps because they were more immediately focused on what to do with him now: fifteen years old and restless, rebellious, religious, he was clearly so full of bliss and vinegar, something had to be done to make sure he was set on a path leading him closer to God, not farther away. Canada was for childhood and America was for adulthood, and Nebraska hadn't worked out as a place to grow up from one to the next. But he had to go somewhere, ideally somewhere where he could resume his schooling and wouldn't get into any trouble. The summer of 1952, Clem and Ella decided to send their wayward boy Richard on to a place called Cisco, Texas, where Ella had some distant relatives. This was, by the most basic definition, somewhere, and hopefully it was somewhere where he could go to school and avoid trouble. This proved a faint hope.

CHAPTER FIVE

A Jackrabbit-Shooting Cisco Kid Turns Arbiter Elegentarium

Shotgun loaded, Dick Neuhaus stood up in the Model A's rumble seat and squinted against the hard Texas sunlight. He was searching for targets as the two young men hammered down the fairway in the roadster. "There's one!" he yelled down to his buddy Keith, pointing to their right with the barrel of his uncle's gun, and so Keith veered toward the dead-brown green, the target itself little more than a blurry smudge hopping past a faded putting flag. They hit a bump and Keith winced, less for himself than for what these small-town safaris were doing to his Ford—fabric top, blue body, red spoke wheels, it was very fine, and he was very fond of it. After all, he'd only bought it a few weeks earlier, in September 1952, with his very first paycheck as the new teacher for a one-room Lutheran schoolhouse in Cisco, Texas. Actually, no, his roommate that year in West Texas bought the car with Keith's very first paycheck, but Richard John Neuhaus magnanimously allowed that they could share it. And when they weren't just cruising around the quiet streets of town, or heading down the road to Abilene mostly for the sake of just heading down the road, or scoping out a new quarry pond for a swim, the two of them liked to drive on over to the Cisco Country Club—whose main attraction, a golf course, was really more what you might call a "goat patch." There, they would chase after jackrabbits and blow them away until the supper hour. Driving back, the boys wondered if it'd be chicken-fried steak that night, or if their sweet old lady hostess would surprise them again by baking lemon pies for dinner, a whole one apiece.

After school those days, Keith would return to the house where they were living—the home of World War II veteran Erwin Prange and his wife, Dorothy, called "Grammy Gus," who were relatives of Ella Neuhaus whom Richard would later describe as his "shirt-tail cousins." Keith was certain to find Dick, four years his junior, knocking about as usual, either reading a book that looked well beyond his age, never mind this place, or killing time out back in the shed, throwing pearl-handled daggers into the wall. These daggers were among Erwin's cherished hoard of German military goods, which he'd brought back with him after the war and kept in a chest that Dick had found quickly, ignoring the SS officer's long coat and also the electric train set (which no doubt reminded him of the version he'd enjoyed in the attic abode of his Canadian childhood) for the throwing knives and shotgun buried underneath. The daggers Neuhaus eventually wrecked, cracking and splitting the handles from repeated throws while waiting around for Keith to come home from school. The shotgun was put to use at the Cisco Country Club, not always as intended either: one time, going after a jackrabbit, Neuhaus aimed a little too low; he didn't just miss, he shot off the roadster's radiator cap. Had pastor and deer hunter Clem Neuhaus received a detailed report of his son's activities in Cisco, this one in particular would have no doubt been troubling: he wasn't just raising hell, he was missing his targets too.[1]

Neuhaus was also missing school in a regular way: he never attended while in Cisco and, in fact, would never return to high school. Not that Keith knew any of this specifically; in fact, he knew very little about his housemate Dick except that he was from Canada, was a pastor's son, and clearly, by age sixteen, had vocations for religious and intellectual life and for getting into trouble: late at night, he talked, and talked, and talked—about God, about ideas, about outsized plans involving both and adolescent schemes that seemed to involve neither. On this latter part, he had clearly done something wrong to be sent to Cisco, as Neuhaus himself would later acknowledge candidly: "For my sins, part of my misspent youth was misspent in Texas . . . in Cisco, a depressed and dust-driven town that was kind to me and is perfectly evoked in the film *The Last Picture Show.* Of West Texas it was said that there is nothing wrong with it that some water and a few good people would not remedy. To which the response was the same might be said for hell." Neuhaus did not regard his own time in Cisco, misspent though it largely was, as hellish, even if he seemed like something of a "hellion" to those around him, his buddy Keith included. Indeed, another of Neuhaus' contemporaries from his year in Cisco recalls hearing about him before meeting him: rumor was, some PK from Canada was "driving the poor pastor crazy because he was disputing him by asking questions he couldn't answer."[2]

Peter Bogdanovich's *The Last Picture Show* was set in 1952, exactly contemporaneous with Neuhaus' own time in West Texas; its visuals captured the look and feel of the place while its story line reflected the restless mood the place encouraged among its residents: "Everything is flat, and empty here, and there's nothing to do," complains one character, who, like many others, looks for mostly reckless things to do to fill up that vacancy. Neuhaus did very much the same, if, of course, on his own distinctive terms. Beyond shotgun-and-dagger hijinks and road tripping around the dusty flatlands and playing hell with the pastor, and also having more wholesome fun as part of the local Grace Lutheran Church's Walther League and quarry pond swimming and enjoying the occasional beer with some of the "good old boys" in Breckenridge, up the road from dry county Cisco, Neuhaus eventually found a more profitable use for his year-long sojourn in West Texas. He traded up from a part-time job pumping gas at the local Humble Oil stop by persuading Grammy Gus to lend him enough money to buy and start running his own gas station, a venture that involved his also becoming, by his own lifelong proud measure, at age sixteen, "the youngest member of the Texas Chamber of Commerce." The station was nothing much to speak of and, one assumes, didn't require a significant investment on Dorothy Prange's part; otherwise it would be unclear how or why she would have put up the money, as persuasive as Neuhaus could be. It was located a few miles outside Cisco, at a stark crossroads visited by rural folk who did not mind the minor markups on town prices that their teenage clerk-cum-owner charged for the foodstuffs and Bull Durham tobacco he sold them.[3]

This offered an otherwise somewhat aimless young man a focus for his days, but being a country crossroads gas station owner wasn't the life and work God was calling Richard John Neuhaus to pursue. Indeed, by his own reckoning, his time in West Texas, in keeping with much of his youth, was "misspent," but Neuhaus would later also write, "I've never regretted the time in Cisco, a depressed and dust-driven town that was kind to me." This kindness came, in part, through the hospitality of lemon pie suppers and friendships forged during Abilene road trips and golf-course target practice, and also through the experience of running a small business—a very small business, to be sure, yet the kind of life-lived badge he would later wear proudly, making more of it than perhaps others might, whether as the entrepreneurial intellectual he proved to be or as a Cold War–era proponent of free market economics. But years before this, and independent of his teenage small business venture, his portion of West Texas kindness came most consequentially in the form of an unexpectedly striking Christian example, and in the vocational planning, if not plotting, that was done on his behalf that year.

The former of these significant kindnesses he wrote about many years later in *First Things;* and while Richard John Neuhaus considered every moment of his earthly life, from kitchen sink baptism forward, as available material for his writing and preaching, he only wrote substantially about one experience from his time in Cisco (aside from Chamber of Commerce boasts). This suggests how generally misspent that year indeed was, but also how comparatively affecting this one event proved. Among Neuhaus' Cisco buddies was a boy named Tyler, who was "thought to be a bit slow" or, back in the day, "retarded." This mattered less to Neuhaus than Tyler's bearing: "There was a wondrous calm about him, as though he had a secret world where he really lived." Whether it was his attic abode or his capacious book-lined imagination, the same might be said for the young Neuhaus, yet what matters most here is the implied difference between these two boys: no one who spent more than five minutes with him would describe the teenage Richard John Neuhaus as possessing "a wondrous calm." Tyler, a devout Baptist as Neuhaus recalled, won over their crowd less with his faith, or his calm for that matter, than with his fearlessness: "One hot day some of us were swimming in a rural tank," Neuhaus would write, many years later, "which is what Texans call a man-made pond for watering cattle. The rest of us were impressed by, indeed envious of, Tyler's fearlessness in diving from a huge rock into what must have been no more than five feet of water. He was unruffled and told us—not bragging, but with smiling ingenuousness stating the obvious—'I'm under the shadow.' "

Tyler was quoting Scripture and, from Neuhaus' immediate vantage, clearly living from it as well. Psalm 91 promises, "He that dwelleth in the secret place of the most High shall abide under the shadow of the Almighty. . . . He shall cover thee with his feathers, and under his wings shalt thou trust." In typical latter-day Neuhaus fashion, given his habit and gift for yoking together the quotidian and the cosmic, the plainspoken and the sophisticated—with himself, in thoughts, words, and experiences, as the hub and integrator—he connected Tyler's example to the Swiss theologian Hans Urs von Balthasar's study of the Catholic writer Georges Bernanos. According to Neuhaus, Tyler and Bernanos each in his way "lived under the shadow" not of death but of God the Almighty, and so in this juxtaposition of two very different Christian examples that each in its way influenced their evoker, both devout men were "standing fearless on the heights [and] falling into the mystery of grace."[4]

The teenage Richard John Neuhaus likely did not conceive of Tyler's tank-diving as a faithful fall into a muddy West Texas pool of God's own grace. Nevertheless, the humility and immediacy of faith of this slow-minded teenage Baptist afforded Neuhaus an example that took shape in stark, oppositional relief to the figure he was himself cutting throughout much of his "misspent youth," notwithstanding his Damascus moment in that Great Plains boarding school dorm room. This sense of a vocation misspent, even wasting away, was particularly felt by Neuhaus' pastor in Cisco, Jim Hanning. "We gotta get him to do something," he remonstrated with Neuhaus' housemate Keith, because otherwise this very talented, very energetic young man was basically drag-racing away his life along a slack loop in Cisco, with little effectual concern or pressure coming from his parents in Pembroke, who, at this stage in his life, appeared to have been content with his simply being under some (distant) family supervision. Nor was there any pressure or concern coming from school authorities, because he never attended to begin with, or from the old couple he was living with at the time. Not that Neuhaus wasn't generating his own kind of pressure: late at night in the Prange living room, and also on dusty drives back and forth to Abilene, Richard talked endlessly, both with Keith and at Keith. The topics were theology and ideas and politics only when they weren't his penchant for grand plans: no, he would not follow Keith's lead and court a girl, he would found a Lutheran monastic group. But outside a Flannery O'Connor short story, you can't get very far at answering God's call by trying to be a monastery-founding theologian and intellectual polemicist as a high school dropout gas station owner knocking around in West Texas.

There was, it turned out, a little Lutheran school in Austin that Erwin Prange and Keith and the Grace Lutheran pastor all recommended as a better place for Dick to try if the plan was for him to spend a second year in Texas—as it was by default, since no one else in Neuhaus' life had any other suggestions at this stage. The school itself was a two-track place that accepted students into its high school program and also into its collegiate stream. The gas station wasn't doing a great deal of business, and the poor pastor was tired of answering Neuhaus' overwhelming and enthusiastically arcane theological questions, and so Richard agreed to give it a go. Reflecting a very different time and circumstance for American higher education, the application form for the Concordia Lutheran College of Texas was a single sheet and involved only a few questions, to be backed up by the requisite official paperwork. Beyond the standard biographical information, the application form requested information on whether the prospective student would pursue studies in ministry, teaching, or classics; also, "Who pays expenses?" (in Neuhaus' case, it was his paternal grandmother); it asked for an account of the applicant's prior schooling, and of his memory and aptitude; and it finally required a statement on "conduct and disposition" (there were, fortunately for this applicant, only two lines provided for this last statement).

By all accounts, Neuhaus didn't particularly resist the idea of going to Concordia-Austin, or pursue it with any great excitement either. Instead, one sunny day in early September 1953, he walked up to the registration lines at the college. Surveying the signage, he realized he had two options: high school or college. Weighing the relative merits of each, he chose the lineup for college. Scanning through his sheaf of papers until he found Neuhaus' application, the admissions officer informed the confident-looking young man standing in front of him that, regrettably, it was incomplete. "We have not received your high school transcript," he said. To which Neuhaus immediately answered, "I hope you will receive one soon"—and with that one line, he talked and walked his way into college.[5]

Two years later, the 1955 edition of the Concordia-Austin yearbook featured the photograph of a handsome young man sporting a light blazer, a crisp white shirt, and an elegant tie: if not as broad-shouldered or scholarly looking as some of the others in the graduating class, he was, nevertheless, the most refined-looking. He had a short, sharp haircut that set off his prominent nose and ears, but more noticeable still was his assured-looking smile: there was no shyness, no uncertainty in this graduate's face. And the caption accompanying this poised portrait suggests his distinctive, outsized presence on campus:

> RICHARD JOHN NEUHAUS,
> Pembroke, Ontario, Canada
>
> *Choristers, Vice-President of 8:40. Scholar, ARBITER ELEGENTARIUM, subject of the Queen; when most "normal" students had gone to bed Dick was sure to be wide awake, expounding his sundry and various theories.*

As these things tend to be, the yearbook caption is driven by a combination of affection, admiration, and sarcasm, which specifically attest to the ways in which Neuhaus thrived at college. While other graduates were identified by the sports they played or positions they held in various clubs, Neuhaus was distinctively, if not exclusively, identified by his status as a "Scholar." His extracurricular involvements were more creative than sporting: he sang in this school choir too—but it was all male and mostly rural Texan in composition, no panty raids happening here. He also cofounded a drama society that he named after the curtain-raising time on Broadway, an early suggestion of where Neuhaus was setting his sights, even from a Lutheran junior college in Texas. One classmate's personal edition of this yearbook featured a telling scrawl across Neuhaus' picture: "POPE," it read in looping blue ink, just as this had been his father's nickname at seminary and in Pembroke. In the son's case, this handle had less to do with Neuhaus' future religious trajectory than with sarcastically capturing his overly developed sense of himself as a putatively infallible authority on the religious matters before him.[6]

Concordia-Austin was indeed a far ways from either Broadway or Rome; it was an undistinguished but enduring little place modeled on the German gymnasium system of schooling—a six-year sequence designed as a suite of advanced studies intended to transition students from early high school to early college. The Missouri Synod had adapted the German system to its own purposes throughout America, predominantly to prepare its finest young men for seminary studies and ministry, or for careers as teachers. Founded in 1925, Concordia-Austin grandly considered itself "the school of the prophets" and adopted as its motto "With God we shall do valiantly." But to do anything at all required much kindness from its benefactors—local Missouri Synod Lutherans who gave modest sums of cash, and also books and even foodstuffs, with members of nearby congregations sending the school crates of grapefruits and oranges. This also required ingenuity from its enterprising president, George John Beto, a Missouri Synod pastor who would eventually become a prominent and influential reformist figure in the Texas justice system.

While leading Concordia, Beto was known for his fund-raising skills: he would preach to a congregation about the mission and struggles of his school and ask for pledges of support, and then reliably receive checks from congregants as they shook his hand and blessed his work on the way out of the service. He was also an avid hunter; on happy occasion the men of the college were treated to fresh deer steaks courtesy of his rifle. Most importantly, though, Beto was a God-loving man with a booming voice that he devoted to proclaiming the Gospel; he habitually derided Edward VIII for abandoning the duties of the British throne out of mere feelings for some American divorcée; he favored Stetson boots, blue two-piece suits, and a ten-gallon hat; he struck a figure of masculine piety, a Texas version of muscular Christianity, that appealed to his students, Neuhaus in particular, as he would later recall in writing about his admiration for Beto in an issue of *First Things*. Not that this admiration prevented him from getting in trouble with the college president.[7]

One of Neuhaus' college contemporaries recalls his controversial role in a school drama society performance of *Stalag 17*, a Broadway play about a clutch of American airmen scheming and suffering under German control in a World War II POW camp. Written by Donald Bevan and Edmund Trzcinski, the play was adapted for the screen and became a successful movie directed by Billy Wilder and starring William Holden, which was released right around the time Neuhaus started at Concordia-Austin. One of his first notice-winning moves was to found the 8:40 Society in collaboration with the college president's son. The new drama club was dedicated, according to its charter, to helping students "develop speech facility and social presence." Neuhaus himself needed little such assistance, of course, and when the society decided to mount a production of *Stalag 17* for an audience featuring some local donors to the school and also church leaders from nearby congregations, the authorities allowed it after some changes were made. Al Leja, the English teacher, one of few faculty members with a doctorate, crafted audience-friendly euphemisms for the script's notable profanities. Partway through the actual performance, however, Neuhaus went off-script, or more accurately, he went back to the original script and began swearing onstage, shocking if not offending most of the audience, the potentates particularly, and earning himself a disciplinary session in the president's office. All of this further confirmed his classmates' sense of him as "not exactly what you'd call a person who went along with what the rules said."[8]

There were, to be sure, many rules for life at Concordia-Austin: up at 6:30 every day, breakfast, chapel, then class, lunch, class, supper, study hall, and another thirty minutes of chapel before lights out at 10 P.M.: no drinking and no girls, but efforts were made to find both in greater Austin on weekends, when the upperclassmen were allowed to stay out until 11 P.M. In all these rules, there was no formal stricture on conversation itself, and here was where Richard John Neuhaus really won notice. Though called a "Scholar" in his graduation entry, he was in fact an inconsistent student, excelling in subjects only when they appealed to him—like English with Dr. Leja, who, notwithstanding Neuhaus' departures from his wholesomely doctored *Stalag 17* script, took a great interest in him and encouraged his literary and intellectual appetites. In the meantime, Neuhaus muddled through courses that didn't appeal to him, which generally included the language training in German, Latin, and Greek. While his roommate and future lifelong friend Robert Louis Wilken would be dutifully studying for his languages classes at night, Neuhaus would be reading *The Brothers Karamazov* or the philosophy of George Santayana or consuming the latest issue of *Time* magazine, each its own indicator of someone with extraordinary interests in a student body populated mostly by farm boys and future country preachers. As Neuhaus himself would later observe, of his youthful reading of Santayana in particular, it was borne of a sense he had that this was "someone to be read if one aspired to a respectable measure of familiarity with the important thinking of the time." And while Santayana didn't persuade Neuhaus in the substance of his ideas, he impressed upon him the importance of having a "sensibility and style" that could be effectual for someone seeking to become a public thinker successfully working in and in fact advancing "something like an American intellectual tradition."[9]

Retrospective framing notwithstanding, these are outsized notions of future plans for any junior college student, never mind for someone coming through a minor Lutheran school in Texas. Indeed, Neuhaus won notice from faculty and students alike as "very bright, somewhat dislocated" and also a "free spirit" in a very confined educational and cultural situation, according to one former classmate, largely because of his status and indeed behavior as "the resident intellectual," as Neuhaus himself would later describe his collegiate presence. This was all most apparent to Wilken, a New Orleans native with plans for a life in ministry who would himself go on to a consequential career as a scholar of early Christian history, a crucial contributor and interlocutor for Neuhaus in his various publications and projects, and eventually a fellow Catholic convert. But back in his college days, he could only study for so long before he and everybody else in their four-man dormitory would be interrupted by Dick

Neuhaus, who was once more grinning, ready to share another of his theories or plans. Another of his Concordia-Austin contemporaries, asked if he ever heard Neuhaus going on at night, laughed and answered, "We all heard him."[10]

As to what he went on about, it was a combination that would remain consistent throughout Neuhaus' life: religion, politics, books—he had ideas and opinions on all of this and also, always, on how any given operation could be run better or be checked by dramatic statement and action. In one memorable instance, Neuhaus was advocating a student strike, no doubt against some element of the school's authoritative structure or restrictive strictures upon its students. So caught up in making his case, Neuhaus didn't notice the chill and hush descending on his listeners, who watched as President Beto entered the room and made his way toward the rebel-rouser, stood behind him, and calmly observed, "Brother Neuhaus, if you don't like it here, you can leave." As Neuhaus himself later acknowledged, in retelling this story abashedly, "I stayed, and that was the end of the insurrection." He stayed, and didn't exactly thrive academically, but certainly did so socially and intellectually and spiritually, and was, as his yearbook entry noted, an authoritative and eloquently talkative night owl—the "arbiter elegentarium" who, while most of the "normal" students were asleep, was "sure to be wide awake," "expounding" for an audience impressed, annoyed, persuaded, and anything but indifferent to "his sundry and various theories."

Almost twenty, he had really started into the flourishing time of his brilliant and rebellious youth, and at Concordia-Austin had found the best fit so far for his talents and energies, if not nearly the best fit finally. That happened shortly after Concordia College bid farewell to its Class of '55, and some of these promising young men, Dick Neuhaus and his good friend Robert Wilken included, headed to St. Louis to attend Concordia Seminary. This was the synod's premier seminary, and then in the years of its greatest success in forming new pastors to discern, embrace, and minister to the world the promise and potential of God's love—Lutheran-framed,

Missouri-stamped. There is no evidence of Richard John Neuhaus ever struggling with his decision to enter seminary, or considering any other vocation. If never stated outright, this seemed to have been the long-understood and singular option for him, and Concordia-St. Louis proved an ideal setting. This would be the place where smart, daring, devout, and fine-talking Dick Neuhaus would become smart, daring, devout, and fine-talking Pastor Richard John, ready to take on the world and win it for Christ and His Church. This was the case even though, already in his Lutheran seminary days, he was arguing over just how Lutheran, just how Catholic, that beloved Church had been, was, and was meant to be.[11]

CHAPTER SIX

Goal, Malady, Means: A Seminary Formation in Church and Church Politics

"THIS IS THE DAY THE LORD HAS MADE! LET US REJOICE IN IT! Good morning, gentlemen."

"Good morning, Father Piepkorn!" the seminarians replied immediately, with almost military alacrity. Some may have been subtly grinning to have just won a bet, and others may have been subtly rolling their eyes at their professor's early morning intensity, or at his martial affectations, or at his Romish airs, or at all of this at once. But also, some among the class, including nineteen-year-old Richard John Neuhaus, would have been rapt. In this short, energetic pastor-scholar, he had found a rare model within the Missouri Synod of a catholic-framed Lutheran ecclesial identity integrated with intellectual sophistication and ordered to and by a joyful love of God and the Church. Of course, on just these terms this very same model proved unappealing to other seminary students. But regardless of how they rated his joyful entrance and commanding start to the day's work, when Father Piepkorn rushed into the lecture hall that morning, all of them would definitely have been nervous: Was he going to spring another of his infamous multiple choice tests on them? And would it be in German or in Latin this time? Would the questions be from the footnotes from last week's readings or from last month's? Or would he just start in on them, firing off questions like a scholarly machine gun? Never mind biblical Hebrew five days a week, Piepkorn, first thing in the morning, was the great worry of all new seminarians. After all, the upperclassmen at the seminary could be helpful to the new guys in telling them what to expect from some of the other faculty in terms of teaching and tests. But with "the Pieps," as many students called him, if never to his bespectacled, lantern-jawed face, the only preparation was accepting one certainty: he never asked the same question twice.

When Piepkorn came in, the morning's first wager among the students was decided: it was his military chaplain's uniform today, not his Geneva gowns. Either way, he'd be wearing a Roman collar, that was for certain: in fact, some of the seminarians liked to joke he was so catholic-minded, Arthur Carl Piepkorn wore a Roman collar with his pajamas. And while not everyone at the seminary—by no means—agreed with his arguments for the theological and ecclesial necessity of understanding the Lutheran confession as a reform movement internal to the universal catholic church, some dismissing it as High Church affection, others as theatrical "smells and bells," his students generally respected the seriousness and fullness of his commitments. Calling most every other faculty member either "Professor" or "Pastor," students at Concordia-St. Louis, the Missouri Synod's flagship seminary, called Arthur C. Piepkorn "Father."

But as his chaplain's uniform suggested, they could have saluted him too. That he wore military garb to classes on frequent occasions was no great surprise. After all, he'd served in the army with great pride and distinction from 1940 to 1953—as a regular chaplain during the war itself, then as senior chaplain for the U.S. occupation force in Germany, and thereafter as the commandant of the stateside chaplain school and finally as president of the Chaplain Board itself—before returning to his alma mater and taking up an appointment as a professor of systematic theology in 1951, having also, along the way, married and had four children, served as a pastor for a series of midwestern congregations, and also earned a doctorate in Babylonian archaeology from the University of Chicago. If by 7:40 A.M., the start of morning classes at the seminary, Arthur C. Piepkorn was already going full-throttle, that's because he went full-throttle at life itself.[1]

He was one of the most charismatic and distinctive faculty members at Concordia-St. Louis during one of that historic seminary's most thriving times, and one of the most decisive exemplars and influences on Richard John Neuhaus' life and work. Neuhaus came under his sway in a variety of ways during his five years of seminary (1955–1960)—forming, with Robert Wilken and a few others, a group of ardent devotees who regularly congregated around Piepkorn as he rushed around Concordia's collegiate Gothic grounds, his arms always full of books, his head reliably crowded with abstruse historical facts he was happy to dispense to his happy listeners. Neuhaus and Wilken would attend the brief, formal evening prayer service he held on campus, and both began using a breviary for morning prayers, as he did; at night, they visited with him at his home for more informal discussions of theology and culture and ideas. They also attended more sacrament- and ritual-focused services that Piepkorn led on Sundays. These more Catholic-seeming services happened off campus, at a time when the Missouri Synod was already moving closer to the sensibilities and practices of American Protestant Fundamentalism. For all this—and particularly for their close and devoted association to Piepkorn—Neuhaus, Wilken, and their crowd were regarded by their fellow seminarians as the High Church intellectual set at Concordia. And while Piepkorn revealed to Neuhaus a fullness of possibility internal to Lutheranism itself, his most basic contribution to Neuhaus' seminary-era formation was the combination of the contemplative and the active life that he embodied, whether in class, on campus, at his home, or before the altar. "In wonder before the truth, he was a child," Neuhaus would later recall of his beloved teacher, while "in conveying the truth, a master."

But what more specifically was this truth that he delighted in and delighted in teaching his seminarians? Neuhaus persuasively accounted for this in a 1984 speech he delivered at the Lutheran School of Theology in Chicago, on the occasion of the first awarding of a prize named for Piepkorn that Neuhaus helped found and fund. For Piepkorn, as a theologian and teacher, and for Neuhaus, as a willing disciple, the historical reality of Christianity after Martin Luther was never meant to forge a permanent ecclesial division from the universal Church, as Neuhaus argued in summarizing the governing premise of Piepkorn's theology: "The Reformation was not against the Church catholic but to make the Church more catholic." Advocating for this premise, Neuhaus continued, Piepkorn "opened our Lutheran self-understanding to the full resources that are rightfully ours" and rightly garbed what was otherwise, he observed dismissively, "a skeletal tradition, skipping from Paul to Augustine to Luther to whatever was the reigning theological fashion of the day." Instead, Lutheranism properly understood and ordered could claim continuity with "Ambrose and Abelard and Teresa and Bonaventure and Thomas," or so proposed the then Lutheran pastor Neuhaus, who further told his Lutheran listeners, paraphrasing his Lutheran seminary teacher, that these figures "must be doctors of our church if our church is part of the only Church that Christ has." This being the case, Lutheranism, rightly understood, wasn't an end in and of itself, but possessed a great "ecumenical vocation and destiny . . . to heal the breach of the sixteenth century and be an agent of visible unity of all Christians." Mindful of his immediate audience for this encomium to Piepkorn, Neuhaus acknowledged that his sense of Lutheranism and of the Church was "controversial in some circles still today" and indeed that "Piepkorn's legacy should be seen as part of an ongoing contestation within American Lutheranism." Neuhaus' most dramatic response to this contestation made national news six years after he gave these remarks, when he converted to Catholicism. But decades before that, while Neuhaus was a student at Concordia-St. Louis, American Lutheranism's internal struggles were already playing out, in a variety of ways, on campus. Unsurprisingly, Richard John Neuhaus was far from an indifferent bystander in these struggles.[2]

Concordia-St. Louis was known in Missouri Synod circles as the "theoretical" seminary, in contrast with Concordia-Springfield, Clem Neuhaus' alma mater, which was the "practical" institution. The latter was intended to prepare pastors for missionary work, and the former for more intellectual and scholarly endeavors. The seminary itself began as a log cabin schoolhouse serving eleven children, in 1839; by the time Richard John Neuhaus arrived, in 1955, his tuition paid for by his grandmother—who had so wanted her son Clem to become a minister and, likewise, at least one grandson, whom she'd already put through junior college in Austin—the seminary was the leading institution in the Missouri Synod. The attention and resources it commanded as it grew reflect as much. The synod devoted millions of dollars to building up a campus on the west side of St. Louis that, in its size and design, was worthy of the synod's own size and designs on answering Theodore Roosevelt's famous 1910 prediction that "the Lutheran Church is destined to become one of the two or three greatest and most important churches in the United States." A remarkable one hundred thousand people turned out for a ceremony in June 1926 to mark the completion of the seminary's ambitious building campaign, which had produced a linked set of imposing and—this being the advantage of the chosen architectural style—already historic-looking Collegiate Gothic structures. Various buildings were named for historic figures from the Missouri Synod (principally, C. F. Walther), from the Reformation (Martin Luther, William Tyndale), and from the early Church (Athanasius). Its Lutheran pride aside, the campus boasted the only Gothic smokestack in all of America.

According to one historian, the attention and resources devoted to Concordia-St. Louis reflected its signal importance in conceptually and physically manifesting "Missouri's unity, loyalty, devotion, and sacrifice": it constituted a strong, stable, and sizeable foundation for the training of future generations of men committed to preaching and teaching God's Law and Gospel. It was indeed needed: the Missouri Synod's rolls effectively tripled between 1935 and 1960. And so, when he reached campus in September 1955, Neuhaus was one of 750 seminarians being taught and trained by a faculty complement of almost fifty, including Piepkorn and also the newly appointed dean of the chapel and homiletics professor, Richard R. Caemmerer. The latter would become a second major influence on Neuhaus' formation during seminary, specifically with his emphasis on the irreplaceable importance of preaching. As Neuhaus himself would later remember, Caemmerer taught that "every sermon should be composed of three parts: goal, malady, means," corresponding to (1) the Christian's hopes and ambitions; (2) the sins and errors that prevent their achievement; and (3) the Gospel's capacity for overcoming the malady and "bestow[ing], as a gift from God, the opening to the goal."

By Wilken's recollection, Piepkorn and Caemmerer all but competed with each other to influence their shared set of admiring students. Each man unsurprisingly focused his energies on transmitting to his devotees what he regarded as the most important dimension of Lutheranism for these new pastors and future Church scholars to understand and help advance. Neuhaus was influenced by their combined efforts: from Piepkorn, it was establishing Lutheranism's full ecclesial heritage and its definitional commitment to greater catholic unity; from Caemmerer, it was establishing the significance of the sermon as a pastor's greatest opportunity and therefore responsibility for teaching, guiding, inspiring, and challenging his flock to live out the Gospel. Neuhaus was simultaneously influenced by the time and energy each man devoted to forming and mentoring young people, which, in time, he would more than match in his own ways.[3]

Aside from the impact of these professor-pastors, Neuhaus' more immediate friendships and also antagonisms with his fellow seminarians were arguably just as formative. Before leaving Austin, Neuhaus and Wilken and some of the others going on to St. Louis had agreed they would not room together at the start of their time in seminary. Already solid friends, they thought it wise to expand their circles in their new environs. Neuhaus was assigned to a room designed and built in the 1920s as part of the seminary's expansion, a combination bedroom and study intended for two students. His roommate was a New Yorker named Jack Elliot, a future biblical scholar who was more of a studious type than a sociable intellectual like Neuhaus. Indeed, from the very start of his time at St. Louis, Neuhaus did more than just expand his personal circle; he was "kind of a plague on all houses," observes one fellow seminarian, John Heinemeier, who would later serve as Neuhaus' associate pastor at his first and most significant church assignment, St. John the Evangelist in Brooklyn. On first meeting Neuhaus in seminary and observing his gadfly energies, Heinemeier recalls being most taken aback by his boldness, which was evident to others in Neuhaus' willingness to argue points of doctrine and implications of theology in the classroom, in the dining hall, in the dormitory, and all points in between.

He was never but willing, even happy, to join an argument—and not about whether the Cardinals' Stan Musial was a greater ballplayer than the Red Sox's Ted Williams or some other such typical young man's local trivia from the time, but about the catholicity of the Lutheran confession; about the nature and implications of biblical inerrancy; about the risks and rewards, in practical and higher order terms, of ecumenical engagements with other Lutherans, and also with Catholics, and also of interfaith encounters with Jews; about his much admired Adlai Stevenson's prospects to make Dwight Eisenhower a one-term president in running against him in the 1956 elections; about how much attention, and just what kind of attention, the seminarians should be paying to the racial situation outside the seminary walls, in St. Louis, in the neighboring parts of the South, in America itself, after the landmark 1954 *Brown v. Board* Supreme Court decision in favor of school desegregation. To Neuhaus, all of this seemed self-evidently to matter and justify hours of debate and plans for action, even if it didn't matter as immediately to many of his fellow students, students like Heinemeier and others of similar background, who had come to St. Louis from small-town and rural and decidedly homogenous German congregations. For them, Concordia-St. Louis was a challenge and an opportunity. For Neuhaus, Concordia-St. Louis was all opportunity—to start living out, more fully and credibly and effectually, the vocation he had discerned as very much his own: to be a bold Christian and a bold intellectual and a bold cosmopolitan and a bold operator, all at once, all as one.[4]

By Christmas 1955, the effects of his seminary experiences were already evident in Pembroke, when Neuhaus came home as part of an almost complete family reunion: all eight children save the two eldest, Mim and Fred, were there, along with assorted new spouses. Tom and George, Neuhaus' immediately older twin brothers, had made the greatest effort to get back. They had joined the army in 1950 and by 1955 were stationed in the Southeast Asian nation of Laos, where the United States was developing a military presence to support the local government as a bulwark against the growing Communist presence in neighboring Vietnam. Unsurprisingly, as America's long and difficult involvement in Southeast Asia was just beginning, everyone wanted to know what things were like over there, the seminarian included. At the same time, Tom and George peppered Dick with questions about seminary life. He was clearly thriving, to judge from the energetic Christmas sermon he preached at St. John's. In the future, however, as politics began to play more of a role in Neuhaus' sermonizing, the senior pastor would begin to request advance copies of his son's planned remarks, ostensibly to ensure they were accessible for the small-town congregation, but also, no doubt, to ensure they were in keeping with Clem's understanding of *echt* Lutheranism, *echt* Missouri.

Indeed, while others in Pembroke took note of Dick's newly advanced ways—for dessert one night, he requested a bowl of ice cream and a cup of coffee, and then suavely poured the one onto the other like he was sitting in the middle of Paris, not Pembroke—Clem wasn't entirely convinced that his son was thriving in all the right ways at seminary, on his own mother's tab no less. While the rest of the family caught up and reminisced and enjoyed this rare time—it might have been at least a decade since that many had all been back at 357 Miller Street together, and they wouldn't come together again until the early 1970s, when the patriarch was on his deathbed—Clem and Dick were at it again, as usual, as always, arguing church and politics and church politics at the dining room table. What Clem might have noticed, and been particularly troubled by, was the new substance informing his son's always-sharp opinions. He had stronger arguments now for understanding relations with other Lutheran denominations as ecumenism rather than unionism; on working toward rapprochement with Rome as fulfilling Luther's original vision of the Reformation, not destroying it; on reading the Bible in critical and historical terms as adopting an intellectually mature fidelity to God's word, not waging a heretical attack on it; on understanding involvement with the nascent Civil Rights Movement as vital mission work to be preached about and pursued, as opposed to a complicated distraction from real preaching, real mission. In short, Concordia-St. Louis was encouraging Richard in all these ways, not to his father's approval by any means, nor to universal approval even at Concordia itself.[5]

In time, the internal debates among faculty, students, and administrators at the seminary, and between the seminary and its governing synod, would become so pronounced that Concordia would break apart, signaling the end of a remarkable era of growth, ambition, and intellectual vitality. Indeed, at the very apex of this era, the fissures were already emerging, even in seemingly harmless ways. For instance, Friday afternoons at the seminary were a welcome time for the bookish set in the 1950s, and not simply because classes were done until Monday. Rather, this was the appointed time for Concordia students to conduct their weekly book auction, a practical way to share out titles and raise some funds in the meantime. Gathered together, the bidders competed with one another as much for the laughs as they did for the books: coming up with witty remarks and sarcastic valuations, whether of the book up for bids or of the successful bidder, was a skill that enjoyed premium status during the auction. And every Friday, during that time at Concordia-St. Louis, there was one sure and reliable target, Bronx native Herman Otten, who could always be counted on to buy the alarmist and hard-Right books that came up, books with titles like *Collectivism on Campus* and *McCarthyism: The Fight for America.*

According to historian James L. Burkee, Otten was arguably the Missouri Synod's "chief antagonist" and also its "most infamous figure" during its postwar conflicts and schisms. He was already infamous by the time Richard John Neuhaus joined him at Concordia-St. Louis, in no small part because of the bruising stridency with which he railed against (what he regarded as) evidence of creeping liberalism and covert heresy and assorted political and religious conspiracies at the seminary. Otten was influenced and driven, in these respects, by both internal and external developments and discoveries. He was, for instance, fairly fixated on potential Communist threats on campus, these being the early days of the Cold War. Domestically, such threats were dramatically framed by McCarthy's public accusations of Communist infiltrations at the State Department and his Senate Committee hearings to investigate the presence of Communist sympathizers in broader American life, and also by the Hiss-Chambers trial, in which an ex-Communist turned avowedly conservative intellectual accused a fashionably liberal lawyer and intellectual of spying for the Soviet Union during his time at the State Department. Taken together, McCarthy and Hiss-Chambers firmly identified Communism as a less-than-clear but clearly present danger in American life. And as far as Otten was concerned, Communism was only one such danger threatening Concordia and its mission to train the Missouri Synod's future pastors and leaders; the other, scandalously, was to be found among Concordia's very own faculty.

Indeed, in making this case Otten was following a model that gained national attention in 1951 when William F. Buckley, Jr.—who would become modern American conservatism's most influential figure and in time a close Neuhaus friend and collaborator—published *God and Man at Yale,* an indictment of his alma mater's faculty for its destructive, leftist ways in the lecture halls. Buckley accused Yale professors of willfully teaching students ideas and inculcating them with ideologies that ran directly counter to the university's founding religious and cultural principles and simultaneously betrayed its alumni's expectations of fidelity and continuity. Otten was convinced that similar subversion was at play at Concordia-St. Louis, specifically around the concept and nature of biblical inerrancy.[6] Defending and extending biblical inerrancy as core to its self-understanding and even to the very integrity of Christianity itself, Missouri put out Franz Pieper's *A Brief Statement of [Its] Doctrinal Position* in 1932, which emphasized, in strong fidelity with the founding documents of Lutheranism, that "since the Holy Scriptures are the Word of God, it goes without saying that they contain no errors or contradictions, but that they are in all their parts and words the infallible truth, also in those parts which treat of historical, geographical, and other secular matters." The position was restated emphatically in the 1930s because by then, historical-critical biblical scholarship was firmly established as a basic premise of approaches to Scripture in both the secular academy and in liberal Christianity.[7] This was a premise, just as these were competing sources of influence and authority, that the Missouri Synod was keen to repel. But by the 1950s, particularly at its most intellectually accomplished and ambitious seminary, the Missouri Synod was in fact witnessing internal challenges to its revered concept of biblical inerrancy.

In 1957 and 1958, some Concordia professors and seminarians were questioning whether the synod's commitment to this principle was too rigid and, as such, stifling of new thinking and methods meant to renew the faith for modern times, not wreck it by association with the same. Self-appointed heresy hunter Otten began reporting about these notions, which came up in class discussion and also published work, to seminary authorities. He also recruited a group of like-minded fellow students who were sympathetic to his crusade, if not as loud and confrontational about it, and debated his foes around campus. He did so while proudly carrying around the latest issues of Buckley's fledgling *National Review* magazine—the lead venue in American conservatism's postwar rise to decades of decisive national influence. His periodical choice marked Otten as a self-conscious conservative trying to stop the dangerous forces of relentless, secular-derived concepts of progress and liberalism in a student body where the leading lights were cosmopolitan and self-consciously progressive and liberal-minded. Indeed, Neuhaus was a prime adversary-cum-target for Herman Otten—after all, with his buddy Wilken, he'd already outmaneuvered an Otten ally to secure the editorship of the student newspaper, which was, Otten and others charged, a hotbed of dangerous liberalism. During its Wilken-Neuhaus run, the paper featured a regular column entitled "Discerning Periodical Spirits," thought up and written each issue by Neuhaus. He used the column to discuss and recommend articles he'd read elsewhere that, in his considered and already considerable opinion, were worth reading.

A forerunner of the popular, occasionally infamous "While We're At It" section of *First Things*, "Discerning Periodical Spirits" would have been exactly the kind of wide-ranging forum welcomed by seminary liberals as a means and source of opening the synod's future ministers to the world at large and simultaneously identifying, through its recommendations, important if little-known readings, people, places, and problems in that world in need of Missouri ministering. But to seminary conservatives like Otten, this opening up was more accurately a reckless abandoning of Missouri's internal strengths, evident in its doctrinal integrity and continuities, for the dangerous allure of the new and fashionable, which, ironically, is a charge Neuhaus would himself later level at the synod, and also at liberal mainline churches and left-leaning Catholicism. Yet by 1992, in looking back at this particular endeavor and its reception, Neuhaus would revel in the fact that his paper was "the favored foil of the seminary's conservative critics" because its pages considered "the chronology of Genesis, the historicity of the Resurrection, and why it was all right for Catholics and Protestants to pray together." Indeed, Neuhaus' paper at once reported on and contributed to the tumultuous situation on campus, at a time when, by his own acknowledgment, "Concordia Seminary was churning with controversies beyond numbering." Throughout these controversies, whether in the pages of the *Seminarian* or in their various direct debates, Neuhaus played the willing progressive while Otten offered rearguard pushback: in a sense, each young man likely benefited in his development along his chosen ideological line thanks to his encounters with the other. For Otten, Neuhaus was a cosmopolitan "slick" who heralded a hollowed-out, trend-chasing future for Lutheranism. For Neuhaus, Otten was a parochial reactionary who embodied the inward-focused, stiff-minded past of the Lutheranism he had encountered in various small-town forums—in Pembroke, in Seward, in Austin, and now even in big city St. Louis.[8]

But in St. Louis, he also found resources and exemplars that encouraged him to resist the predictable pushback, which came to a head after many heated exchanges in the cafeteria and residence, when Otten dramatically threw down a direct challenge to Neuhaus, daring him to sign a statement Otten had composed that purported to capture Neuhaus' position on biblical inerrancy (stating that the undersigned explicitly repudiated biblical inerrancy). By Otten's own recollection, Neuhaus refused the challenge, and typically laughed him off at that, which, for Otten, was still more evidence of Neuhaus' behaving just like the smug "slick" he was. But of course Neuhaus had more political smarts than to sign such a statement and effectively give Otten an autographed cudgel to come after him with. Indeed, Otten was constantly bringing evidence of what he charged was false doctrine and other heresies to the administration's attention, which encouraged a spirit of mistrust, conspiracy, and accusation among the student body. In fact, the students soon broke into rival camps that met in secret and traded in rumors and heated letters and filched papers and, beyond debating their opponents, began spying on them as well. At one point, Neuhaus and Wilken went so far as to try to tape-record a faculty meeting about the controversies on campus, but they couldn't finagle their way into an adjoining room and their espionage effort failed. These controversies only intensified, and eventually, Arthur Repp, Concordia's academic dean, called a meeting of all seminarians. In a tense silence they gathered in the chapel, where Repp declared, "A terrible thing has happened at our seminary. Eight men have charged eight others with false doctrine. And now we have to do something about this."[9]

Importantly, given Concordia's exalted position and demographic influence within the Missouri Synod, and the theological nature of the charges being advanced, the Concordia battles that Neuhaus joined and witnessed weren't simply a variation on the typical hothouse dramas to be found most any time in any small college community. Indeed, what was done—who said, wrote, taught, and believed what at Concordia-St. Louis, leading up to Repp's announcement and thereafter—represents the Missouri Synod's contribution to the broader "epic struggle between the forces of modernism and conservatism in American religious life" that has been under way since World War II, contends James Burkee. Neuhaus avoided taking any direct fire—meaning that, while at seminary, he was never formally charged with heresy by Otten; this would happen a few years later. In small part, he relied on his political smarts, but also, and here setting a pattern that would carry throughout his public life and professional career, despite how closely involved he was with an inwardly focused debate, he was always already engaged in matters that took him elsewhere, both intellectually and physically.

While at seminary, he read *The State and the New Testament,* a 1956 treatise by Lutheran Scripture scholar Oscar Cullmann that advocated for the Gospel-driven necessity of Christians' engaging with the secular state, which Neuhaus later invoked as "the one book that launched me into serious concern about church-state relations." Aside from this early intellectual attentiveness to the relationship of religion and politics, Neuhaus ventured into greater St. Louis out of various and intersecting interests. He took graduate courses in sociology at Washington University (Concordia's offerings in this respect were clearly limited compared to his developing interests in how people and communities live together and pursue discrete and common interests). With Wilken and other catholic-minded Concordia students, he also attended Mass at Our Lady of the Holy Cross, because it was celebrated—in traditional vestments, the brocade designs rich with medieval imagery—by Monsignor Martin Hellriegel, a then leading figure in Catholic liturgy circles for whom the renewal of the Mass involved a self-conscious rededication to its centuries-old rituals rather than a radical reform to reflect modern sensibilities.

In understanding how Neuhaus understood himself, in terms of his religious and cultural position along the Left/Right spectrum, his early interest in Roman Catholicism, coupled with his being so decisively formed and influenced by the catholic-minded Arthur Piepkorn, marked him as a liberal by rigid Missouri standards, even though his later critics on the religious and secular Lefts would regard these very same interests as evidence of a longstanding crypto-conservatism. The same left- or right-wing critique could be leveled at him for his Jewish interests and connections. In addition to his seminary-time interest in Catholic liturgy, Neuhaus also attended his first Passover after becoming an admirer of Sol Bernards, an activist-minded progressive rabbi who worked in interreligious affairs for the Anti-Defamation League and visited the seminary in this capacity. As their interactions warmed, Bernards eventually invited Neuhaus to join his family for Passover, the first of many that Neuhaus would observe with the rabbis he would count as mentors, friends, and collaborators. No doubt, their conversations would have touched on Bernards' public work as a defender of workers' rights—in 1959, he testified before Congress regarding a General Electric decision to change the location of one of its factories—and his interest in Civil Rights, which would have dovetailed with Neuhaus' own, which first developed during his time at Concordia, through a summer assignment to an inner-city congregation in Detroit and also, if to a lesser extent, through a vicarage year spent at a Chicago church.[10]

These experiences exposed Neuhaus to the hard economic and social realities of urban black life in America, and also the church's capacity and position and prophetic responsibility to offer succor and seek justice. In Detroit for that summer assignment partway through his seminary training (other summers were spent up in Pembroke, working as an itinerant salesman for the Fuller Brush Company and as a salesclerk for a local auto parts supplier) Neuhaus had his first exposure to inner-city ministry at Zion Evangelical Lutheran Church, an imposing Romanesque building on Military Avenue. There, he served under Kenneth Runge, an ambitious congregation-builder committed to inner-city ministry who was also a prolific author of Lutheran hymns and tracts. Military Avenue itself, lined with modest homes on either side of the church, didn't look particularly different from the immediate environs back home, around St. John's Lutheran on Miller Street in Pembroke, Ontario, but the demographics—a white congregation situated in a predominantly black neighborhood—and the larger social context certainly were. By the late 1950s, Detroit was some fifteen years removed from the three-day race riot that took place in July 1943 and left twenty-nine dead, hundreds injured, and more than a thousand arrested. But racial tensions certainly had not abated; instead, at best, some telling modes of imperfect accommodation had developed, as Neuhaus discovered in religious terms on Sunday mornings that summer. Before the service began, church ushers arranged themselves on Zion's front steps. Anytime black people approached, the ushers would intercept them and, in an awkwardly Christian manifestation of liberal white guilt, provide cab fare and send them off to the nearest black Lutheran congregation.[11]

Neuhaus' summertime in Detroit would have framed the possibility and great need for an urban-focused Lutheran ministry that took up the challenge of Civil Rights and race relations, rather than sidestepping it.[12] But thereafter, if Neuhaus had been keen to discern whether urban ministry and Civil Rights work were the defining elements of his particular vocation, he was likely disappointed by his 1958–59 vicarage year. Neuhaus was assigned to Pilgrim Lutheran Church, which was located on Chicago's North Side, about seven miles from the downtown core, in a leafy neighborhood with a good Lutheran preparatory school right across the street. Daily congregation life at Pilgrim, in other words, seemed to have been at notable remove from the poverty and conflicts that characterized life for Chicago's black population, which predominantly lived on the South Side, and Neuhaus would have likely been directed to focus his energies on the immediate concerns and operations of the congregation, which were not notably focused on Civil Rights or urban ministry.[13]

At least we can surmise as much from the fact that he never wrote about his vicarage year on Chicago's North Side, which is especially notable given how much he wrote about seemingly more minor places and times in his early life, like Seward and Cisco. Chicago would certainly figure later on in Neuhaus' life, and dramatically at that, but his vicarage year was something he mentioned only in passing, and in general terms, as when he remarked in one interview that thanks to this vicarage year, following as it did upon his time in Detroit, "I fell in love with the city, with the idea of city ministry." His vocation may have developed in reaction to the more conventional congregation work he did at Pilgrim, but there is no way to know for certain. What is telling, nevertheless, is Neuhaus' wording: he fell in love with the city, with an idea, with the idea of a city ministry, but not with any minister's daughter. This latter outcome was a frequent occurrence for seminarians in their vicarage year. It had happened for Clem Neuhaus and also, to Richard Neuhaus' open surprise and dismay, for his friend Robert Wilken. He would discover this on New Year's Eve, 1958, when Wilken came up to Chicago to visit, bringing along Neuhaus' seminary roommate Jack Elliot and also his new girl, Carol.

The quartet had dinner one night at an Italian restaurant in the city; conversation around the table was dominated by the recent election of a new pope, the joyful John XXIII, who seemed to these young Lutherans like a promising and needed figure for what felt like a coming new era for Christianity and the world alike. But at one point in an otherwise jovial dinner, Neuhaus suddenly asked Wilken and Elliot to leave the table. He wanted to talk to Carol, alone. He let her know what he thought of her romance with his best friend. He didn't think much of it, in fact. "Do you realize what Robert's lights are?" She clearly didn't, at least as far as Neuhaus was concerned. That's because she didn't know that in their later seminary years, Wilken and Neuhaus both had been quite taken with Father Piepkorn's emphasis on the virtues of celibacy for ordained ministers. And she clearly also didn't know that Wilken and Neuhaus had all but made a pact to both pursue, upon ordination, urban ministries at a time when historic (and white) Christian congregations were abetting the so-called white flight from America's decaying, race-conflicted cities by committing more of their attention and resources to churches in the new, pristine suburbs. She didn't know—or, worse, she didn't care, because she could actually tell Robert's lights weren't Richard's: after seminary, Wilken would marry her and pursue further studies, eventually becoming a family man and accomplished scholar of early Church history. And onward from their New Year's Eve one-on-one in Chicago, his wife and his best friend would never be on especially warm terms.[14]

Neuhaus went from his vicarage placement back to Concordia for a final year, where one of the most influential books he read was Jaroslav Pelikan's *The Riddle of Roman Catholicism.* Pelikan was a onetime Concordia professor who went on to an illustrious career at Yale as a historian of Christianity. Aside from that particular book's emphasis on ecclesial Protestantism's continuities and heritage in the early (Catholic) Church—emphasis that would have coincided with Piepkorn's teachings—Neuhaus would have no doubt been influenced by Pelikan's lament for the decline of specifically Protestant urban ministry in postwar America, while urban Catholicism continued and, in this vacuum, even thrived. Pelikan argued that this decline was the result of the Protestant churches' respective conflicts about race relations within their own congregations, which he worried were being resolved in the wrong direction: "Each settlement in the direction of 'separate but equal' Protestant churches weakens the Protestant message in its witness to the universality of the Gospel," a statement that resonates with Martin Luther King, Jr.'s more famous and pithy observation that Sunday morning, eleven o'clock, was the most segregated hour in America. Indeed, Neuhaus would have understood the realities of this Jim Crow–like approach to the Gospel during his Detroit summer, in witnessing a Sunday morning cab-fare approach to race relations, and perhaps, if not as immediately, from what he witnessed while in Chicago. He wanted to do something about this, and he would, but, as he would discover upon learning from the seminary administration of his first assignment as a new pastor, he would have to wait. Years later, Neuhaus would acknowledge, gratefully, that the seminary "took the risk of training and recommending me for the Church's ministry." Right after he finished his studies, however, the seminary didn't risk much with him. Instead, he was given a year in effect to cool his heels, to encourage his endless energies in more conventional, more traditionally Missouri ways than he had been drawn to during his seminary years. The son of a small-town pastor, he would begin his ministry as the very same.[15]

With his baby sister, Johanna, sent down to St. Louis on behalf of the family to tag along somewhat awkwardly at the various festivities, Neuhaus graduated from Concordia in June 1960. Fittingly, he went home to Pembroke for his ordination, which made the local newspaper. "ORDAINED BY HIS FATHER," runs the caption under a picture of the grave-faced, Geneva-gowned Clem Neuhaus looking down at his white-robed, Roman-collared son—who is staring just as hard at his father as his father is staring at him. The two are standing before the altar where the ordination took place. The newspaper also reports that following his ordination, Neuhaus was off to New York to preach at his new church, St. Paul's Lutheran, which was located in the all but invisible town of Massena, in upstate New York. Richard John Neuhaus would spend a very quiet year ministering to this congregation, before answering a call to take over a church in Brooklyn—a church that was poor, failing, and stuck in a rough part of town. And leaving behind his seminary life and early years, this was exactly where and what Neuhaus wanted to make the axle point of his always moving, always turning ministry. As it took shape in the tumultuous 1960s, this ministry would prove always godly, often unruly, and frequently controversial. It would lead him to people, places, and action that in turn brought out Richard John Neuhaus as an ambitious, even aggressive new player in American religion, politics, and culture.[16]

Part II

FROM BROOKLYN TO AFRICA, AND MANY POINTS IN BETWEEN, 1961–1974

"Here I am, a Canadian-reared, Texas-educated, Missouri Synod Lutheran writing from black Brooklyn where I have lived almost the whole of my adult life."

Richard John Neuhaus, *Worldview* magazine (1972)

CHAPTER SEVEN

A Young Pastor Discovers "the Glory and Tragedy of Life in This City"

Making his way through the happy people gathered on the street enjoying drinks and swaying to the music, Richard John Neuhaus smiled and waved hello to the many members of his congregation in the festive crowd. They were all enjoying the late summer gathering that his new Brooklyn church, St. John the Evangelist, was putting on in partnership with the local neighborhood association. It had been announced with decidedly humble posters—handwritten in capital letters, with rough, penciled star shapes framing the words "BLOCK PARTY"—that promised a steel drum calypso band and free food. Neuhaus would keep one of these posters among his personal effects for the rest of his life, a minor but fitting memento of the Brooklyn Lutherans he served as pastor from 1961 to 1978, whose lives, by most postwar American measures, were bleak and poor. Yet as Neuhaus soon discovered, developed, and fortified, these were lives that were also joyful and faithful to God and to the work of the Church in the world, in the city, in the streets, in the projects. But today, at least, was a day meant for enjoyment, not work. Everybody was having a good time, Pastor Neuhaus included, who offered a crooked grin to any joking invitations to join his congregants and dance. Having attended his solemn, highly ritualized services, of course they knew better than to expect that from their new young pastor. They also knew by now that regardless of the mugginess, or the fact that it was a Friday night party, he'd be wearing his dark clerics and sporting a crisp white Roman collar. And they also knew by now that the pastor wouldn't turn down a can of cold beer if you offered him one.

Eventually Neuhaus made his way to a free card-table chair. Someone took his picture while Neuhaus sat, sipped, and surveyed his situation. So this was urban ministry. Day's end, late August 1961, the humid New York air was ripe with sweat and garbage. It was loud too, with the raucous voices and music of a full-on block party, but this was only part of the greater loudness of life in the city: the calypso band and party-makers had to compete to be heard over the din of the constant bumper-to-bumper cars lining Broadway and Bushwick, two nearby major thoroughfares, never mind the noisy, apocalyptically bad traffic on the Brooklyn-Queens Expressway. Along with the Williamsburg Bridge, the borough's closest entry point into Manhattan, the expressway, a massive slab of horizontal concrete, shaped the middle horizon between this little corner of Brooklyn and the great, towering City itself. As for this little corner, Maujer Street in the Williamsburg district of the borough, the local landscape featured an aging red brick Lutheran church with sharp Gothic features on one side, and a row of squat-boxed brown brick housing projects on the other. By and large, the people milling about Neuhaus at this party were residents of these projects. And as far as he could tell, they were already keen for Jesus and grateful for the securities and fellowship of church life, if not yet fully formed in their understanding of the faith.

So yes, this was urban ministry. This was the ministry Neuhaus had experienced, to some extent, as a seminarian on summer assignment in Detroit and during his vicarage year in Chicago; the ministry he'd read about in Jaroslav Pelikan's work as receding, at least in its Protestant element, just as many American cities were also failing; the ministry he'd discerned was his to take up alongside his friend and fellow seminarian Robert Wilken (and to which he remained committed after Robert married and went off to graduate school instead); the ministry he remained committed to even after, or maybe especially after, seminary officials assigned him to a sleepy small-town congregation in upstate New York upon his graduation and ordination, as a punishment of sorts for his troublemaking at seminary; the ministry that became his less than a year into his life as an ordained pastor, when he answered a call from a Lutheran congregation in Brooklyn whose demographics were, one could put it diplomatically, "in transition." And this was where Richard John Neuhaus wanted to be; this was where he was sure God was calling him to be. But surely God could call on some others, to come help out?

By summer's end, 1961, Neuhaus realized just how badly he and his new congregation needed help—and not because St. John the Evangelist was failing, as might be expected in light of its recent history as a congregation and its location in a depressed inner-city neighborhood, but because it was, in fact, thriving. The church was founded in 1844 and joined the Missouri Synod in 1861. Originally, it served the local German immigrant farming community that had settled in the northern part of Brooklyn, across the East River from Lower Manhattan. Reflecting both large-scale European immigration to the United States from the mid-nineteenth century through to World War I, and also American Lutheranism's own robust growth during this period, the congregation, which was white immigrant agrarian and then working class in its composition, grew and thrived. By 1883, it had built a grand new church at 195 Maujer Street, and by 1909, a school. Thanks to its size and strength, during the 1910s and 1920s St. John the Evangelist served as a mentor church for newer and smaller Lutheran congregations in the area, including a mission church that shared the same name in the Glendale district of the next-door borough of Queens.

The Great Depression severely weakened the church's capacities, just as it inflicted hardship across the country and in New York as well. One effort at a constructive response took shape on a spring day in 1936, when Mayor Fiorello La Guardia showed up across the street from the church for a groundbreaking ceremony, to inaugurate work on New York City's second major public housing project. Known as the Williamsburg Houses, the residences inspired Betty Smith's 1943 novel *A Tree Grows in Brooklyn,* which for generations of readers in America and around the world has evoked the daily difficulties and relentless search for human dignity that characterize life in modern American housing projects. With the opening of the Williamsburg Houses, the demographics of the neighborhood began to change. For decades, this part of Brooklyn had been dominated by European immigrants, German Lutherans notably, and also Romanian and Hungarian Satmar Jews. By the late 1940s, while the Jewish community continued on, expanding notably in the 1930s as Jews fled the growing Nazi menace, other European immigrants had begun leaving the area just as more African-Americans were moving in. The phenomenon of "white flight," an unfortunate and undeniable part of the broader narrative of postwar American urban decline, decisively affected the congregation of St. John the Evangelist. In 1953, then pastor Martin Steege effectively abandoned the church to the downtrodden and now predominantly black neighborhood. Taking the church's formal charter documents with him, he resituated the congregation in Glendale, at what had been a mission station of St. John the Evangelist.

The original church kept going under Richard Klopf, who had been Steege's assistant and in turn rose to full pastor after Steege left. As the new pastor, Klopf made two decisions that led to the remnant congregation's rejuvenation and also made plausible Richard John Neuhaus' arrival as his successor. First, rather than focus exclusively on the few white congregants who remained with the church, he made inroads with the local black population and began to develop a racially integrated congregation during a decade, the 1950s, when American public life was in upheaval over race relations, reacting most notably to mounting resistance against Jim Crow laws in the South. Second, Steege changed the church's culture of worship; he was a Lutheran invested in an understanding of the confession as purest in its most original, sixteenth-century incarnation, which meant he pursued a more ritualized, Catholic approach to liturgy and also instituted confirmation classes centered around the Lutheran text traditionally used for such instruction, Luther's *Small Catechism.*

St. John the Evangelist, circa 1961, must have seemed like an almost providential opportunity for the bored young pastor stuck upstate, where he was leading a little Lutheran congregation in the sleepy small town of Massena. Indeed, it is no great surprise that Richard John Neuhaus answered a call to lead a racially integrated congregation in a poor district of New York City, no less one that had committed itself to a more Catholic understanding of Lutheran worship while pursuing the core practices and documents of historic Lutheranism. Neuhaus was installed as pastor about a month shy of his twenty-fifth birthday, on the second Sunday of Easter, April 9, 1961. A choir of pre-seminarians lent their strong young voices to the occasion. A few days later, having moved in next door to a red brick three-story residence that had already seen its best days, much like the old grand piano it unexpectedly counted among its possessions, Neuhaus wrote his friend Robert Wilken, announcing the liturgical date of his becoming pastor and highlighting the elevated tenor of the event: "Installed Misericordias Domini—much pomp, ceremony, and incense." That was all his friend would hear from him for six months. As Wilken would later recall, in a 1971 sermon he preached at St. John the Evangelist to mark the tenth anniversary of Neuhaus' pastorate, this extended silence from his otherwise voluble friend and a relentless letter-writer suggested "he had been swallowed up by the city and his new congregation"—happily so, necessarily so. Indeed, Neuhaus immediately took up the work of the congregation and the community and quickly realized just how much work there was, just how much need, how much opportunity to do the work of God and the Church in the city: to provide important cultural and community-building elements and services that were otherwise lacking on Maujer Street, like a new elementary school, home visits for the elderly and infirm, a youth group to keep kids off tough and dangerous streets, and foremost, for all, to catechize and evangelize the people. And so Richard John Neuhaus went looking for help.[1]

In early September 1961, Neuhaus addressed a hall packed with eager new students at Concordia College Bronxville, a Lutheran junior college located north of Manhattan, in Westchester County. He'd made the journey in the company of other Lutheran pastors from the city who were likewise seeking assistance for their ministries. For the young people in the audience, Pastor Neuhaus stood out. Elegantly dressed, trim and energetic, with dark eyes set between a sharp nose and a broad, expressive brow, he cut a handsome figure. But more distinctive was the nature of his message—not its eloquence, or its assured integration of the dictates of the Gospel and the work he was calling them to take on, but instead the urgency and intensity of his invitation. Knowing only too well the expected trajectories of students attending an institution like Concordia-Bronxville, Neuhaus asked them to consider doing something more courageous for Christ than simply becoming teachers or pastors and running off to the suburbs. Instead, he asked them to consider committing themselves to urban ministry in New York, and he made a point of dismissing any romantic notions of what that might involve.[2]

As he would also do in future books and essays that touched on his early years at St. John the Evangelist, Neuhaus emphasized the hard realities of the place they'd be committing to: there were at least three burned-out buildings in the vicinity of the church, and many, many abandoned storefronts interrupted by pawnshops, bargain stores, liquor outlets, and meager grocery stands. The sidewalks were dirty, covered in spit and trash, and the local population divided sharply along racial lines, with aging Italian barbers complaining that their old clients were moving out and that the new people, "these other people," arrived with their own barbers. But for Neuhaus, all of the obvious difficulties that he was describing to his

Bronxville collegiate audience had to be viewed from the perspective of the Gospel, which only made the Christian call to charity and justice all the more pressing. Indeed, upon finishing his talk, Neuhaus told his audience he needed help right then. And he truly meant right then! He needed Sunday school teachers, door-to-door evangelizers, and lay church workers to administer to the sick and poor whom the church encountered every day simply because of its geography. He needed well-formed, enthusiastic young Lutherans.

All of which is also to say, beyond the clear need for public work and witness that the new pastor of St. John the Evangelist wanted to satisfy, this same twenty-six-year-old young man was also in need of creating a sympathetic religious community around himself. He'd been part of just such a community in various forms throughout his life, but now, as an unmarried young pastor starting up a new assignment, with no senior pastor to mentor him or family to come home to or significant friends or colleagues to call on in his new city, Richard John Neuhaus would have been longing for the leisurely bonhomie and mutual encouragement to vocation that he had enjoyed in seminary, college, boarding school, and back home in Pembroke. There was nothing like this to be had on Maujer Street when he showed up in 1961. And so, beginning a practice that would hold for the rest of his life, when confronted with the absence of the religious or intellectual community that he thought was good and necessary and also personally longed for, Richard John Neuhaus worked hard to create that very community—and, in so doing, inevitably made himself its central figure.[3]

This happened almost immediately at St. John the Evangelist, as a group of young people from Concordia-Bronxville answered his call, attached themselves to the church, and immersed themselves in the daily work of urban ministry. Neuhaus didn't let them understand their relationship to the church or their duties as a mere Lutheran version of the Peace Corps, or even as an opportunity for vocational discernment or practical training for a church-related career. Instead they were to see it as their becoming a religious community in and of themselves, whose work was ordered to and by an active and regular prayer and sacramental life. There were obvious practical advantages to this community frame—the rigor it developed, the distinctive source of fellowship it afforded them together, the contemplative repose it afforded for each in what was otherwise a very active day. That said, Neuhaus regarded daily Eucharist and also group prayer—which took place at the start and end of each day and was based on formal prayers taken from the Lutheran breviary of the holy hours—as primarily a means of ensuring that his young urban ministers didn't lose sight of why they were pursuing this calling: both for and because of Christ. Neuhaus needed them to know this in order for them to be effective in their shared ministry, but more importantly because he regarded his volunteers as souls that were his responsibility to minister to. In turn, Neuhaus could enjoy the fellowship he was otherwise lacking, while also now being able to more substantially pursue the work of the church around Williamsburg, whether it was providing instruction in the faith through Sunday school, ministering to the basic social needs of a very poor neighborhood, or sending friendly young faces into the projects to knock on doors and invite folks to attend a Sunday service that promised a worship that was wondrous and transporting, and one thigh-thumper of a good sermon to boot.

Forty years after attending her first of many Neuhaus services at St. John the Evangelist, June Braun could still vividly attest to their appeal and power. A freshman Concordia-Bronxville student in 1961, she'd initially signed up to help at another urban church but kept hearing about what was happening at St. John's from her school friends and was intrigued enough to see for herself. Importantly, her interest wasn't in the particular work to be done, or in the people to work with and to serve, neither of which were notably different from what she was already experiencing elsewhere in Lutheran Brooklyn. Nor was she pulled over by the promise of a charismatic pastor alone. Instead, for June and many others who joined Neuhaus' congregation and his urban ministry in the early

1960s, the principal draw was the Sunday service itself, and more precisely its rare combination of transporting liturgy and bold, imperative preaching. Neuhaus' predecessor at St. John's, Pastor Klopf, had been similarly committed to liturgical practices that were solemn and ritual-focused, features enhanced by a choir that intoned traditional hymns throughout. Forming the service this way, Klopf was drawing on traditional small-*c* catholic traditions internal to Lutheranism along the lines of Arthur C. Piepkorn's ideas and practices. Klopf was also ordering the liturgy to and around the significance of the sacrament—the Eucharist—that was the very heart of the service itself. Yet by some accounts, Klopf may have been almost too solemn, too ritual-minded. Taking over, Neuhaus added a greater verve and vitality to the services, perhaps nowhere more so than in his preaching, and in this way integrated the influences he had received from his two most decisive seminary teachers, Piepkorn on liturgy and Richard Caemmerer on preaching.

"The church is the family of God," he preached that first Sunday June Braun attended one of his services, proposing a premise, vision, and indeed a call to action that carried at once universal and local meaning, as she soon discovered. In universal terms, Neuhaus wanted his congregants to know that their worship was in continuity with centuries of Christian prayer and practice and in solidarity with contemporary, ecclesial Christians from around the world, who were not, for that matter, exclusively Missouri Synod Lutherans. Indeed, unlike his more rigorous counterparts within the Missouri Synod, Neuhaus was very much open to ecumenical connections with Catholics and Mainline Protestants. After his first couple of years in Brooklyn, this openness would really begin to grow, in no small part because it provided a religiously framed context for his intensified involvement in the major currents of 1960s American life, while also attesting to his ongoing first-person commitment to work, as a Lutheran, toward what he often described as the project of healing the "breach of the sixteenth century" between Roman Catholicism and Reformation Protestantism. Doing so, however, would simultaneously open him up to charges of unionism, radical liberalism, and heresy from his opponents within Missouri, like his old seminary antagonist, Herman Otten, culminating in Otten's filing heresy charges against Neuhaus in 1969.

Such concerns were far from Neuhaus on Maujer Street in the early 1960s. Indeed, the local nature of God's family, embodied in St. John the Evangelist, was then his primary focus. This focus meant extending and expanding his predecessor's commitment to building a racially integrated congregation. It also meant preaching the oneness of family that was God's church, and preaching the need for a genuine, which is to say a genuinely, Christian community in the midst of a massive and alienating city. These were subjects that appeared in many of his sermons, which his congregants distinctively praised as "real thigh-thumpers." Beyond the liturgy, Neuhaus encouraged connections between his new young crew of urban ministry workers and the poor black congregation members who lived in the projects across the street, through informal means like social calls made on Sunday afternoons. Importantly, these visits came about through friendly invitations from the black congregants, rather than any kind of programmatic outreach from the white church workers, suggesting the former's sense of genuine belonging at St. John the Evangelist and likewise a sense of shared responsibility for attesting to the congregation's sense of itself as one family under God.[4]

During Neuhaus' early years as pastor, his church's vitality made it an exemplary kind of racially integrated, religiously orthodox Christian community in an era when racial division and/or religious heterodoxy more generally marked embodiments of American Christianity. But there was another, more surprising practice in place at St. John the Evangelist: in addition to two English-language services, Neuhaus led a German-language service, every Sunday. He did this out of sympathy and admiration for a small number, no more than twenty, of older Williamsburg residents of ethnic German stock who continued to attend church on Maujer Street, even though many of their co-congregants had left as part of the 1953 white flight to

Glendale. For Neuhaus, this was no remnant of a gone congregation, but a living element of the present one, and he ministered to them too, using the language of worship they'd always known. In making this decision to reintroduce a German-language service, Neuhaus inadvertently created something of an ironic symmetry across two generations of Lutheran pastors in his family. Some twenty years earlier, Clem Neuhaus had suspended German-language services at his St. John's in Pembroke, Ontario, in order to demonstrate the fullness of his immediate allegiances during wartime. Twenty years later, Richard John Neuhaus resumed a German-language service at his St. John's, in order to demonstrate his immediate allegiance to what remained of the founding community of the congregation.[5]

Those who departed had taken with them not only the church's charter but also much of its financial support, and while the new congregants were enthusiastic for Neuhaus' services and his new ministry group, they weren't in positions to help maintain the congregation as had their predecessors. The most obvious sign of this limit was the pastor's salary: there simply wasn't one. Neuhaus had to get a job. He found work as a chaplain at King's County Hospital, a sprawling complex that sat some five miles south of Williamsburg, in the East Flatbush district of Brooklyn. A position pursued for the practical purpose of supplementing his nonexistent pastor's salary, and one he seems to have kept for no more than a couple of years, the chaplaincy proved profoundly affecting to the young Neuhaus, exposing him to some of the darkest realities of urban life and of human suffering, while also revealing the surprising dignities of birth and death in a place where a great deal of both took place. Neuhaus would write about his formative time at King's for years afterward, in letters to friends and also in his books, and he kept for some time an unusual souvenir of his time there.

During one of the twenty-four shifts that he would work in the early 1960s, around midnight during a summer heat wave, Neuhaus watched ambulance attendants rush in with a woman drenched in her own blood. She was a complete wreck—her face strafed with bits of broken glass, one of her forearms so bashed up that broken bones had pierced the flesh. She was pronounced dead on arrival by the hospital intern who received her alongside Neuhaus, but then they both saw life still persisting in her eyes. They immediately responded to the presence not of a fresh corpse but of a fellow living human being, albeit one in the final moments of an excruciating death. Without speaking to each other about it, as Neuhaus would later write in *As I Lay Dying,* his autobiographical exploration of the mundane and mystical dimensions of death, the two of them tried to restore some portion of dignity to the woman before she died. "I think we both understood what she was owed, and that is why slowly, almost ritually, we picked out the glittering shards of glass from her pretty black face. I put the diamonds in a small plastic bag and kept them for years," he remarked, before concluding, "I no longer know where they are. I remember the smell, though, the smell of blood, which smells only like blood." As a writer, Neuhaus was willing to evoke the unexpected image of tiny diamonds in order to mark just how strangely glittering was the evidence of extreme violence marring the dying woman's face. But he didn't take a similar literary opportunity to conjure up the smell of blood: blood was blood, and nowhere more evident than in the emergency ward of King's County, which he described as a "bedlam [filled] with the victims of shootings, knifings, brawls, beatings, and accidents labeled 'cause unknown.'" Once the young woman died and her body was removed, eventually buried in the potter's field on an island in New York's East River, Neuhaus puzzled over what had happened to her, who had done this to her, before commending the woman's soul to the God who knew and claimed her even if no one else did. And then he went to minister to the next patient.[6]

Sometimes these patients ministered to him. The most memorable of these instances occurred in the death ward, where those deemed beyond recovery lay dying on beds crammed close into one another. "On hot summer days," Neuhaus would later recall, "they would fitfully toss off sheets and undergarments. The scene of naked and half-naked bodies groaning and writhing was reminiscent of Dante's *Inferno,*" and rare was the shift where Neuhaus didn't pray over two or three people for whom he was their last companion before death. The patient that affected him most was a bald, seventy-year-old man named Albert. One summer morning, Neuhaus visited with him and read aloud from the Bible. As might be expected, he chose the Twenty-Third Psalm, "The Lord is my shepherd; I shall not want." That evening, returning to visit with Albert, Neuhaus tried to embody, as best he could, the Psalm's sense of an abiding, merciful presence, as he later recounted: "I put my left arm around his shoulder and together, face almost touching face, we prayed the Our Father. Then Albert's eyes opened wider, as though he had seen something in my expression. 'Oh,' he said, 'oh, don't be afraid.' His body sagged back and he was dead." Neuhaus admits he was "stunned" by this turn of events: that as Albert was dying, he offered Neuhaus consolation, the very fact of which—the inherent dignity and abundant charity signaled by a man offering this to his ministering chaplain with his last breaths—moved Neuhaus greatly in the moment and in recollecting it years later in *As I Lay Dying.* That Albert had cause to offer Neuhaus consolation strongly suggests the difficulties that this twenty-six-year-old pastor must have had in confronting death itself, which figured often in his hospital chaplaincy work, whether as the aftermath of rage and violence visited upon a young woman or in the quiet moments following an old man's deathbed prayers.[7]

Neuhaus' time at King's also revealed to him some of the difficulties that surrounded life's early moments. Witnessing these difficulties—like a baby boy born unwanted, who would become a ward of the city—only intensified his still-fresh commitment to the ministry he had taken on in becoming an inner-city pastor. This much is evident in a remarkable twenty-one-page letter that Neuhaus wrote Wilken on his breaks during one long day at the hospital. The letter's most revealing moments occur when Neuhaus returns to his pen and paper right after watching a birth:

> *I just saw "baby boy Washington" enter life with a cry. He does not yet know how much he will have to cry about. His mother is unmarried and does not want him. He will be turned over to the city for a life of not being wanted. This is true for more than one third of all the hundreds of babies delivered here. I don't think his prospects are very good for finding love, happiness, joy, purpose. . . . I am not depressed—only filled with wonder. Wonder at the glory and tragedy of life in this city. In a little while I will drive home and can count on being struck again by the New York skyline—a never failing object of adoration. The city and the potential of the civilization it represents—to this I am religiously committed. And to the ways of the God who brought it into being. "What is man, that you keep him in mind?" Little baby boy Washington—fear not, He has redeemed you. He has called you by the name you do not yet have, you are His! I cannot guarantee you that this is true. It may be a pious illusion. But it is better than what is called the truth by men, but just must be illusion. You are not alone.*

Nowhere is Richard John Neuhaus' sense of self and world, circa 1961, more evident than in this letter to Wilken, in no small part because the letter's purpose is as much about letting his friend know about his new life in New York as it is a pretext for making sense of that very life for himself. And to do that is to make sense of life for the people around him, including for a newborn child whose future, like that of so many others, seems bleak from the moment of birth. Indeed it did, by most every measure and truth devised by men alone—and so would be, but for God's redemptive claim upon every human life, baby boy Washington's included. Why does Neuhaus directly address the child in a letter to Wilken? Is this a rhetorical flourish? After all, there is no denying the highly literary quality of the writing, the intensification of feeling and drama made possible by this sudden switch to addressing a baby he would never see again. But ultimately Neuhaus is not performing here for his friend;

he is not psychologically working through the events of a difficult day at work, or even giving his literary muscles a workout otherwise denied by his consuming duties as a full-time pastor and part-time hospital chaplain. By the end of this letter, Neuhaus is praying. He is praying for this child, that the child may know he is not alone, and he is praying for others like him. And he is praying to God with praise, thanksgiving, and petition, all for having been given a demanding new ministry marked by urban glories and tragedies that fill him with wonder and only confirm his commitment to doing God's work in the world. This was a world whose intensifying conflicts would soon command much more of his time and energy, his words and his prayers.[8]

CHAPTER EIGHT

From Brooklyn Pastor to National Newsmaker

Talking back to Lyndon Baines Johnson, Richard John Neuhaus made national news for the first time on October 25, 1965. Earlier that month, in response to the antiwar protests that were spreading across the country, the President had expressed rather maudlin astonishment that so many were so aggressively protesting America's expanding war effort against Communist forces in Vietnam. Johnson was, in his words, filled with "surprise that any one citizen would feel toward his country in a way that was not consistent with the national interest." A few days later, Neuhaus shot back, "It concerns us that the President should be amazed by dissent," as the *New York Times* reported, as part of its coverage of a daylong ecumenical conference in Manhattan, where some one hundred Protestant, Catholic, and Jewish clergy met to discuss U.S. foreign policy in Vietnam and its domestic pressures and corollaries. Alongside Abraham Joshua Heschel and Daniel Berrigan, a publicly acclaimed rabbi and a Jesuit priest who would soon become a distinctive icon of 1960s anti-establishment foment, Neuhaus emerged that day as a national religious leader in the growing antiwar movement, a development that dovetailed with his increased presence in the Civil Rights Movement. And so began the first major arc of Richard John Neuhaus' public life.

He entered into that public life as he would always remain in it, up to his death: as a man of God who found in that office and vocation both the means and the imperative that ordered his considerable ambitions and energies into protest-framed activism, controversy-making, and coalition-building; into politically engaged ecumenical and interfaith work; and into theologically informed cultural critique and analysis, whether in print publications or in speeches and interviews. The same was true of press conferences, where he could be reliably assured that the national media would quote him, for instance, caustically disputing the President of the United States. In and through all of this, Neuhaus would develop a remarkable and often conflicting array of friends, colleagues, and collaborators well placed across the intersecting worlds of American religion, intellectual life, media, academia and policy circles, political action groups, and the various branches and offices of the federal government. Just as he did in his church life with his young urban ministry recruits, Neuhaus would become a hub for a series of spokes extending outward to form a wheel the pace and direction of which he largely set himself. He did this with a combination of outsized charisma and outpacing energy, which he committed to advancing the goods of religion in and for public life, while often advancing himself as the exemplary embodiment of the very same. He found many loyal friends, sympathetic colleagues, and willing collaborators, who over the years were largely matched by, and sometimes themselves joined, a roster of vehement foes, hostile critics, and willing detractors.[1]

Neuhaus' life and work dramatically expanded in its scope and reach from 1965 onward. This took shape through a series of decisive events both personal and public, with each of these contexts informing and affecting the other. His own voluminous writings, paired with his all but continual presence in the national media and in American religious, intellectual, and greater public life from this period onward—as both a subject with influence and a figure of interest—afford abundant evidence to explore and analyze. But for the time between 1962 and his *Times* appearance in late October 1965, there is comparatively little hard evidence of how Neuhaus was spending his time, beyond continuing to lead his congregation and also discerning what it would mean for him to contribute to the broader work of early 1960s liberalism's defining projects: the expansion and enshrinement of civil rights for African-Americans; the increased protection and support of society's most vulnerable and powerless members; and the speaking of moral truths to military-industrial powers that were otherwise positioning the United States to wage a major war in Southeast Asia, even while many at home were questioning its motives, aims, and legitimacy. In time, Neuhaus and his congregation both would be variously and controversially involved in all of these projects.

Unsurprisingly, for a white Northern pastor leading a majority black church, the entry point was the Civil Rights Movement. Across the nation in 1962 and 1963, Civil Rights advocates and tentatively sympathetic political leaders adopted a variety of measures to advance the cause. City buses were boycotted in Albany, Georgia, to protest segregated seating; a Voter Education Project took shape and began registering black voters elsewhere in the American South; President John F. Kennedy issued an executive order prohibiting racial discrimination in all federally funded housing; and most dramatically, in the summer and fall of 1962, a young black man named James Meredith was admitted on federal court orders to the University of Mississippi. His subsequent effort to register for classes occasioned an extended and heated political dispute between the Kennedy administration and the governor of Mississippi that led to rioting, mob violence, and the stationing of some twelve thousand federal troops around the campus, who were sent in to guard Meredith's right to a higher education. Come 1963 in neighboring Alabama, members of the Southern Christian Leadership Conference (SCLC), with its president, the Reverend Martin Luther King, Jr., the most prominent among them, began an extended antisegregation campaign in Birmingham that pursued a program of nonviolent resistance to unjust laws and was met with brutal force. In addition to arresting thousands, local law enforcement, led by "Bull" Connor, Birmingham's public safety commissioner, went after the peaceful protestors with fire hoses and police dogs. In April 1963, King himself was arrested. While imprisoned, he wrote one of the most famous epistles in American history, the "Letter from Birmingham Jail." Decades later, writing and blogging about King for *First Things,* Neuhaus would recommend it as an unqualified "classic," praise it as "deservedly enshrined in the telling of the American story," and confidently predict that "as long as the American experiment continues," citizens "will read and be instructed by" King's letter.

No doubt Neuhaus read and was instructed by it upon its 1963 appearance in venues like the *New York Post*, the *Atlantic Monthly*, and the *Christian Century*. For someone with Neuhaus' interests, sensibility, and position at the time, King's letter represented at once a stirring call to action and an influential exemplary version of what it would mean to bring theology, Scripture, and the Christian tradition to bear upon matters of grave consequence in contemporary public life. To argue for the ethical imperatives, the Christian precedent, and the national implications of refusing to obey unjust laws in Birmingham, King cited the words and ideas of St. Paul, St. Augustine, and St. Thomas Aquinas; he cited figures of civil disobedience from the Old Testament and the exemplary persecuted witness of the early Christians; he cited key revolutionary events and founding documents of the American Experiment in addition to drawing on the writings of Martin Luther, Paul Tillich, Reinhold Niebuhr, Martin Buber, T. S. Eliot, Thomas Jefferson, and Socrates. And rather than only citing the Gospel teachings of Christ, King invoked the crucified Christ as the ultimate figure of the extremism that King and his fellow protestors were called to emulate. In dying for our sins, he wrote, Christ went to his death as an "extremist for love, truth, and goodness."[2]

Beginning with his commitment to Civil Rights but developing from there into every question of public consequence that he took up in his life and work, Neuhaus would consistently advance arguments housed under the overlapping canopies of the Christian tradition and the American Experiment, as does King with his "Letter from Birmingham Jail." More directly, Neuhaus answered King's call for greater action on the part of the white clergy by preaching extensively from the pulpit at St. John's about the religious imperative to support Civil Rights. This was predictably well received by his black congregation, even if the accompanying calls to join in a national social justice movement developing around events taking place in the American South, framed as a necessary way of living out the Gospel, may have been more demanding and unexpected for a church that had cause enough to focus its time and energy on more immediate social and economic challenges. These matters significantly occupied Neuhaus' daily concerns, as Robert Wilken and his wife, Carol, discovered in the summer of 1963. Over dinner at a little restaurant in Greenwich Village, Neuhaus made scant effort to hide how little he thought of people who didn't forsake the grand opportunities of the greater world to devote themselves to the poor and unwanted in rarely considered places like the housing project district of Williamsburg. Wilken, an academic and family man passing through New York en route to visit Europe, felt this rebuke rather directly: his and Neuhaus' diverging paths after seminary remained a source of tension between them, insofar as it occasioned the latter's all but open disapproval. This disapproval was also taking a broader, more ideological form, as Wilken noticed on another visit with Neuhaus during his early time in New York. The two of them attended a musical performance at Lincoln Center. During the intermission, milling about with the wealthy concertgoers, Neuhaus raised a hand in protest at the scene and said, "Robert, do you realize all the money that's being spent on this, and how many poor people there are in this city? With their suffering, why are we doing this?"[3]

Indeed, rather than mixing with elites, Neuhaus pursued only greater involvements with the marginalized masses, as when he attended the August 1963 March on Washington. The SCLC organized this daylong event in order "to use the capital as a parade ground for human rights," as declared Roy Wilkens, another Civil Rights leader. A host of prominent Civil Rights leaders and liberal-minded public figures, clergy, musicians, and celebrities attended alongside thousands of ordinary citizens, black and white. Identifying another element in the mix, in citing a formative commitment to postwar liberalism as a defining feature of future neoconservatives, Justin Vaisse notes that Neuhaus participated in the March on Washington, as did Penn Kemble, Joshua Muravchik, and Paul Wolfowitz. But this grouping is only obvious in retrospect, for they didn't attend together or even know one another at that point. Likely these other figures would have been among the white "students and over-earnest intellectuals" that King biographer Taylor Branch identifies among the tens of thousands of whites joining the many more thousands of blacks who covered the "vast acreage between the Capitol and the Washington monument" that August 28, 1963. But not Neuhaus, who would have been elsewhere in the massive crowd, surrounded by the black members of his congregation with whom he likely attended the event, traveling from Brooklyn in one of the two thousand buses from across the country that carried marchers to Washington. That day, the pastor and people of St. John the Evangelist, alongside some two hundred thousand others, would have heard a succession of songs and speeches that culminated with King's "I Have a Dream" address, which closed with his famous vision of "that day when *all* God's children, black men and white men, Jews and Gentiles, Protestants and Catholics, will be able to join hands and sing . . . 'Free at last! Free at last! Thank God Almighty we are free at last!' "[4]

Returning to Brooklyn, the sonorous timber of King's voice still in his ears, Neuhaus turned his attention to Civil Rights activism within the Missouri Synod, writing a letter on "Racial Demonstrations" to the widely read *Lutheran Witness* newsletter in September 1963. The letter, as Missouri Synod historian James Burkee notes, bluntly advocated for increased participation in these activities "'precisely in order to antagonize' conservatives in the church and society," and thereby force a greater reckoning with the nation's undeniable racial injustices for otherwise unwilling Missouri Lutherans and other conservatives. Beyond provocation-minded letter writing, Neuhaus also increased his involvement with the Lutheran Human Relations Association of America (LHRAA), a broadly Lutheran organization initially dedicated in the 1950s to integrating congregations but that in turn began to pursue nonviolent protest for Civil Rights in the early 1960s, which included "kneel-ins" as an ecclesial complement to the sit-in movement. In time, Neuhaus would become its most prominent New York representative, just as his antiwar activism began in earnest as well. His brother Tom noticed elements of the former when he saw Neuhaus briefly in November 1963, stopping in New York in transit on a leave from his military assignment at an American base in Germany. Shortly before and after the brothers met, two historic events of lasting consequence took place. On November 1, 1963, South Vietnamese President Ngo Dinh Diem was overthrown; on November 22, U.S. President John F. Kennedy was assassinated. Though neither brother could fully know it then, these events would each in its way herald a tumultuous era in American life, an era that they engaged in very different ways. In time, Neuhaus would dispute the Vietnam War extensively with his brother Tom and his brother George, who both fought there on multiple tours. But this brief meeting in New York, before Kennedy was killed and before the geopolitical ramifications of Diem's overthrow began to be felt, was cordial, and the more significant impression Neuhaus gave his brother was of his enthusiastic immersion in the work of leading his congregation and in becoming more involved in the Civil Rights Movement.[5]

The latter took practical shape through a series of speeches

Neuhaus made in 1963 and 1964 under the auspices of the LHRAA and through his developing connections in an East Coast college chaplaincy network, and also through his participation in the Missouri Synod's Atlantic District annual conventions, where he quickly emerged as a progressive leader by way of his Civil Rights advocacy. Within a year, he would win both notice and notoriety for his efforts inside the Missouri Synod. In 1964, however, he was engaging more than Lutheran audiences: he began taking his charismatic appeals on behalf of Civil Rights and urban ministry and much else to places like Harvard and Yale, where future close friends and decisive collaborators like Michael Novak, Leonard Klein, and James Nuechterlein were then students. Novak recalls being immediately taken with Neuhaus' commanding presence in a meeting room, borne of his energetic, faith-informed convictions and calls to action, which were framed and matched by intellectual voraciousness and voracious name-dropping. Indeed, Novak—soon a major public intellectual and prodigious writer in his own right, whose overlapping interests in Catholicism, democracy, capitalism, and the American Experiment would become closely intertwined with Neuhaus' work over the years—left his first meeting with Neuhaus under the impression that "he seemed to know everybody."

To Novak, Neuhaus was also willing and able to talk about everything: "religion, politics, modernity . . . ecclesiastical and academic gossip, how to beat those threatening Republicans (Nixon, Rockefeller and their ilk, not to mention Goldwater in 1964), Vatican II, ecumenism . . ." Leonard Klein had heard of Neuhaus from friends in New York, who spoke more about the appeal of his liturgy than his activist work. Intrigued, he attended a talk Neuhaus gave in New Haven under the auspices of Yale's campus chaplaincy, which was then led by William Sloane Coffin, Jr. Within a couple of years of this visit, Coffin would become one of Neuhaus' most prominent colleagues in the religious wing of the antiwar movement. Klein himself would later work closely with Neuhaus in 1960s activism, and in the 1970s on a Lutheran religious newsletter, and eventually also convert to Roman Catholicism. He was a divinity school student when he first saw Neuhaus at Yale in 1964 and was taken by his double commitment to liturgical renewal and Civil Rights activism. Klein was also influenced by Neuhaus' commendations of Wolfhart Pannenberg, a Lutheran theologian working in Germany, whose writings were then untranslated and effectively unknown in American theological circles. After this first meeting, Klein was so engaged by Neuhaus' example, he asked to spend the following summer at St. John the Evangelist, where he learned from and helped advance Neuhaus' ministry.[6]

Nuechterlein, who was a graduate student at Yale at the time and would eventually serve as the editor of *First Things* under Neuhaus for more than a decade, first met him off-campus. He was a lay delegate to the Missouri Synod's Atlantic District Convention, where Neuhaus, in attendance as a Brooklyn pastor, attempted to persuade his fellow Missourians to recognize the need for a more activist kind of ministry in order to live out the Gospel in meaningful, effectual ways in 1960s America. This effort was far from easy. While no one in any northern districts of the Missouri Church would actively or publicly oppose Civil Rights, few were willing to endorse it or any tacitly sympathetic measures. This wasn't necessarily out of racist sentiment, but rather because of a more traditionalist construal of Lutheranism's Two Kingdoms theology. The theology itself extends the Lutheran binary of Law and Gospel into a broader context while affirming "the characteristically Lutheran habit of thinking in two realms," in this case by "putting the Word and Sacraments into one, [and] public life and human rights into the other," as theologian Carl Braaten explains. The key question in modern American Lutheranism is what kind of relationship there ought to be between the Kingdoms of God and Grace, insofar as they together constitute, in Braaten's formulation, "two modes of divine activity in the world," one mode with a sacred and the other with a secular frame and focus.[7]

At one end of the doctrinal spectrum, some Missourians held

that the Two Kingdoms are two strictly separate realms that Christ Himself distinguished in His Gospel call to render unto Caesar and unto God the things that belong each to each. As Lutheran theologian George W. Forell straightforwardly noted in a 1945 article, "Each man is a member of a secular realm and of a spiritual realm. It is important to realize the difference between these two realms and to keep them separate. . . . Luther himself pointed frequently to the difference between the two and reiterated the need for a clear separation." By extension, then, the Church, as earthly crucible and conserver of God's Graces, is called to keep itself separate from worldly affairs, as are its ministers. At the other end of the spectrum, however, were Missourians who held that these Kingdoms needed to be distinguished from each other but not kept artificially separate, precisely because they naturally, necessarily, and mutually overlay each other, to form a full account of a Christian's responsibilities in this life. The question, for those who construe the theology this way, according to Braaten, "is whether the church and its missionary outreach can join [together] in the creative task of bringing the vertical line of justification through faith alone [the Kingdom of Grace] to bear upon the vertical line of the kingdom striving for justice in an evil world." Neuhaus passionately believed so—and King's rejection of a separatist account of the sacred and secular in his "Letter from Birmingham Jail" would have afforded a convincing real-time demonstration of why. Indeed, Neuhaus squarely occupied this side of the spectrum in 1964 and long thereafter, even if the political imperatives he responded to and the activist projects he advanced would themselves shift in profile and principle from politically and culturally progressive to conservative.[8]

In 1964, the early stage of his public life, Neuhaus was clearly a progressive force in Missouri's Atlantic District. As intensely as he held to this line, it didn't prevent his offering more dispassionate counsel. During one of his campus visits in 1964, Neuhaus met a young man in crisis. John Robert Hannah was a seminarian who had decided to pursue an army chaplaincy. In light of rising antiwar sentiment on college campuses and in broader American life, and more intensely in response to hearing Neuhaus speak against the war effort, he was now questioning his decision. He wrote Neuhaus to this effect and asked for advice. In reply, Neuhaus told Hannah that while his own conscience would not allow him to follow the trajectory Hannah had chosen—he noted that he had himself briefly served as a military chaplain before resigning—he could understand this as a vocational choice that Hannah had clearly discerned with care and concern. Neuhaus did not conceal or overplay his own position on the matter, despite the obvious opportunity he had to influence this seminarian to his liking. Why? Perhaps Neuhaus was, in a minor way, avoiding an unwelcome repeat of his own related experience. Near the end of his time in the seminary, Neuhaus was convinced to join the army by Father Piepkorn—a very proud military chaplain and a persuasive influence on his devoted seminarians, among whom Neuhaus was first: others, including Wilken, also joined at his urging. His vocational interests clearly elsewhere, Neuhaus resigned, well before doing so would have been a more dramatically political act. And when the pattern emerged in reverse a few years later—Neuhaus was now in the position of counselor, and his counsel by that time would have been to join most anything other than the army—he refused to extend it and left the matter for Hannah to decide by the dictates of his own conscience.[9]

There were no similar complications when it came to Neuhaus' Civil Rights advocacy among his fellow ministers. At Atlantic District conventions in the early 1960s, he delivered speeches and advanced motions to convince his fellow Missourians that church and mission were called to come together and join the Civil Rights Movement. He had little success, and would try again in 1965, under more dramatic and personally charged circumstances. Before that, in mid-June 1964, Neuhaus made a more local appeal along the very same lines when he gave a paper entitled "Should We Save Brooklyn Lutheranism?" to the Brooklyn Lutheran Council.[10] His answer, obviously, would have been yes, and the measures he would have inevitably advocated to do so—a combination of liturgical renewal, urban ministry, and Civil Rights activism—would no doubt have been informed by his own experiences and commitments at St. John the Evangelist and elsewhere. This otherwise minor paper retains significance as the first that Neuhaus thought to record in his personal papers as a distinct publication. A signal of a sensibility at once practical and well organized, but also rather self-regarding, the notation suggests that he knew, by June 1964, that his ministry was beginning to take on a more public cast and should be chronicled as such.

A year later this would become fully the case, when Neuhaus talked back to Lyndon Baines Johnson while talking to the *New York Times*. A Lutheran pastor taking on the President in the middle of but one of so many protests was well in keeping with the atmosphere of 1965, when the United States entered its most tumultuous and conflict-ridden period of the twentieth century, and Richard John Neuhaus began what would turn out to be a lifelong balancing act between his local ministry and his national ambitions, between his activist commitments and his intellectual energies, and between his political alliances and his personal friendships. Across all of this he kept strong his commitment to God and His Two Kingdoms, though this would often be disputed by opponents and critics whom Neuhaus frequently engaged and sometimes helped along in his words and deeds, as a man of God and a patriotic American. This would always be a complex and imperfect and disputable combination that would, in 1965, introduce Richard John Neuhaus to the Missouri Synod's national stage and to broader American public life. He would prove a faith-filled and fierce player in a fraught and fierce time.[11]

CHAPTER NINE

Missouri's Militant Instrument of God's Peace

Waiting his turn to speak, Richard John Neuhaus couldn't help but look across the crowded delegate floor to the queue of pastors standing before the other microphone. He focused on one man in particular. Given his height and size and grave composure, Clem Neuhaus would have likely stood out to anyone, but his son Richard was only a few feet away, and he was ready to voice his passionate disagreement with his father, again. Only this time, the two of them would not be arguing at the Neuhaus dining table after Sunday lunch; they would be arguing in front of hundreds of fellow pastors, themselves variously caught up in the debate that the Missouri Synod confronted at its 1965 national convention in Detroit. Was the church called to commit itself to the struggle for Civil Rights in solidarity with a broader coalition of churches and denominations? Or, in committing to the struggle for Civil Rights, was the church abandoning its historic and sacred identity and mission? Working from opposed understandings of Two Kingdoms theology, the son was convinced of the former; the father, of the latter. Debating from the delegate floor a series of Mission Affirmations forwarded by Missouri moderates and disputed by conservatives—the most contentious being specifically the establishment of the "principle of an interchurch approach to mission," which, in practical terms, would justify involving Missouri more formally in the religious segment of the Civil Rights Movement—Richard and Clem each tried to convince their brother pastors of what he believed to be the only right course forward.[1]

The father-and-son duelists only intensified the tension in the delegate hall. James Burkee observes: "Moderate victories in 1965 exposed growing polarization in the church. . . . Perceptions [of tacitly condoned unionism and universalism] pushed delegates and even family members into opposing camps, ideologically," an intensification Burkee personifies in Richard and Clem's convention floor clash. Indeed, for years afterward, whether in conversation with friends or more formally with historians of the Missouri Synod's divisive postwar period, Richard Neuhaus would recall this event with complicated feelings. While always proud of his early and consistent involvement in the Civil Rights Movement, he regretted that he never convinced his father to change his mind about it. James Nuechterlein, Neuhaus' longtime colleague at *First Things*, observes that Neuhaus "talked a lot about his father," notably about their debates at home and in public. His remarks suggested to Nuechterlein a long-standing and unmet desire for approval on Neuhaus' part; no doubt the father and son's very public dispute over Civil Rights in the 1960s would have both exacerbated and further prevented satisfying this. Clem, who enjoyed some formal standing at the convention because of his status as an Ontario District vice president, didn't budge on his conservative views about the synod and whether it had political and ecumenical responsibilities, just as his son was emerging, in Burkee's words, as "Missouri's revolutionary for civil rights."

This status, developed through Neuhaus' growing involvement in the LHRAA and through his various writings on the subject for Missouri publications like *Lutheran Witness* magazine and also for the catholic-minded scholarly journal *Una Sancta* that he would eventually edit, would have been solidified by his contributions at the 1965 Detroit convention to the successful passage of the Mission

Affirmations. The passage represented a "BLESSED REVOLUTION in the Synod's thinking and practice," as Neuhaus grandly put it to another Lutheran newspaper at the time. His old seminary foe Herman Otten fully agreed that this was a revolution for Missouri, but he saw no great joy in this. For conservatives like Otten, involvement with Civil Rights was a malformation of what it meant to proclaim the Gospel; it was a rejection of the call to obey civil authorities and follow secular laws in keeping with (at least one reading of) Two Kingdoms theology. At the helm of a small but active cadre of reactionary activists competing for influence within the synod, Otten immediately took to print and also aggressively lobbied the synod leadership to regard Neuhaus and his fellow moderates' victories as troubling evidence of (reckless) liberalism, (destructive) unionism, and (dangerous) Communist sympathies.[2]

Neuhaus' involvements outside the already fractious confines of the Missouri Synod only encouraged these characterizations. By the time Neuhaus spoke at the Detroit convention, in late spring 1965—marking the start of the most significant twelve months of his life and work to date—he had already participated in the March 21, 1965, freedom march from Selma to Montgomery in support of black voter rights. The march had followed only days after the Johnson administration sent legislation to Congress that sought, through federal oversight, to ensure the right to vote in parts of the country where blacks had been historically and systematically disenfranchised. In Selma, Martin Luther King and other established Civil Rights leaders were joined by new allies like New York Rabbi Abraham Joshua Heschel, who had a prominent place at the vanguard of the marchers, one man over from King, and would soon become a significant figure in Neuhaus' life and work. Heschel introduced Neuhaus directly to King and made him a small and grateful part of King's work, and more significantly, he decisively influenced Neuhaus' understandings of Judaism and of what it meant to be a man of God in public life. Leaving Selma, however, Neuhaus would have been only a member of the greater mass of thousands of black and white marchers at that point, rather than any kind of leader in his own right. While marching, he would have witnessed the tension and stakes of the event, with military jeeps forming a colonnade at every crossroads along the route, news of an unnamed white minister in an advance car getting beaten up, and one counterprotestor standing beside the Pettus Bridge out of Selma holding a sign that read, "I hate niggers."[3]

Beyond his contributions at the Detroit convention, Neuhaus drew on his personal experiences in situations less public and dramatic than the Selma march, as part of his advocacy for Civil Rights within Missouri. In December 1965, he led an LHRAA conference in Chicago that was devoted less to discussing Missouri's position on race and politics than to finding practical means of putting the Synod's Mission Affirmations from the national convention into action. Speaking from his status as the pastor of an inner-city black congregation, Neuhaus captivated the room by drawing from his experiences as a chaplain at King's County Hospital: he told his fellow pastors a terrible story of a young black woman sitting in a hospital waiting room, a sick baby in her arms. They waited, and waited, and waited, in vain: no one came to the mother and child's aid. After three hours, the baby died. Faced with such realities in his very midst, how could a pastor confine himself to his pulpit?[4]

As fraught as the Civil Rights situation was in the United States by 1965, in Alabama and other Southern states most obviously but also in minor ways and places like a Northern inner-city hospital, it didn't command the exclusive focus of the national conversation. Following the August 1964 Gulf of Tonkin incident—a North Vietnamese attack on an American naval vessel—the Johnson administration secured congressional approval to expand the American military presence in Vietnam. The President signaled these plans in his 1965 State of the Union address, where he framed the growing war effort as a defensive strategy meant to block the worldwide advance of Communism, and to aid the imperiled people of South Vietnam. A month later, U.S. forces initiated Operation Rolling Thunder, a systematic and sustained bombing of North Vietnam targets; in March, American Marines began arriving in central Vietnam to protect U.S. air bases; by July 1965, American ground forces had dramatically increased to 125,000, a figure that would more than double in the coming years, while casualties increased from a few hundred to tens of thousands. These developments in Southeast Asia met growing resistance at home, where, by the mid-sixties, there was already organized dissent on the secular political Left and from peace- and justice-focused religious groups who demonstrated against America's involvements in Vietnam, U.S. foreign policy more generally, and the Cold War's nuclear arms race. Peace marches took place in New York and Washington; campus protests and teach-ins happened at the University of Michigan, UC-Berkeley, and elsewhere; organizations were founded, and declarations and manifestos written, as with the Students for a Democratic Society (SDS) and their Port Huron Statement—these elements collectively attested to the emergence of three main sectors of leftist dissent and activism focused directly against the Johnson administration. There was a radical Left, dominated by the SDS; a pacifist Left, populated by an array of organizations, including the Committee for Non-Violent Action and Women Strike for Peace; and a liberal Left, led by organizations like the Committee for a SANE Nuclear Policy, Americans for Democratic Action, and, by late October 1965, the country's first formal religious organization dedicated to ending the war in Vietnam, which Richard John Neuhaus cofounded, thereby beginning what would prove a lifelong, religiously informed engagement with national politics.[5]

By the autumn of 1965, prominent American government officials were aggressively trying to discredit the growing antiwar movement. Attorney General Nicholas Katzenbach suggested it was infiltrated by Communists and subject to federal prosecution, while FBI Director J. Edgar Hoover opted for a simpler, ad hominem approach: "Anti-Vietnam demonstrators in the U.S. represent a minority for the most part composed of halfway citizens who are neither morally, mentally nor emotionally mature." As Mitchell Hall explains in his comprehensive history of the antiwar group that Neuhaus helped lead, "In response to these attacks, an ad hoc group of about 100 Protestant, Catholic, and Jewish Clergy from New York City organized an ecumenical forum to evaluate America's Asian Policy. Representatives of the group held a press conference in the United Nations Church Center on October 25, 1965." It was during this press conference that Neuhaus issued his first notable public comment, that tart response to Lyndon Baines Johnson's lamentations over dissenting citizens, while further observing that efforts from "the highest levels of government" to suppress dissent could eventually "subvert the very democracy which loyal Americans seek to protect."

Neuhaus' comments may not have been as alarmist and provocative at the time as they might seem today, in part thanks to the context created for them, at least among religiously minded peace and justice advocates, by John XXIII's 1963 encyclical *Pacem in Terris*. There, the pope proposed, "Authority is a postulate of the moral order and derives from God. Consequently, laws and decrees enacted in contravention of the moral order, and hence of the divine will, can have no binding force in conscience . . . indeed the passing of such laws undermines the very nature of authority and results in shameful abuse." Neuhaus, himself an early admirer of John XXIII, would always be rather taken with this particular strand of thought about the legitimacy of state authority. In fact, he would later invoke and also quote directly from *Pacem in Terris* on questions of abortion and on the place of religion in public life more generally. Claims over the possible subversion of democracy by state authorities would also recur in various forms at politically significant moments throughout his public life. Indeed, Neuhaus had a particular interest, if not penchant, for provocatively accusing a democratically elected American government of pursuing actions that undermined American democracy itself. It is unclear how much his first notable version of this recurring prediction surprised his fellow speakers during the post-forum press conference at the UN in 1965, but Neuhaus was himself surprised when one of them, the rabbi Abraham Joshua Heschel, suddenly told reporters that a formal group would be organized to mount resistance to the war. It would exist for as long as the war went on and be made up of religious leaders who would work to "mobilize [religiously informed] opposition to United States intervention in Southeast Asia," as Hall notes. After the news conference, Heschel challenged his unprepared colleagues to help him fulfill his press conference promise. "Are we then finished?" he asked Neuhaus and others. "Do we go home content, and the war goes on?" The question answered itself.[6]

At the helm were Heschel, Neuhaus, and also Jesuit Daniel Berrigan. The latter would almost immediately run afoul of Catholic authorities, both from his order and from the Archdiocese of New York, because of his public involvements with the organization. He was in fact ordered to remove himself from the organizing committee, and then effectively exiled for a span to pursue church duties in South America. That November in New York, Neuhaus and Heschel arranged an empty chair onstage beside their own to represent Berrigan's suppression and forced absence at a conference on the war. Speechmaking and dramatic imagery aside, the conference yielded a resolution, supported by the four hundred clerics in attendance, that "the conflict in Vietnam, according to our religious convictions, is not a just war." But could this statement, stark and strong on its own terms, have any effect on national politics and policy making? What might be necessary for that to happen? Media interest in the emerging movement that Neuhaus, Heschel, and Berrigan (in absentia) were now leading, and the great number of fellow clerics and also laypeople looking for their leadership, together suggested that a religiously informed and religiously led antiwar movement was filling an obvious lack in the broader protest movement, otherwise dominated by secular leftists of various affiliations. The emerging religious antiwar movement also established a countervailing force to the uncritical patriotism and support for the war coming from other religious leaders in the United States, perhaps from no one more prominently than New York's Francis Cardinal Spellman. Facing pickets at home over the perception that the American Church was punishing priests like Berrigan for their antiwar activities, Spellman spent Christmas 1965 in Vietnam, celebrating Mass for the troops. In an interview with the *New York Times* while in Saigon, he effectively codified the then religious conservative's baseline position on Vietnam: "The Cardinal was asked 'What do you think about what America is doing in Vietnam?' and he answered 'I fully support everything it does.' . . . He added: 'My country may it always be right. Right or wrong, my country.' "[7]

For Neuhaus and his fellow organizers and their supporters, the United States was doing a great deal of wrong in Vietnam and had to stop, both for the good of the people caught up directly in the conflict and to restore the moral dignity and stature of the United States itself. The broad response to their early efforts suggested to the new group's leaders that their effort to agitate for peace could and should move beyond New York. To that end, on January 11, 1966, a group of clergy met at the apartment of John C. Bennett, president of New York's Union Theological Seminary, where they decided to take their movement national. They named themselves the National Emergency Committee of Clergy Concerned About Vietnam. The organization's initial members, noted journalist Francine du Plessix Gray, then covering Clergy Concerned's beginnings for the *New Yorker* in a series of intensely observed articles that would eventually become an important, almost real-time history of 1960s religious radicalism, "read like a Who's Who in the American Church." One of its leading members was William Sloane Coffin, Jr., whom Neuhaus already knew through his visits with Coffin at Yale. Neuhaus would remain close with Coffin for at least a decade—filling in for him at the Yale chaplaincy now and then, and hosting him at his Brooklyn church on occasion, where Coffin would play on its broken-down grand piano while the two of them smoked cigars, sipped whiskey, and passed the night by belting their way through *The Lutheran Hymnal*.

Eventually, they would break, during a public debate in the

mid-1970s about the right ordering of orthodoxy and social justice in American church life, an event that Neuhaus would regard as a personal and doctrinal betrayal on Coffin's part. In 1966, however, they were very much of a shared mind on the matter before them, as Coffin's first public comments about their new organization suggest. He was an obvious choice to speak to the media at Clergy Concerned's beginnings. Coffin was a Presbyterian minister with an elite East Coast pedigree and a notable office at Yale. He was also a recognizable member of the early 1960s Freedom Rider movement that had agitated for desegregation in the South. Already a religious figure of some prominence in American life, Coffin stepped forward to announce the committee's formation at a press conference following the meeting in Bennett's apartment. "The moment is crucial," he declared, "for it may well be that morally speaking the United States ship of state is today comparable to the *Titanic* just before it hit the iceberg. If we decide on all-out escalation of the war in Vietnam, then to all intents and purposes of the human soul we may be sunk. We plead therefore with our fellow clergy to support our government's effort to negotiate an end to the war and to prevent its further escalation."[8]

The dramatic texture of Coffin's remarks underscored the committee's core contention that ongoing, indeed intensifying war in Vietnam posed an irreducibly moral challenge to the nation—rather than only a logistical or political one, as other opponents might hold. As such, clergymen, speaking out on matters of grave public concern from their religiously framed positions, had a distinctive contribution to make, if not a responsibility to carry out, in convincing the government to end the war before it further imperiled the nation's moral standing and condition. In Gray's estimation, such presumption was especially provocative: "Clergy Concerned was proposing the startling notion that the issue of war and peace was a valid concern of all churches." This was startling to ordinary citizens and ecclesiastical authorities alike, because both of those groups were now "suddenly confronted with these distinguished churchmen protesting the illegality and the immorality of the Vietnam war." These churchmen began making this case right away in January 1966. They sent a telegram to President Johnson after their founding meeting, in which they called for an end to the bombing and a commitment of future American aid in Vietnam to humanitarian causes over and against more armaments.

They kept up the pressure thereafter, with a steady stream of related telegrams and public statements. At the same time, relying on donated office space on Riverside Drive courtesy of the National Council of Churches, committee members began a nightly phone operation to organize local chapters intended to create support and also collect notes of concern and protest. Within days, Hall records, there were chapters in twenty states, from across the country. From the start, the organization had two interlocking aims: to grow and mobilize support, denomination by denomination, for a religiously framed program of dissent over the war in Vietnam, and to draw on that support to pressure the nation's political leaders to pursue negotiations for peace. That was an unlikely prospect in CCAV's early days; from the 1964 Gulf of Tonkin Resolution through ensuing bombing campaigns and troop buildups, the United States was clearly committed to a significant military escalation of its war effort in Vietnam.[9]

At its conception, there were twenty-eight Protestants on CCAV's national board, alongside seven Jews and five Catholics. At twenty-nine, Neuhaus was the youngest member and the only one from the Missouri Synod. He also possessed one of the lowest public profiles, certainly by comparison to the most prominent members, who included Martin Luther King, Jr., Bennett, Heschel, Coffin, and also Robert McAfee Brown—another Presbyterian minister who was then a professor of religion at Stanford and a notable figure in Civil Rights in addition to ecumenical developments. Leading a minor congregation in an inner-city part of an outer borough, Neuhaus wasn't devoting a notable name and influential platform to a new organization and grave cause he cared deeply about, as might have been the case for already established men like King, Coffin, Brown, and the others, and as would be the case for Neuhaus himself later in life, when he became an almost inveterate signer of sundry policy statements and public declarations. In his 1966 organizing for CCAV, Neuhaus essentially developed a notable name and helped build an influential platform for himself. Reading Oscar Cullmann's *The State and the New Testament* while in seminary, Neuhaus had begun thinking seriously, if only theoretically, about religion and public life. Becoming involved with Civil Rights from within the Missouri Synod, he started to take action, working alongside clergy from other faiths—who were themselves looking to national leadership from a Baptist minister—while making a name for himself, notoriously and otherwise, within Missouri. In sum, by cofounding Clergy Concerned, Neuhaus found the cause, colleagues, and combined religious and political terms that formed him in his vocation thereafter to make a case for religion's importance to American public life, which was just as often making a case for his own.[10]

In the months after Clergy Concerned's January 1966 founding, Neuhaus immersed himself in the consuming work of turning a newly founded organization into an effective and influential national protest movement. With Bennett, Heschel, Coffin, and also David Hunter, deputy secretary of the National Council of Churches, Neuhaus formed a steering committee to grow the organization. "[Planning] meetings were called ad hoc, usually by Neuhaus," Hall notes, drawing attention to his outpacing energies at the time, passionately focused as they were on advancing Clergy Concerned's contributions to the national debate about Vietnam. The committee's explicitly religious identity and terms of dissent were distinct when set against the broader antiwar movement; so too was its understanding of dissent itself as a sincere expression of love of country: "Do not let the hawks monopolize patriotism," Coffin emphasized in early letters to local chapters. Neuhaus was especially committed to this position, and indeed, a few years later at his church in Brooklyn, he would preside over one of the era's most distinctive antiwar demonstrations, a liturgical-political mix of dissent, patriotism, and Christian ritual that helped earn him a reputation as "one of the most militant peace organizers in the United States," as du Plessix Gray would later observe.

Neuhaus wasn't always and only militant in his antiwar work. On March 29, 1966, he led a peace march down Fifth Avenue alongside New York Rabbi Lloyd Tennenbaum and Daniel Berrigan, then freshly returned from his South American exile. The marchers, some sixty in total, included ministers, rabbis, priests, and nuns; wielding banners that read "Peace" in English, Hebrew, and Latin, as the *Times* reported, they "held brief services at two Protestant churches and a synagogue" and also at the United Nations Church Center before completing their act of witness at St. Patrick's Cathedral. There, Neuhaus was part of "what was probably the first interfaith service in the cathedral's 106-year history," as the *Times* further noted. With Mass under way at the cathedral's main altar when the group arrived, a monsignor welcomed the demonstrators on behalf of Auxiliary Bishop Joseph Flannelly and then led them into the Lady Chapel. The demonstrators-cum-worshipers had a ten-minute service—though not before the monsignor barred photographs of the event by reporters, and also refused to give his name, suggestive of the need for much discretion on the part of the Catholic host. The service itself featured the 75th Psalm ("The horns of the righteous shall be exalted," it concludes) and prayers for peace by St. Francis of Assisi and Pope Paul VI, the former involving Francis's famous plea "Lord make me an instrument of your peace" and the latter cribbed from Paul VI's October 1965 peace-themed homily from his Mass at Yankee Stadium.[11]

A few days after the peace march made a little New York ecumenical history, the national committee vowed, in keeping with Heschel's founding promise, to keep the organization in existence until war's end. Thereafter, it decided to change its name in order to better reflect the substantial support it was generating among clergy and laity alike. The newly minted Clergy and Laity Concerned About Vietnam (CALCAV) next hired as executive director, in May 1966, a recently ordained minister, Richard Fernandez. He came to the organization via his teacher at Andover-Newton Theological School, Harvey Cox, a publicly engaged minister, activist, and intellectual known for his closeness to Martin Luther King, Jr. Cox would in turn prove a significant collaborator and like-minded friend for Neuhaus in CALCAV, before becoming more of a religious and public life sparring partner in the years that followed. Hiring Fernandez was yet more evidence of CALCAV's growing success, but also of the demands that its leaders otherwise had on their time. With an executive director in place, Neuhaus was able to pull back a little from the organization's daily workings and focus more on staging provocative public events, like a "peace fast" that began on a muggy Fourth of July, 1966, at the Community Church on Thirty-Sixth at Park Avenue. Alongside Heschel and Berrigan, Neuhaus lead 150 others in the forty-eight-hour fast, the purpose of which, he told a *Times* reporter, was to serve as "a call for repentance, to turn away from the madness that we see at least in the Administration's determination for a military victory." And when he wasn't fasting for peace against military madness, Neuhaus continued on with his duties at St. John the Evangelist, where he remained sole pastor until well into 1967, at which point he was formally released from his conventional pastoral responsibilities to devote himself, with the proud blessing of the congregation, more fully to the national activism and also the public writing he had undertaken.

A few weeks after the Fourth of July peace fast, Neuhaus left New York and went north to visit his parents, then living in Simcoe, Ontario, where Clem had answered a call after leaving St. John's Pembroke. The occasion was the fortieth anniversary of both Clem's ordination and Clem and Ella's marriage. Richard was invited to preach. Tensions between father and son, who hadn't seen each other since they'd debated a year before in Detroit, might have abated for the span of a celebratory service and a cordial picture-taking by the local newspaper, but no more than that. In a contemporaneous letter, Clem informed Richard that he would have to submit all future sermons in advance. Clem justified the request by explaining that Richard, unfiltered, was simply too intellectual for his small-town Canadian congregation—but given the active tensions between them, there was certainly more to this than merely sparing Clem's salt-of-the-earth congregants too much learning for a Sunday morning. In fact, Neuhaus never preached at his father's church again. Their differences were too great, about the direction of the Missouri Synod in general and on Civil Rights in particular, and also over the war in Vietnam—which Clem strongly supported, not least because two of his other sons, twins Tom and George, were in-country Green Berets.[12]

Indeed, in all but direct opposition to his father and fellow pastor, Neuhaus was extending the 1965 Missouri Synod Mission Affirmation into new areas, working to stop the war and doing so in thoroughly ecumenical terms, organizing alongside Episcopalians, Methodists, and members of other moderate Protestant denominations, not to mention Jesuits and rabbis. By 1966, Missouri's revolutionary for Civil Rights was fashioning himself into a bold and sharp instrument of God's peace for Vietnam. Two years later, even bolder, even sharper, this instrument would find itself blunted when Chicago's finest gave Neuhaus the bum's rush, throwing him out of the Democratic National Convention for the trouble he was making on the convention floor as an antiwar delegate. With this badge of radical honor, and the connections he'd made and the standing he enjoyed in the religious Left and in broader Movement politics, Neuhaus might have soon become fully established as a moral and intellectual leader of the American Left itself, perhaps even a clergyman counterpart to the SDS's Tom Hayden. But this was not to be. At the height of his radical leftist phase, Neuhaus would begin questioning his place in the Movement. While he largely agreed with much of the radical Left's diagnosis of the problems afflicting American life in the 1960s, he did not believe in their ultimately mundane prescriptions. The question then was for how much longer could Richard John Neuhaus hold together his sacred ministry with his political activism, his religious beliefs with his ideological affiliations? He had become a leading clergyman of the American Left, only now to discover that the American Left was moving away from his clergyman concerns.

CHAPTER TEN

1968: Passionate Diatribes and Tumultuous Receptions

Peter and Brigitte weren't expecting him, and they certainly weren't expecting him to look the way he did, but they were relieved to see Richard, nonetheless. Everyone was talking about what had been going on in Chicago. With the Democratic National Convention in session that August 1968, warring factions within the party contested for the presidential nomination: Bobby Kennedy was gone, assassinated two months earlier in Los Angeles, and so the choice was between establishment liberal vice president Hubert Humphrey and antiwar insurgency candidate Minnesota senator Eugene McCarthy. While their supporters struggled against each other inside the cavernous International Amphitheatre, the city streets became a smoky battleground. An array of antiwar and anti-establishment groups clashed with aggressive police forces serving under Chicago Mayor Richard Daley. With his "massive bull temper," as Norman Mailer memorably described Daley in his remarkable report on the convention, "The Siege of Chicago," the mayor was committed to maintaining public order in his town, bluntly and brutally if necessary. The Austrian academic couple summering on Long Island knew all of this from the television coverage and newspaper reports. But what of their friend the Brooklyn pastor, a McCarthy delegate prone to protest and pontificating? At least now he was here, standing at their front door. He wasn't hurt and he wasn't in jail, at least not anymore. Still, unlike most times they saw him, he wasn't just ready to move on to the next protest, the next march, the next meeting, even the next late night argument around their kitchen table. He was "shaken," they would remember, years later, by what he'd seen and gone through, in Chicago, by just how brutal the police were, and likewise by how violent and increasingly anti-American the greater leftist political movement was becoming.

Late August 1968: Peter and Brigitte Berger opened the front door of their Montauk summer house and found an exhausted and beleaguered Richard John Neuhaus standing on their stoop. He told them he'd come straight from Chicago. Neuhaus' involvements at the convention and in that cauldron-like city during those chaotic and historic days were more than personally significant—he had attended not just as a McCarthy delegate positioned against the eventual nominee, Hubert Humphrey, but also on behalf of CALCAV, no less in place of an ailing Reinhold Niebuhr, arguably the most respected and influential theologian in postwar American public life. As Niebuhr's replacement, Neuhaus addressed the party's national committee, requesting that it adopt an amnesty program for conscientious draft resisters and army deserters as a plank in its campaign platform. The national committee declined the request. He would have been disappointed, no doubt, but Neuhaus had other business to keep him busy during the convention. When he wasn't on the delegate floor or in committee rooms, he ran a pro-peace press conference in tandem with Paul Newman; he helped get a drunken, riled Norman Mailer back to his hotel room after he tried to punch out a couple of Chicago cops; with television cameras rolling, he was himself forcibly removed from the convention floor in a seersucker suit and Roman collar in an altercation where a fellow Manhattan delegate's credentials were questioned by a convention official and a struggle ensued, with CBS Television's Mike Wallace getting punched in the face by a policeman and also ejected when he tried to cover the melee, as the *New York Times* would report.

Neuhaus wasn't mollified by his rough treatment inside the convention center. Outside, he led a peace march across Michigan Avenue, defying a police order not to cross an imaginary line they'd drawn at 18th Street; for this he was arrested and spent a night in a Cook County jail cell, where with others he listened by radio to Hubert Humphrey's acceptance speech in an atmosphere too angry to grant the nominee's sincerity in invoking St. Francis of Assisi's famous "Make me an instrument of Thy peace" prayer. Neuhaus was eventually convicted on charges of "disorderly conduct" along with other marchers, including the journalist Murray Kempton—with whom, one night earlier in the convention, Neuhaus sipped bottles of Heineken in a hotel room, chatting about the situation their politics and political colleagues had created. In his recollection, Neuhaus and Kempton "pondered our awkwardness in having to spend as much time . . . distancing ourselves from others in the Movement as in distancing ourselves from the opponents of the Movement." Leaving aside for now this late night cold beer lamentation, the rest of these events and experiences represented, in one sense, the successful culmination of Richard John Neuhaus' 1960s activism and emergence as a religious figure of influence and consequence in national affairs. Indeed, during what might have been the very conversation concerning Neuhaus' selection to speak on behalf of CALCAV at the convention, in place of the far more prominent figure originally intended to deliver the remarks, Reinhold Niebuhr reportedly said to Neuhaus, "I'm told you're the next Reinhold Niebuhr." It's hard to imagine a greater affirmation of the trajectory he was on, en route to Chicago.[1]

But how dramatically different were those few fierce days of political fighting and street fighting compared to his first encounter with Chicago, in that quiet placement year near the end of his time in seminary! Afterwards, taken aback by what he'd experienced in the city, Neuhaus took some time on Long Island, with the Bergers, to catch his breath. Berger considered himself a conservative, at least in contrast to Neuhaus considering himself a radical in those days, and he would serve as Neuhaus' primary interlocutor in the coming years, even while Neuhaus' radical activities intensified and began to attract FBI interest. During this same period, Neuhaus would also more critically think through the implications of his continued involvement in "the Movement," as he would refer to it two years later, in his first book. It would be coauthored with Berger, and was a book that began in their late-night conversations and eventually constituted Neuhaus' first notable reckoning with the American Left, after nearly five years of almost total immersion in two of its leading projects (Civil Rights and antiwar protest).[2]

It's not surprising that Neuhaus turned to the Bergers for a respite at summer's end 1968. Two years earlier, he had first contacted Berger, an Austrian-born Lutheran sociologist then teaching at the New School, to see if he would write a review for *Una Sancta,* the Lutheran theology journal that Neuhaus had written for after seminary and began editing by the mid-sixties. In all likelihood, Neuhaus took notice of Berger following the 1966 publication of the latter's now canonical study of the development and sharing out of morally significant meaning in public life, *The Social Construction of Reality.* The review assignment mattered less than the connection it forged, which took shape first over lunch at a little Italian restaurant on West 11th. As Berger would later recall, that opening conversation was convivial, and also substantial: among other things, they discussed the question of God's justice with respect to the death of children. Their conversation would expand dramatically through years of twice- and thrice-weekly dinner engagements and rounds of drinks well into the wee hours at the Bergers' run-down brownstone in Brooklyn's Cobble Hill neighborhood, which was about a twenty-minute drive away from Neuhaus' church on Maujer Street.

This affectionate and cerebral friendship and influential collaboration formed around Neuhaus and Berger's shared interests in discerning and articulating morally and religiously grounded arguments for ordinary citizens' responsibilities and involvements in a shared public life. And while all of this intellectual socializing and social intellectualizing—incidentally, these two phrases together account for the catalyst and context and contours of many of Richard John Neuhaus' most important friendships over the years—easily explains why Neuhaus and Berger became strong friends so rapidly, the emergence and importance of this friendship, for Neuhaus, stands out for two other reasons. With his wife, Brigitte, a formidable intellectual in her own right and a consummate and wry host—years later, she would fondly recall Neuhaus as "the guest who came to dinner, and never left"—Peter Berger was generally sympathetic to Neuhaus' prime public causes and activist involvements during the 1960s and likewise to his ministerial work. Moreover, on occasion the Bergers and their children attended Neuhaus' services at St. John the Evangelist, and Berger also had some limited involvement with CALCAV. That said, Berger played no significant part in Neuhaus' broader pastoral or activist networks, which was important.

Neuhaus was close to others, of course, in broad terms, including the young people engaged in various dimensions of urban ministry at his church and the network of like-minded colleagues he'd developed through his Civil Rights and CALCAV work. Robert Wilken also remained very important, as he always would, and, by 1967, he had even come to New York and was teaching at Fordham, which meant they saw each other with greater frequency than earlier that decade. By this time, Wilken had also introduced Neuhaus to another figure who would prove of great significance, indeed consequence, in his life and work, Avery Dulles. The son of U.S. secretary of state John Foster Dulles, Avery Dulles was a Catholic convert then teaching at Woodstock Jesuit Seminary. Dulles served on the editorial board of *Una Sancta* and, a couple of times at their meetings, which were held at St. John the Evangelist, took Communion from Neuhaus—"It was the sixties," explained Wilken, as a shorthand explanation for what's otherwise an extremely liberal act of ecumenical fellowship, particularly for Neuhaus, given his formation in the closed Communion context of the Missouri Synod.

Dulles would go on to a heralded career as a theologian and also eventually serve as Neuhaus' personal seminary instructor and catechist in preparation for his 1991 ordination as a Catholic priest, by which point they had self-evidently grown very close. In the late 1960s, however, Neuhaus was far closer to people like Berger, and also Rabbi Abraham Joshua Heschel. The latter was a prolific author, professor of theology at the Conservative Jewish Theological Seminary, and, with his beret-capped head of prophet-like white hair and flowing beard to boot, a media-friendly figure of national prominence involved in Civil Rights, ecumenism, and the antiwar efforts of CALCAV. But by Neuhaus' own admission, this was no friendship of equals, no matter how he valued their hours spent in conversation over cigars about Jewish and Christian theology. It was, instead, more of a mutually affectionate mentorship model, a variation on Neuhaus' formative mentorship under Piepkorn at Concordia: indeed, Neuhaus would dedicate his 1975 book *Time Toward Home: The American Experiment as Revelation* to both men, by then deceased, whom he describes in the dedication itself as his "fathers in God."[3]

For his part, Berger was mostly unconnected to any of the other main elements in Neuhaus' world or his past (as Wilken was). Rather, he lived and worked a sympathetic space apart. Hosting an intellectually voracious bachelor and bad cook who was otherwise almost constantly in motion, Peter and also Brigitte were glad to sit down with him at the kitchen table and dine, drink, observe, listen, discuss, and debate. Their most distinctive contribution, for Neuhaus himself, was the contemplative retreat that their family life and intellectual interests afforded him from what was, otherwise, days and years of relentless, action-oriented daily life as a pastor and activist. Since returning from his parents' wedding anniversary celebration in July 1966, through to his going to Chicago in August 1968, Neuhaus was engaged every which way. In any given seven days, he might give a talk at Dorothy Day's Catholic Worker house on a Friday night, then head down to Washington on Saturday morning in an old Volkswagen bus for an antiwar rally, picking up Bill Coffin and a few others along the way, then return to New York in time to lead Sunday services at St. John's in English and in German before going on to a Sunday afternoon peace gathering in the city, where he'd give a rousing address and his accompanist Joan Baez would sing a soothing song, and then the two of them would go for coffee (and nothing more, though the lifelong celibate Neuhaus would later joke with friends and even with his big sister Mim that Baez was an old flame).

Come Monday, he'd be fielding interview requests from *Time* magazine or the *New York Times* about CALCAV's latest statement or protest, at which point the standard workweek began for a senior pastor at a thriving urban parish now with a growing school in operation too, where Tuesday and Wednesday and Thursday evenings not spent with the Bergers were inevitably spent in teleconferences with CALCAV colleagues from around the country, or in more direct planning meetings for the coming weekend's set of antiwar events in Washington or Civil Rights protests in the city. All of this was going on alongside the conscience statements, letters to the editor, and policies for CALCAV that he was writing, at least when he wasn't working on his Sunday sermons or filling in for Bill Coffin at Yale Chapel or arguing back and forth with family members about George and Tom, then in the midst of multiple tours in Vietnam.[4]

This was the shape and pace and scope of Neuhaus' life for months if not years at a time during this period. Some occasions certainly stand out: advocating in the *Times,* as a well-known antiwar cleric, for the abolishment of the clergy draft-exemption policy because "the total exemption of clergy does American religion a great disservice" in cordoning off the clergy from such a major part of national life, never mind from the souls of the soldiers; and then showing up in the *Times* again, this time peering out from the steps of a Manhattan military induction center while chained to fellow protestors and to a draft resister, Barry Johnson, who showed up to let the army know he wouldn't be showing up; attending an off-the-record session with Defense Secretary Robert McNamara, alongside

Bill Coffin and Abraham Joshua Heschel and other colleagues from CALCAV, who presented a paper in hopes of persuading the secretary to pursue a more moderate course in the war instead of escalation; and quietly giving sanctuary to draft resisters at St. John's.

He also hosted events for CALCAV on Maujer Street, culminating in a 1967 antiwar "Service of Conscience and Hope" in the church itself, attended mostly by outsiders rather than by members of the congregation. The service featured remarks by Rabbi Heschel, who called his listeners to action by declaring, "Some are guilty, all are responsible." The service also featured a debate between a draft resister and an enlistee who nevertheless took Communion together after their exchange before some five hundred attendees, who were there mainly to serve as sympathetic witnesses. At a different point in the service, under a fuggy haze of marijuana smoke that mixed with traditional incense, two hundred young men turned in their draft cards, which were sent on to the Justice Department. As the draft cards were turned in, the people in the pews were singing "America the Beautiful," which is likely the last thing any of them would have proposed. But they hadn't; the pastor presiding over the service had, and on this, he wouldn't budge. If, as Susan Sontag argued in *Styles of Radical Will* (1969), "the key to a systematic criticism of America" was a criticism of American involvement in Vietnam, then for Neuhaus, this criticism was finally patriotic. It was the best possible means of calling the United States back to its morally sound, even exemplary, principles, the abandonment of which was represented by the war in Vietnam.

On this very point Neuhaus would later cite a sympathetic conversation he had with Norman Thomas, the Presbyterian minister who was a repeat Socialist candidate for the presidency, while on the speaker's platform at an antiwar rally in 1968 (or 1969). The two men watched as the crowd burned the American flag, which led Thomas to say to Neuhaus, "Richard, don't they understand that our purpose is not to burn the flag, but to cleanse the flag?" But of course, those involved in protesting the war weren't of a singular purpose, as Neuhaus would increasingly acknowledge. Indeed, at what was arguably his own signal antiwar event, Neuhaus sensed that the great majority of people in attendance at the "Service of Conscience and Hope" regarded his invitation to sing "America the Beautiful" as a scandal, "much as though someone were to suggest to Bob Hope and Billy Graham at Honor America Day that the crowd should join in singing the 'Internationale.'" He persuaded them, nonetheless, by telling them (in his recounting) that this "was not a description of the present America we knew but a song of hope for the America which, by actions such as the conscientious resistance of [this] day, would one day be realized." The result, he observed, was "the lustiest and most heartfelt rendition of 'America the Beautiful' that I ever heard."[5]

This was all bold, intense, and distinctive work and action leading up to his attending the 1968 Democratic Convention, work and action that would continue after Chicago as well, even if Neuhaus was by then growing somewhat uneasy with his place within the radical Left, just as his words and actions were solidifying it. Following his eventual break with the broader American Left and turn toward a greater political conservatism, he was reticent later in life about the extent and particularities of his 1960s-era antiwar activities, reticent at least compared to how willingly, proudly, and disproportionately he discussed the other element of his 1960s leftist life. This wasn't simply his Civil Rights work, largely pursued under the auspices of the LHRAA, or his leading a significantly African-American congregation in Brooklyn, but his personal encounters and what he regarded as direct collaborations with Martin Luther King, Jr. These were minor for King if memorable for Neuhaus—no time more than when, alongside fellow New York activist-organizer Allard Lowenstein, he had a private meal with King, who was accompanied by Andrew Young, executive director of the SCLC. In Neuhaus' remembrance of the event, the four men enjoyed "a leisurely and convivial lunch" that was charged with suppressed laughter over an absurd case of mistaken identity: "The restaurant had been alerted that 'the famous Dr. King' was coming," Neuhaus would later recount, "and the waiter assumed that the white man in the clerical collar must be he, so throughout lunch addressed me as 'Dr. King.'" Neuhaus went on to note that King took advantage of this rare public privacy and smoked "throughout lunch, a regular habit that he usually indulged only in private. Among other things, we talked about the abiding wisdom of Reinhold Niebuhr and the need to recognize the distinction between the morally imperative and the historically possible, agreeing also on the moral imperative to press the historically possible. It was the last time I saw him."[6]

Writing about this encounter decades later, Neuhaus claimed that it happened "a few months before [King's] death" in April 1968. This is unlikely—authoritative King biographer Taylor Branch places him primarily in Memphis in the months leading up to his April 4 assassination, and makes no mention of any notable engagements in New York during this time. Neuhaus' mistake can be accounted for as either a simple memory slip or as an understandable dramatic intensification in retrospect of his small but bona fide personal connection to one of the most significant figures in American history. More likely, based on Branch's work and also Mitchell Hall's history of CALCAV, Neuhaus lunched with King about a year before he died, in early April 1967, when King was twice in New York under the auspices of CALCAV. On April 4, a year to the day before he died, King spoke before three thousand people at Riverside Church, and a few days later he agreed to become co-chair of CALCAV. King did so in the midst of national media criticism of his remarks and also a groundswell of popular support for the antiwar position that King had boldly advocated from the Riverside pulpit, when he declared, "I knew that I could never again raise my voice against the violence of the oppressed in the ghettos, without having first spoken clearly to the greatest purveyor of violence in the world today—my own government."

Eleven days after making this stark and provocative connection between U.S. domestic and foreign policy, King was back in town on April 15, to speak to a much larger crowd, some four hundred thousand demonstrators gathered from a host of antiwar organizations, who had marched en masse from Central Park to the UN. In New York and a leading figure in CALCAV, Neuhaus would have had multiple occasions in these couple of weeks to be in close contact with King and, for instance, go to lunch. Indeed, suggesting this closeness, there's at least one photograph of Neuhaus sitting right beside King, while others confer in the background, which was taken during an April 4 news conference related to the Riverside address. And while Neuhaus was certainly present at other major occasions involving King—whether it was Civil Rights events like the Selma march, or a February 1968 antiwar march to Arlington Cemetery, a photograph of which shows Neuhaus in the second row, just behind Heschel and King, whose arms are linked—there's no hard evidence of any substantial, personal connection between them that might justify Neuhaus' recurring claims about their closely working together. He made these claims in passing when discussing King in various issues of *First Things* and also across his books: "I count it among the great graces of my life that I was for a time, until his death . . . permitted to work with Martin Luther King, Jr., as a kind of liaison between himself and the peace movement" (*Freedom for Ministry*, 1979); "in the two years prior to his death . . . I would work closely with Dr. King as he was striving to bring the Southern [Civil Rights] movement to the North, and to merge it with the powerful dynamics of the movement against the war in Vietnam" (*America Against Itself*, 1992); "It was a grace of my life to work personally with Dr. King for several years as a liaison between his Southern Christian Leadership Conference and other social movements of the time" (*Doing Well and Doing Good*, 1992); "I count it one of the great blessings of my life to have worked closely with Martin Luther King, Jr., especially during the three years before his assassination on April 4, 1968" (*Catholic Matters*, 2006).

The similarity of these passages and their consistent lack of detail suggest the claim was overdetermined. More accurately, Neuhaus worked closely and personally with people who worked closely and personally with King during these years: fellow CALCAV leader Harvey Cox, who played an important role in first introducing King to sympathetic young white Northerners, and also Heschel, who, according to his biographer Edward K. Kaplan, developed an immediate and intense connection with King based on their overlapping commitments to a biblically framed argument for minority justice, to nonviolence, and to bearing socially and politically engaged witness in American public life. Of course, Neuhaus shared in all of these elements with both Heschel and King, and in the work to which it led, but he felt this sympathetic connection far more intensely than King did.[7]

Neuhaus kept that sense of connection as active as he could even after King's assassination, beyond talking and writing about him on occasion for the rest of his life. Indeed, shortly after King's assassination, and attesting to his bona fides in King's circle, Neuhaus hosted King's widow, Coretta Scott King, and also King's close associate and successor at the SCLC, Ralph Abernathy, for an evening service at St. John the Evangelist. She spoke and he preached—and Neuhaus remained in touch thereafter, receiving Christmas cards from Coretta and her children that he kept among his personal effects just as he kept the "BLOCK PARTY" invitation from early in his time on Maujer Street. To mark the one-year anniversary of King's death, which fell on Good Friday, 1969, Neuhaus preached an anniversary service held at St. John the Evangelist. In his sermon, Neuhaus proposed King's suitability for sainthood. He didn't seem particularly mindful that this was an unorthodox proposal, coming from a Lutheran and concerning a Baptist, but instead pressed the case in polemical and dramatic terms: "If the rest of the Church is inhibited in celebrating Martin Luther King as a saint, it is a judgment upon the Church and not upon the man. If we refuse to acknowledge contemporary sainthood, we in effect declare the death of God and of his power to generate extraordinary personal events." This cause predictably went nowhere past a roused-up memorial service in Brooklyn, for which Neuhaus also composed a memorial prayer related to the installation of a portrait of King in the church itself. This prayer was also framed in turn, and hangs to this day at the back of the church. More impassioned than eloquent, more dramatic than contemplative, it is a testament to its author's always ardent and finally religious valuing of King's life and work.

THE REVEREND MARTIN LUTHER KING JR. SAYING TO THE CHURCH CATHOLIC, BY RICHARD JOHN NEUHAUS

He lived for justice
and for the healing of Your wounded world.
But in everything he spoke and organized,
he lived and died for You, Almighty Father.
In him, You showed us what we might be;
In him, You called us to deeds of courage.
In him, You gave witness to Your way through our time.
We confess that we were not ready for him,
Our world was not worthy of him,
By the word of the ancient prophet and by the life of Your Son,
You prepared us for Your servant, Martin.
His death is judgment upon us and upon our children.
We do not plead ignorance.
We dare to ask forgiveness.
Lord Jesus, touch his wounded face and make him whole,
In the transfigured glory of his black manhood.
Embrace him in the sight of those noble ones
Who have loved Your Father's will more than life itself.
Command the angels to sing in jubilee,
And the trumpets to sound.
Bring us to the time when all eyes shall see the glory of Your coming.
Bring us to the Kingdom we desire yet more earnestly,
Because Martin will be there.

Bless and hallow and sanctify this portrait, we pray,
To the sustaining of the memory of Martin Luther King
And to the service of his dream,
In the name of the Father, Son, and Holy Spirit. Amen.

April 4, 1969: Neuhaus preached the memorial service where this prayer was first uttered, but he wasn't the presider. That was John Heinemeier, the new senior pastor of St. John the Evangelist. He had arrived in 1967, just a few years out of seminary, and was very much committed to urban ministry and Civil Rights. By the time Neuhaus was in Chicago for the Democratic National Convention, Heinemeier had assumed the great majority of the senior pastor's duties.[8]

Thereafter, Neuhaus continued to preach on the Sundays he was on Maujer Street (about half the time, in Heinemeier's recollection), but he had little to do with the daily business of running St. John's as a congregation or as an urban ministry. The people of St. John the Evangelist were encouraging of this transition, mindful of how much Pastor Richard had done to revive the church, and of how committed he'd been to the congregation, having had to work a night job as a hospital chaplain in his first year because there were no funds to provide even a modest pastor's salary. Moreover, they were proud that their very own pastor had become a man on the national stage while living and worshiping with them on Maujer Street over the years. With Heinemeier now installed, Neuhaus was no longer immediately responsible for the daily life of the church. He could devote himself that much more to working for Civil Rights and against the war in Vietnam. And that's exactly what he did in the fall of 1968, after first turning to the Bergers for some needed respite following his time in Chicago. Neuhaus' already bold critiques of America's situation in Vietnam became bolder still, and also took on an international dimension. In October, as part of a CALCAV initiative, Neuhaus went to Paris and Stockholm with Harvey Cox and a few others to minister to deserters and resisters, and also to

St. John's Lutheran Church and the Parsonage, 357 Miller Street, Pembroke, Canada. Neuhaus grew up here, a pastor's son born and baptized "on the Canadian frontier."

Neuhaus family (provided with permission to use by Johanna Speckhard and Mildred Schwich)

The Neuhaus family, Pembroke, 1936. With their other children surrounding them, Ella Neuhaus sits beside her husband, Clemens, holding their new baby boy, Richard John, on her lap.

Neuhaus family (provided with permission to use by Johanna Speckhard and Mildred Schwich)

Neuhaus as a boy in Pembroke, mid-1940s. This was the sharp-dressed and "uneducable" little Lutheran professor who talked his way around town.

Neuhaus family (provided with permission to use by Johanna Speckhard and Mildred Schwich)

Neuhaus going over a musical score with his sister Johanna, mid-1950s. He probably enjoyed being photographed while smoking a cigarette more than getting the song right.

Neuhaus family (provided with permission to use by Johanna Speckhard and Mildred Schwich)

Neuhaus in the mid-1950s. Here was a young man keen to enlist in a grand cause, and also cause some trouble, as school authorities in Canada, Nebraska, and Texas all discovered during his teenage years.

Neuhaus family (provided with permission to use by Johanna Speckhard and Mildred Schwich)

Neuhaus at school, early 1950s: His Concordia College yearbook caption observed that "while most 'normal' students had gone to bed, Dick was sure to be wide awake, expounding his sundry and various theories."

Neuhaus family (provided with permission to use by Johanna Speckhard and Mildred Schwich)

Neuhaus' ordination, presided over by his father at St. John's, Pembroke, July 1960. Father and son stare at each other with far more gravity than affection: as pastor and pastor in a tumultuous decade of American life, they would continue to face off, with increasing tension.

Neuhaus family (provided with permission to use by Johanna Speckhard and Mildred Schwich)

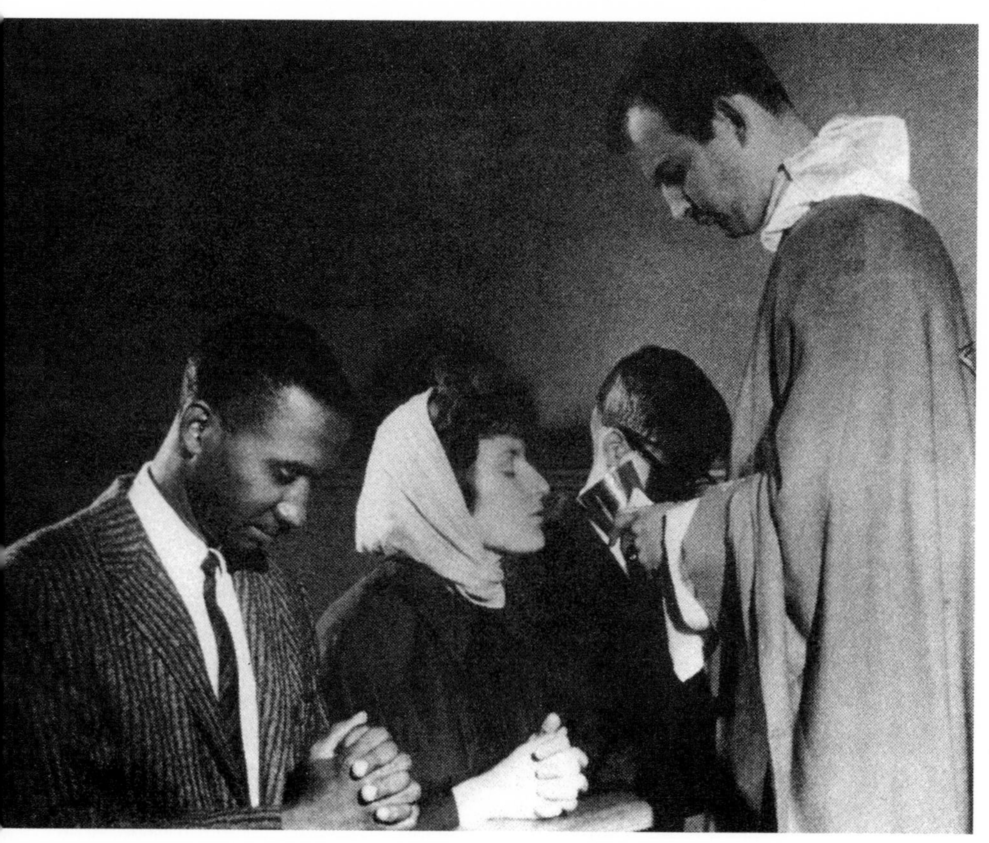

Pastor Neuhaus at St. John the Evangelist, Brooklyn, early 1960s. Neuhaus would embrace urban ministry and Civil Rights simultaneously.

Neuhaus family (provided with permission to use by Johanna Speckhard and Mildred Schwich)

Neuhaus in the March on Washington, D.C., February 1968. Now a leading clergyman of the American Left, Neuhaus participated in many antiwar demonstrations during this period. Here (far left), he's walking close by two men he greatly revered, Rabbi Abraham Joshua Heschel (in beret) and the Reverend Martin Luther King, Jr., along with Ralph Abernathy (to King's right), and Rabbi Maurice Eisendrath (carrying the Torah).

Neuhaus Estate/Institute on Religion and Public Life (provided with permission to use by George Weigel and Robert Wilken)

Neuhaus sitting for a television interview with Bill Beutel, late 1960s. He would continue to hold forth for television audiences and other media for the rest of his life.

Neuhaus Estate/Institute on Religion and Public Life (provided with permission to use by George Weigel and Robert Wilken)

Neuhaus and Peter Berger, Brooklyn, early 1970s. Close friends and collaborators for decades, the two men came up with many ideas for books, magazines, conferences, and other publicly minded cerebral pursuits.

Neuhaus Estate/Institute on Religion and Public Life (provided with permission to use by George Weigel and Robert Wilken)

Pastor Neuhaus at work, mid-1970s. At odds with his left-wing colleagues in religion and politics and ideas, by this period he was beginning to look elsewhere.

Neuhaus family (provided with permission to use by Johanna Speckhard and Mildred Schwich)

speak at European antiwar rallies, where he raged eloquently about how the war in Vietnam was God's means of punishing the United States for its imperial overreach, as Harvey Cox would recall years later.

He made similar points at home during this period, never more notably than on October 5, 1968. Neuhaus was in Baltimore that day, for the beginning of the trial of the "Catonsville Nine," the Berrigan brothers and seven other Catholic antiwar activists who had removed some three hundred draft files from a draft board in Catonsville, Maryland, in May of that year, burned them in the parking lot, and then prayed until the police arrived and arrested them. They were tried five months later, and after the first day's court proceedings were done, protestors gathered at St. Ignatius church hall in the Mount Vernon district of Baltimore. The religious and secular Left were both there in strong numbers, as Francine du Plessix Gray reported, covering the events for the *New Yorker* and eventually publishing her book-length study of the religious antiwar Left, *Divine Disobedience.* The protestors filled the hall past capacity. They were chanting, singing, passing around papers advocating for a host of leftist causes—not just petitions calling for amnesty for draft resisters, but also calls to boycott United Fruit Company products, support Cesar Chavez and Mexican farm workers, and so on. The papers also sported clever critical slogans, like "WANTED: JESUS CHRIST: This man is threatening the American way of life." Telegrams of support for the Catonsville Nine were read out by loudspeaker, from Bill Coffin, Coretta Scott King, Ralph Abernathy, Benjamin Spock, and Tom Hayden. The main speakers were Dorothy Day, Noam Chomsky, Harvey Cox, and then Neuhaus, who delivered the standout address of the night, as Gray reported:

> *Neuhaus accused the government of murder, accused Johnson of betrayal, accused Johnson of "selling out the American dream of liberty for the mailed fist of repression." . . . Neuhaus's passionate diatribe, and its tumultuous reception, carried the demonic side*

> *of the sacred. The rage of this austere young man in a pearl-gray pastoral suit, the terrifying fervor of the young face surmounting the starched white collar, recalled the Parliamentary Fast Sermons of the pre-Cromwellian decade, those jeremiads . . . which precipitated the beheading of Charles the First in 1648. Seldom had the* vox populi *which deposed Lyndon Johnson sounded more enraged.*

While the crowd went wild at the speaker's blowtorch eloquence, the men standing at the back of the hall took note. They were FBI agents, monitoring the proceedings just as the FBI would be listening to Neuhaus with interest a few months later, in early February 1969, when he gave a sermon at a CALCAV service in Washington. Earlier that day, Neuhaus had been part of a delegation alongside Heschel, Coffin, Coretta Scott King, and others—"militant pacifist leaders," the *New York Times* described them—that spent forty minutes with Henry Kissinger, national security advisor to recently inaugurated President Richard Nixon. Three decades later, writing in *First Things* about Kissinger's memoirs covering this period, Neuhaus noted that Kissinger promised CALCAV's representatives that "if a year later we did not see persuasive evidence of a policy of U.S. withdrawal of troops from Indochina, he would join our protest." Such an offering suggests in part why, as Hall argues, this meeting with the new president's top foreign policy advisor "seemed a significant improvement over the past two years, when President Johnson had refused all meetings with the group." But Neuhaus wouldn't wait a year to see what Kissinger did with their proposal that the new administration shift U.S. policy in Vietnam and against draft resisters at home, toward peace and development for the former and mercy and amnesty for the latter. He wouldn't even wait a day. That night at a CALCAV-sponsored event, with the FBI recording the proceedings, Neuhaus declared the Vietnamese people nothing less than "God's instrument for bringing the American empire to its knees."[9]

And so Richard John Neuhaus reached the most radical position in his public life on the Left. But even still, as Peter Berger remembers from their late-night conversations in Cobble Hill during this period, he was already questioning his continued status and placement on the Left, just as its various parties and movements—on the antiwar front, on the Civil Rights front, and on social and cultural matters as well, whether campus politics or sexual politics—were splintering and combusting at an accelerating rate. How could Neuhaus make sense of this fractured, factious scene, and of his own continued involvement with it, while still working toward the political and social goals that had been driving his life and work for almost a decade? He stepped out intellectually, and then stepped back in politically: he went to Mexico with Berger to write a book about it all, and then he came back to Brooklyn and ran for Congress.[10]

CHAPTER ELEVEN

A Thoroughly Radical Writer Makes a Radical Run for Congress

On September 21, 1969, Neuhaus and Berger finished writing their first book together, *Movement and Revolution.* It took the form of extended essays by each, on common concerns regarding the conceptions and stakes of radicalism and revolution as means of effecting meaningful change in contemporary American social and political affairs. As the book's first sentence makes clear, the authors were working from religious first principles and understood this work as shared, ongoing, and personal: "The conversation of which this book is part began with theology rather than politics." The implication about the authors' shared self-regard is rather striking: the book isn't, as one might expect, the greater outcome and expression of matters begun as informal dialogue between two friends. Instead, it's a selection from that greater dialogue, intended to offer a timely example of what it means to consider matters of shared concern from conflicting positions. To be sure, with due humility near the end of this same preface, they note, "We do not regard ourselves as so important that our conversation will be of intrinsic interest to others"; rather, "It is precisely because our understandings emerge from conversation about issues that are not unique to us but grip millions of thoughtful Americans that we hope this book will be useful to others."

Doubleday, their publisher, hoped millions of book-buying Americans would agree when the book was released in February 1970. Its publication was acknowledged in a brief *New York Times* notice, alongside the fourth volume of Dumas Malone's biography of Thomas Jefferson, an anthology of wedding poetry from around the world, and a book promising, on title alone, to reveal *The Secrets of Voodoo.* The *Times* glossed Berger and Neuhaus' work as "a dialogue on American radicalism," though it didn't spell out the purposeful conflict at the book's core. Berger approached questions of radicalism and revolution as an avowed conservative; Neuhaus, as an avowed radical. What exactly, though, did these self-professed labels mean? Elsewhere in the preface, Berger and Neuhaus propose distinctions rather than definitions: "The radical believes politics to be more crucially significant for the realization of man. For him, a larger sphere of human life must be 'politicized.' The conservative, on the other hand, is suspicious of the political enterprise itself. The slogans and promises of political change seem to him more threat than promise." Likewise, they continue, the conservative seeks stability and continuity between past, present, and future, while the radical welcomes an "age of discontinuity" as "an age of new possibilities." Together, Berger and Neuhaus are convinced that some kind of change is needed, a conviction borne by the frankly framed bona fides they also establish in the preface: "While we are not insensitive to the influence of our respective zip codes on our political views, both of us are personally involved with the struggle to humanize urban America."[1]

After dedicating the book to Brigitte, whom they playfully but respectfully described as "wife to one, friend to the other, adamant critic of both," they signed off on the preface from Brooklyn, New York, in all likelihood from the kitchen table in the Bergers' Cobble Hill house where so many of their conversations took place. On the

Feast of St. Matthew, 1969, as they date it in the preface, or September 21 for the secular set, Neuhaus and Berger were probably still suntanned from their summertime work on the book, thanks to the locale where the notes and writing took place: Cuernavaca, Mexico, a place of "dazzling sunlight" as Berger would warmly evoke it later. The book's Mexican composition came about after Berger was invited to lecture on sociology and economic development at the Centro Intercultural de Documentación (CIDOC) by Monsignor Ivan Illich, a charismatic and progressive-minded Catholic priest and intellectual "with a great gift for public relations," according to a contemporaneous profile by Francine du Plessix Gray. Illich set up the institute in the early 1960s, ostensibly as a missionary training center; its governing ideology was a graft of Vatican II–era Catholic progressivism—the Church working in and with and for modern society, with and for all people of goodwill, regardless of creed—onto straightforward leftist anti-Americanism: "I would like to start, under your auspices, a center of de-Yankeefication," Illich brashly and persuasively informed the local bishop in Cuernavaca.

Illich regarded the institute, in its missionary training auspices especially, as a means of resisting the encroachment of conservative-leaning U.S. missionaries into Latin America, which he believed would inevitably bring along and then impose wreckful middle-class presumptions and values on the local poor. But he wanted the institute to be more than merely a means of resistance: CIDOC also served as a spiritually ordered intellectual meeting place for discussing new means and models of improving the lot of the poor. Berger was invited under the latter context, and he brought along his family and also Neuhaus, who lived that summer in an apartment atop the garage that was attached to their guesthouse. Neuhaus and Illich were an obvious match: they were both charismatic, eloquent, and handsome young men of God; they were both ambitious, entrepreneurial, fierce, and righteous (if not self-righteous) about the importance of their respective intellects and publicly focused ministries. Unsurprisingly, they couldn't stand each other. This was, in both

Peter and Brigitte Berger's amused recollections, a palpable, mutual dislike from first impressions onward, and it never changed during Neuhaus' time in Mexico. And so Berger divided his intellectual commitments in Cuernavaca between the two, lecturing with Illich at CIDOC and working on the book with Neuhaus back at the guesthouse.[2]

The book was published in early 1970 under the editorial direction of Midge Decter, who had edited Berger's earlier work and would in turn be a notable figure in Neuhaus' life and work for decades—as an editor of his books and at *First Things,* and also in the context of her marriage to Norman Podhoretz, the prominent Jewish neoconservative intellectual, longtime editor of *Commentary* magazine, and himself a future Neuhaus friend and culture war ally. The question and indeed quality of one's political and ideological allies and foes runs throughout Neuhaus' section of the book, which follows Berger's "Between System and Horde: Personal Suggestions to Reluctant Activists." For his part, Berger offers an elegant and dispassionate account of what political involvement might look like when ordered to and by "the motive of compassion." Berger's primary intention is to describe a cross-political community of the compassionate—compassionate conservatism *avant la lettre,* as it were—that would afford protections from and an alternative to the mutually dehumanizing choice between a politics dominated by the "system," or the structures and levers of power and control at the command of the impersonal modern state, and a politics dominated by the "horde," or the reactionary, rejectionist, violent, and aggressively populist movements self-consciously set up in direct opposition to the system. Berger concludes his contribution by endorsing the inherent liberties of the individual in a democratic society as the best possible source and indeed focus of all meaningful political action. His argument is sober-toned and measured. It reads like a set of eloquent remarks meant for a graduate seminar. What follows is a whole other kind of eloquence.[3]

"It is a mass movement of revulsion against mindless slaughter in

Vietnam," opens Neuhaus' half of *Movement and Revolution,* which he titled "The Thorough Revolutionary." It's an exhaustive effort to make sense of what it means to be a revolutionary in contemporary American life, and it can be exhausting to read in its vehemence. Symptomatically, the opening paragraph offers eight successive sentence-length definitions of "the Movement." Only then does Neuhaus think he's complicating the term, before candidly declaring it a "phenomenon so amorphous and fractious" but also "the most hopeful among the forces reshaping American life." Fine and well, but what then is it? In aggregate, *"The Movement is the cluster of persons, organizations, world views and activities located on what is conventionally called the Left and acting in radical judgment upon the prevailing patterns, political, economic, social, and moral, of American life."* Neuhaus proceeds to subject the Movement to his own radical judgments, some sympathetic and others critical, while simultaneously drawing attention to his status as an actor within it.

As such, "The Thorough Revolutionary" is significant for our understanding of Richard John Neuhaus' life and work in two respects, and bears more attention than some of the other books he would publish in the 1970s. First, it represents the first major instance of the double persona that Neuhaus would deploy in the rest of his writing career: he is at once a robust actor and contributor to the events and ideas under consideration, and a removed commentator on the very same. This double persona would continue to prove substantially accurate if also rhetorically convenient: just as Neuhaus-as-actor could be a major player in any number of political and intellectual groups and milieus but never finally of any one of them, Neuhaus-as-author could align himself with the same program of strong sympathies but with qualifications afforded by the critical distance of being a removed commentator. Beyond offering this first iteration of a recurring actor-commentator presence in his writing and in American public life, "The Thorough Revolutionary" is more immediately significant as a sourcebook for understanding Neuhaus' developing break with the Left and turn to the Right, in no small part because it captures the critical questioning and conversation that he was engaged in with Berger in the late 1960s. This reconsideration would intensify after his time at the DNC in Chicago, 1968, and in turn took its fullest form in his first book.[4]

While Neuhaus' conversion to Catholicism in 1990 conclusively signals a religious migration that was catalyzed by his openness to Piepkorn's ecclesial Lutheranism in the 1950s, there is no single event that comprehensively accounts for and solidifies Neuhaus' intellectual and political migration from Left to Right—that is, at least prior to his involvement in the 1975 Hartford Appeal for Theological Affirmation, to be discussed in the following chapter. But before he could be said to fully have gone over to the Right (that is, by the early 1980s), Neuhaus tried for years to find and sustain a viable position for himself on the Left. The effort was thorough if not ultimately successful, and it began in substantial form with his contribution to *Movement and Revolution,* with an essay that comes out of a young man's basically unsettled sensibility.

In print, Neuhaus comes across as one deeply invested in the matters under consideration but also deeply unclear about the nature and the quality of his connection to the others likewise invested. He is also having a great time figuring it all out, as a writer not nearly as constrained by word counts as he was in his wide-ranging journalism, which, in 1970 alone, notably included essays appearing in two flagship leftist journals, one arguing for amnesty for draft resisters and deserters in the *Nation* and the other in the *New York Review of Books* defending Martin Luther King against a salaciously detailed biography. This same year, he also wrote book reviews and opinion pieces, emerging from more explicitly religious positions and taking on not just cultural but also ecclesial and theological concerns, for religious publications like *Commonweal,* the *Christian Century,* and *Lutheran Forum.*

But by comparison to these pieces, constrained by space and by the nature of the assignment in each case, it is in his half of *Movement and Revolution* that Neuhaus finds the generous space and open premises to really fire up his literary and intellectual engines. And even while his purposes are substantial and serious, Neuhaus' prose is showy, snappy—he observes, for instance, that the most zealous among new radicals "become masters of one-Leftmanship, ever prepared to go one step further to demonstrate they really belong to the community of the saved." His arguments are often explicitly biblically informed, but in a cocky, clever preacher's kid kind of way: "Paraphrasing Jesus, he who would preserve his autonomy would lose his autonomy"; "With TV [as in televised] politics, as with God, all things are possible." The author wears his cosmopolitan learning proudly, drawing critically and commendably from the works of Albert Camus, Frantz Fanon, the Founders, Kierkegaard, Herbert Marcuse, and even a nineteenth-century Russian monk's writings on the nature of a Revolutionist, alongside more immediately relevant analyses of the American scene from then important sources like James Baldwin's *The Fire Next Time,* Michael Harrington's *The Other America,* C. Wright Mills' *The Power Elite,* and Staughton Lynd's *Intellectual Origins of American Radicalism.*[5]

Neuhaus' authorial sensibility, throughout, tends to the contrarian. For instance, after tracing a genealogy of the Movement forward from its conception as a Civil Rights–focused concern through to its broader engagement with American politics, culture, and economics at home and abroad, he notes that its "distinctive dogma" is that "evil is inherent in, and not accidental to, the American Way." He then glosses his analysis and distances himself from the more doctrinaire adherents within the Movement by explaining that this is "a dogma in the pejorative sense of the term," insofar as it overdetermines one's thinking, acting, and positioning with respect to American life while also creating a too rigid standard for good standing within the Movement itself. This distancing discloses a pattern that shows up elsewhere in "The Thorough Revolutionary." Neuhaus zealously, indeed brilliantly, articulates an array of provocative radical positions—on Israel as Imperial America's Middle East bully pawn; on Black Power as the only viable power for racial uplift in America; on the Cold

War anti-Communist argument for intervention in Vietnam as a political mask for what is actually an economic campaign to consolidate global inequality for American domestic advantages; on similarities between Nazi Germany and the United States with respect to war-making and attacking their minorities (at points throughout his career, Neuhaus was too given to Nazi analogizing). But he invariably gives voice to these radical positions within a rhetorically cooler, almost sociological frame, and also with elaborate qualifications and caveats. It is difficult, in other words, to locate Neuhaus fully in any one articulation of Movement ideas and practices, even while it's obvious that he has a closely observed sense of these ideas and practices, a sense that he accentuates via occasional autobiographical insertions about statements he's personally heard from the speaker's platform at rallies, in high-level activist meetings, and so on—not to mention, as we would expect, insights he's gained from personally "working with Dr. King," as he informs the reader.

The most controversial element in this Pastor's Personal Tour of American Radicalism, however, concerns Neuhaus' writings about revolution: its necessity, its legitimacy, its effects. Decades later this writing would come up in a rather melodramatic and finally unpersuasive exposé of Neuhaus by an ex-colleague, Damon Linker. He would draw on Neuhaus' rhetorically frank willingness to consider revolution in the pages of *Movement and Revolution* as early evidence of Neuhaus' extremist tendencies, which, Linker argued, found their full expression in Neuhaus during the 1990s and 2000s, by which point he had supposedly become a "Theocon" intent on transforming late secular America into a semi-medieval theocracy. Leaving aside Linker's too breathless argument for now, he certainly found in this first book ample evidence of Neuhaus' openness to considering revolution, if not downright enthusiasm at the prospect:

> *"We" are for revolution. A revolution of consciousness, no doubt. A cultural revolution, certainly. A non-violent revolution, perhaps. An armed overthrow of the existing order, it may*

be necessary. Revolution for the hell of it or revolution for a new world, but revolution, Yes.

Neuhaus' effort both to engage as actor and analyze as critic, in this particular passage, rests almost entirely on his scare-quoted "We." This is a qualified self-inclusion that is immediately forgotten for the passionate excitement of the prospect he then gets to conjure up from within this snug-fitting guise. To be sure, Neuhaus later adopts a more careful stance, writing about the "responsible revolutionary" as someone who understands the grave stakes of his actions, and the need to establish legitimate grounds by appeal to normative standards of justice. It is clear he thinks this kind of candid determination and ethical thinking is necessary, given the shirking romanticism he has witnessed in the Movement and which he identifies among idealistic campus radicals and others likewise unwilling to consider the ugly, bloody realities of what revolution practically (meaning physically, even lethally) involves. Positioning himself against each of these types, Neuhaus explicitly declares, "I affirm the right to armed revolution," and wants his readers to know he means it: "This is not merely a theoretical affirmation; I believe there are situations in which the right can be morally exercised"—provided that this right follows upon a justice-minded assessment of its need, an acceptance that responsibility for its execution and consequences rests on the individual actor, and also, importantly, the conviction that "there is a reasonable hope for success."[6]

In other words, the Richard John Neuhaus who emerges in the pages of *Movement and Revolution* is a serious radical. He is committed, credentialed, and just as critical of all pretenders to the same title as he is of their common opponents. Later in his career, often in the back pages of *First Things,* Neuhaus would make much of his marked distaste for the kind of oppositional labeling and strict, reductive definitions and differentiations that seem inherent to political-intellectual movements and likewise to church politics: Conservative vs. Neoconservative vs. Liberal vs. Neoliberal; Traditional Catholic vs. Vatican II Catholic vs. JPII Catholic, and so on. In general terms, this taxonomic tendency is at base motivated for its various practitioners by a desire to establish orthodoxy, not just against obvious dissenters but also, perhaps more importantly, against competing construals of the very same orthodoxy. Disavowals aside, from *Movement and Revolution* onward, Neuhaus was himself just as given to this tendency to define and counter-define in political, intellectual, and ecclesial terms. While comprehensible within the frame of his becoming a politically engaged religious leader and public intellectual from the late 1960s through to his death in 2009, his willingness to define and counter-define owes a significant debt to his Lutheran identity and specifically to his formation within the Missouri Synod. After all, from the sixteenth century forward, this was a confession that had been always already given to rivaling claims of ecclesial and theological orthodoxy. These were claims that clashed against those of Rome, and also within broader Lutheranism and within the Missouri Synod, across their histories and right into the seminary battles and convention floor debates that Neuhaus joined.

In other words, when Neuhaus turned his attention to the tenets and tendencies of the radical Left and engaged in an extended combination of diagnosis, definition, and differentiation, he was primed for this work by his Lutheran formation as much as he was by his activist experiences in the 1960s. Based on those experiences and likewise the publication of *Movement and Revolution,* Neuhaus was obviously a man of the Left as of 1970.[7] But what was a man of the Left to do, in 1970, to bring about the kind of changes he was convinced America so desperately needed? The book's brief conclusion offers some suggestions, as Neuhaus and Berger differentiate themselves once more. The conservative remains convinced America has not yet reached a state where revolutionary action is needed "to achieve the changes demanded by justice," while the radical contends "this is not yet clear" and that "it will only become clear as we intensively press such efforts." In this sense, for Neuhaus, continued reform work is the best course of action: if it fails, this "will strengthen the revolutionary struggle that will then be necessary." If it succeeds, this means "achieving a more just society without the enormous suffering of revolutionary struggle." And for both men, as this capture of a portion of their ongoing conversation concludes, "there [exists] an agenda of urgent actions which alone can force the verdict of the future." Just what was next on Neuhaus' agenda for forcing just such a verdict?[8]

"The Reverend Richard J. Neuhaus, a Lutheran clergyman, [is] seeking a House seat from Brooklyn," reported the February 2 edition of the *New York Times,* as part of a broader story about McCarthy and Kennedy supporters, all of them pro-peace radical Democrats who had decided to run for public office in the 1970 midterm elections. The plan was for radical caucuses to form, district by district, and then hold their own primaries in advance of the official party primary. The goal: to unseat establishment and status quo incumbents while running on a strident antiwar/pro-peace plan, and in turn defeat the Republicans in the general election. Much later in life, Neuhaus would cast a critical and sheepish eye on his decision to enter electoral politics in the winter and spring of 1970, explaining it away as "a fit of vocational absentmindedness," out of which he "ran for Congress . . . and thank God, lost." Neuhaus made this comment in the midst of a remembrance of Allard Lowenstein, a Democratic activist with whom Neuhaus had been close in the early 1970s, not least because Lowenstein was then a Nassau County congressman leading the movement in New York to recruit and run radical pro-peace candidates against establishment candidates in the primaries.

This all took shape, in Neuhaus' case, under the auspices of the Brooklyn Reform Democrats Association (BRDA), which was set up in the 14th Congressional District, a slice of multiethnic Brooklyn—Italians, Puerto Ricans, and African-Americans made up its sizeable minority communities, alongside smaller but still notable Polish and

Jewish enclaves—that included parts of Red Hook, South Brooklyn, and also Neuhaus' own Williamsburg. The BRDA's mandate was to select a candidate who would run against incumbent Democrat John J. Rooney. As the *Times* Washington correspondent Clayton Knowles reported, Rooney became "a target because, as chairman of the Armed Forces subcommittee of the House Appropriations Committee, he is viewed by many Liberal Democrats as a spokesman for the military at the cost of other national programs." Neuhaus put it more sharply, calling Rooney "the single most reliable friend the Pentagon has in Congress" in an interview he gave to the *Times* in early February that led to a brief article focused expressly on his anti-Rooney candidacy. Members of Rooney's district who wanted him ousted had two choices in the BRDA radical primary: Neuhaus or Peter Eikenberry, a lawyer then serving as general counsel to the Bedford-Stuyvesant Development and Services Corporation.[9]

Over nine days in March 1970, the candidates debated each other at a series of public forums throughout the district, giving electors a chance to consider their relative merits in advance of a March 23 vote. In forum after forum, culminating in a raucous homecoming reception at his very own Williamsburg Reform Democrat Club, Neuhaus charged up his audiences with a dramatic stump speech conjuring vivid images of the ongoing carnage in Vietnam, which Congressman Rooney was helping along in his Armed Forces Appropriations chairmanship. But Neuhaus didn't need to convince his antiwar, propeace audiences of any platform; he had to convince them that he was the right man to lead it, and his pitch was pragmatic if implicitly egotistical: it would take a candidate with a national presence and a national network to generate the campaign donations and publicity needed to take down Rooney: in this race, it would take Neuhaus. Eikenberry knew he couldn't compete with Neuhaus' rhetoric or his prominence, nor did he try. Instead, he argued that he was the better candidate to defeat Rooney because he was local, not national: he was an experienced organizer with extensive grassroots connections throughout the district, which would prove crucial to the ground operation at the formal Democratic primary in late June 1970.

In fact, Eikenberry's argument carried the day: on March 23, 1970, he defeated Neuhaus in the BRDA primary by three votes (154–151). By his own admission, this was thanks to a stronger get-out-the-vote operation, which involved his "personally dragg[ing] three people out of their homes in the last hour of the voting," as he would write in a recollection of the 1970 radical primary and then formal primary. He won the first only to lose the second to the incumbent (49%–45%) on June 23, 1970. Eikenberry lost to Rooney despite his local organizing operation, despite receiving the endorsement of the *Times* editorial board, and despite receiving support from the likes of Dustin Hoffman, John Kenneth Galbraith, and Arthur Schlesinger, all of whom appeared at fund-raising events leading up to the party primary. Notably absent among Eikenberry's supporters during his bid to get rid of Rooney was the other man apparently passionately committed to this goal.[10]

Was Neuhaus a sore loser? Or was he duly chastened by the defeat in higher order terms? Did he discern in it evidence that supported a stricter construal of what it meant to live out Two Kingdoms theology, which is to say, that his vocation to public life, as a man of God, was never meant to involve such a formal, indeed explicit, involvement in secular politics? The first possibility isn't charitable enough, while the second seems too charitable. Neuhaus himself had little to say about his dalliance with electoral politics beyond diagnosing it, some twenty-five years later, as a case of "vocational absentmindedness." At the time of his candidacy, his co-pastor at St. John the Evangelist, John Heinemeier, was "frankly astounded" by Neuhaus' decision to run, as were others close to him in the congregation. "This blew our minds," Heinemeier remarked, years later. Nevertheless, they helped out with what they regarded as a "very odd, heady enterprise," in no small part because members of the congregation beyond the inner circle were proud and excited by the prospect of their beloved pastor becoming their man in Washington.

Indeed, multiple telephone lines were installed in the church office as part of the campaign mobilization effort, while the church basement served as a meeting space for political organizing meetings.[11] But none of it proved enough, and Neuhaus was defeated and never tried again, and he thanked God on both counts.[12]

And so 1970 witnessed Richard John Neuhaus become both a published author and a failed politician, a sharp-tongued commentator on radicalism and a passionate if fickle radical candidate. What are we to make of this combination of efforts? Neuhaus was clearly looking for a mode of public engagement that would be at once more efficacious than the endless activism—the marches, speeches, rallies, meetings—he'd been involved with for years, in no small part because he was witnessing firsthand in these involvements ideological fissures and greater differences that he decided to make sense of through writing, but also, in a sense, to overcome through politicking. Outwardly, in both cases, he was working toward a goal shared, by 1970, by an increasing number of Americans, if from different vantages and according to different logics: the end of the war in Vietnam. Inwardly, he seemed at odds with his established position in the Movement, and with local New York and broader national life both, at least judging from the critical elements and unclear sympathies that characterize his part of *Movement and Revolution* and judging from his seemingly sudden decision to run for Congress, which none of his living contemporaries interviewed for this biography seem to have been consulted on before he announced.

What Neuhaus would diagnose as "vocational absentmindedness" seems more accurately a case of vocational dissonance. As always, he wanted to serve God, he wanted to lead people, he wanted to change the culture. By 1970, he was attempting to align and integrate these ambitions through life and work as a Brooklyn clergyman intellectual-cum-activist author politico. He would keep attempting the same, involving the same roles in the years to come, even as their ratios and orientations would begin to change. But in the meantime, he needed to step away for a span. Shortly after the run for Congress didn't work out, Neuhaus learned that Peter Berger was going overseas on a research trip. Neuhaus decided to join him. What better way to take a break from everything New York than to spend a few months touring around Africa?

CHAPTER TWELVE

The Lonely Radical Looks Elsewhere

There was no formal reason for Neuhaus to journey to Africa in spring 1971. Since he was traveling on personal terms rather than under the auspices of any sponsoring organization, the trip was only possible thanks to his securing a paid sabbatical from St. John the Evangelist. In fact, as Peter Berger would later recall, members of Neuhaus' congregation considered this trip a gift to their pastor, in gratitude for ten years of work for the Kingdom in Williamsburg and beyond. More than grateful, they were proud that their pastor was going to Africa. Strong feelings for Pastor Neuhaus persisted despite his increasing detachment from the daily life of the congregation in the late 1960s and into the early 1970s, a detachment that would be more squarely solidified upon his return from Africa when he moved into his own separate apartment inside the staff house on Maujer Street. He became even more detached thereafter, by becoming associate editor of *Worldview* magazine, the Carnegie Religion and International Affairs (CRIA) monthly, which, in time, also involved his moving his daily affairs from Brooklyn to Carnegie's Manhattan offices on the Upper East Side. Indeed, by the mid-1970s, and with Harvey Von Herten joining as a new assistant pastor to John Heinemeier, Neuhaus had effectively ceased to be a significant part of the life of the congregation, beyond preaching at one of the Sunday services.

But this growing distance had no effect on departure day for Africa in 1971. Members of the congregation even accompanied Neuhaus to the international departures gate at JFK to see him off, among them a host of older ladies who were "full of motherly solicitude," Berger remembers, as Neuhaus readied to board an Air Afrique flight for Dakar, Senegal. And as Neuhaus himself would later observe, his personal interest in going to Africa in 1971, beyond no doubt wanting a break from his political-intellectual-ecclesial activist life in New York, "was undoubtedly related to my work in the civil rights movement and my years as a pastor of a large black parish in Brooklyn."

He offered this context in a preface to his 1986 book *Dispensations,* which explored the place and power of Christianity in South Africa's apartheid-framed public life. More immediately, he briefly but pointedly referenced his time in Africa in the preface to his first single-authored full-length book, *In Defense of People,* which was published the same year as his trip. Its front cover promised "an evocative polemic against an ecology movement that puts the 'rights of nature' above the 'rights of man' "—but the book proved overwritten and overly smug in its relentless put-downs. Worse, it indulgently showcased the author's seemingly infinite array of impressive connections and matching reading list. In a rightly cutting assessment, *Kirkus Reviews* accurately captured the book's hopped-up tone and disparate tendencies:

> *With a dose of Maileresque pontification, a few forays into hippie argot, and a relentless downpour of the most colorful and diverse namedropping, Brooklyn pastor Neuhaus spins a uniquely personal and sometimes incomprehensible Christian panegyric to the human race. How John Mitchell, Marshall McLuhan, Arthur Schlesinger, Leonard Bernstein, and the* New York Times Magazine *can be splashed across a handful of pages;*

> *how Neuhaus can believe that the "uplift literature of Consciousness III is to the ambitiously radical what Amy Vanderbilt was to another generation"; and how Che and Gandhi can be melded with "joining the rustic tribal commune of totally biodegradable existence" is breathtaking. Jack Newfield, Garry Wills, Norman Podhoretz, John Gardner, Gaylord Nelson, James Buckley, Irving Kristol, the Founding Fathers, Abraham Lincoln, the Mayflower Compact, Hannah Arendt, Charles Péguy, Walter Lippmann, Joseph McCarthy, G. K. Chesterton (in that order) and so many others make another mad dash to the relevance finishing line. Are Malthus, Ehrlich, and Garrett Hardin (Population times Prosperity equals Pollution) correct? When the cosmic dust settles we find that Neuhaus doesn't think so, but instead wants to focus on reconstructing the American myth, using the churches to covenant a 20 billion dollar assistance fund for the poor nations. Outasight and into the pop-ecoculture-Jesus-freak-quasi-radical-pseudo-intellectual miasma.*[1]

Published in fall 1971, shortly after he returned from Africa, *In Defense of People* was a caustic survey-cum-attack on what Neuhaus regarded as an emergent ecology movement made possible by implicit race and class privileges and governed by an anti-humanist sensibility and animus toward the global and local poor. Neuhaus locates the most strident and influential version of this sensibility in the ideas and prescriptions of Paul Ehrlich, author of *The Population Bomb* (1968), an alarmist future-focused analysis of demographic growth as planetary peril. Rejecting this line, he argues that Ehrlich and simpatico intellectuals, academics, and public policy types promote severe restrictions on reproductive rights in the Third World—population control via forced sterilizations and abortion on demand—only ostensibly in order to preserve the planet from human exploitation. In actuality, they were working to preserve and extend their own First World way of life over and against Third World human lives that, by their narcissistic standards, don't merit the same. The success of this effort, Neuhaus charged, was thanks to their opinion-making influence in American public life: "Intellectuals," he declares with remarkable detachment, are "those who mint and market the metaphors by which public consciousness is shaped."

Unfortunately, Neuhaus himself was too interested in intellectual minting and marketing of his own: he warns of "Antipopulation Vietnams" and crows that "the moral decision is not for us to go on a diet but to redistribute the food." He spends more time on rhetorically winning formulations than on soberly prosecuting his important, baseline argument, that "we should not permit ourselves to be seduced into mislocating the crisis of our times" away from a focus on helping the suffering poor of the planet, to focus on a planet putatively suffering because it is overpopulated by the poor. As Neuhaus personally discovered and reported in one of the book's many autobiographical insertions—elsewhere he dedicates the book to his parents and, as the seventh of eight children, wryly expresses gratitude to them "for their not stopping at two"—this anti-poor position wasn't focused only on people in the distant Third World but also targeted the very people he served as pastor:

> *A distinguished medical proponent of abortion on demand once assured me that no one should be forced to be born who was not guaranteed "the minimal requirements for a decent existence" [essentially, the standard family, education, and economic elements of secure and stable middle-class American life]. When I [Neuhaus] pointed out that, by his criteria, most of the people I work with in Brooklyn should have been aborted in the womb, he responded with utmost sincerity, "But surely many, if not most, of the people who live in our horrible slums would, if they could be objective about it, agree with me that it would have been better for them not to have been born."*

This exchange proved a crucial experience in Neuhaus' life and work. While deepening divisions in CALCAV and the Supreme

Court's January 1972 *Roe v. Wade* decision provide national-political contexts for his ongoing shift from Left to Right, the encounter he describes above afforded him his most visceral sense of why he could no longer be a clergyman of the Left. As he would write elsewhere, in a variation on this anecdote that involved a Princeton professor rather than a direct conversation with a blithe abortion rights advocate, there was too great a "discrepancy between my perception of the people of St. John's and the claim that they were living lives not worth living [because] none of them could begin to qualify by the noted professor's index of a quality of life." Powerfully motivated in his ministry, writings, politics, and activism by a sense that the right-ordered purpose of liberalism was to defend the weak from the powerful, by the early 1970s Neuhaus began to understand his commitment to the rights of the poor and the racially oppressed as of a piece with his commitment to the rights of the unborn, which would occupy an ever greater primacy in the coming years. From the beginning, however, this integration of rights for the poor and rights for the unborn placed him at a critical distance from a Left in which private rights—made possible by and indeed protecting implicit race and class privileges—trumped responsibilities for others.[2]

Neuhaus' trip to Africa itself yielded a few valuable encounters and friendships that he would draw on over the subsequent years, though without ever explaining how he came to meet any of those involved in the first place. During his time in Africa, he would later recount, he enjoyed "a leisurely lunch spent in conversation with [then president of Tanzania] Julius K. Nyerere, in the very elegant mansion built for the former British governor in Dar es Salaam"; while in Johannesburg, he met with the South African cleric Beyers Naudé, who introduced him to others in his anti-apartheid circle; and in Senegal, he had an emotional experience at Gorée Island, the infamous collection-cum-departure port for Africans taken in slavery to the New World. But despite visiting some twenty-five different countries over the course of a few months, Neuhaus did not write much in formal terms about his 1971 time in Africa, beyond these scant references. Rather, he returned with some amusing anecdotes that he enjoyed retelling thereafter, and one in particular. According to his longtime assistant Davida Goldman, Neuhaus liked to describe his experience of reading the material in the seat pocket in front of him while waiting to depart from one African locale to another. "Welcome to Pan-African Airlines," the brochure declared. "Over two thousand safe takeoffs, and many safe landings!"

Near the end of his trip, after a series of safe landings, he did write two letters to Robert Wilken. The first, sent on thin blue aerogramme paper embossed with the photograph of a smiling African woman snuggling a cheetah outside the Nairobi Hotel Intercontinental, is business-minded. Wilken appears to have been Neuhaus' consigliere with respect to his prepublication plans for *In Defense of People:* Neuhaus asked him to help establish the possibility to publish an excerpt of the book with *Harper's* magazine (which worked out, producing an October 1971 article), and he also included in this letter an addition to the acknowledgments page of the book itself, featuring a brash reference to his being "in Africa checking out terms of the 'Covenant with the Poor'" while the manuscript's final proofs were looked over in New York at the offices of his publisher, Macmillan. He wasn't checking out these terms, however, in Nairobi: the second half of this letter details just how very "Western" the city felt to him compared to other parts of the continent, not least because the "place [is] crawling with British, German, and a growing contingent of Americans," including Vice President Spiro T. Agnew, who was in town to meet with Nairobi president Jomo Kenyatta. Neuhaus was profoundly underwhelmed: "Met Agnew briefly yesterday, as he was passing through. Dismal fellow, [he] was on his way to a golf course one hour after arrival."

The rest of the letter to Wilken suggests how much his life and work back home remained in the front of his mind. He wonders about the progress of a CALCAV plan to release personal correspondence between Lyndon and Ladybird Johnson (that seems never to have materialized); he asks for details about a recent LCMS Atlantic District convention; he wonders if Herman Otten's heresy charges against him were publicly released and, if so, about the reactions.[3] He admits to homesickness for Brooklyn, but also, more sheepishly if just as honestly, he admits to feeling excited about the new living (and working) situation awaiting him upon his return: "The fixing up of the apartment in the staff house has assumed inordinate proportions in my mind. Almost daily I think of it, and of the work I will do there." *There,* instead of the work he'd been doing for ten years, a few doors down Maujer Street, in the pastor's office; though a passing admission, this offers strong evidence of Neuhaus' longing and his plans to pursue matters independent of his pastoral assignment, while still formally affiliated to a congregation. Formally, but also rhetorically, partway through the opening chapter of *In Defense of People,* Neuhaus invokes Williamsburg, Brooklyn, as the place "where I am now and hope to be for as long as the black and Puerto Rican people of Williamsburg put up with my ministry and my eccentric wish to write on the side for readers who do not live in Williamsburg." The reality of Neuhaus' efforts, from 1971 forward, and notwithstanding his passionate rejection of the quality-of-life reading of the people of St. John the Evangelist, more accurately suggests that the conventional operational duties of a pastor became a side pursuit for him. Indeed, the prioritizing of intellectual engagement would become a standard practice for him throughout his clerical life as both a Lutheran pastor and a Catholic priest.[4]

Two weeks after writing to Wilken, Neuhaus wrote him again. He was about to leave Africa and the Middle East behind to meet with Berger in Rome for a quick European coda to their trip. This letter provides a greater sense of how he was enjoying his time overseas. Addressing both Wilken and his wife, Carol, Neuhaus wrote them from Jerusalem in late July on stationery from the Gloria Hotel, close by the Jaffa Gate. After a few remarks about the Holy City, to be expected from a first-time visitor—how small and living it felt to be there, rather than grand and historic; how physically close together were the Mount of Olives, Mount Calvary, and other signal sites of Christ's time on earth; how intermixed were the city's history, commerce, tourism, social life—he acknowledged feeling more generally tired out by the double experience of "travel and serious talk," so much so that he hadn't bothered to contact many of the people he'd been recommended to meet while traveling. He also admitted to feeling overwhelmed by "the experiences and problems of Africa" that he had firsthand witnessed, and also feeling anxious, if not annoyed, about news of lagging work on the apartment he was to occupy upon returning, and likewise about internal tensions at CALCAV and how this might affect his continued involvement with the organization. But then he turned to higher concerns, telling Wilken that he went to the Western Wall and prayed for the person and ministry of an old friend from their St. Louis seminary days, the rabbi Sol Bernards. He closed, "A thorough exploration of the social and political realities of Israel will have to wait another time. These days have been in the nature of personal and religious pilgrimage—an activity that has lost none of its meaning! Shalom! Richard."

In composing this letter, Neuhaus knew there was much to be said and done about Israel's situation; he knew there was much that he, personally, would want to say and do about it—but not this time. Prayer and pilgrimage were more important, always, and right then, they were more personally needed than the development of yet another set of "thorough explorations of social and political realities." Two letters, an airplane anecdote, those references to a few important people and places encountered—that is effectively the sum total of Neuhaus' 1971 trip recollections. In other words, the trip didn't yield a lode of material for a new book or articles or some new major initiative or project. And this is a good thing. It is evidence that not every element of Richard John Neuhaus' life was always already framed by its value for his various and voracious ambitions and interests. It is evidence that he could acknowledge a situation—like "the experiences and problems of Africa"—that was simply too much for him to take care of with his quick mind and sharp tongue. It is also evidence that he knew there were moments in his life—being on his own, in the Holy Land, for instance, tired out from serious travel and serious talk both, and so taking the time to pursue a "personal and religious pilgrimage"—where the needs and dictates of his spiritual and religious life mattered to the exclusion of any number of intellectual and professional concerns that would otherwise be fully integrated into that life. The limited outcomes of this trip are also evidence that Richard John Neuhaus could, in fact, now and then, relax.

That said, he wasn't feeling relaxed when they first touched down in Africa, as Peter Berger would recall in his own favorite anecdote from their time together there (which lasted a few days, before they parted company to pursue their respective itineraries). Following a death-defying nighttime cab ride through Dakar, Neuhaus and Berger were deposited in their hotel. Berger slept a little, showered, shaved, and then found Neuhaus at his door in the early morning hours, "with a very distressed look on his face. He said in a solemn voice, 'I have bad news for you.'" Anxious to see a doctor immediately, Neuhaus explained to his friend that his "testicles were rapidly and painfully swelling," Berger explains. The hotel manager arranged for an English-speaking doctor to come by, who assured the patient that the swelling was an inoculation side effect that was, gladly, undone with a new injection. Returned to normal, Neuhaus was ready to begin his African adventure, though for years afterward Berger would needle him with reminders of his early morning bad news declaration in Dakar.[5]

Late summer 1971, Neuhaus returned from Africa and was greeted by very different kinds of bad news: one set was political, the other personal. The former concerned CALCAV, and at least it was expected, as Neuhaus had intimated in his Jerusalem letter to Wilken. By that year, Neuhaus had realized that he could no longer remain a leader in the organization through which he had become a national figure. Its politics and his were no longer in concert. In fact, as Mitchell Hall explains, in the months leading up to his departure for Africa, Neuhaus already found himself at odds with the dominant strains in CALCAV even while continuing to exert influence at the national leadership level. In April, shortly before his departure, he had proposed a campaign to extend and develop CALCAV's national reach by intensifying its appeal to local churches and synagogues across the country to join its ongoing mission to end the war in Vietnam. This proposal went forward alongside parallel interests from elsewhere within the organization to consider the deeper moral implications, for the United States itself, of both its foreign and domestic policies. The latter element of this plan would lead to Neuhaus' break with CALCAV, a break telegraphed in part by the organization's decision to change its name during this period to CALC, literally dropping "About Vietnam" from its formal identity because that was considered too restrictive. To establish the terms and plans for its latest campaign, the newly minted CALC looked ahead to an August 1971 organizing meeting in Ann Arbor, which roughly coincided with the fifth anniversary of its founding.

The Ann Arbor conference was far from a unifying event. Now moderate-seeming CALC members, Neuhaus included, focused on extending their antiwar campaign as it had developed through the years, but they had to compete for attention and policy influence with more radical-minded delegates who were openly operating in solidarity with the South Vietnamese National Liberation Front (NLF), or Viet Cong, one of the United States' major opponents in the war. The sympathizers went so far as to fly "the Viet Cong flag at the head of [a] peace parade" that took place around the time of the conference, as Hall notes. And beyond the sharp differences over Vietnam then on display, there were also divisive efforts to situate CALC's antiwar work in a more systematic criticism-cum-campaign with a domestic focus, a "campaign," Hall explains, "for social justice that linked the domestic issues of racism, sexism, poverty, and police repression to foreign policy." Neuhaus wanted CALC to remain focused on the war in Vietnam, but to address what had become, by 1971, a pragmatic question: "With Vietnamization,"[6] as Hall reports based on an interview with him, "Neuhaus felt he no longer had to argue that the war was wrong, only how to get out." Meanwhile the new dominant currents in CALC, particularly after the Ann Arbor conference, were interested in turning the organization's mission into a broad-based criticism of American society that had more in common with the secular liberal currents of the counterculture than with Clergy Concerned's religiously framed and informed origins. And so, by late 1971, Neuhaus withdrew from a leadership role in CALC, according to Hall, even though it would be another three years before he fully broke with the organization he had cofounded.[7]

During those three years, Neuhaus also lost three significant people. The first was his father. When Neuhaus returned from Africa, Clemens Neuhaus was still pastor of a Lutheran church in Simcoe, Ontario. Aged seventy-one, he was still going, still full of zeal for the Gospel and for the work of the Church, but also, more mundanely, he was still going because he had to: as a pastor, he was afforded a salary and lodging for himself and Ella. Retirement would have offered little more than a pension and, in all likelihood, required his having to rely on the hospitality and support of his children. This wasn't the sort of arrangement that would have appealed to a man like Clem Neuhaus, long accustomed to ruling a household and congregation both. But his health was clearly failing by late 1971. He was diagnosed with lung cancer. It was so far advanced that they didn't even bother treating it. Mim, the eldest, went to Simcoe to help Ella take care of Clem in his final days. She spent a great deal of time on the phone with her brothers—Fred calling from California, telling her to do one thing and reminding her that he should be heeded because he was the oldest son, and Richard calling from New York, telling her to do something else and reminding her that he should be heeded because he was the pastor.

By January 1972, the end seemed close, and so the entire family assembled in Simcoe for the first time in years, most of the siblings traveling from various points in the States, and the twins securing compassionate leave from their units in Vietnam. The siblings argued about what to do with their father's personal effects, and they argued about the war in Vietnam, and the whole time, in Mim's recollection, Ella was in the kitchen, cooking for the family, "just as if nothing's happening." But neither Ella nor any of the children could avoid the doctor's conclusive assessment: Clem was confined to his hospital bed, and in early February his doctor informed Mim that he didn't have more than a couple of weeks, and it would be right for the children to say good-bye while there was still time. She came back to the house and delivered the sad news. It was firmly rejected by one family member.

"Just listen to me," Richard declared, dismissing Mim's report so brusquely it still annoyed her some thirty years later. "I did work at King's County Hospital," he continued. "Dad doesn't even look anywhere near death. You haven't seen death. He's going to be fine. He's not going to die." With this, Richard told everyone to go home. Everyone went home. Clem died a week later. Everyone came back. There was no remorse on Richard's part. He was too busy criticizing some of the decisions Mim made about the funeral. As for the funeral itself, Neuhaus served as one of his father's pallbearers, along with the other brothers. That was the extent of his involvement in the service, and his taking part as a pallbearer only draws more attention to the strangeness of the situation. Why wouldn't the pastor son preside over the pastor father's funeral? Were their kitchen table and convention floor debates so finally corrosive of their relationship? Was Richard still upset that Clem had commanded him to submit all sermons in advance if he ever wanted to preach at Clem's church again? If so, this was a command Richard respected after a fashion, by never preaching at that church again, even at Clem's funeral.

None of Neuhaus' surviving relatives have any particular account for why he didn't preside at Clem's funeral, and indeed, it's common practice in the Missouri Synod for the local pastor to preside, even when the family of the deceased includes a clergyman. Not that Neuhaus likely complained about this, anyway. Most every person who recalls Clem and Richard's relationship notes their similarities—primarily their matching if opposed portions of supreme self-confidence and stubbornness when it came to ecclesial and intellectual arguments—and also the heatedness of their debates. Both of Neuhaus' sisters, as well as his colleague and friend James Nuechterlein, recall Richard's longing to win his father's attention and also earn his father's respect, if not as a fellow sportsman than as a fellow clergyman. But no one describes any significant or deep affection on either man's part for the other. Indeed, years later, as Nuechterlein recalls, Neuhaus would on occasion wistfully recall a memory of walking with his father when he was about five years old, and Clem remarking, "Dickie, you sure are a good walker." The wistfulness came less from the richness of this father-son experience itself than from the memory's standing out in Neuhaus' mind as a rare moment of focus, affection, and encouragement from his father, who otherwise had a family and congregation to run, and other sons more immediately adept at winning their father's attention.

In the years following his father's death, Neuhaus would write about him on rare occasions—as with "Like Father, Like Son, Almost," his 1994 *First Things* remembrance, which was more nostalgic and bemused than moved or moving. He would, in turn, develop a stronger relationship with Ella, faithfully calling her at least once a week and enjoying her visits to New York (as part of a broader slate of regular visits she made by bus to her children living across the country). This closeness was helped along by Ella's decision to move back to Pembroke following Clem's death, a move that coincided, in the early 1970s, with Neuhaus' decision to begin spending part of every August there. He would often spend this time living with his mother in the simple cottage owned by members of the family, near Pembroke, on the Quebec side of the timber-strewn Ottawa River that afforded them burnished views of their hometown while they sat on the deck to watch the sun go down.[8]

Clemens Neuhaus died on February 12, 1972. Ten months after losing his father, Neuhaus lost a significant father figure, Abraham

Joshua Heschel. After a long and consequential life as a notable religious intellectual and activist rabbi who excelled at bringing the sacred to bear upon questions of public import in American life, whether over Civil Rights, the war in Vietnam, or interfaith relations, Heschel died on December 23. Mindful that Heschel's Christian friends wouldn't be allowed into the synagogue for his funeral, his wife, Sylvia, called them to come to the house. "Neuhaus was among the first" to arrive, according to Heschel's biographer, Edward K. Kaplan, and he knelt and prayed by Heschel's bedside, where he was soon joined by the Berrigan brothers. There seems to be no comparable moment of prayerful leave-taking on Neuhaus' part with his father, whether because he was so wrongly confident that Clemens would live on, or because in some respects Heschel's passing was more immediately, in fact more intensely, felt. As both example and enabler, Heschel was arguably the most important figure in Neuhaus' 1960s emergence as a clergyman on the national stage. It was with Heschel (and Berrigan) that Neuhaus cofounded CALCAV; it was through Heschel that Neuhaus met King; and it was because of his endless hours spent in conversation with Heschel, discussing theology and much else, that Neuhaus developed what became a lifelong commitment to fostering stronger Jewish-Christian relations in America. With Heschel gone, and Peter Berger already having broken with CALC because of its radical turns, Neuhaus was that much more on his own in the organization. It was in the context of the organization's later memorial tribute to Heschel that Neuhaus would all but fully break with CALC himself.

Before that happened, however, another more far-reaching break took place, which coincided with the death of a third important figure for Neuhaus. "In mid-December 1973, Arthur Carl Piepkorn died after entering a barbershop bordering the seminary," recounts James Burkee. Neuhaus' beloved, decisively influential seminary teacher, Piepkorn passed away from a heart attack mere days after he was informed that he was to be forcibly retired from teaching at Concordia-St. Louis, ostensibly because he was past the nominal retirement age of sixty-five. More accurately, as Burkee recounts, Piepkorn was pushed out as part of the culmination of a broader campaign against putative "moderates" at Concordia, waged by traditionalists (who received constant encouragement and supporting evidence from Herman Otten) who worked back channels and also maneuvered at national conventions to convince Missouri's overall leadership that the synod itself was imperiled by heterodox elements at its flagship seminary. Their argument was that Piepkorn and many other faculty members' interests in historicist approaches to Scripture and their openness to ecumenism and social justice concerns like Civil Rights were a collective betrayal of *echt* Missouri, which is to say, *echt* Lutheranism, because they respectively challenged biblical inerrancy, encouraged unionism, and undermined Two Kingdoms theology.

Onward from his student days under Piepkorn and also Richard Caemmerer, Neuhaus was a notable Missouri moderate, part of a faction that found itself on the losing end of the confession's internal battles, as the synod's leadership, specifically Missouri president Jack Preus, increasingly aligned the confession's sensibility and sense of identity and purpose with dominant strands of American biblical fundamentalism—literalist, anti-cosmopolitan, and stand-alone. Moving in this direction, the synod simultaneously rejected the reform-minded and integrative, ecclesial Christianity that Piepkorn passionately believed in and taught as the formulation of Lutheranism most in authentic continuity with the confession's sixteenth-century founding. But Piepkorn's vision was in the decided minority in Missouri, and shortly after his death, the remaining moderate group at the seminary went on strike after the overseeing Board of Control fired seminary president and moderate defender John Tietjen. The faculty were ordered to return to work, refused, and were also fired. They departed dramatically on February 19, 1973, as Burkee describes it: "Leaving the quadrangle, they boarded up the entrance to the seminary with two large frames marked 'EXILED' and began a staged march out of the campus that would soon lead to a formal separation from the LCMS."

In turn, this faction would found a seminary in exile, called Seminex, and form a new Lutheran body, the Association of Evangelical Churches (AELC). Neuhaus would join AELC while still maintaining his association with Missouri, until the latter removed him from its rolls because of his affiliation to the former. For a cradle Missourian, the son of a conservative LCMS pastor no less, this must have been a difficult break for Neuhaus, a break he tried to prevent by establishing the "dual rostering" arrangement with the AELC and LCMS that predictably didn't last for very long. In all this, Piepkorn's death would have been a personally felt loss that, in its surrounding context, signaled a broader loss: if there was effectively no place for someone like Piepkorn in the LCMS, circa 1973, what kind of place was there for his most devoted student?

This same double sense of loss figured in Neuhaus' relationship to Heschel and CALCAV. It came into especially sharp relief when Neuhaus attended the organization's 1974 memorial for Heschel. Listening to the remarks offered about his beloved mentor—and, at least in Hall's detailed history, tellingly not invited to deliver any remarks himself, as might have been expected given his personal relationship to Heschel and their close association especially within CALCAV—Neuhaus was outraged by one speaker's remembrance in particular. As Neuhaus told Hall, it amounted to "a strident, leftist cliché. It just became appallingly clear to me, that in no way did I believe what this organization was about anymore." In late 1974, Neuhaus was essentially finished with the group that had made him a nationally prominent clergyman of the Left. A year later, when he and a few others tried—and failed—to win broad support among his leftist colleagues for a public condemnation of the new Communist government in Vietnam because of its broad human rights abuses and specific targeting of religious minorities, he knew it was really over: for his onetime allies, leftist political solidarity trumped concerns over the higher dictates of religious freedom and human dignity. And so he was effectively finished with the Left itself in political-intellectual terms by 1975, though he had been moving in this direction from at least 1971, judging from his rant, *In Defense of People,* which he published that year against its rising elements following his return from Africa.[9]

In a contemporaneous piece for the *Christian Century* magazine, tellingly titled "The Loneliness of the Long-Distance Radical," Neuhaus declared the Movement "dead" because the majority of its members had abandoned its higher ethical aspirations—to bring peace and justice to the poor and war-trodden at home and abroad—for the intoxications of personal liberation-cum-libertinism. Not for Neuhaus was then–Hillary Rodham's 1969 Wellesley College commencement declaration that the rising generations in American life were "searching for a more immediate, ecstatic and penetrating mode of living." Indeed, he wondered autobiographically in his *Christian Century* essay, what were those to do who remained committed to reaching "the Kingdom of God" rather than being now committed to achieving "the perfect orgasm"?

But of course he had his answer ready. They would only press on in their mission, "until wars end and the prisoners are released, until the blind see and the hungry are fed," and they would do it, at least Neuhaus would do it, now, without any illusions about the people they were running with: "To be sure, from time to time the radicals will find themselves part of what look like mass movements. But because they are radicals they won't count on it." By 1974 and moving into 1975, there wasn't much from the past fourteen years that Richard John Neuhaus could count on to provide the means and platform for him to keep working for God's Kingdom as he had been since coming to New York in 1961. He was, as ever, engaged in politics of all kinds—ecclesial, intellectual, ideological—but in the principles, premises, and positions he was committed to he found himself lonelier and lonelier. But surely, there were others just as committed as Neuhaus was to defending the most vulnerable at home and abroad from the most powerful and their so-called qualities of life. Surely there were others who understood this defense as beginning and ending in the service of God and His Church. Surely, there had to be others. They just needed someone to get them going.[10]

Part III

FROM HARTFORD TO ROME, VIA THE NAKED PUBLIC SQUARE, 1975–1990

"I've known authors to go to great lengths to promote their books. But arranging a presidential campaign, isn't that a bit much?"

Television interviewer to Richard John Neuhaus (1984)

CHAPTER THIRTEEN

Appealing for Right Religion, Appalling the Left

"It stands athwart history, yelling Stop, at a time when no one is inclined to do so, or to have much patience with those who so urge it." So William F. Buckley, Jr., described the defiant posture of his new magazine, *National Review,* upon its 1955 founding. In time, Buckley's formulation would come to serve as a shorthand definition of what it largely means to be a conservative in modern American life. And by this definition, Richard John Neuhaus fully became a conservative over a few wintry days in Hartford in January 1975, about twenty years after Buckley set the terms. These were days spent developing what would become the Hartford Appeal for Theological Affirmation. If little known now, compared with his earlier and later involvements and exploits, the Hartford Appeal is profoundly significant to understanding the life and work of Richard John Neuhaus. In fact, the Hartford Appeal is finally a more important event in his religious-political career shift from Left to Right than his contemporaneous break with CALC over Vietnam and the ethics of American power at home and abroad. This is because the Appeal signaled in simultaneously theological and public terms the end of Neuhaus' collaborations with American Christianity's liberal-activist community, his transformation into one of that community's most implacable critics, and his emergence as one of conservative Christianity's foremost apologists, intellectual leaders, organizers, and operators.[1]

About a year after the Appeal first appeared, by which point media coverage was in full swing—*Time, Newsweek,* the *New York Times,* and the *Times'* Sunday magazine all devoted attention to it, with Neuhaus a recurring interviewee—and a liberal counter-Appeal called the Boston Affirmations was in the offing, Neuhaus co-edited a series of essays about the statement, its intentions, and its effects. In his contribution to *Against the World for the World: The Hartford Appeal and the Future of American Religion,* Neuhaus explained the Appeal's origins and necessity by situating what happened in Hartford in a broader context: "It is said that the mood of the seventies is one of retreat; more specifically, that the churches are retreating from the commitment to social justice that motored the civil rights movement, the antiwar protest, and related crusades of the past fifteen years. It is not insignificant that the Hartford Appeal, issued January 1975, came at the precise midpoint of the decade." He concluded: "Hartford is an appeal to call a halt to retreat." Neuhaus' "halt to retreat" lacks the force and flair of Buckley's declared plan to stand "athwart history" itself, "yelling Stop." But in at least one respect the Appeal proved comparably significant to the rise of the Buckley-led modern conservative movement two decades earlier: it both exposed and intensified the post-Vietnam factionalization of publicly engaged Christian ministry in the United States along activist-oriented liberal and doctrine-focused conservative lines. In his own writings about this split, Neuhaus would reject it as producing a false binary, even while he contributed to such distinctions for the rest of his career with voracious criticisms of liberal Christianity for uncoupling the Gospel's call to work for justice and mercy from the Gospel's revelation of Christ as the Son of God and the universal savior of mankind.[2]

Indeed, if in less dramatic terms, Neuhaus' sense of this lamentable division was at work in the very conception of the Appeal itself. The idea came out of the Brooklyn think tank also known as the Bergers' Cobble Hill brownstone, where one evening in January 1974, Neuhaus and Peter Berger decided to have some fun. Fun, that is, as only religiously minded intellectuals like Neuhaus and Berger would understand it: "Neuhaus and I thought it would be fun to make a list of the major themes in mainline Protestantism that irritated us," Berger recalled in a memoir. They shared this "negative list" "with a small number of theologians who, we thought, would agree with it. Most of them did," Berger further notes, "and with enthusiasm." Thereafter, to discover if something of greater substance and influence might come of this initial enthusiasm, Berger arranged for a conference to be held at Hartford Seminary, where some twenty-four theologians were recruited to discuss and debate the list in greater detail. The theologians came from across the range of American Christianity, though they were weighted toward the strongly ecclesial (Catholics, Lutherans, Orthodox) and the historic Protestant Mainline (Episcopalians, Methodists, Calvinists).

Each participant in the majority, in fact everyone other than Pastor Neuhaus of St. John the Evangelist in Brooklyn, was either a faculty member at a major seminary or university (like Yale Divinity, Notre Dame, or New York's Union Theological Seminary) or a high-ranking official in the administrative apparatus of a major church. Least credentialed, Neuhaus was nevertheless the vital center of the Hartford roster, which featured those who were already close to him then—his co-organizer Berger and also Robert Wilken, Avery Dulles, Bill Coffin—and those who would variously collaborate with him in the years to come, including Methodist theologian and noted pacifist Stanley Hauerwas, heralded Lutheran theologian George Lindbeck, rising Calvinist leader Richard Mouw, and prominent Orthodox priest Alexander Schmemann. With the Hartford Appeal, and as would prove the case throughout his life and work, Neuhaus drew on his distinctive gift for identifying like-minded people from across a series of religious, intellectual, political, and cultural contexts. But this was no mere cerebral-curatorial habit; he was equally adept at persuading them to come together for projects and meetings that reliably led to more projects and meetings and also forged strategic alliances and rich personal friendships and led to much late-night drink and talk—all of which Neuhaus focused, first and last, on questions of public and religious significance.[3]

Beyond its beginnings as a bemused late-night list-making session in Brooklyn, the Hartford Appeal pursued a serious and provocative premise. The signal problem of the contemporary Church, the preamble declares, is "an apparent loss of a sense of the transcendent" among its leaders and members, "which is undermining the Church's ability to address with clarity and courage the urgent tasks to which God calls it in the world." This loss is evident in a set of "pervasive themes" characterizing the mood, mind-set, and practices of contemporary American Christianity, themes that present ideas and construals that are "superficially attractive" but, subjected to the shared scrutiny of some two dozen theologians, prove "false and debilitating to the Church's life and work." The thirteen themes that the authors of the Appeal formally rejected, listed below, serve in turn as a comprehensive summary of the positions that Neuhaus would assail in the years to come:

Theme 1 · Modern Thought is superior to all past forms of understanding reality, and is therefore normative for Christian faith and life.

Theme 2 · Religious statements are totally independent of reasonable discourse.

Theme 3 · Religious language refers to human experience and nothing else, God being humanity's oldest creation.

Theme 4 · Jesus can only be understood in terms of contemporary models of humanity.

Theme 5 · All religions are equally valid; the choice among them is not a matter of conviction about truth but only of personal preference or lifestyle.

Theme 6 · To realize one's potential and to be true to oneself is the whole meaning of salvation.

Theme 7 · Since what is human is good, evil can adequately be understood as failure to realize potential.

Theme 8 · The sole purpose of worship is to promote individual self-realization and human community.

Theme 9 · Institutions and historical traditions are inimical and oppressive to our being truly human; liberation from them is required for authentic existence and authentic religion.

Theme 10 · The world must set the agenda for the Church. Social, political, and economic programs to improve the quality of life are ultimately normative for the Church's mission in the world.

Theme 11 · An emphasis on God's transcendence is at least a hindrance to, and perhaps incompatible with, Christian social concern and action.

Theme 12 · The struggle for a better humanity will bring about the Kingdom of God.

Theme 13 · The question of hope beyond death is irrelevant or at best marginal to the Christian understanding of human fulfillment.[4]

To each of these, the Hartford group offers a cogent and critical response, a response determined by the group's deliberative sessions.[5] To claim that Neuhaus was the primary author for these responses is admittedly speculative. But everyone interviewed for this biography who ever participated in a meeting with Neuhaus, from his 1960s CALCAV days through his 2000s work with the group Evangelicals and Catholics Together, among any number of other conservative colloquia, at some point describes his incomparable talent, if not genius, for intervening in an involved, occasionally abstract discussion with a rapidly formulated statement that articulated the common understanding in the room. At times, these contributions were provoked by Neuhaus' tendency to grow impatient with particularly abstract conversation, and also with conversations that he wasn't personally, exclusively dominating. (The New York area pastors who, beginning in the mid-1970s, regularly gathered on Wednesday nights at Neuhaus' apartment for an evening of cigars and Scotch and lively, heady conversation, for instance, knew that their host would single-handedly provide all three.) But personality traits weren't the main factor. Neuhaus was always keen to advance a mature discussion to new considerations, and also to ensure that the discussion itself—while important in its own right for religious and intellectual reasons—also produced material that could help defend, change, or challenge the wider culture, such as the times demanded. In this particular instance, the Appeal critically insists that the stated positions are too much of a piece with the dominantly secular-liberal spirit of the time. The responses propose correctives, derived from the first principle of biblically founded beliefs in the Kingdom of God, the Divinity of Christ, and the ultimate importance of prayer and liturgy—"We worship God because God is to be worshiped"—all set over and against a Christianity either willfully captive to the times or lacking the courage to contradict them from the resources traditionally and institutionally embodied in Gospel and Church.[6]

The Hartford Appeal generated almost immediate public interest and controversy. In February 1975, *Time* magazine breathlessly framed it in historic terms that also intimated the beginnings of a full-on culture war inside American Christianity itself: "Christian history is replete with bone-rattling documents of theological protest that capsuled the pressing issues of the day: Martin Luther's 95 Theses, which sparked the Reformation, Pope Pius IX's 19th century Syllabus of Errors, and the German Confessing Christians' Barmen Declaration against Nazism. The technique has fallen into disuse, but it was dusted off last week by a group of . . . Christian thinkers [from] nine denominations. After a weekend war council at the Hartford Seminary Foundation in Connecticut, they joined in a dramatic warning that American theology has strayed dangerously far afield." *Time* went on to report that while no names were named in the published statement, there were nevertheless some obvious targets during the sessions themselves, including Harvey Cox,

Neuhaus' CALCAV ally and onetime Paris bunkmate. Cox was a target because, in his best-known work, *The Secular City,*[7] he advocated a free-form approach to Christianity liberated from institutional structures. Meanwhile, for its subordination of theology to politics, the Marxist-informed liberation theology movement emerging from liberal Catholic circles was another target, one that Neuhaus would return to over the years as he became a committed, indeed strident anticommunist. In addition to Cox and liberation theology, there was at least one institutional target in mind, the ecumenical World Council of Churches, which, Neuhaus told *Time,* is nothing less than "a gargantuan exercise in [the very] cultural capitulation" that the Appeal was lamenting. This wasn't the first time Neuhaus used a broad public platform to go after a religious institution with vim and vehemence because it was failing to live out its sacred purpose and promise, and it certainly wouldn't be the last.

The same month he was chatting with *Time,* Neuhaus also published an energetic and wide-ranging piece in the *Christian Century,* "A Pilgrim Piece of Time and Space." It was accompanied by a flattering (if very 1970s) photograph of the pastor, aged almost forty, with thick muttonchop sideburns blending into shaggy locks that didn't exactly obscure his receding hairline. Staring pensively into the distance, his elbow on a lectern, his hand stroking his chin, here was someone you could imagine *Christian Century* inviting, as it had, to offer some observations and formulations "on the state of religion, theology, the nation, and oneself." He had much to say on all these items, much of it in keeping with the concerns that drove Hartford, and he was frank about the cleavage he saw in American religious life, where the sources of a revival were, and where his own allegiances lay. They certainly weren't with churches that had capitulated to an increasingly secularized and mundane culture—"What is called mainstream Protestantism witnesses to a massive enervation. It seems in large part a house of the dead, the dying, and the decadent; it cranks up machinery from past crusades, it sucks the blood of whatever 'movement' creature shows signs of life . . . and it generally confuses the consequences of incompetence with the consequences of bearing the cross." And so, "for the shape of things to come," Neuhaus continued, "I look especially to the Roman Catholics, the evangelicals, and the Lutherans" because these churches evidenced "a theological vitality and earnestness of mission" in and of themselves, never mind by comparison to the incompetent zombie-vampire ranks of the Protestant Mainline.

Telegraphing with remarkable accuracy the very realignment he would be instrumental in bringing about by the early 1990s, Neuhaus discerned in 1975 an emerging coalition made of three distinct elements. First, post–Vatican II Catholics keen to confront the surrounding culture out of the deep resources of their church and tradition, a movement to be distinguished from the media caricatures Neuhaus colorfully summarizes as "lesbian ex-nuns robbing banks to support the revolution." If we ignore these "sideshows," Neuhaus argues, then we might "see that Catholicism is positioned to redefine the vital center of Christianity in America," a premise he would explore with increasing interest in the years to come. The second element in the coalition was the evangelicals, for their activist energy undergirded by the unassailable firmness of their theological imperatives. Third, and least, Neuhaus notes Lutherans, emphasizing their reformist and unifying capacities, though he isn't particularly confident: "Lest I be accused of self-serving, I assure the reader that being a Lutheran gives me innumerable reasons to despair of Lutheranism contributing anything helpful to the larger church."

At the end of this punchy contribution to the magazine's ongoing "New Turns in Religious Thought" series, Neuhaus turned more personal. "The *Century* editors ask about influences on my thinking," he noted. Much of the list is predictable enough: Piepkorn, Heschel, King, and also the German Lutheran Wolfhart Pannenberg, whose systematic exploration of the meaning of God's intervention in history through the revelation of the person of Christ represented, as far as Neuhaus was concerned, "the most ambitiously architectonic theological enterprise of our time." In terms of earlier influences, he cites St. Augustine, Tillich, Schleiermacher, and Troeltsch, and also Dostoevsky, whose "Grand Inquisitor" section from *The Brothers Karamazov* Neuhaus hailed as "the only thing I have ever read that I would want to see added to the biblical canon . . . It is the story of the church's temptation until the kingdom comes." The most ardently framed inclusion in his list of influences, however, is "Paul, above all Paul, always Paul: I Corinthians 4:5 is the style, Romans 14:8 is the bedrock of confidence." For style, in other words, it's Paul's admission "Judge nothing before the time, until the Lord come, who both will bring to light the hidden things of darkness, and will make manifest the counsels of the hearts." For the bedrock, it's Paul's assurance that "whether we live, we live unto the Lord; and whether we die, we die unto the Lord: whether we live therefore, or die, we are the Lord's."

First and last convicted by this sense of claim and belonging, Neuhaus didn't end his set of influences on this seemingly fitting note. Rather, he ended in more personal terms, by describing his home in New York—his homes, that is, including the *Worldview* magazine offices "on the posh upper east side of Manhattan" that afforded him a community of "authors, academics . . . and divers experts on international affairs and the like." His other efforts at this time, he noted, ranged from "keep[ing] a left hand in city politics and spend[ing] too much time in board and committee meetings . . . dealing with peace, race, urban affairs, and so forth," to "a number of church-related projects dealing with public policy and . . . the editorship of *Forum Letter,* a monthly commentary on what [was] happening in American Lutheranism and the larger church." Conscious of how varied this list would seem to anyone other than himself, Neuhaus declared that all of the people involved in these concerns "are very agreeable about my wandering in and out of their worlds." At the end of the day, however, his firmer sense of home remained his life and work on Maujer Street, and it inspired from him some of his most moving prose from this period: "The question of who I am or what I do always begins and ends with, and I suspect will always return to, my being a pastor here in this pilgrim piece of time and space that is St. John's Church, Brooklyn." His suspicion would prove wrong a few years later, but not his sense that for all the many exploits he pursued, the source and summit of his life and work was his vocation as a pastor and, in time, a priest.[8]

A few months after Neuhaus wrote about himself for the *Christian Century* and was written about by *Time,* the latter's prediction proved right: the Hartford Appeal generated great conflict. As Neuhaus recounted decades later, shortly after the Appeal was released, Bill Coffin came to him in distress. This must have been sometime after late January 1975, which is when Coffin wrote Neuhaus a warm letter about the Hartford session, describing his "happy grateful mood" and telling Neuhaus, "I'm glad you thought of me and I'm glad I was smart enough to come." Coffin, the long-standing Yale chaplain and nationally prominent social and political activist of impeccable liberal Christian credentials, was in agreement with Neuhaus that the continued work of the Church in the world needed a firmer, more explicit grounding in theology. This was likely why he had signed the Appeal in the first place. But Coffin's mood changed as Hartford began to stir controversy. In Neuhaus' recollection, Coffin "was under strong pressure from others to choose between Hartford and those who understood themselves to be the objects of Hartford's criticisms." No doubt thanks in part to the quality and strength of their long-standing friendship, Coffin was initially willing to stay with Neuhaus on the Hartford side despite the pressure he was getting from other quarters. In fact, Neuhaus and Coffin came forward together as the Appeal's most prominent signatories when the National Council of Churches organized a debate over its claims at Manhattan's Riverside Church, on June 14, 1975. A decade earlier, while Martin Luther King spoke out against the war in Vietnam under the auspices of CALCAV, Neuhaus had been in this same church, his status self-evident as a leading member of the radical religious Left. His status was evidently otherwise after Hartford, as Neuhaus squared off with Coffin against Harvey Cox to debate the claims and implications of the Appeal.

The debate didn't go as Neuhaus might have been expecting. "Halfway into the discussion," he remembered, "Bill joined the other side in criticizing Hartford." In fact, according to a transcript of the debate, Coffin was against him from the start. Perhaps goaded by the moderator's admitting to being "perplexed" at seeing Coffin's name on such a conservative document, Coffin began his remarks by disavowing his connection to the Appeal. He recalled that his first impression, upon receiving the initial statement from Neuhaus and Berger, was that it was going to be "strictly anti-left" in its focus rather than broader in its targets and concerns. But he joined on anyway, he told the audience, mostly because "Dick is persistent," if likewise resistant to Coffin's counsel that the Appeal was going to stir up a great deal of trouble. At Riverside, Coffin conveniently forgot about his late January "happy grateful mood" about Hartford, and he spent the rest of the debate working in tandem with Cox, battling against the chief troublemaker himself, Neuhaus. At the most heated moment, Coffin angrily interrupted Neuhaus in the midst of an extended account of Hartford's claims to declare, "When you say 'Hartford says'—says you!" and Neuhaus tersely responded that he was describing the Appeal in objective terms. And as Neuhaus would later recount, for all intents and purposes, "the friendship effectively ended that day at 475 Riverside. We saw each other from time to time after that, but it was not the same." Neuhaus said nothing else about this break beyond describing it as a "sharp parting of ways." That might be putting it mildly: it happened in public, in a prominent setting, and it had to sting in its combination of personal betrayal and theological division.[9]

In a larger context, Coffin's turn was for Neuhaus still more evidence of establishment Christianity's loss of nerve before an adversarial movement that he had himself been part of, scant years before. In fact, in the same 2006 *First Things* remembrance of Coffin where he recounted the Riverside turnabout, Neuhaus also described his firsthand experience of the willful capitulation of America's historically leading churches and related organizations while he was himself still in his radical Left period. Writing about it decades later, Neuhaus ironically regretted that the Movement was in one sense too successful: "We, the young radicals, were on fire with anti-establishment rhetoric, and I was rather taken aback when the establishment evidenced such eagerness to be part of the movement against itself. . . . There was a great fear of being out of step with the young and their putative revolution. Eugene Carson Blake of the National Council of Churches, featured on the cover of *Time* as 'Mr. Protestant,' John Bennett, president of Union Seminary, and so many others happily signed up with 'The Movement,' and I wondered what was going to happen to the institutions that they headed—the institutions that I had thought were running the world. Now we know." At the time, however, persuading establishment church leaders to speak out on Civil Rights and the injustice of the war in Vietnam from their powerful and influential pulpits was exactly what Neuhaus was working for, and he would have counted support from the likes of Bennett and Blake a success for the fledgling CALCAV. Only in retrospect did he fully recognize that the radicals and the establishment supporters were mutually engaged in seeking each other's recognition, for their causes and institutions.[10]

Neuhaus was convinced, by 1975, that this dynamic of mutual approbation worked to the expense of traditional doctrine and practice, and the breakdown of historic institutional integrity rather than its timely revivification. For years afterward, he criticized organizations like the National Council of Churches and the World Council of Churches, and the Protestant Mainline itself, for capitulating to an increasingly liberal and less traditionally Christian culture in America, instead of challenging it. Of course, Neuhaus had earlier gone after the same organizations in the years leading up to Hartford because he was convinced they were shirking their duty to challenge a conformist mainstream culture abetting injustice at home and abroad, and were doing so by hiding behind their historic institutional integrity. But by the early 1980s, and with notable public effect, he would go after these same institutions again, this time from an anticommunist position. Moving in that direction by the mid-1970s, he was then mindful that neither the latest iteration of the Movement nor the traditional sites and sources of Protestant power in American life were viable contexts for him to pursue his own publicly focused ministry. And so Neuhaus took it upon himself to find platforms of his own, which he established in no small part by writing and working against the radical allies he had left behind, and against the establishment opponents who had too willingly accepted defeat by those radicals.

Of the platforms he either created or commandeered in the mid-1970s, the Hartford Appeal was the most prominent and influential. Less prominent but profoundly important to Neuhaus was his involvement, in 1976 and thereafter, with the founding and development of Lutherans for Life, which would eventually become one of the relatively few non-Catholic pro-life organizations that possessed national reach.[11] Other efforts during this period now look more like preparatory work for his more notable pursuits in the 1980s and thereafter, like (as he noted in his *Christian Century* article) his taking on the editorship of the *Lutheran Forum Letter* in 1974, a monthly newsletter put out by the American Lutheran Publicity Bureau. Over the next sixteen years, Neuhaus would comment on the goings-on inside the fractious world of late American Lutheranism, using a combination of caustic wit and serious criticism and also consistent apologetics in support of a catholic understanding of Lutheranism as a reform movement internal to the Church universal. *Una Sancta,* the Lutheran journal he worked on as an editor in the 1960s, was defunct by 1970 due to low subscriptions, and so *Forum Letter* became a way to stay engaged and influence American Lutheranism in the years after the breakup of Concordia Seminary and the deepening divisions within the Missouri Synod. But beyond his elbows-out public presence in the Synod, Neuhaus also sought a larger platform for his ideas and concerns through his contributions as editor and writer for *Worldview* magazine.

Neuhaus began contributing to *Worldview* in the late 1960s, and became an associate and eventually a senior editor in the 1970s and early 1980s, serving alongside his friend and the magazine's longtime editor in chief, James Finn. The two of them first met in the mid-1960s, when Finn interviewed Neuhaus during his ascendant Movement days for a book of conversations about (as the title went) *Protest: Pacifism and Politics.*[12] Thereafter, by Neuhaus' own measure, they spent "thousands of hours in conversation over drinks and good food," often involving Finn's wife, Molly, in something of a repetition of Neuhaus' friendship with the Bergers. Their primary work together was during the 1970s on *Worldview,* the publication Neuhaus later described as "a forerunner to *First Things.*" Independent of Neuhaus' rather self-important account of its importance, *Worldview* itself was on its own terms a distinctive publication with an ambitious purview ordered to and by ideas and concerns that were confidently religious in their sources. The magazine was founded in 1958, under the auspices of a religion, ethics, and international affairs organization founded by Andrew Carnegie in 1914. By the time Neuhaus was involved, the organization was known as the Council on Religion and International Affairs (CRIA), and *Worldview* was its monthly venue for contributors to engage contemporary international affairs out of the "West's perennial tradition, which is deeply, essentially rooted in the values of the Judeo-Christian, classical humanist view of man and society." This was, in other words, a perfect venue for Richard John Neuhaus. And over the years, he wrote opinions and reviews on a typically remarkable array of subjects and people, including the "troubles" of Northern Ireland, the writings of Wolfhart Pannenberg, the (latest) failures of the NCC and WCC, and Prime Minister Pierre Trudeau's program for a new multicultural Canada. He also used its pages to pick more than a few fights. He vigorously disputed prominent leftist intellectual Michael Harrington's claims about Martin Luther King's turn toward socialism in late life (citing, of course, "personal conversations with King" along the way) and more gingerly argued with Princeton ethicist and admitted "big brother in the faith" Paul Ramsey about whether Neuhaus was licensing revolution with his writings and remarks or only vigorously establishing its stakes and terms.[13]

His most notable confrontation in *Worldview* was with his once and future close friend and collaborator Michael Novak. Across multiple issues of the magazine in 1972 and 1973, Novak and Neuhaus clashed in heated, personal terms. This began when Neuhaus panned Novak's book *The Rise of the Unmeltable Ethnics,* arguing that it over-privileged the significance of one's ethnic origins and ethnic community as substantial, even mystical sources of strength and identity and resistance in a WASP-dominated America. In other words, Neuhaus thought Novak was advocating for ethnicity—rather than citizenship or religious affiliation—as the strongest possible grounds for a greater cultural flourishing. Novak pushed back, hard, insisting that Neuhaus was an irreducible German Lutheran desperate to conceal his origins and meanwhile rise up in American life by going around in person and print as a deracinated cosmopolitan elite. But Neuhaus got the last word, in *Worldview* at least, noting that Novak's arguments were "uncommonly deficient," before composing an autobiography that delightedly exaggerated the charges made against him by Novak, whom Neuhaus declared was America's leading "angry ethnic":

> *Here I am, a Canadian-reared, Texas-educated, Missouri Synod Lutheran writing from black Brooklyn where I have lived almost the whole of my adult life, a son of Maimonides and Melanchthon, a descendant of* stetl *and* bierstube, *an intellectual offspring, says Novak, from Jonathan Edwards; I am, it must be*

confessed, a veritable melting pot. My illegitimacy fully warrants the disdain of the ethnically pristine one-man immigrant Slovak community of Bayville, Long Island.

And with that, Novak and Neuhaus didn't speak for a decade.[14]

Throughout Neuhaus' writing for *Worldview,* Vietnam was a recurring concern, even as his positions changed in focus and feeling. In 1967, he had written sympathetically about bold advocates for peace and mercy emerging from the ranks of America's traditionally establishmentarian churches. By 1980, he was lamenting the war as "the squandering" of "American global power," which, "considering the alternative"—the Soviet Union—was clearly "benign and essential." He also wrote repeatedly about the place of religion in American public life, especially in the lead-up to Jimmy Carter's victorious 1976 presidential run against Gerald Ford, including "Why I Am for Carter," a dense and analytical declaration of support in seven theses that appeared in an October issue of *Commonweal.* In this article, Neuhaus praised Carter's integration of social justice imperatives with public policy decisions, while also dismissing as romantic, pointless, and electorally counterproductive the Eugene McCarthy write-in campaign of fall 1976. In the pages of *Worldview,* he was less strategic and partisan, and more expansive in his hopes for what a Carter presidency might mean: "The Carter era could signal the end of the public hegemony of the secular Enlightenment in the Western world," he dramatically predicted that summer. He was also keen to write about Carter's candidacy in a way that established his own set of higher order and contrarian terms for understanding the nature of American politics.[15]

Thus motivated, in his *Worldview* articles Neuhaus downplayed arguments from supporters and sympathetic pundits that a Carter presidency carried the prospect of uniting the country in racial and regional terms, even while writing in the same vein in *Commonweal.* In fact, Neuhaus argued, the stakes were greater, and likewise the promise. The actual prospect of a Carter presidency, Neuhaus proposed, had to do with a restoration of how "we understand morality in public life," particularly in the post-Watergate era.[16] Not just a restoration, but actually a renewal and a welcome reconceiving, Neuhaus proposed, insofar as Carter struck him as a politician capable of bridging the gap between secular elites and religious masses, and credibly articulating, as no president had since Woodrow Wilson, and before him Lincoln, "the Jewish-Christian foundation of public morality." Later in life, in fact "all the time" by his own accounting, Neuhaus would counsel his readers and audiences from Psalm 146, "Put not your trust in princes." Yet he later clearly did so, in many ways, with George W. Bush, and to a lesser extent with Ronald Reagan, and enthusiastically then with Jimmy Carter. In 1976, assessing the candidate, Neuhaus was convinced that Carter would be a salve for an American public life that, in his diagnosis, was suffering from secular-religious divisions that directly mapped onto the demographic estrangement of the elite from the masses. These dual divisions, he argued, weakened and eroded the nation's culture and lead institutions, and likewise diminished the citizenry's experiences and understandings of a common national life. These divisions needed to be exposed, their damage undone, and a program of unifying national renewal developed in their place, and Neuhaus was confident that Carter would be an exemplary figure for this. But what might such a program of renewal involve? Neuhaus had a few ideas.[17]

CHAPTER FOURTEEN

Books to Empower People and Pastors Alike

If Neuhaus liked to invoke Psalm 146 about the danger of hoping for too much from politicians, and to recall Paul's letters about God's vouchsafing of the immediate and ultimate realities of every human life, he was also certainly familiar with Ecclesiastes 12:12: "Of making many books, there is no end." And even by his own robust standards, his literary output between 1975 and 1977 was remarkable: three books in as many years and work started on a fourth that would be published two years later, the most significant among them the shortest (coauthored by Peter Berger), in addition to his regular writing for *Worldview, Forum Letter,* and a host of other publications, as well as a tour-de-force commencement address at his displaced alma mater. The books weren't uniformly successful, but taken together they make clear the full spectrum of his interest and ambition: to be an influential voice on matters of immediate importance for pastors, community leaders, fellow intellectuals, policymakers, and politicians alike. The latter trio made up the primary audience for a book he wrote to coincide with the 1976 bicentennial, 1975's *Time Toward Home,* which afforded a significant moment to consider the state of the nation as far as Neuhaus was concerned.

For many Americans, he lamented in the preface to his most

substantial effort from this prolific period, the "celebration promises to be more requiem than revival," coming close on the heels of a tumultuous thirteen years in American life that were punctuated by assassinations, a divisive and victory-less war, wave upon wave of political and social protest, and a president resigning in disgrace. But in spite of all this evidence of American decline, Neuhaus was hopeful. He wanted others to be hopeful as well, and promised his readers that this book would offer some "practical steps for reviving the vision of the commonweal to which the American experiment must be directed." Importantly, the viability of these practical steps depended on an initial openness to "trying to view the American experiment with religious seriousness." But why be open to this formulation as a means of understanding and approaching politics, in a nation where church and state are constitutionally separated under the religion clauses of the First Amendment, for their mutual good? Because, Neuhaus would argue consistently in his writings on this subject, an absolutist construal of this separation misapprehends the very nature of how people understand themselves, their rights and responsibilities, and their common life together. As would run one of Neuhaus' core formulations for the rest of his intellectual work, in the preface to *Time Toward Home* he proposes that "politics is a function of culture" and "at the heart of culture is religion."[1]

This was no abstract theory, coming from this author. To work for change in the world is to engage in politics, Neuhaus well understood by the mid-1970s. And likewise, thanks to his formation in Lutheran Two Kingdoms theology matched to his experiences in and beyond the Movement, he knew that politics could never be its own absolute, and indeed would be dangerous and heretical were it so. Rather, politics draws from and contributes to culture, the shared principles, premises, and practices that attest to a people's values and shared self-understanding. But—and this is the stark contrast between believing and nonbelieving thinkers on these matters—the values and self-understanding, for believers, aren't self-generated. They are derived from the shapes, sources, and systems of ultimate meaning, which is to say, from religion. Framed by this politics-culture-religion formulation early in *Time Toward Home,* so begins in earnest the ever two-track nature of Richard John Neuhaus' major writings about the place of religion in American public life. For the rest of his career, he would always be making two cases simultaneously: First, and explicitly, that the political, social, and cultural institutions of American public life should be open to religiously informed positions (and persons) in their ongoing deliberations about how best to know and seek the good for the people of the United States. Second, and implicitly, that Neuhaus himself could offer, in his own positions and person, the very best in religiously informed contributions to American public life. Based on the evidence put forth in *Time Toward Home,* however, it would be a few years still before Neuhaus could more persuasively claim as much.

Indeed, as Lutheran theologian and bioethicist Gilbert Meilaender would observe in an admiring 2009 remembrance of his longtime colleague, *Time Toward Home* wasn't one of Neuhaus' better-known books, but instead was important as an early statement of some of the major concerns that would motivate his mature work—particularly, Meilaender noted, the idea that "God has a stake" in the American Experiment itself, and that denying this premise risks creating a condition where an incorrigibly religious people's source of transcendent authority and purpose is relocated to the state itself. Neuhaus' effort with *Time Toward Home* and future books is to propose a middle way between theocracy and secular totalitarianism, a way easily captured in his eminently quotable statement to *Time* magazine when it profiled him in positive terms upon the fall 1975 publication of the book: "When I meet God, I expect to meet him as an American." If so, then God should be prepared to meet a rather long-winded American, with sharp opinions and extensive citations on everything under the sun, at least judging from that latest book. Far more temperate in tone, *Time Toward Home* suffers nonetheless from the same grab-bag tendencies and cerebral loquaciousness that impaired *In Defense of People.* "This is a book of theology, cultural criticism, politics, philosophy and ethics," Neuhaus informs us early on, no less "among other things," before acknowledging that the result might be "a reckless careening across interdisciplinary lines or a synthesis of usually diverse angles of vision."[2]

At its best moments—when Neuhaus isn't muscling in clever metaphors or needlessly showcasing his bona fides as a very well-read intellectual with strong social justice and populist credentials to boot—the book offers a strong vision of revival, rather than a requiem, for American public life upon the nation's bicentennial. He locates the potential for revival in and through the forging of "a society of democratic pluralism publicly committed to a transcendent commonweal." This commitment would be made possible by the church taking on a robust presence in American life, he argues, in terms that resonate with the contemporaneous Hartford Appeal, provided that it first accomplishes "an imaginative re-appropriation of its own tradition, a theological recovery of nerve, a new confidence in the distinctiveness of its own truth claim, a new courage to live in dialectic with the larger culture." The distinctiveness of the truth claim that a confident church brings to larger culture, according to Neuhaus, is its capacity to articulate and sustain what he describes as a covenantal account of the American Experiment itself. Figuring out exactly what Neuhaus means by "covenant" isn't easy. Neuhaus is not exactly drawing on Covenant theology itself, which has a substantially Calvinist pedigree. Rather, he repositions its traditional emphasis on the successive, biblical unfolding of God's decisive promises to humanity into an American historical-political context that begins with the Puritans' own biblical self-understanding of their New World community as a covenantal act made before and with and under God.[3]

With this precedent in mind, Neuhaus uses his covenantal model to remind readers of the significance of religious truth claims in the American past. He proposes the covenant model as a means of involving religiously grounded reason and morality in American public life as alternatives to then regnant notions like an American "civil religion," which he argues risks sacralizing the nation itself, and especially as an alternative to the influential ideas of philosopher John Rawls, whose *Theory of Justice* (1971) offered a secular "contractual" model for social cohesion based on a balance of individual self-interest and fair-minded treatment of the self-interest of others. Rawls' work received sustained attention in *Time Toward Home,* more so than any other author's. Neuhaus considered his ideas dangerously alluring to the elites of American life, people of decisive public influence in the academy, media, politics, public policy, and the judiciary. The dangerous allure was in how Rawls' work brilliantly and elegantly encouraged these elites along in their ongoing move away from traditionally construed transcendent sources of meaning and value toward a mundane, exclusively rationalist understanding of human behavior and society itself, an understanding, in other words, that excluded religion from public life.

With its proposals around a covenantal model of American purpose and self-understanding, *Time Toward Home* tries hard to make a case for the importance of including religion in public life. But the effort undermines itself, in a sense. The book is too much of a ramble, too convoluted in its set of auto-politico-religious interests, too full of declarative sentences piling up one upon the other, all seeming to serve as a definitive statement about the relationship between religion and public life in America, at least until the next sentence. In other words, it reads like the rough notes of a hyper-keen diagnostician assessing symptoms in search of an exact prescription. Indeed, it would be almost a decade still before Neuhaus would find the right phrasing and fitting moment—a "naked public square," a presidential election campaign impacted by the rise of a self-consciously religious voting bloc—to establish the vital and hierarchically ordered interplay of politics, culture, and religion as crucial for the health and prospects of a pluralist democracy. In so doing, he would simultaneously solidify his accompanying position as America's foremost spokesman and proprietor for this vision.

Not that he didn't try and try again in the meantime, as with his 1977 effort *Christian Faith and Public Policy: Thinking and Acting in the Courage of Uncertainty,* published by Augsburg, a Minneapolis-based Lutheran press. Developed under the auspices of the Lutheran Council USA, the book came out of Neuhaus' Council-sponsored meetings with a variety of American Lutheran leaders and intellectuals, including those close to him, like Berger and also fellow Concordia Seminary graduate and religion scholar Robert Benne, and those in positions of political influence, most notably Illinois congressman Paul Simon. Early on, Neuhaus explains that all involved agreed that the book "represents the views of the author in conversation with consultants" whose aim is "to relate Christian faith and public policy" in a contemporary context, which inevitably involves the "advance [of] Christian thought and action in the political arena," all of which is in support of "embolden[ing] man to embrace more fully the ambiguities and the obligations of Christian citizenship." But it is not an easy book to embrace: "There are at least nine reasonably discrete ways in which the church can be instrumental in relating Christian faith to public policy," one chapter begins, preemptively sapping the energy of even the most sympathetic reader; another provides five ways that the church "relates to the interests of the state" followed by five ways that the state "relates to the interests of the church"; still another chapter proposes a remarkable fifty-seven different religiously informed propositions "by which public policy decisions might be reached"; all are accompanied by detailed analyses and cross-references to points raised in earlier chapters. The baseline questions at work across this awkward amalgam of consultative writing and elaborately structured analyses, prescriptions, and imperatives are those running throughout Neuhaus' work on religion and public life: First, why are questions of politics meaningful to Christians? Second, as the book's closing line puts it, "*how* can Christian faith be made publicly effective"?[4]

The Augsburg book focused on public policy rather than on electoral politics as the means to make Christian faith publicly effective. It may have enjoyed some currency within the small world of late 1970s Lutheran policy wonk types, and likely reached readers through the personal networks of the various individuals involved with the project and through any formal channels that the Lutheran Council USA possessed for placing books in the hands of rank-and-file pastors and individual congregations. But *Christian Faith and Public Policy* doesn't figure much in either contemporaneous or later estimations of Neuhaus' work, not by comparison to its predecessor *Time Toward Home,* and certainly not by comparison to the other book he published in 1977, *To Empower People.* If *The Naked Public Square* would prove the book that made his most influential and lasting contribution to American public life itself, *To Empower People,* cowritten with Peter Berger, was the book that proved his most influential and lasting contribution to American public policy. Years later, both men would reflect on the surprising and lasting success of this work, particularly in terms of how much effect it had relative to its length—little more than fifty pages—and likewise relative to the effect of the hundreds upon hundreds of other pages they wrote in tandem and individually, in the 1960s and 1970s. For Berger, "perhaps the ultimate sign of success is that the [book's governing] term, *mediating structures,* which we concocted, is now used without mention of its origin, it has become a common noun like *fridge* or *coke,*" at least in discussions of the relationship between the state, the individual, and the various institutions that mediate between them in modern life.

That said, Berger confessed in a retrospective appraisal that he was skeptical of "claims [that] have been made that *To Empower People* has had a great influence on social policy in the United States, such as on various reforms of welfare or on the developments that led to the [2001] faith-based initiative." Neuhaus shared Berger's pleasant surprise at the book's ongoing success, if not his skepticism about its influence. In 1992, he would jauntily quote and then commend his own prediction from *To Empower People* itself, that its proposals "could become the basis of far-reaching innovations in public policy, perhaps of a new paradigm for at least sectors of the modern state," by noting in turn that indeed this " 'New Paradigm' was subsequently adopted by some political leaders and social policy experts and is today being advanced with varying energy and effect at both the federal and state levels of public policy." He was even more explicit in his estimation of its success in a 1993 *First Things* item, matter-of-factly explaining that the proposals in *To Empower People* were "entertained by the Carter administration, praised by the Reagan administration, and officially embraced by the [George H. W.] Bush administration."[5] And when a twentieth-anniversary edition was published and reviewed in glowing terms by Adam Wolfson in the *Public Interest*, Neuhaus couldn't resist quoting at length from his estimation of the book's significance, particularly Wolfson's sense that Neuhaus and Berger had anticipated major public policy work by the likes of Francis Fukuyama, Robert D. Putnam, and Daniel Bell with their slim 1977 "study and appreciation of civil society."[6]

So what was so significant about the fifty pages that Neuhaus and Berger wrote up after yet another conversation at the Bergers' Brooklyn brownstone? The answer involves a combination of good timing and good writing, most immediately instigated by Brigitte Berger's living room suggestion "to Neuhaus and me that some radical reformulations of social policy were much needed," as Berger recalls.[7] This was a need Neuhaus was interested in answering, specifically through a fresh approach to government policy that would be practically effective and ethically coherent, if from a consciously Christian position. But rather than seek a book deal in New York, Berger and Neuhaus went to Washington. Berger approached the American Enterprise Institute (AEI), a conservative think tank, which invited them to (in Berger's words) "write a paper outlining what such a reformulation [of social policy] might look like," and which published the effort in 1977, just as its own influence was reaching its summit.

AEI was founded in 1938 in reaction to the expansionist implications of New Deal–era government. It began to wield greater influence through its involvement in Barry Goldwater's 1964 presidential run and then achieved more permanent influence during the early years of the Reagan presidency, when, according to historian Sidney Blumenthal, many of its associates joined the administration where "the notions that it had promoted were being turned into policy." In other words, what Berger and Neuhaus were proposing—essentially a new approach to solving "the dilemmas of the welfare state"—was perfectly suited to AEI's long-standing mission, and to its more immediate late 1970s interest, in influencing public policy from a conservative position. The new approach they were proposing, Berger and Neuhaus explain early on, would resolve "contradictory tendencies . . . [in] current thinking about public policy in America . . . between wanting more government services and [calls for] less government." Rather than issue a vulgar conservative demand for the dismantling of the entire welfare state, or a simplistic liberal plea for its ever-greater expansion, Neuhaus and Berger outline a realist-minded middle way: "We suggest that the modern welfare state is here to stay, indeed that it ought to expand the benefits it provides—but that *alternative mechanisms are possible to provide welfare-state services.*"[8]

And yet, beyond the auspices of its publication, the coauthored publication was also just well written. The remainder of *To Empower People* makes a concise and focused case for the practical and ethical goods of what Neuhaus and Berger call "mediating structures" as precisely these alternative mechanisms for "expand[ing] government services without producing government oppressiveness." Throughout, and in marked contrast to the combination of pyrotechnics and turgidity that marks much of Neuhaus' other book writing during this period, the prose here is sober and the argument clear, that if "neighborhood, family, church, and voluntary association" were "more imaginatively recognized in public policy, individuals would be more 'at home' in society, and the political order would be more 'meaningful.'" They focus on these four institutions particularly because "they figure prominently in the lives of most Americans" and "are most relevant to the problems of the welfare state with which we are concerned." But in fact, the authors are concerned with more than the immediate problems of the welfare state. Throughout the work, Neuhaus and Berger return to the basic problem of life in a modern society dominated by corporate and more so by governmental and bureaucratic "mega-structures": individuals facing alienated, atomized lives before and under a massive and impersonal state. This ultimately leads, they contend, to the detachment of "the political order . . . from the values and realities of individual life." And "when that happens," they warn, "the political order must be secured by coercion rather than by consent. And when that happens, democracy disappears."[9]

Their stark and smart phrasing yokes domestic policy concerns to anxieties about the specter of totalitarian states, and in turn suggests a Cold War–era imperative to use mediating structures to keep vital and strong "the values and realities of individual life" within a thriving democratic political order. And unlike pronouncements about imperiled democratic legitimacy that show up elsewhere in Neuhaus' career, their appearance in *To Empower People* never overwhelms the work's other elements, which include specific policy recommendations to be undertaken through mediating structures, and also acknowledgment of the significant pedigree upon which they draw: detailing the intellectual genealogy of their proposal, Berger and Neuhaus cite Edmund Burke's "little platoons," Émile Durkheim's "little aggregations," and Tocqueville's positive valuation of the local association's importance for a healthy democracy, among others. In larger terms, their ideas resonate with the longstanding Catholic concept of subsidiarity, as Berger would later acknowledge. And while they don't cite the source in *To Empower People* itself, Berger and Neuhaus are clearly motivated by the same concerns that animated the 1931 papal encyclical *Quadragesimo Anno,* in which Pius XI formally declared that "it is an injustice and at the same time a greater evil and disturbance of right order to assign to a greater and higher association what lesser and subordinate organizations can do. For every social activity ought of its very nature to furnish help to the members of the body social and never destroy or absorb them."[10]

The specific furnishings of help that Neuhaus and Berger discern are impressive in their anticipation of future public policy concerns and priorities, including heightened investment in local neighborhoods as sites and sources of felt cohesion for citizens, and defense of the inherent autonomy and agency of the family to care for the well-being of children over the divisive and imposing power of bureaucrats and social service agencies. In 1977, if not in later years for Neuhaus, this defense includes not just traditional families but also "lesbians and gays, liberated families. . . . Indeed, virtually any [family] structure is better for children than what experts of the state can provide." Berger and Neuhaus also recommend school vouchers as a means of achieving much needed "radical reform in the area of education," and the importance of local decision making over federal or judicial impositions. Otherwise, they warn, "the people of Kokomo, Indiana, must accept public promotions of pornography . . . because such promotions are protected by precedents established in Berkeley, California." The theme, again and again, is that "people in communities"—whether through their neighborhoods, their churches, their families, their volunteer organizations, or ideally through overlapping involvement in all of these at once—"know best what is needed for the maintenance and development of these communities," rather than bloated and distant government departments. But lest any reader confuse Berger and Neuhaus for rearguard foes of the modern liberal state, they also repeatedly stress that their "argument is not against modernity but in favor of exploring the ways in which modernity can be made more humane."[11]

A cowritten work, *To Empower People* resists a forensic analysis of what was written by Berger versus what was written by Neuhaus, with one notable exception: the section on religion's place in public life seems primarily to come out of Neuhaus' ongoing preoccupations, and indeed it provides a telling indication of the increasingly precise terms that would govern those preoccupations. The problem, the authors argue in this section, is that a "view that the public sphere is synonymous with the government . . . has been especially effective in excluding religion from considerations of public policy." This is in spite of the observable evidence that religious organizations like the Salvation Army are much better at "helping the truly marginal" than government bureaucracies that rely on "generalized categories" rather than engaging with the complex realities of individual persons. As such, Neuhaus and Berger recommend, religious institutions should be "utilized as much as possible as the implementing agencies of policy goals." Mindful of accreted resistance to such a proposal, they argue that too much contemporary thinking about church-state relations has relied on a misreading (purposeful or otherwise) of Jefferson's "Wall of Separation" metaphor for that relationship, treating it as the authoritative interpretation of the First Amendment itself. But, Neuhaus and Berger argue, "the religion clauses of the First Amendment . . . should not be understood as requiring absolute separationism," which they declare "theoretically inconceivable and practically contrary to the past and present interaction of church and state." In fact, absolute separationism works against the anti-establishment imperative in the First Amendment, while a reasonable openness to religion is its best guarantor, they argue, or more likely, as the language very strongly suggests, Neuhaus argues here:

> *As long as public space is open to the full range of symbols cherished in [a] community, there is no question of one religion being "established" over another. [But] public policy is presently biased toward what might be called the symbolic nakedness of the town square.*

By 1977, Neuhaus already had the diagnosis and was closing in on the phrasing that would make him a figure of permanent influence in American life. But this was only one element, briefly mentioned, in the broader set of diagnoses and proposals that feature in *To Empower People*—proposals that were in fact taken up following the paper's publication when the AEI, in conjunction with the National Endowment for the Humanities, sponsored an expanded research project based in New York. It focused on the conceptual and practical implications of using mediating structures in five areas: health care, housing and zoning, welfare and social services, education and child care, and criminal justice. Each area was to be explored by a panel of academics and policy experts under the leadership of distinguished panel chairs, including Harvard sociologist Nathan Glazer and community organizer Robert Woodson from the National Urban League. The specific impact of this project is unclear, beyond introducing Neuhaus and Berger's terminology and diagnoses into public conversation. But its immediate and lasting success didn't tempt Neuhaus into becoming a policy wonk. After all, this intellectual work was always secondary to his main vocation. This became clear later in 1977 when he was invited to give the James A. Gray Lecture for Duke Divinity School's two-day intensive "Commencement and Pastor's School," a lecture and seminar that led to his next book, *Freedom for Ministry*. More immediately, Neuhaus' vocation, and indeed the circumstances of its early development, became powerfully clear when he was asked to give the commencement address at his displaced alma mater, which was now calling itself Concordia Seminary in Exile.[12]

Delivered on May 13, 1977, the day before his forty-first birthday, Neuhaus' address was delivered by a preacher rather than by a partisan. Remarks in the latter guise might have been more expected, given the circumstances of the occasion. After all, this was the first full graduation ceremony for Concordia Seminary in Exile ("Seminex") following its dramatic break and departure from Concordia-St. Louis in 1973, and the seminary chose as its commencement speaker a devoted student of the late Arthur C. Piepkorn and of Seminex leader Richard Caemmerer, a speaker who also happened to be the editor of the lively *Lutheran Forum Letter,* a speaker with a long-standing reputation for theological and ecclesial rabble-rousing in the synod itself. In other words, Neuhaus' allegiances would have been as clear as his reputation for sharp and caustic polemic. And so as he stood behind the simple lectern and gripped its thick wooden beams, no doubt many of the faculty, graduates, and family members gathered in the borrowed gray stone grandeur of Washington University's Collegiate Gothic quadrangle were expecting a rousing defense of the ecclesial principles—and politics—that had brought them together that day in pained but hopeful exile.

But Neuhaus' focus was firmly on what was to come, rather than what had already come to pass. He wanted the newly ordained to know that whatever difficulties they had endured as Seminex's first graduates, these were mere prologue to the difficult realities of being pastors in the world beyond the dramas of seminary life: "If you are to be shepherds of His sheep and the servants of His servants, then abandon the lust for happiness in the discovery of joy," he challenged them in his deep and sonorous voice. But this too would be a hard-won joy, he emphasized, rejecting the romantic optimism expected of speakers at such occasions: "I have heard commencement speakers wish for graduates success, prosperity, and success. I would wish you no less. But I would alert you to your more likely lot of failure, necessity, and tears." These were words spoken by a seasoned pastor to a field of green pastors. He wanted them to know that in their various church assignments they would be dealing with and ministering to fallen people and damaged souls. And this is why, Neuhaus explained, he chose as his commencement theme 2 Corinthians 2:4, St. Paul's complex assurance to his readers that "I wrote you out of much affliction and anguish of heart and with many tears, not to cause you pain, but to let you know the abundant love that I have for you." Neuhaus in turn explicated the seeming contradiction of joy in tears with citations of Old Testament precedents and prophets and also the words of Rabbi Heschel; he cited great Lutheran pastors of the past, and Luther himself, encouraging a fellow pastor who was under attack from all sides to "only keep your eyes fixed on what Christ has done for you and for all men in order that you may learn what you should do for others."

And then Neuhaus elaborated upon Luther's version of an *imitatio Christi* imperative by describing what all pastors are called to do for others: to devote themselves to a life of love and sacrifice in spite of inevitable discouragements. "When you doubt—and you will doubt—that [your congregants] are the people of God, remember their baptism, their communion, and their profession of faith. These objective marks, and not their agreement with you or their liking for you, are the signs that they are God's elect." And this in turn suggests the ultimate disposition a pastor is called to sustain: "To be grateful for your people is to think highly of your people, for their sake, but always and above all for Christ's sake." This foundational claim for ministry—that an imperfect pastor's love for his imperfect people is ordered to and by his love for Christ—begins and ends with the good and securing news of Christ's perfect love for him and for all people. Living out of this theologically and experientially rich and difficult conviction, Neuhaus explained, it's no wonder the joys of a pastor's life are born of many tears, as St. Paul knew so many centuries before. He then matter-of-factly offered a persuasive standard for these new pastors to measure their coming life and work: "You could do a lot worse than to have it said of your ministry that they could not distinguish between the sound of joy and the sound of weeping."

Having first firmly and even movingly established these realist-minded, biblically anchored first principles for the newly ordained to rely on and be grateful for in embarking on their careers as ordained pastors, only then did Neuhaus finally address the ecclesial-political context of this particular occasion. "You who graduate from Concordia Seminary have additional reason to be grateful, for your have received advance training for life in exile," he acknowledged. Was this, at last, a turn toward the caustic eloquence so many had come to expect from Richard John Neuhaus? No, it was a stunning sublimation of a painful experience of church politics into a theological lesson about the universal condition of Christians living short of God's kingdom. Rather than smartly schematize a possible reunion with the original Concordia, or colorfully lament why it wouldn't be possible, Neuhaus rejected such this-worldly preoccupations and called on the community of a seminary in exile to do the same: "Exile is not a misfortune to be remedied except by arrival in the Promised Land. And there is no promised land short of the Promised Land. Exile," in other words, "is not the exception but the normative form of faithfulness" in the earthly time before heaven's eternity.

Having delivered a timely reminder, Neuhaus then ended his remarks concerning the Seminex situation on a more admiring note, calling on the graduates to be grateful that their teachers decided to take the difficult step of founding a new seminary to remain faithful to the teachings and doctrines of the church, four years before. This was a decision, taken not without its share of tears, that was now joyfully bearing the fruit of so many new pastors entering the world to carry out the work of the Gospel. None of which would have been possible, Neuhaus concluded, suddenly no longer addressing the graduates but speaking with them, as a fellow graduate, were it not for the men who left Missouri's flagship seminary to found Seminex: "Their decision made it different for all of us; such witness is a rare gift; and we are grateful." This was a gratitude Neuhaus would repeat in the opening lines of his next book, even in his own struggle, in the coming years, to find places, platforms, and positions fitted to his own unusual gifts, which included a rare and fierce ambition for public Christian witness.[13]

CHAPTER FIFTEEN

Seeking Freedom for His Own Kind of Ministry

Author, book critic, public intellectual, political activist, religious journalist, theologian—these are but some of the designations Neuhaus accumulated as his career developed in the late 1970s and early 1980s. Together, they afforded the platforms and premises for advancing his ambitions and his vocation for public Christian witness. But they were all secondary to his primary self-understanding as an ordained Lutheran pastor. That said, his most substantial written treatment of the life and work of a minister actually came only after he left his most significant pastoral assignment. "This book was written in the year after my departure from the Church of St. John the Evangelist in Brooklyn, New York, where I had been pastor for seventeen years," Neuhaus explained in a prefatory note to *Freedom for Ministry*, an autobiographical guidebook-cum-apology for a robustly traditional approach to the work of Christian ministry in the late twentieth century. He began writing it in 1977 as the annual Gray lecture at Duke Divinity School, and published with Harper & Row two years later.[1]

Rather than offer yet another set of polemical and elaborate broad-gauge analyses, criticisms, and proposals about the state of the American Church and about the intellectual-political textures of American public life, it's a first-person account of the challenges, demands, and possibilities inherent to the work of Christian ministry. Throughout, Neuhaus emphasizes that a minister must always understand his sacred office as the difficult but necessary integration of higher-order theological responsibilities with immediate sociocultural responsibilities. Which is to say, Neuhaus proposes that a minister must be an exemplar to his congregation of "the pursuit of holiness": showing them in word, deed, and person what it means to be "holding out for the fullness of God's rule in our lives and in our world." Leading an exemplary life in joyful obedience to God is far from easy, Neuhaus acknowledges later in the book, because it means "learning to hold on" to a higher-order sense of ministerial vocation in a world that would either deny any higher-order sense of ministerial vocation, or render it mere mundane social work. Rejecting these options and encouraging his minister readers to do the same, with *Freedom for Ministry* Neuhaus offers a thoughtful account of how to hold on to one's vocation to ministry and in so doing, for the sake of God, Church, congregation, and self, also why to hold on.[2]

But in leading just such a life himself, Neuhaus decided in 1978 he could no longer hold out and hold on from Maujer Street, and early on in *Freedom for Ministry* he frames the leave-taking from his first and most significant pastoral assignment in emotionally charged terms: "I miss St. John's very much," he confesses, so much so that he even "considered writing a chapter on the pains of leaving a people and a parish that, if possible, one loves too passionately." But if this intense devotion, which was undeniable in the 1960s, was still fully in effect by 1978, why then did Neuhaus leave his beloved St. John's after nearly two decades if there was no one but himself responsible for this decision? Without denying the overall sincerity and depth of his affection for St. John's, or his rightful pride in the decisive contributions he made to its renewal, or the profound importance of this assignment to his formation as a pastor, activist, and thinker, Neuhaus' decision to leave in 1978 would not have been as difficult as he makes it seem in *Freedom for Ministry.* After all, he had largely transitioned away from the daily life of the congregation by the early 1970s, and after returning from Africa had moved out of the pastor's residence into a separate apartment maintained by the church. But beyond preaching regularly at one of the Sunday services when he was in town during the rest of the decade, his ties to the congregation increasingly figured only in his author bylines and as a noteworthy and certainly earned source of experience and credentials to draw on in his writing and public life, as with the early pages of *Freedom for Ministry.* Over the years, he would consistently look back fondly on his years at St. John the Evangelist, which he affectionately nicknamed "St. John the Mundane" to contrast it with the grand (and, to Neuhaus, grandiose) Episcopal Cathedral Church of St. John the Divine in Manhattan. And if his poor and lowly and Gospel-fired Brooklyn congregation was mundane by comparison to that rarefied and elite warren of liberal Christianity, that was only to its greater credit.[3]

Neuhaus' departure from St. John the Evangelist was in keeping with a broader pattern of transition that marks his life and work in the late 1970s and early 1980s, as he searched with only limited success for an office that both reflected and advanced his ongoing interests in making first-person contributions of religion to American public life. This effort began with his establishing the conceptual and practical terms of his status and responsibilities as a pastor after leaving St. John's. In 1978, Neuhaus accepted an associate pastor position with Trinity Lutheran Church in Manhattan's Lower East Side, on 9th Street at Avenue B, across from Tompkins Square Park. Trinity Church–Lower East Side was a multi-bricked three-story building that looked far more like the low-rise apartments beside it than any of the Gothic or Romanesque churches that Neuhaus was more accustomed to, based on his assignments to date. Not that he was particularly involved with this congregation either. He led a Sunday service, lived on his own in an apartment on East 27th, and otherwise spent the majority of his time at his

Worldview office on the Upper West Side, and on his various intellectual and public pursuits.

Living by himself on East 27th, Neuhaus might have been on his own for perhaps the first time in his life. He wasn't happy with the arrangement. If he was going to keep on with his books and declarations for a national stage, he needed to find a home that would be far more than a room of his own. He needed to be part of a religious community in the city, ideally on his own terms. All of this was evident to a fellow pastor at Holy Trinity, Larry Bailey. Soft-spoken, refined, and sympathetic to an ecclesial formulation of Lutheranism similar to Neuhaus', Bailey had first met him in the 1960s while he was a seminary student passing through Brooklyn. When Neuhaus joined Trinity, they developed a good rapport, had dinner together once a week, and when Neuhaus expressed his dissatisfaction at living on his own, and raised the idea of their sharing a residence while founding a religious community in the city, Bailey agreed. Neuhaus provided the conceptual framework—which involved common evening prayer each day, taken from the Lutheran Book of Worship, and a shared meal for members of the community every Saturday—and Bailey did the legwork, at least when he wasn't at church or, in time, teaching at a Lutheran high school in the Bronx. And so while Richard kept preaching, writing, and declaring, Larry went into Lower Manhattan in search of some pastor-friendly real estate. By 1979, they had settled on a place, 338 East 19th Street, a simple gray four-story town house with wrought-iron black balconies, which sat halfway between First and Second Avenues. They bought it for $65,500, with Neuhaus contributing two-thirds of the purchase price, presumably out of his writing and speaking fees rather than pastor's salary. Bailey and another (temporary) partner, Tom Dorris,[4] made up the remainder.

The building was located in a nondescript part of the Lower East Side, if within close proximity to far more defined New York neighborhoods like Stuyvesant Town, Union Square, and Gramercy Park. Dating from the mid-nineteenth century, it hadn't been well maintained by its prior owner, and required some $10,000 in initial repair work. Neuhaus occupied the main-floor apartment, which also had a rough basement, where he kept a writing space, and direct access to a small garden. Bailey took a smaller upper-floor unit. The rest of the units would, in time, be filled out with people also interested in the idea of living as a religious community in the city. But 338 initially came with tenants who continued to live there in rent-controlled protection under the new ownership. They were certainly not part of the new ownership's ethos, which was captured in the name of the not-for-profit organization that Neuhaus and Bailey founded as the religious community that would own and run the building: the Community of Christ in the City.[5]

An extensive file of paperwork kept in Neuhaus' personal papers suggests how complicated this three-person real estate purchase and simultaneous religious community founding was, but in time these matters were resolved, and Neuhaus would live here for the rest of his life. Indeed, 338 East 19th Street would develop into the fuller religious community he wanted to be part of, meaning one that he could preside over without having to run (superintending matters and community dinner duties both fell to Bailey). And because it was very much Neuhaus' place, 338 also became an operations hub, social club, and intellectual salon for him and for his circles of friends and colleagues. Some thirty years after branding the attic at his parents' Miller Street home in Pembroke "Dick Neuhaus' Abode" in spidery black cursive, he once again could lay claim to a place that was his, on his own terms, and in the heart of New York City, no less. His residential situation effectively resolved in 1979 with the move to 338, Neuhaus' ecclesial and professional situations were not yet, at least not in keeping with his more entrepreneurial and elastic sense of ministerial vocation.

This was a sense that he had come to over the years at St. John the Evangelist and was able to enjoy largely thanks to the arrangements he was able to secure with a supportive congregation and with his fellow pastors, and likewise because of the tacit permission he received from his superiors in the Missouri Synod's Atlantic District. But he couldn't simply presume the same arrangement in joining a new congregation in Manhattan, or in becoming a pastor with a new Lutheran body for that matter, having affiliated himself with the recently formed Evangelical Lutheran Church of America (ELCA) in the wake of the Concordia Seminary breakup and broader Missouri Synod conflicts of the 1970s. And so, in order to secure the arrangement he sought, Neuhaus simply proposed the "call" he wanted to answer, in a November 1979 letter to Rudolph Ressmeyer, who had been his LCMS Atlantic District superior and was now his ELCA East Coast Synod bishop. Neuhaus submitted to him "a formal request for a call from the East Coast Synod [to be] on assignment to urban ministries," which he glossed as his status with Trinity Church as an associate pastor and also as an affiliated pastor with St. Peter's Lutheran on Lexington. In these capacities, his ministry involved the "regular ministry of preaching, teaching, and minister of the Eucharist."

As for the other six days of the week, Neuhaus proposed that they would be taken up as they already were, with "teaching responsibilities [through] *Lutheran Forum* and *Worldview*, lecturing in New York and elsewhere to church and secular groups, research projects on religion and society, and my own writing." All of this could be effectively framed and contained within the ecclesial rubric of "urban ministries" such as Neuhaus construed these. He was successful in proposing and answering his own call within ELCA, as unconventional as this would have been for a standard Lutheran pastor. This would be in keeping with a pattern that would hold across multiple church affiliations in the mid-1980s. Yet it clearly wasn't enough to fulfill his sense of premise and platform for his public ministry, as Neuhaus' other efforts during this period suggest.[6]

In fact, a few months before making his request to Ressmeyer, Neuhaus applied to become the president of CRIA, the Carnegie Religion and International Affairs organization that sponsored *Worldview* and hosted Neuhaus and his *Worldview* colleague James Finn at its Upper West Side offices. His letter of application, addressed to CRIA trustee Jerald Brauer, the prominent University of Chicago Divinity School theologian, marks the beginning of a period in Neuhaus' life and work wherein he would repeatedly seek affiliations with publicly focused, independently financed and mission-driven intellectual institutions—what we generally call think tanks today—as the primary means for pursuing his religious, intellectual, cultural, and political interests. But his efforts weren't immediately successful, and this is not surprising, at least judging from how Neuhaus approached the presidency of CRIA in his letter of application. "I have some rather definite ideas about what CRIA is and what it should be," he declared in his opening remarks. Having candidly admitted to this, he faithfully followed through in the rest of the letter. His ideas about how to solve CRIA's apparent identity crisis included, foremost, a change in its scale. CRIA had to move from being a "New York–centered operation . . . to play [instead] a leadership role in the national discussion" of "international issues that engage religion and ethical reflection." Neuhaus was also convinced that CRIA was in the meantime failing to live up to its historic role as an educating institute capable of shaping and right-ordering American understandings of international affairs by framing them in ethical and religious terms. To detail this basic mission failing, he invoked his own 1973 analysis of the organization's situation (even then, as far as he was concerned, it "was not actualizing its potential") before remarking, "On re-reading the paper now, including its very critical sections, I find myself in substantial agreement with what I thought then."

The formulation is stunning, whether for its chutzpah or its egotism, and regardless, Neuhaus was magnificently heedless of how negatively such formulations could be received, especially as indications of the kind of leadership and self-affirming sensibility he might bring to the office of CRIA president. He didn't help matters later on in the letter by insisting that were he president, he would logically serve as "the public presence of CRIA in the many forums in which religion and international affairs are joined," but he wanted the trustees to know that he would not take on the job if all of his public positions were to be held captive to this role. Working this out, he acknowledged, would require "a great deal of restraint and trust" on the part of both CRIA's president and its trustees. But most any trustee reading Neuhaus' letter would have likely been skeptical of his capacity for restraint, given the letter's blunt proposals, blunter criticisms, and brash presumptions. And they would have been likewise skeptical of his overall intentions for the presidency, because he included in his own letter of application a parallel request and endorsement for his friend and *Worldview* colleague James Finn to become CRIA president ahead of him. The implication was obvious: Neuhaus was confident that his vision of what CRIA could be would come into effect whether he was leading it or Finn. This likely wasn't the most adept move for himself or for Finn, and indeed both men were passed over for the job. It went instead to Robert J. Myers, a former CIA station chief in Cambodia and State Department official who had also served as publisher of the *New Republic* before coming to CRIA as its president. In time, and owing largely to his growing public presence as a willing scourge of liberal churches while maintaining links to CRIA via *Worldview,* Neuhaus would clash with Myers, and soon thereafter end his association with both the magazine and its sponsor.[7]

Never one to put all of his plans in one place, even in the midst of applying to become president of CRIA or at least securing the position for his colleague, Neuhaus was also trying to found a religiously focused think tank of his own. Throughout 1979, he was in correspondence with colleagues and friends to gauge their interest and potential support for "the Lexington Center for Religion and Society," which would be housed at St. Peter's Lutheran Church in midtown Manhattan, at Lexington and 54th. It's not surprising that Neuhaus was interested in affiliating his work with St. Peter's. The church's long-standing double mission was, first, ecumenical—its mid-nineteenth-century origins were in collaborations between

German Lutheran immigrants and an Irish Catholic businessman—and, second, strongly focused on urban ministry, which in this case wasn't Maujer Street urban ministry but instead ministry in the great skyscraper canyons of midtown Manhattan. Indeed, in late 1977, through an arrangement with Citibank, St. Peter's opened a striking new glass-walled complex centered around a sleek, sharp-angled, graceful church that rose up beside Citibank's famous white-blocked fifty-nine-story tower, which sits on massive stilts that were necessary to preserve the church's long-standing occupancy of the grounds below.

Nowhere else in Manhattan is there any (Lutheran) church so dramatically, intimately, and self-consciously situated near the summits of worldly power, and this is exactly where Neuhaus wanted to be. But what exactly did he propose doing, while there? Simply too much, and not all of it prudent, according to the people he reached out to about his proposed center. He informed *Commonweal* editor Peter Steinfels, Notre Dame theologian (and future foe) Richard McBrien, and Harvard sociologist Nathan Glazer, among others, that "the Lexington Center [would be] a non-sectarian educational and research institution focusing on religion and public policy, religion and the arts, and theological studies. . . . [It seeks to be] an unparalleled meeting point for research and diverse approaches to the role of religion in shaping the city and the society of the future," through lectures, public debates, courses, conferences, all located at "the stunning new Saint Peter's Church." While his correspondents were sympathetic to the idea of a think tank focused on religion and society, and also encouraging of Neuhaus' energies, Steinfels and Glazer were convinced that the center's array of proposed foci were simply too broad to yield substantial results in any one category. And when Neuhaus in turn offered potential areas of specific focus—like U.S. nuclear policy, and the positions that American religious leaders had taken on it—McBrien pointed out that such topics, particularly as Neuhaus was already framing them, were too easily subject to politicization and in turn would lean to the unwelcome transformation of an avowedly "non-sectarian educational and research institution" into a sectarian political outfit.[8]

In the end, the Lexington Center at St. Peter's never came to anything beyond laying the intellectual and conceptual groundwork for the kind of think tank Neuhaus would pursue more successfully in the coming years. In the meantime, he remained affiliated with the church while also maintaining his association with Trinity–Lower East Side, and in 1981 went so far as to apply to be senior pastor at St. Peter's, perhaps because he regarded the leadership of a congregation so situated as well aligned with his sense of an intellectual-cultural urban ministry. He was, however, turned down for this position as well. As it explained in its decision letter, the call committee was convinced that Neuhaus was clearly more suited to serving the needs of the church and its community through his ongoing public engagements. If disappointed, he was nonetheless gracious, indeed more gracious than he had been in his CRIA presidency effort: in his response to its decision, he acknowledged to the call committee that his sense of the ministry at St. Peter's was different from the committee's own, and that this basic misalignment wouldn't have made for a successful pastorate from either's vantage. Even more unexpected than any of these efforts, in 1982 Neuhaus put himself forward for a position in pastoral theology at Yale, seeking to replace the Catholic priest and heralded theologian of Christian spirituality Henri Nouwen. While Neuhaus had been a regular fixture on college campuses since the 1960s, and occasionally taught courses for seminaries—a 1979 summer session for Princeton Theological Seminary led one of his students, Methodist Paul Stallsworth, to become a future associate in Neuhaus' institute and magazine work—the idea of his submitting in sustained, long-term fashion to the conventions of academic culture is dubious. Yale thought so too, and gave the job to someone else.[9]

When he wasn't pursuing these various efforts to secure a clear and substantial office for his publicly focused ministry, Neuhaus was far from idle. Indeed, in the late 1970s and early 1980s, he faithfully fulfilled his idiosyncratic ELCA call. He continued writing for *Worldview* and put out *Lutheran Forum* every month; he regularly reviewed books and wrote opinion pieces for *Commonweal, Christian Century,* and other publications; and he sat for interviews with publications like *Newsweek,* which sought his views on the recently elected Pope John Paul II's electric effect on people around the world and in New York, as evidenced by his October 1979 visit. Under these circumstances, Neuhaus offered only the first of what would prove many, many admiring words about John Paul II, in this instance drawing attention to the pope's "challenging some of the basic structures of the modern age . . . and telling us 'God is alive and well and calling you to radical discipleship.'" He also gave talks in locales as far-flung as Messiah Lutheran Church in Fairview Park, Ohio, on Lutheran-Catholic relations, and the Harvard Club, New York, on priest and democracy thinker John Courtney Murray's ideas about the interplay of the sacred and the secular in America. The latter would have served as a crucible, among others, for developing the ideas and arguments that took full shape in *The Naked Public Square.*[10]

During this period, Neuhaus also became involved with President Carter's White House Conference on the Family initiative, which pursued a nationwide participatory dialogue on how to strengthen the American family. By his own account, he served as a "presidential appointee" in its New York state conference and led at least one hearing under its banner. In late 1979, he received an admiring note from then–New York lieutenant governor, Mario Cuomo, thanking him for his excellent work "in handling the November 9, 1979 hearing . . . I am told that, as expected, your questions were to the point and perceptive." Cuomo ended his letter to Neuhaus by expressing hope to see him at future Conference activities, but this was not to be. As Neuhaus would later lament in briefly mentioning his experience with the Conference partway through *The Naked Public Square,* it was "ill-fated" in no small part by the success that gay rights and feminist organizations had in changing the initiative's initial wording from "Family" to "Families."[11] Presumably at the same

November 1979 New York hearing that Cuomo referenced in his letter, Neuhaus debated a gay rights activist about whether the focus of the Conference should be on strengthening the state of the family among the traditional ranks that made up the great demographic majority, or on changing government policy to be more inclusive and supportive of nontraditional family arrangements. The experience left Neuhaus convinced that it was "absurd" for a "national commission [to] spend millions of dollars recommending the overhaul of family law in America on the basis of such 'revolutions' . . . Yet it is but one in a long list of absurdities by which desire is disguised as a declaration of fact."[12]

At odds with the leftward direction taken by the Conference—signaled for him by the shift from "Family" to "Families"—and no doubt disappointed that Carter wasn't more supportive of the traditionalist position, Neuhaus didn't stay involved with it for very long. But by 1981, he had found a far better focus for his interests and concerns, particularly his intensifying anticommunism, which had been signaled, for instance, by a February 12, 1979, *New York Times* Letter to the Editor. Neuhaus wrote to dispute the paper's recent coverage of the predominantly Latin American liberation theology movement and related debates about the nature and permissibility of political activities by Catholic priests. Positively citing recent remarks by John Paul II on the matter, Neuhaus argued that the Church is always for the liberation of people from poverty and injustice and in turn emphasized that this liberation should be from any and all political oppressors, Left or Right. This could best be done, he further argued, through the defense and promulgation of democratic pluralism, rather than by deploying Marxist dogma as a normative guide to Christian witness and action. Neuhaus would develop this very same argument in far more significant ways in 1981, when he became a founding member of a new organization, the Washington-based Institute on Religion and Democracy (IRD). Its founding statement, which he composed, very much echoed these arguments in advocating religious freedom, politically independent churches, and pluralist democracy over and against the totalitarian structures and strictures of Marxist-Leninist thought and Communist regimes.

In remarks he gave in 2005 to mark the organization's twenty-fifth anniversary, Neuhaus described IRD as "one small, but not insignificant, Christian effort in the latter part of the twentieth century to retell the American story relative to God's providential purpose and most specifically to God's creation of human beings wired for freedom. That's how we started." In more practical terms, IRD started through early 1981 discussions involving Neuhaus, Methodist activist leaders Ed Robb and David Jessup, anticommunist organizer Penn Kemble, and also, if unexpectedly given their personal animosities, Neuhaus' old friend then foe Michael Novak, who was now a research fellow at the American Enterprise Institute. The two of them reconciled around the time of the IRD's founding thanks to the mediating efforts of George Weigel, an emerging thinker on Catholicism and international affairs then based in Seattle, who had met each man separately in the prior years and invited them west to give some talks. While fifteen years younger, Weigel would quickly become Neuhaus' most important colleague, especially from the later 1980s until his death in 2009. Along the way, Weigel also became, after Robert Wilken, Neuhaus' closest friend.

His first important contribution to Neuhaus' life and work, however, was ending the rift between him and Novak. To do so, Weigel brought Neuhaus along to dinner at Novak's one evening in Washington, and over bad pizza, the bad blood dissipated: perhaps the sting of their 1970s arguments had lessened with time, perhaps they together (if at Weigel's encouragement) realized that their concerns about religion and American life mattered more than review column sniping. Thereafter, these three men would develop an influential and often controversial collaboration, as religiously minded neoconservative intellectuals and organizers who enjoyed much influence in Washington and Rome both, and in American Catholicism itself, while generating much controversy and criticism in the process. Among their many common interests, from the beginning, the three were confident that orthodox Christianity, and American churches, had signal roles to play in the Cold War–era defense of democracy against totalitarianism, provided the churches weren't already undermining this defense (and orthodox Christianity itself) by other means. With Weigel still a few years away from establishing his own position of influence in Washington and in national and international Catholic circles (which happened with significant encouragement and maneuvering from Neuhaus), the already established Novak and Neuhaus pursued this shared concern most immediately by establishing IRD with Penn Kemble and others.[13]

The IRD founders were convinced that the national leadership of major American churches—namely, the United Methodists, the Episcopalians, and the Presbyterians—and their associated organization, the National Council of Churches, were enabling the spread of Communist doctrine and with it the suppression of religious freedom, democracy, and Christianity itself, by using their various outreach offices to send aid to left-wing social and educational programs in Soviet bloc countries. Meanwhile, at home, these churches were suppressing alternative views about how to achieve social justice within their own ranks. These diagnoses and concerns aligned very well with regnant neoconservative ideas about the Cold War, principally Jeane Kirkpatrick's famous 1979 article for *Commentary* magazine, "Dictatorship and Double Standards," which excoriated the Carter administration for its failure to compete with the Soviet Union in its military buildup and expanding influence around the world, particularly in Latin America and Africa. The problem wasn't in the Carter administration alone, as far as Kirkpatrick was concerned. She further identified a dangerous "affinity of liberalism, Christianity, and Marxist socialism" among American liberals in general and specifically in "Left-leaning clerics whose attraction to a secular style of 'redemptive community' is stronger than their outrage at the hostility of socialist regimes to religion," all of which needed to be combated domestically just as the United States needed to combat the Soviet Union abroad. With such positions enjoying strong currency in the new Reagan administration—Kirkpatrick was picked by Reagan to serve as the U.S. ambassador to the United Nations—and in surrounding conservative circles, IRD had little trouble getting off the ground. It secured $300,000 in annual funding from conservative foundations—including the Scaife Family Charitable Trust and the Smith Richardson and John M. Olin foundations—and Ed Robb became the head of its organizing committee, if not its most newsworthy spokesman.[14]

IRD set out with two aims: first, to expose Communist-friendly enabling efforts in American Christianity, and second, to support alternative efforts that pressed for pluralist democracy and religious freedom—or at least for anticommunist resistance that could, in turn, lead to these same ends. This imperfect latter distinction was immediately evident in May 1981, when IRD sponsored a "Committee to Save El Salvador" that staged a demonstration at the Lincoln Memorial. The demonstration was designed to counter simultaneous demonstrations being held at the Pentagon and elsewhere over the Reagan administration's providing aid to the military government of El Salvador, which was then battling Marxist forces for control of the country in the early days of what would prove to be a twelve-year civil war. In its coverage, the *New York Times* referred to IRD as "a pro-Administration group," which was accurate insofar as it aligned with the administration on the paramount importance of combating Communism and preventing the Soviet Union from increasing its Central American sphere of influence beyond Cuba and Nicaragua to places like El Salvador. However, IRD's contribution to the national debate over U.S. support for the El Salvadorean government was minor compared to the explosive effect it soon had on the question of the NCC and related churches' support for Marxist and Communist elements around the world.[15]

Neuhaus was a prime figure in these efforts. The first was a January 1983 story in *Reader's Digest,* featuring IRD member David Jessup (not identified as part of the organization), who shared his outraged discovery that United Methodist Sunday collection money was systematically being routed to "the governments of Cuba and Vietnam and the pro-Soviet totalitarian movements of Latin America, Asia, and Africa," among other unsavory destinations, through the "relief and development arm of the National Council of Churches." About a week after *Reader's Digest* ran "Do You Know Where Your Church Offerings Go?" *60 Minutes* devoted two-thirds of its regular Sunday evening hour to a similarly themed story narrated by Morley Safer, entitled "The Gospel According to Whom?" As Safer explained early on, the program explored and exposed the role of the NCC and other Mainline Protestant organizations in directing the proceeds of "active Christian charity" from well-intentioned, unwitting sources like the people of First United Methodist Church of Logansport, Indiana, into "causes that seemed more political than religious and causes that seemed closer to the Soviet-Cuban view of the world than Logansport, Indiana's." This was an effort that "they," meaning the congregation in Logansport, "didn't like." Nor did Neuhaus: "I am worried, I am outraged when the church lies to its own people" about the Communist-friendly destinations and Marxist ideological ends of the monies it was collecting, he told Safer in an on-air interview, before he really let loose on what it meant for a church to tell lies and actively support, in funds and in-person visits, anti-Christian regimes:

> *"The height of hypocrisy is to pretend that in painting a rosy picture of the sufferings of the poor, in making excuses for those who oppress the poor, that one is speaking on behalf of the poor, [and] so we have religious leaders who go to countries which are massively repressive regimes, in which Christians are in jail, have been tortured, have been killed by the thousands, and they go to those countries and our religious dignitaries consort with the persecutors of the church of Christ. This is evil. This is wrong. It discredits the church's social witness. It undermines any elementary notion of justice. We have to turn this around."*[16]

The NCC filed formal complaints with both *Reader's Digest* and *60 Minutes* over these stories, outraged by what they regarded as unjust and inaccurate depictions of their activities, and mindful of how devastating such reports would be to their levels of support in Cold War–era America. The NCC also knew that the IRD was the principal player behind this double takedown, and—as per Neuhaus' closing exhortation to Safer—that "they have set out to do us in, and they must be taken seriously," as one NCC spokeswoman told the *New York Times.*

Indeed, NCC president James Armstrong, who came off as defensive and cowed during his *60 Minutes* interviews by comparison to the strident and convinced Neuhaus and other IRD colleagues, "denounced the institute from the pulpit of Riverside Church," the paper further reported. Ever thereafter, liberal Christian leaders regarded the IRD as a continual scourge and fearsome intellectual-political wheelhouse of the emerging religious right wing.[17] Meanwhile, Neuhaus' IRD activities didn't endear him to his colleagues at CRIA or elsewhere.[18] In fact, CRIA president Robert Myers wrote Neuhaus with orders to vacate his office. The timing of this order had obvious implications: Myers wrote Neuhaus on January 31, 1983, only a few days after the *60 Minutes* episode ran. He was convinced that Neuhaus' activities "created an image problem" for the organization, not least, Myers charged, because "your high public profile [has] overshadowed" the work of CRIA.[19]

Later that same year, Neuhaus met John Howard, the founder and president of an Illinois-based conservative think tank called the Rockford Institute. Unlike Myers, Howard was persuaded, indeed quite taken, with what Neuhaus had to say about the current situation of religion in American life, as he explained in an interview. Over a long lunch at the Biltmore Hotel in New York, later in 1983, Howard told Neuhaus of Rockford's plans to found and fund a New York arm for its operation. He wanted it to focus on exploring the place and purpose of religion in American society from a conservative vantage, through articles, journals, studies, public statements, public talks, conferences, and seminars. Howard asked Neuhaus if he would direct it. After years of trying to find a platform and position for himself and his work, here was a sympathetic admirer from an established institution offering it to him directly! Nevertheless, Neuhaus stipulated a condition for his acceptance: as part of his duties as director, he wanted to put out a monthly survey of his own, on religion and public life. Howard thought it was a great idea, and so the Rockford Institute Center on Religion and Society was founded by March 1984, with a $200,000 annual operating budget supported primarily by Rockford and also by the John M. Olin Foundation, the Pew Memorial Trust, and the Smith-Richardson Foundation.[20]

Neuhaus' new directorship was first reported in November 1983, as part of an incendiary profile that *Harper's* magazine ran on him titled "Going to Extremes: A Sixties Radical Converts to an Eighties Reaganite." This was the first of what would prove repeated media efforts to make sense of Neuhaus' shifting political and cultural career and his consistent presence and influence in American public life. In this case, the effort was framed by a contrast between his CALCAV days and his work with the IRD—with references to his upbringing and family life supplied through interviews with his older brother Fred, who basically described and dismissed all of Neuhaus' 1960s radicalism as little more than a rebellion effort against his conservative father. The broader article, by Minneapolis-based journalist Philip Weiss, is similarly cynical, arguing that Neuhaus' "stunning" shifts from Left to Right, from McGovern supporter to Reagan apologist, and from a Brooklyn urban ministry to a Manhattan urban ministry, were motivated by "worldly hungers that are themselves key strains of the conservative gospel: the desire to influence policy and the pursuit of material reward"—rewards that Weiss discerned in a rather fantastical description of dingy 338 East 19th Street as a "well-appointed" and "handsome Manhattan row house."

Though he was only now reaping these awards as a prominent neoconservative, Weiss alleged, Neuhaus' lifelong efforts had been governed by a "blind faith" in the holy rightness of his own worldview, a faith that remained consistent whether as a "righteous radical or as a stern apologist for conservatism." Neuhaus was interviewed for this article, and while his remarks as published were framed as obvious evidence of his suffering from "a fundamentalist vision" of the world, he nevertheless spoke eloquently of the need to approach the difficulties of contemporary life out of a "vital center" of thought and action that would be capable of facing the "horror[s]" of abortion, poverty, unjust wars, and Marxist-Leninist totalitarianism with a morally serious hope that such horrors can be turned back by drawing on the best of American democracy and the Judeo-Christian tradition. One year later, he would make this case again, in much fuller and very timely terms, in a book that established him as a figure of permanent influence in the American public square.[21]

CHAPTER SIXTEEN

1984: The Naked Public Square Campaign

On November 7, 1984, Neuhaus' publisher wrote him the kind of letter that every writer hopes someday to receive. "You will be interested to know," Wm. B. Eerdmans reported, "that we are at the moment out of stock of *The Naked Public Square,* having sold out the first printing." The letter was sent the day after the 1984 presidential election. As one television interviewer put it to Neuhaus in the lead-up to Election Day, "I've known authors to go to great lengths to promote their books. But arranging a presidential campaign, isn't that a bit much?" Neuhaus relayed this clever question in an October 1984 letter to his much admired colleague overseas, the German theologian Wolfhart Pannenberg. "The response to *The Naked Public Square* has been nothing short of astonishing," he continued, before quipping, "Of course Reagan and Mondale [have] helped." Indeed, Neuhaus was mindful that the unprecedented interest in him and his ideas had a great deal to do with the timing and circumstances of the book's arrival: "As with most books that 'catch on' in this way," he mused, "I think it's largely a matter not of saying so much that is new but of providing some metaphors by which people can think about things that had confused them."[1]

Indeed, Neuhaus wasn't saying much that was especially new in *The Naked Public Square,* at least not in the context of nearly twenty years of his writing and advocating for religion's place in American public life. In fact, as early as his 1967 interview with James Finn for his book on protest, pacifism, and politics, Neuhaus was lamenting the retreat of religion into private spheres and calling instead for clergymen "to understand their role as clergy in the public sphere." This was an understanding that he clearly lived out, and likewise wrote from, throughout the 1970s and early 1980s, with works like *Movement and Revolution, In Defense of People,* and *Time Toward Home,* and in the specifically religious portions of *To Empower People.* He did the same in his many talks and articles during this period, perhaps nowhere more directly on track toward the particular terms and concerns of this book than in his 1981 Harvard Club New York remarks on John Courtney Murray's ideas of the sacred and secular elements in American democracy, and his 1982 consideration in *Worldview* of the rise of the Moral Majority, "Addressing the Naked Public Square."[2]

This being the case, and leaving aside for a moment the specifically political and electoral circumstances of its 1984 reception, what in fact was so new about his most famous book? First, it was his incisive and perfectly timed attentiveness to the late 1970s through early 1980s rise of Christian fundamentalists as a sizeable and organized presence in American public life and politics, and his understanding of their motivating grievances, as he described these early on in *The Naked Public Square:* "Groups such as [the] Moral Majority kicked a tripwire alerting us to a pervasive contradiction in our culture and our politics. We insist that we are a democratic society, yet we have in recent decades systematically excluded from policy consideration the operative values of the American people, values that are overwhelmingly grounded in religious belief." The second new element was his creation of a provocative and powerful metaphor that captured this sense of systematic exclusion. "The naked public square," as a term, had a crucially calming effect on the rest of the book's argument and likewise its prose, by comparison to its predecessors. No longer did Neuhaus seem to be striving, every few sentences, to deliver a crowning statement about religion and public life, nor was he endlessly laying down snaking topic lists and convoluted systems for understanding the subject at hand. And he finally refrained from indulging in the caustic and clever put-downs that had tended to take up too much time in his earlier work.

He was, instead, at last fully in command of his subject and his terms of argument, which expanded over sixteen chapters that explored an array of overlapping realities and perceptions, historic and contemporary, about religion's place in American life. The explanatory proposition threading throughout, of course, was that politics is a function of culture, and that culture is a function of religion. Among his particular emphases were the rupturing and divisive effects of morality understood in private, individual, and relativized terms against the public, communal, and normative; the lamentable failure of the Protestant establishment to sustain theologically serious and irreducibly theological positions before an ascendant secular liberalism; and the unappealing prospect of "a Christian America" that sought exclusive and singular authority in public life, a prospect that Neuhaus emphasized would only continue to lead many people to prefer the exclusive and singular authority of secularity in public life, that is "until Christians can believably propose that there is greater safety under a sacred canopy that brings all institutions and belief systems, and most particularly religion [itself], under judgment. The canopy is that to which Judeo-Christian religion points," and *The Naked Public Square: Religion and Democracy in America* is Neuhaus' most masterful effort to point this out.[3]

This mastery is nowhere more apparent than in his accomplished reformulations and distinctive extensions of the ideas and premises of Jesuit theologian John Courtney Murray. To be sure, Neuhaus engages many other notable thinkers in the book—Tocqueville, whose most famous work, *Democracy in America,* Neuhaus invokes with the subtitle of his own, and also Alasdair MacIntyre, John Rawls,

Clifford Geertz, Michael Novak, and Reinhold Niebuhr, among others—but none matter so much as Murray, and specifically the catalytic power of Murray's idea (in Neuhaus' cogent capture) "that the democratic reality [of the United States] could not be sustained on narrow secular grounds." In American Catholic circles at least, Murray was the earliest and most eloquent proponent of a religiously informed approach to democracy, which was simultaneously a religiously informed apology for democracy itself. Murray based this proposal on his discernment of "the evident coincidence of the principles which inspired the American Republic with the principles that are structural to the Western Christian political tradition," as he framed it in his 1960 book *We Hold These Truths: Catholic Reflections on the American Proposition.*

Almost twenty-five years later, Neuhaus fully assimilated and then innovatively built on Murray's discernment by engaging a moment in American life when the "evident coincidence" that Murray wrote about was far from evident to secular elites, and far more providential than coincidental to Christian fundamentalists. And "the naked public square" served as a provocative and punchy phrase for explaining the dangerous cause and effect of these oppositional positions and groups, which, Neuhaus argued, were ironically collaborative in their ideas and actions: "By building a wall of strict separationism between faith and reason, fundamentalist religion ratifies and reinforces the conclusions of militant secularism," he explained at one point, while elsewhere emphasizing that proponents of exclusive secularism resist and ridicule exclusively faith-based propositions for politics and public policy. Writing from a perspective positioned beyond these mutually reinforcing antagonists, Neuhaus expressed his great frustration with both groups: together, they were preventing any salutary drawing on the Judeo-Christian tradition and biblically informed formulations of the good in the larger deliberative processes and practices of modern democratic life.[4]

Running alongside this frustration throughout the book are explicit warnings and tacit propositions. The explicit warnings concern the strength and well-being of the democratic system itself, which Neuhaus argued were under threat if the current tensions between aggrieved fundamentalists and exclusionist secularists turned into dangerous conflicts. The stakes couldn't be higher, as far as he was concerned: "It may be that the only alternative to civil war is to engage [Christian fundamentalists] in civil discourse. For that to happen, our definition of civil discourse cannot exclude what they want to talk about. They want to talk about God in public." Sympathetic to what the fundamentalists wanted, Neuhaus was bluntly critical of how they were seeking it. He castigated them for contributing to their very own exclusion from the public square insofar as they had no "convincing and coherent theory of democratic governance." In its place, the fundamentalists worked out of their reliance upon biblical inerrancy, an approach to questions of faith and reason whose inherently divisive effects and intellectually unpersuasive elements Neuhaus had already experienced firsthand, during his seminary days and thereafter in the Missouri Synod. And while he nevertheless supported the fundamentalists' willingness "to assert the public meaning of the biblical message," he was convinced that "the way in which that assertion is made is profoundly disturbing on several scores"—not least this reliance on biblical inerrancy, which, he argued, encourages a closed loop of inerrant-by-association biblical preachers quoting from the inerrant Bible, which in turn actuated "its refusal to engage the Christian message in conversation with public and universal discourse outside the circle of true believers." In other words, there was no viable theory of religiously informed democratic governance to be found here for a pluralist democracy. Of course, this didn't mean such a theory wasn't possible.[5]

Rejecting other models to make way for his own, Neuhaus proposed just such a theory by modeling an integrative form of civil discourse—what he more often calls a "public philosophy," meaning a philosophy whose propositions intend to inform and effect citizens' lives even while the higher truth-claims that order and motivate the philosophy and its propositions originate in sacred sources and their institutions. To prevent both the potential theocratic and Erastian outcomes, this public philosophy has to be articulated in publicly available terms, terms that are comprehensible and acceptable beyond the ambit of one's personal beliefs and confessional commitments. Neuhaus' model of just such a public philosophy in *The Naked Public Square* confidently draws biblical wisdom and the Judeo-Christian tradition into critical, constructive conversation with post-Enlightenment thought and modern political theory, in support of a universally appealing proposition in American life: "democracy is an experiment well worth protecting and moving toward the fuller realization of its promise." And this was a reachable promise that could begin to take shape if the good people each of Cisco, Texas, and of Manhattan stopped thinking and speaking about religion and politics like they had grown accustomed to, and more like the author of *The Naked Public Square*, who was mutually sympathetic, critical, and seeking to generate a discourse that was dispassionate and dialectical rather than demonizing and divisive. And were this to happen, perhaps then "the hopeful prospect" would arise, as the book's final statements put it, that the United States would "move beyond present polarizations" and its citizens, Left and Right, God-fearing and God-less, would seek to understand and live out in common "the newness, the fragility, the promise, and the demands of religion and democracy in America."[6]

That said, in 1984 when the book came out, the hopeful prospects and immediate demands of American democracy were yoked to the drama and stakes of a presidential election charged with questions over the place of religion, and of religiously motivated citizens, in public life and politics. As the *New York Times* reported in one of many stories it ran about religion and politics during the election year, "the historic controversy over mixing religion and politics, dormant for many years, has become a prime issue in the current Presidential campaign." At the center of this controversy were Christian fundamentalist leaders like Jerry Falwell, who was righteously and simplistically calling for a religious politics that could secure the very salvation of the country itself. As Neuhaus noted while discussing Falwell in *The Naked Public Square,* this otherwise minor Virginia mega-church leader had come to play a significant part in public life and electoral politics from the late 1970s through the mid-1980s. In founding the Moral Majority in 1979, Falwell sought to operationalize his righteous conviction that biblical religion had to figure substantially in politics and public life, in order to stop a national moral decline that had started in the 1960s and 1970s. This decline was abetted by what Falwell called "the [previously] deafening silence of the pulpit" on matters like abortion, women's rights, gay rights, school prayer, and coarsening popular culture, and likewise the pulpit's hesitancy to advocate for the positive role that biblical religion could play in all of these contexts and in government itself.[7]

So motivated, and amply supported by his followers, Falwell and the Moral Majority deployed considerable financial resources and influence over millions of Christian voters while campaigning successfully for Reagan over Carter in 1980, and were primed to do likewise for Reagan over Mondale in 1984. Reagan himself openly courted this demographic, and the Republican Party aligned parts of its policy platform with their interests and concerns. The result, according to scholar John H. Simpson, was that "the religious new right" succeeded during this period in "politicizing socio-moral issues in such a way that Reagan was able to identify himself with the views of a majority of Americans on those issues." But by 1984, the effect of Falwell and the Moral Majority's generating electorally focused enthusiasms from millions of churchgoing, now reliably Republican voters had a logical countereffect on Reagan's Democratic challengers. On the campaign trail, vice presidential candidate Geraldine Ferraro invoked the dangerous influence of "extremist right wing" movements in American life, while Walter Mondale characterized Falwell's relationship to the Republican Party during a presidential debate as nothing less than "an abuse of faith in this country."[8]

Mondale, Ferraro, and like-minded politicians and commentators were convinced that Falwell and his followers were running roughshod over the First Amendment and imperiling American democracy, with the encouragement and to the benefit of Reagan and the Republican Party. Falwell and his forces, meanwhile, were convinced that they were restoring much-needed traditional moral values to American public life and government while simultaneously empowering millions of God-fearing, USA-loving citizens to renew that democracy itself. In fall 1984, Neuhaus and his new book were the preeminent sources in attempts from across the ideological spectrum to address this situation. In the months after *The Naked Public Square* was published, Neuhaus was repeatedly asked to discuss matters relating to the relationship of religion and politics, church and state. His efforts included a heady September session on William F. Buckley's PBS talk show *Firing Line* that saw a quick-witted exchange about the comparative moral stature of Mother Teresa and a San Francisco transvestite performance artist nun named Sister Boom Boom.

As always with Buckley, there was something serious to the seeming lark: appreciating that Neuhaus' work mattered beyond its campaign trail fodder, he compared these dissimilar figures to reveal the broad consequences of permitting religiously informed understandings of value in public life. *Time* magazine took a more straightforwardly sober approach that same month, inviting Neuhaus to address "the proper relation of religion and politics" and more specifically whether "the current campaign controversy [over Falwell and his movement's role in the campaign] was salutary or harmful." Neuhaus' response was essentially a cogent summary of *The Naked Public Square,* and ended with this barely veiled self-recommendation:

> *America lacks a coherent, morally grounded public philosophy. We do not have the vocabulary to debate moral issues in the public square. This could be severely damaging, if not fatal, to the American democratic experiment. The present confusion, however, can turn out to be a watershed moment in American politi-*

> *cal and cultural life if we begin to reconstruct a public philosophy, one that is responsible to, and in conversation with, the religious-based values of the American people.*[9]

This was, in fact, a watershed moment for Neuhaus himself, whose lifelong work would proceed and develop at an accelerated and elevated level with the publication of this book. Having described intellectuals in earlier writings as "those who mint and market the metaphors by which public consciousness is shaped," this is exactly what Neuhaus fully became and conclusively accomplished with *The Naked Public Square.* Book review editors, news producers, and opinion makers immediately thought as much, and in time so too would politicians, policy makers, and scholars.[10] That fall, Neuhaus emerged as America's most prominent and discussed authority on religion and public life, if not as a universally accepted authority on these matters. Indeed, as conservative columnist George F. Will suggested with his judiciously framed endorsement, Neuhaus' work was "the book from which further debate about church-state relations should begin." That debate quickly filled out the book reviewing pages of American newspapers and journals: in the second half of 1984 alone, some fifty different reviews of *The Naked Public Sphere* ran in major national outlets, various city dailies, religious publications, intellectual and political magazines, and scholarly venues. Notable among these was the respectful and critical attention from Harvey Cox in a full-page consideration for the *New York Times Book Review,* which profiled Neuhaus alongside the review and thereafter selected the title as one of its "Notable Books of the Year."[11]

In general, religious and intellectual publications divided in their responses largely based on their own politics. The basic consensus among the reviewers went something like this: Neuhaus had correctly and articulately diagnosed a very contemporary problem in the United States: determining the nature and necessity of religion's place in public life. Some reviewers were convinced he was also correct in his analyses of the related symptoms and in his proposed prescriptions. Others held to the contrary. The dissenting critics cited plenty of evidence for the continued presence of religious elements and figures in American public life, and moreover questioned how a book that detailed the rise of the Religious New Right into political consciousness and public power could simultaneously argue that the American public square had been denuded of its religious elements. Others drilled into Neuhaus' formulations, wondering exactly how personal belief in Christ or adherence to specific religious doctrines could practically inform broad public policy in a country with no established religion. Still others expressed a combination of gratitude and admiration for Neuhaus, for his embodying in his book a proposal for a morally serious and cosmopolitan public life that wasn't captive to the mutually reinforcing extremes of Christian fundamentalists and secular elites. Even Herman Otten, Neuhaus' longtime Missouri Synod antagonist, gave positive attention to the book in his newspaper, *Christian News,* crediting the author with rightly going after his former friends on the Left for their godless excesses and excessive godlessness. Taken together, these dozens of responses, while divergent in their estimations, were a collective testament to the unprecedented attention that Neuhaus received for this work in 1984 and thereafter.[12]

He was still going strong at year's end. In early December, he spent an evening discussing the book with a reading group at Grace Church, New York City. At the far end of months of book-related work in the national media, he'd have been forgiven for skipping a comparatively minor engagement like this, but he went, perhaps in part to gauge the response of ordinary readers. A few weeks later, on December 20, he met with a very different set of readers, in Washington. Neuhaus was at the White House to deliver remarks in the Roosevelt Room on religion and public life in the context of the recent election, for an audience made up of administration officials, cabinet members, senators, and other religious and political leaders. While it would seem obvious that the success of *The Naked Public Square* led to this invitation, plans for it seem to have first taken shape months before the book took off, when Neuhaus spent some time with a high-ranking member of Reagan's administration thanks to the connections he was making under the auspices of his new job as the director of the Center on Religion and Society. These connections led to Neuhaus' being invited, in July 1984, to the annual get-together of the historic and elite Bohemian Grove, a Monte Rio, California–based private club known for its highly restrictive and male-only membership drawn from the highest ranks of American politics, business, and culture.

Neuhaus was there under the auspices of Bohemian member and Rockford president John Howard. While at the Grove, Neuhaus met with Edwin Meese III, who had been a leading campaign operative in Reagan's 1980 run against Carter and had since become a prominent and influential counselor to the President. Based on the letter Neuhaus sent Meese afterward, it appears that while at Bohemian Grove the two of them explored the idea of "a conference on Christian ethics and the political life" for members of the administration. Which is to say, for a second Reagan administration: Neuhaus was clearly confident, by August 1984, that the fall campaign would make this possible: "I will be back in touch with you to plan something on that [the proposed conference] for after the election," he promised, before signing off, "Please [be] assured of my prayers for your important ministry."[13]

How are we to understand such assurances, coming from a Lutheran pastor to a presidential counselor during an election year roiled by questions of religion's involvement with politics? Was Neuhaus simply offering a more rarefied and discreet version of the "vulgarized moralism" that figures like Falwell were introducing to national life during this same period, as Neuhaus himself describes this phenomenon in *The Naked Public Square*? Readers of that 1983 *Harper's* profile, persuaded by its account of Neuhaus, would no doubt think as much. But Neuhaus would have rejected this charge and might have differentiated between these efforts by emphasizing the meaningful difference (in context and consequence) between public statements and private communications. He might further have suggested that as a pastor, it was his vocational right and indeed responsibility to offer prayers to any person he spent time with, whether a construction worker or a presidential counselor. It was likewise incumbent upon him, as a pastor, to encourage that person to understand his profession in higher-order and ethical, even evangelical terms, indeed as nothing less than a ministry.

All of this is plausible and reasonable, but it doesn't finally counteract the perception and implication that—just as in prior years he was fully committed to trying to influence American public life through Democratic presidential candidates and party politics—by 1984 Neuhaus had consciously and actively aligned his plans for the very same with the Reagan administration and the Republican Party, an alignment that would continue for the rest of his career.[14] In other words, in the fuller context of Richard John Neuhaus' life and work, the interplay of his party politics and his higher positions on religion and politics finally suggests a basic consistency and tacit circularity: regardless of the party and president he was engaging, Neuhaus was always working to develop and advance a "public philosophy" that justified religion's role in the right ordering of American public life. At the same time, he was always seeking to win the most politically influential audience possible for his own vision of what that right ordering would involve, whether this meant an end to an unjust war, racial discrimination, abortion, or embryonic stem-cell research. And in order to succeed in this respect, he was always trying to persuade his listeners to develop an openness to religiously grounded reasons for why they were called to work to end such injustices, which is to say, an acceptance of his public philosophy for the right ordering of American public life.

This is precisely the effort Neuhaus made in Washington on December 20, 1984, when his Bohemian Grove proposal to Meese took the shape of his leading a White House briefing on "Religion and Politics." Largely reprising his *Naked Public Square* arguments as in his *Time* magazine contribution from earlier that year, Neuhaus chose a new and obviously pertinent frame for his remarks, given the location and audience. In his estimation, 1984 would go down in American history as a "watershed year," even more historic and important than the unprecedented election of a Catholic as president in 1960. The support that Reagan received from churchgoing voters "constituted a sharp challenge to the naked public square," he explained, already using his own phrase like it was a well-established term of self-evident meaning, a presumption that made sense given how much it had been used by, about, and beyond him in the preceding months. He then predicted (whether as warning or promise) that this was "a challenge which will become sharper and more effective in the years to come," before concluding, "We must pray and work that it does not lead to religious warfare, but can lead to the construction of a public philosophy emerging from and accountable to the religiously-based values of the American people."[15]

The day after his remarks, Neuhaus wrote his White House host, J. Douglas Holladay of the Office of Public Liaison, a detailed three-page letter that offered in passing some playful crowing about the landslide victory but far more emphasized the opportunity at hand, to make a case for a religiously informed "reconceptualizing of the American experiment." Sometimes, Neuhaus allowed, this meant "'playing hard ball' in the politics of ideas" but more importantly it meant "cultivating persons and institutions who can effectively engage the opposition," meaning persons and institutions that were unlike "Jerry F." and the Moral Majority. Neuhaus acknowledged that the letter, coming a day after his already extensive remarks, was probably "more on this [matter] than [Holladay] asked for, or probably wanted," but he was convinced that the administration was "doing something of enormous potential importance to the future of cultural, political, and religious reconstruction in this country." That being the case, "If I can be of further help," he closed, adding best wishes for Christmas, "please do not hesitate to call on me." By the time Neuhaus wrote this letter, he could send along his best calling card to make obvious the kind of further help he could offer. Eerdmans was on to a second printing, and so, as he noted in his letter to Holladay, he arranged for twenty copies of *The Naked Public Square* to be sent to the White House for distribution, thereby providing political leaders and policy makers with nothing less than his own book-form construction plans for the public philosophy for which he had spent the prior months, if not decades, variously preaching, writing, speaking, organizing, and marching.[16]

Having returned from Washington to New York a few days before Christmas with his White House matters wrapped up, at least until the new year, Neuhaus had yet another invitation awaiting him. This one had nothing to do with *The Naked Public Square.* It came from someone relatively new to New York, someone who was very grateful for all that Neuhaus had done for him that past year in welcoming him to the city: "The past nine months have been modestly eventful," Neuhaus' correspondent noted with studied understatement, before enthusing, "Your contributions have been unique, cherished, and much more deeply appreciated than you may have suspected. I do not use the word *friend* lightly, my dear friend. You will be very much in my prayers during Christmas Mass. Indeed, perhaps you could even be there, at midnight, and join us in the house afterward, with family and a few others? Fraternally in Christ, John O'Connor." Over the previous nine months, in fact, O'Connor had become the most prominent Catholic leader in the United States, which followed upon John Paul II's naming him the archbishop of New York in January 1984 and his subsequent involvements in that year's political campaigns.[17]

Neuhaus had first encountered New York's new archbishop the year before, by way of O'Connor's involvements with the United States Conference of Catholic Bishops' 1983 letter on prospects for war and peace in the nuclear era, "The Challenge of Peace, God's Promise and Our Response." O'Connor's ministry had long been associated with the military, and he was understood to have been the most conservative presence on the commission that produced the letter, evidenced by reports of his arguing that Reagan administration officials be heard out as part of the deliberations, and his unsuccessful effort to have the term "curb" rather than "halt" be used in the letter's arguably most famous statement, "We support immediate, bilateral, verifiable agreements to halt the testing, production and deployment of nuclear weapons systems." Subsequent to the letter's publication, Neuhaus reached out to O'Connor and, by Neuhaus' account, was assured of "his appreciation of the necessity of a strong military posture," a position that Neuhaus also held and advocated. But shared foreign policy positions mattered little to the mutual-admiration society the two men would quickly develop and joyfully maintain from their early correspondence over the announcement of O'Connor's appointment through to his death in 2000, at least by comparison to the unstinting intensity of their pro-life convictions, their willingness to speak out of those convictions, occasionally in provocative terms, and their capacity, if not enthusiasm, for riding the media storms that came of such provocations.[18]

This all looks clear, now, in considering their developing connections in January and February 1984, following O'Connor's telling a television interviewer after he was named archbishop but before he came to New York, "I always compare the killing of 4,000 babies a day in the United States, unborn babies, to the Holocaust. Now, Hitler tried to solve a problem, the Jewish question. So kill them, shove them in the ovens, burn them. Well, we claim that unborn babies are a problem, so kill them. To me it really is precisely the same." Though he was still bishop in Scranton, Pennsylvania, O'Connor predictably made news in New York with the comments, offending the city's Jewish leaders in particular. But he also won sympathetic attention from Neuhaus, who would have been very interested in the issue and in the surrounding media storm. He would have agreed with O'Connor's position on the significance of America's ongoing abortion crisis, not been as offended as others by the Holocaust analogy, and also realized that here was a religious leader of dramatically rising influence in American public life who would benefit from the attentiveness of an experienced hand when it came to discussing religious matters for a New York audience. And so within days of the controversy erupting over his abortion remarks, O'Connor received a letter from Neuhaus, offering good wishes for his new appointment and support for his ministry. O'Connor wrote back a pro forma note, thanking him in impersonal terms for his good wishes, but then he added a far more personal handwritten postscript: "Your support is extremely meaningful to me. Please make contact with me early in the game. We have much to do together."[19]

Neuhaus willingly obliged. After attending O'Connor's March 19, 1984, installation at St. Patrick's Cathedral, he arranged a series of meetings and dinners for the new archbishop over the course of the year. While there's no record of who finally accepted, his invitation list captures a sense of his multiple orbits during this period, all of which he engaged on behalf of O'Connor: he reached out to local Lutheran and other religious leaders, and also to Manhattan intellectuals, ranging from the iconoclastic liberal writer Susan Sontag and *New York Review of Books* editor Robert Silvers to prominent neoconservatives like Irving Kristol and Midge Decter. He did likewise, unsurprisingly, with representatives of the media, like NBC News anchor Tom Brokaw and *New York Times* editorial board member John McKenzie, in this case for a formal December 4 event that Neuhaus created and hosted to introduce Archbishop O'Connor to the city's media leaders. This event didn't take place in the first-floor apartment at 338 East 19th Street. It happened on the twenty-fourth floor of 152 Madison Avenue, in the offices of the Center on Religion and Society. In other words, the event would have served simultaneously as an introduction to John O'Connor and to Richard John Neuhaus, in his new profile as the director of the newly founded Rockford Institute Center on Religion and Society. Neuhaus was no longer only a longtime figure of New York's religious intelligentsia, or more immediately the lately much discussed author of *The Naked Public Square*, or simply O'Connor's self-appointed consigliere. Instead, he was the proprietor of an ambitious new operation dedicated to exploring religion and democracy, and largely on his own terms. In the coming years, these terms would reflect and further enhance his influence in American public life, an influence that was first significantly expanded in 1984 thanks to the Naked Public Square campaign. In 1985 and thereafter, his explorations of religion and democracy would also reflect and develop further his intensifying connections to notable Catholics, and to Catholicism itself.[20]

CHAPTER SEVENTEEN

More and More Catholic Moments, Among Many, Many Others

"Of course the pope's the head of the church," Neuhaus matter-of-factly told Ralph McInenry, one day in Rome, in late 1985. The two of them were standing on a grand cobblestoned boulevard called the Via della Conciliazione. Its name reflects the conciliation achieved between the Holy See and Italy with the 1929 Lateran Treaty, which in turn led to the construction of the road, the primary means of traveling between St. Peter's and the world at large. This was, in other words, the world's most prominent thoroughfare for the two-way passage of sacred and secular powers. As the conceptual setting and center of a life in the public square, this was exactly where Richard John Neuhaus always wanted to be. This ambition and vocation increasingly aligned his life and work with the Catholic Church. He would arrive at this conclusive insight in 1990, based on the ongoing integration of personal commitments and interests that had played out in ecclesial, intellectual, ideological, historical, and also interpersonal terms and reached back through decades of Catholic connections—according to his own account, going all the way back to his youthful sense of a distinctive identification with the Catholic Spooner boys on Miller Street.

This trajectory developed for Neuhaus in closely observed and felt parallel to the ongoing decline of the American Lutheranism and broader U.S. Protestant Christianity that he was formed in and subscribed to for the better part of his life. Indeed, he was still committed to defending his Lutheranism in 1985, when a Catholic priest wrote him a few months before his trip to Rome to inquire why he wasn't Catholic. Neuhaus replied, "It is a question to which I, and I know many other Lutheran pastors, have given careful thought," he noted, before explaining, "There is no insuperable theological obstacle to my becoming a Roman Catholic. However, I am an evangelical catholic who believes that, so long as it seems possible that Lutheranism can be moved toward the fulfillment of its ecumenical duty and destiny [of healing the breach of the sixteenth century, Neuhaus' shorthand for the Reformation], it is God's will I stay where I am in order to advance that possibility."[1]

He stayed on another five years, but these were years in which a much longer trajectory toward Catholicism took definitive shape and exerted notable force, all beginning with his 1985 visit to Rome to cover that year's Extraordinary Synod as a religious journalist writing for *National Review.* John Paul II had called the synod to coincide with the twentieth anniversary of Vatican II, with plans for the bishops of the world to gather and consider how (and how well) the Church had lived out the teachings of the Council since its 1965 conclusion.[2] While in Rome, Neuhaus stayed at the North American College, the impressive residence and grounds that the U.S. Catholic bishops maintain in Rome for the formation and training of American seminarians. He enjoyed a certain celebrity status there, as a news-making New York Lutheran pastor who wore a Roman collar and held clearly sympathetic interests in Catholic matters. He also spent some enjoyable time with John O'Connor, also in town for the synod, which in part involved Neuhaus offering O'Connor advice, solicited or otherwise, about being more wary of the influence of left-leaning Catholics and Catholic publications in America life. Well beyond these American connections, however, Neuhaus enjoyed his few weeks in Rome. Whether attending Mass at St. Peter's, going to various dinners and receptions, or moving in and out of corridor conversations, all of which he noted in his writings about the synod, Neuhaus enthusiastically experienced firsthand the cosmopolitanism, political and intellectual gamesmanship and gossip, and the ritualized grandeurs of the Catholic Church, all at work and in full display at its very center, thanks to an occasion that brought together its leaders and a coterie of advisors and observers from around the world.[3]

The synod itself was focused on deliberating the meaning and outcomes to date of the Second Vatican Council's signal charge, in the 1964 Dogmatic Constitution document *Lumen Gentium,* that the Church and her ministers and laity alike were called to engage with the modern world in evangelizing terms, through the Gospel and in harmony with the continuous, living traditions and teachings of the faith. This was very much the construal of Vatican II's message and meaning for Church and world according to Joseph Cardinal Ratzinger, the accomplished German theologian who had come to international prominence during John Paul II's papacy as the prefect of the Congregation of the Doctrine of the Faith and as the pope's most influential and highly placed advisor, interlocutor, and collaborator. His views on the Council, and on how imperfectly its charge had been taken up in the post-conciliar period to 1985, had become widely known earlier that year, when a German journalist published a book-length interview with him, entitled *The Ratzinger Report.* Its outsized effects at the actual synod itself were evident when another cardinal, Belgium's Gotfried Daneels, told a press conference with obvious frustration that "this is not a Synod about a book, it is a Synod about a Council!" Nevertheless, as Neuhaus would later observe, "Anyone who doubts that the synod was primarily working off Cardinal Ratzinger's agenda has only to make a point-by-point comparison between *The Ratzinger Report* and the interventions and documents of the synod, the most important document being the *Relatio Finalis* ("Final Report"), which called for 'a deeper reception of the Council itself . . . in continuity with the great tradition of the

Church.'" Ratzinger had called for the same in his interview earlier that year, and his vision and plan had clearly won out against others at the synod, as Neuhaus reported in his piece for *National Review*.[4]

"Recovery in Rome, What the Synod Wrought" made clear Neuhaus' sympathetic, indeed admiring, conviction that it was principally Ratzinger who had wrought this recovery in Rome, and that this was for the greater good of the Church and world alike. Not that he was done thinking about these matters, when he returned from Rome to New York in December 1985. He might have earlier that month casually affirmed the authority of the pope over the universal church and, beforehand, told at least one correspondent that there were no "insuperable" theological issues barring his conversion. More immediately important and directing of his interests and plans, however, was his discovery of Ratzinger's singular importance to the future of the Church's conciliation and evangelical efforts with the world at large. What would become clear, in turn, was Neuhaus' interest in aligning his own efforts in the American context with and through Ratzinger and the Catholic Church. Over the next three years, this interest would take shape for Neuhaus in a typically catholic, which is to say all-encompassing, approach, through writings, personal connections, public events, and strategic visits and meetings. If primary, the Catholic Church and its most decisive actors weren't Neuhaus' only focus in the mid-1980s and thereafter, as the pile of papers awaiting him on his return from Rome made clear: "I am still digging out from under all the matters that have accumulated in my absence," he remarked in a late December 1985 letter to Wolfhart Pannenberg, adding "only to discover the holy days are almost upon us."[5]

At the far end of those holy days, and aside from the work he had already begun in support of his ever-increasing Catholic interests—which included securing a contract with Harper & Row for a book about the Catholic Church that he would submit at year's end—Neuhaus turned his attention to a remarkable array of other matters. Throughout 1986, under the auspices of the Rockford Institute and the Center on Religion and Society, he was in negotiations with the Institute on Educational Affairs and its encouraging chairman, leading neoconservative Irving Kristol, to take over *This World* magazine, a five-year-old conservative publication that was suffering from low subscription numbers and a lack of editorial direction. Neuhaus had plans to remedy both of these problems in taking over the magazine as its new editor in chief, having secured funding commitments from the Scaife and Bradley foundations, identified a distinctive audience for the magazine (conservative-minded clergy, educated laity, and religious schools and other institutions), and also articulated a first-principles mission for the magazine under his proprietorship: bringing people over to the right kind of questions about religion and public life, not to any putatively right (or right-wing) kind of politics. He was pursuing this mission and these questions in a variety of venues during this same year. In February, he gave a talk on American religion and foreign policy at the State Department as part of a larger speaker series called "Open Forum" that also included talks by Leslie Gelb, Madeleine Albright, and Jeane Kirkpatrick during this period. That same month, he accepted a White House appointment to serve on the newly created United States Institute of Peace, which was created through congressional legislation calling for the creation of an institution designed "to promote international peace and the resolution of conflicts among the nations and peoples of the world without recourse to violence." That year, he also accepted appointments to serve on the advisory board of the Cardinal Cooke Pro-Life Commission in New York, at John O'Connor's invitation, and became a participant in the "Working Seminar on the Family and American Welfare Policy" at Marquette University's Institute for Family Studies.[6]

At a rate that would only increase for the better part of the rest of his life, Neuhaus was also giving talks and taking meetings all over the country. In March, he spoke at Indiana University on the concept and promise of "democratic morality." In April, he spoke to the Phoenix Rotary Club on "Religion and Politics: Its Yet More

Troubling Future." From Arizona he went to South Bend, Indiana, to give a speech at the University of Notre Dame on "The Obligations and Limits of Political Commitment" as part of a symposium on democracy and capitalism. In early May, while in New York, he lunched with John O'Connor and O'Connor's guest, French cardinal Jean-Marie Lustiger, who asked to see Neuhaus' writings on the recent synod. This same month, he was in Chicago to give a speech at an American Jewish Committee–sponsored conference, the very title of which suggested his influence over such subjects: "Conflict in the Public Square: Religion vs. Secularism." A few days later, he gave another lecture on "Religion in the Public Square," this time to a public affairs institute in Washington, and another lecture, this time on U.S. foreign policy's moral dimensions, in Missoula, Montana.[7]

The honoraria he received for these talks and many, many others were usually a few hundred dollars (though sometimes as much as a few thousand), with similar payments through this period for his freelance writing, and also five-thousand-dollar advances for *The Naked Public Square* and for the upcoming *Dispensations*—beyond the tens of thousands Neuhaus gave to individuals in need and various organizations, the funds were routed into the common account of the Community of Christ in the City along with his salary as director of the Center on Religion and Society. In turn, the Community gave him, as of the mid-1980s, a three-hundred-dollar monthly allowance, most of which likely went to his favorite indulgences, bourbon and cigars. He particularly enjoyed these to cap off a Saturday night dinner at 338 East 19th Street, when community members and any guests would gather in Neuhaus' living room on chairs and couches arranged between a piano and a stone fireplace or, if it was a nice evening, around a patio table in the verdant back garden. The topic, carrying forward from dinner, was often whatever matters happened to be on Neuhaus' mind. Regular attendees knew this meant that as the night wore on, the bourbon flowed, the cigars turned to embers, and discussion and debate would usually turn into a monologue.[8]

Not that there were many complaints. Indeed, beyond the

assuredly interested audience at 338, whose resident population was gradually shifting away from holdovers to willing members—meaning, as one contemporaneous notice put it, "deeply committed Christian[s] interested in a community of prayer and support"—Neuhaus was in constant demand as a speaker, not least in Washington. In June 1986, he was again invited to speak at the State Department. This time the focus was "The Church as a Force for Peaceful Change in South Africa." Afterward, his host reported, "many of those participating in the Conference said your remarks were extremely helpful in giving focus to their developing understanding of South Africa. I agree. Your statement of the moral obligation we [bear] to South Africa was tremendous. . . . Best wishes as you press on with your many roles." These roles included, as of mid-1986, being the author of a new book about the situation in apartheid-era South Africa. This book, *Dispensations,* was published by Eerdmans, which, for a Michigan-based publisher of religiously minded books, had presumably done very well with their first venture with Neuhaus two years before (*The Naked Public Square* had sold some thirty thousand copies in hardcover at that point). One indication of their success with that book was Eerdmans' decision to bring out a second edition, also in 1986, with Neuhaus providing a new preface that featured a mix of at least rhetorical humility—doubting whether it was "the classic and seminal work that critics have kindly declared it to be"—and more than rhetorical brashness: after noting that John Courtney Murray, Reinhold Niebuhr, and Jacques Maritain had advanced arguments "for the connection between biblical faith and democratic governance" in prior eras, he pointed out that this project "has been sorely neglected in our recent history," at least up until now: "I would be gratified greatly if the present book moved others to take up that neglected task. They will not mind, I trust, if I [continue to] have a go at it myself."[9]

With his next book, Neuhaus took a far less swaggering approach. His engagement with the ongoing perils and possible promise of life in South Africa originated three years earlier as a project commissioned by the Council on Religion and International Affairs. In the acknowledgments, he explained this and expressed gratitude to Robert Myers for his support (regardless of the "image problem" Myers had accused Neuhaus of creating for CRIA back in 1983) and also, as ever, to Peter Berger, this time for involving him in a scholarly working group focused on South Africa. From within South Africa itself, Neuhaus particularly credited the cleric and anti-apartheid activist Beyers Naude, whom he had first met in 1971. But all of these individuals were, by the very plan of the book, secondary to those who merited Neuhaus' primary gratitude: "I am grateful to the hundreds of South Africans who generously shared with me their time and ideas," all of which made up the findings promised by the book's subtitle: "The Future of South Africans as South Africans See It." Of course, Neuhaus also had something to say about that future, and about some of the most important people in South Africa working toward it.[10]

The result is a combination of profile journalism and politically framed travelogue. Neuhaus writes about meetings he had with prominent South Africans like Archbishop Desmond Tutu and the political leader Mangosuthu Buthelezi of the Inkatha Freedom Party. He makes a point of interviewing a mixed race ("coloured" in South African terms) student chaplain in the dining room of an otherwise exclusively white hotel, to many harsh glances. At its strongest moments, the book is driven by an attentiveness to voices and sensibilities from South Africa—religious in first principles rather than political—that may not have been receiving as much attention amid the many other efforts to make sense of the country's corrosive racial situation by the mid-1980s. All of this is evident, for instance, in a passage devoted to a Dutch Reformed pastor and Afrikaner who reflects the sense of "dispensation" that provides the book with its title, "an arrangement of affairs in obedience to providence, or nature, or both." This pastor confidently regards his racial group's systematic domination in the country as God's will playing out in and as South African history. In turn, as Neuhaus evokes him, the pastor understands his religious and patriotic duty as aligned with God's will so construed, and he is more than willing to share the Gospel with black South Africans out of this alignment. As such, he is convinced that ending apartheid is tantamount to rejecting his duties before God, country, and black South Africans all, and so he tells Neuhaus: "You can be sure of one thing, man, we're not going to raise the white flag. If the Lord wants us to stand alone, we will stand alone."

We learn all of this because Neuhaus makes it possible for the man to speak out of his first principles, assenting when the man proposes, as he might not to a secular American journalist, "Let me speak to you as a Christian." Neuhaus gives him the opportunity and thereafter analyzes the effort, noting the "sincerity" of the evangelical compunction and even the "ultimate anguish" behind the pastor's righteous defiance, but Neuhaus is blunt in his analysis of the man's sense of religious-racial vocation: "The argument . . . is riddled with contradictions and the logical gaps are glaring." He then concludes, with the kind of comprehensive evaluation-cum-proposal that runs throughout the book, that such representative figures in South African life possess a "moral earnestness" because they "believe they are answerable to a transcendent judgment. That does not make their argument more persuasive. . . . But to belittle it in the name of modern skepticism is, I am persuaded, a sure way to miss out on what is happening in South Africa today and what may happen tomorrow."[11]

Reviewers were more interested in his effort than readers. The book sold poorly, only some three hundred copies in the first year, but it generated respectable critical attention thanks not only to its being published soon after *The Naked Public Square* but also because of the newsworthy immediacy of the subject matter. The most prominent reviewer to consider Neuhaus' propositions was the South African novelist and future Nobel laureate J. M. Coetzee, who wrote about *Dispensations* for the *New York Review of Books* as part of a broader survey of recent work on South Africa, including books about Nelson and Winnie Mandela. Coetzee was certainly critical—he suggested that Neuhaus wasn't as sensitive as he thought to the internal complexities of South African politics in ethnic and intraracial terms, and that his estimations of the African National Congress were distorted by his own anticommunism and selective quoting from party members who espoused particularly virulent revolutionary notions of how to end apartheid. Nevertheless, Coetzee took Neuhaus' effort seriously, and offered strong praise for the distinctive contribution *Dispensations* made to the broader conversation about South Africa: "The best parts of the book—and these parts are substantial—comprise his discussions with churchmen from both sides of the divide about the theology of destiny and the theology of liberation, discussions conducted with rigor and penetration, in a true spirit of inquiry."[12]

Having made this contribution, Neuhaus continued his efforts on other fronts, and by fall 1986 plans had been finalized for the Center on Religion and Society to take over *This World* magazine and put out a first issue by winter the next year, with Neuhaus as editor in chief and an advisory board made up of usual suspects like George Weigel, Peter Berger, and Michael Novak, and also the historian Gertrude Himmelfarb (who was married to Irving Kristol), the Methodist theologian Stanley Hauerwas, and David Novak, a conservative rabbi and scholar of religious philosophy who had been a student of Abraham Joshua Heschel's. *This World* joined the *Lutheran Forum Letter* and the *Religion and Society Report* among the publications Neuhaus was leading and writing for at once, in addition to his contributing reviews, articles, introductions, statements, and so on for a variety of conservative and religious publications. Principal among these venues was *National Review*, which made him its religion editor and regularly published his views on various matters of the day, like religion and the federal judiciary, rivaling versions of patriotism, public policy, socialism, the peace movement, and so on. His views on Catholic matters had the most lasting effects on his future writing and interests, as evidenced by a broad piece entitled "The

Catholic Moment" that appeared in *National Review* in November 1986 and offered the premise, argument, and indeed title for the study he had been working on that year and that would be published in book form the following fall. *The Catholic Moment* would make three major books in four years, matching his late 1970s productivity.[13]

The publisher for his latest book wasn't exactly pleased with his productivity. While grateful to learn from Neuhaus that he would be submitting the manuscript on time, Harper & Row was apprehensive about what he was planning to send them. "I am glad to know we will be receiving the manuscript by December 31 [1986]," Neuhaus' editor wrote him, "but I must tell you we cannot agree to the length of 200,000 words. GOOD HEAVENS! That is over three times the length of the book we had planned! Two hundred thousand words makes a book of almost 600 pages. That's more like 'The Catholic Millennia' than 'The Catholic Moment.'" Never, ever at a loss for words, Neuhaus had an especially large amount to say about the Catholic Church by the time *The Catholic Moment* was published. The book retains significance as a spirited argument for the preeminent importance of the contemporary Catholic Church in the right ordering of world affairs. Neuhaus' evidence rests on the Church's size and global reach, its status "as the world's oldest and most inescapable symbol of moral legitimation," its particular relationship to the United States, and the leadership of John Paul II and also Joseph Ratzinger, all the more evident in an age wherein Neuhaus saw other major Christian denominations—Mainline Protestant churches, notably—as having capitulated to secular liberalism, just as secular liberalism itself offered at best a mundane "closed humanism" that failed to reflect or advance the deepest longings of many believing people around the world. And as he makes clear throughout the book, those longings would best be served by one alignment in particular. "The United States is the dominant power—economic, cultural, and perhaps military—in the world today," Neuhaus declares, while "Rome and the United States are the central influences in the global church today."

In other words, "To 'make it' in the Roman Catholic Church today is to make it either in Rome or in America," even though this means "to make it in one place is to be in tension with the other." As far as Neuhaus was concerned, however—and here he drew extensively and positively both from John Courtney Murray's ideas and from George Weigel's more recent formulations on Catholicism and American democracy in a 1987 book about Catholic thought on war and peace—this could be a productive tension, provided it could be in support of advancing the very best of both contemporary Catholic and U.S. ideas about the human person and political life. Nowhere is this proposal clearer than in his estimation that "there are strong critical elements of the American democratic experiment that are strongly congruent with John Paul's understanding of freedom." Following through on this proposition would become the driving force in his life and work from the late 1980s onward.[14]

The Catholic Moment articulates the religious, specifically American Catholic, dimension of neoconservatism's emphases on advancing morally framed foreign policies and defending democracy as the strongest possible means of winning the Cold War, and in turn establishing the unrivaled power and influence of the United States in world affairs.[15] But in more personal terms, and despite his repeated insistence on the ecumenical frame of his engagements as a Lutheran, the book often reads like an extended justification for a politically engaged religious intellectual's conversion to Catholicism. Neuhaus seems to be not simply writing about Catholicism but instead writing his way toward it, as with early signals like his far-from-detached observation that "eminent converts . . . all have written movingly about discovering in Rome a home in a homeless world, a center of sanity in a world of madness, a refuge from the storms of modernity," only then to dismiss Protestantism "by pathetic contrast" as being "in perpetual heat, ever sniffing about for chances to link up with modernity, to innovate, to accommodate, to make itself agreeable to whomever dictates the manners of the time."

Thereafter, his excitement about Catholicism is obvious in his paeans to the pope—"it seems reasonable to view John Paul II as the most powerful person in the world today"—and in his frank, presumptuous, if not impertinent, estimations of how (meaning, how poorly) many American Catholic bishops publicly affirm and defend the Church's opposition to abortion. The excitement carries through his recurring analyses of Vatican II, its documents, their significance within and beyond the Church, and how he frames and indeed joins the debates over its reception among squishy liberal and reductively conservative Catholics, dismissing both parties to press instead for his own views, John Paul II– and Ratzinger-aligned, about the best possible post-conciliar way forward for Church and world alike. In the midst of all of this, Neuhaus invokes the German theologian Karl Rahner, summarizing one of his formulations as "Being a Roman Catholic was one way of being a Christian, and for many reasons, he believed it to be by far the best way." It's hard to find much disagreement from Neuhaus on this anywhere in *The Catholic Moment.* In short, this is a book written by someone who, under the guise of joining a conversation that he is convinced matters more than any other, seems simultaneously to be catechizing himself and establishing the grounds for joining a faith he has already intellectually accepted as his own.[16]

Respondents to the book certainly took note of the intensity of Neuhaus' Catholic interests, including Methodist theologian Richard Mouw, who wrote him in November 1987 to admit, no doubt speaking for many conservative Protestants during this period, "I continue to observe your work with interest. Privately, I am betting that you will do a Newman and go over to the Roman side one of these days. Or am I seriously misreading recent developments?" Neuhaus wrote back, "No, I'm not planning to 'do a Newman,'" a shorthand reference to nineteenth-century Anglican theologian and cleric John Henry Newman's historic conversion to Catholicism. Rather, he wrote, "Part of the purpose of *The Catholic Moment* . . . is to explain why. Although I'm sure some people will read it as leading to the question, Why not? In any event," he assured Mouw, incorrectly predicting his own near future, "I suggest you cancel your bets." Private responses aside, the bulk of the public response to the book—aside from a positive notice in the *Wall Street Journal* and a respectful one in the *Washington Post*—came from religious publications and critics, many Catholic, with Monsignor George Higgins offering a serious but finally negative treatment of the book in *America* and Michael Novak enthusing about it in the *Cresset.* Lutherans weren't impressed: "Suffice it to say that Luther does not disturb the proceedings in *The Catholic Moment* in any significant way," harrumphed Walter Sundberg in *Reformation.* At some point, most every reviewer noted the apparent paradox, at least for readers not schooled in Arthur C. Piepkorn's ecclesiology, that *Commonweal* editor Peter Steinfels captured crisply for the *New York Times:* "What is a Lutheran pastor doing injecting himself into controversies within the Catholic Church?"[17]

Steinfels posed this question in a January 1988 profile of Neuhaus that attended to the controversy he had stirred in Catholic circles with *The Catholic Moment,* while also reporting on the ways Neuhaus had already started working from his own set of propositions for finding common cause between the leading elements of the Catholic Church and sympathetic Americans: "At Pastor Neuhaus's invitation, Joseph Cardinal Ratzinger, the Vatican official responsible for monitoring Roman Catholic theological orthodoxy, will deliver a lecture in New York this evening (January 27). After his lecture, at St. Peter's Church, at 169 Lexington Avenue near 53d Street, Cardinal Ratzinger, whose efforts to tighten church discipline and reassert papal authority have often met resistance among American Catholics, will participate in a private two-day conference on modern scholarship and the Bible for about two-dozen scholars."

The lecture itself met with dramatic resistance. Shortly after Ratzinger began his remarks before some one thousand listeners gathered at St. Peter's—no Lexington Center ever got off the ground, but Neuhaus nevertheless regarded this as the right place in New

York to host a speech by Ratzinger—a group of gay rights protestors pushed their way into the church. They were chanting "NAZI! FASCIST PIG! ANTI-CHRIST!" Fellow protestors were seated throughout the church, and on cue they stood and joined in the angry chorus against Ratzinger's lead role in articulating and defending the Church's teachings on homosexual relations. No doubt Neuhaus felt vindicated in the requests he had made in advance to New York mayor and friendly acquaintance Ed Koch for a substantial police presence at Ratzinger's public event, reflecting the attention he was sure to receive while in town. After a few minutes of loud and raucous protest, ELCA bishop William Lazareth made his way down to the podium and stood beside Ratzinger, in a show of solidarity. Not that the cardinal himself was visibly perturbed. As the protests waned and the police restored order, an unruffled Ratzinger extemporized, "I think we've had sufficient occasion to listen to this message. It is sufficient now. There are other people here who wish to hear what I have to say, not what you have to say."[18]

The next day, at the beginning of the Ratzinger-led conference sponsored by the Center on Religion and Society, Neuhaus amused his German guest by sharing with him the *New York Post*'s dramatic story about the events of the night before, which was titled "GAY PROTEST ROCKS VATICAN BIGGIE." The conference itself, which took place at the elegant Lotos Club on East 66th, went far more as planned, that is once that plan had finally been agreed on. Neuhaus and Ratzinger had corresponded about a possible event in New York from late 1986 through much of 1987. Ratzinger was open to the idea from the start, but he opted for a more scholarly approach than the one sought by Neuhaus, who wanted the public lecture and accompanying conference to be focused on ecumenism or on "Theology and Public Discourse." Moreover, Ratzinger simply ignored Neuhaus' audaciously forward suggestion that conference invitees be asked to read two works, Ratzinger's *Principles of Catholic Theology* and Neuhaus' own *The Catholic Moment*. Instead, the conference participants gathered "to discuss the contributions of modern biblical scholarship to the Church, to examine the limitations of the historical-critical methods of biblical scholarship, and to explore post-critical sensibilities," a formulation that Neuhaus composed at Ratzinger's direction. Neuhaus invited a combination of Catholics, notably George Weigel, Avery Dulles, and Denver archbishop Francis Stafford, and Protestants, notably William Lazareth, Methodist theologian Thomas Oden, and Lutheran theologian George Lindbeck. John O'Connor opened the proceedings with a disarmingly blunt joke: "In essence, you are looking at the Grand Inquisitor," he said, before introducing Ratzinger in more admiring terms, having already hosted him, Neuhaus, and others for dinner at his residence the night before. Thereafter, O'Connor and Neuhaus gloried in the success of the visit, Neuhaus declaring it "Ratzinger week" in America, marked by generally positive media coverage. In turn, and very much in keeping with the intellectual-ideological project he proposed in *The Catholic Moment,* Neuhaus began planning for something of an "American week" in Rome.[19]

Meanwhile, he continued his Institute on Religion and Democracy–framed conflicts with liberal Christian groups like the Sojourners over U.S. policies toward anticommunist military regimes in Central America. He also turned down the Lutheran Publicity Bureau's request that he use his connections to secure endorsements for one of its publications from the likes of Supreme Court Justice William Rehnquist and Edmund Meese. Instead, he reminded them that "such statements from political figures might be misleading," compared to more credible praise "from prominent church figures and well known pastors." Now very much both of these himself, this status led to overtures he wasn't especially interested in, as when fundamentalist firebrand leader Tim LaHaye sent Neuhaus an effusive letter following a speech Neuhaus gave at a conference on religious liberty. "God has gifted you with intelligence, wit, and sheer guts," LaHaye wrote, which he admired all the more because "most of my ministerial colleagues are gutless wonders, betraying their Lord, their church, and their culture by silence." He asked Neuhaus to keep up the good fight and proposed "a meeting of diverse religious leaders to hammer out an acceptable plan for those who share moral values." Neuhaus, a rapid-fire and robust letter writer always open to praise and collaborations, took a month to reply, and when he did, the letter itself was brief, cordial, almost curt. This was clearly an alliance he didn't want to pursue, especially when a far more appealing one was before him.[20]

In April 1988, Neuhaus had a breakfast meeting with O'Connor, Avery Dulles, Peter Berger, and Michael Novak to discuss a trip that the latter three and Neuhaus were planning to make in June of that year. The catalyst for the trip was the division between how conservative and liberal Catholic thinkers in the United States were framing and promulgating John Paul II's latest encyclical, *Sollicitudo Rei Socialis* ("On Social Concern"), which assessed global inequality from within a Catholic understanding of human dignity and purpose, and from this made criticisms of both capitalist and Marxist systems. Was the pope drawing equivalencies, or were politically motivated respondents spinning his work to their own purposes? Convinced of the latter, at least about those to their left, Neuhaus et al. crossed the Atlantic with a plan "to explore the possibilities of establishing a more sustained conversation between key actors in Rome and some of us in this country who are desirous of placing a more positive construction on the Church's teaching in the United States," as Neuhaus wrote to his colleagues in advance of the trip. He was, in other words, directly and personally trying to fulfill the possibilities tacit in his formulations about the U.S.-Rome double center of global influence he described in *The Catholic Moment.* Just before they left, the selection committee of New York's Riverside Church approached Neuhaus to see if he would consider applying to become senior minister. This might have been a godsend opportunity twenty years earlier, but no longer. Neuhaus declined by explaining, "I believe I am called to my present work for the foreseeable future."[21]

This present work took him, literally, to Rome, along with Weigel, Novak, and Berger. While there, they met with a series of

Vatican officials, including Ratzinger, who was encouraging of their plans, and also with Archbishop Jorge Mejia of the Pontifical Council for Justice and Peace, who was notably displeased—the meeting itself had a "distinctly hostile atmosphere," as George Weigel noted afterward—to learn of Ratzinger's openness to future dialogue with the Americans, and likewise annoyed by Neuhaus' fast-moving and presumptuous plans for Vatican-American collaborations along the axis he had personally spent the last few years creating. Upon returning from Rome, his second significant visit there in three years, Neuhaus attended a state dinner at the White House, where he had "a couple of hours of the most engaging conversation" with the diner beside him, Ronald Reagan. He reported this in a letter to conservative political theorist and moral philosopher Hadley Arkes, the author of a 1987 book *First Things,* whose premise and title would prove important to Neuhaus in the coming years. He also told Arkes about the "intellectual business with the Vatican" that he'd lately been pursuing. This would turn out to be part of the more conclusive pursuit of a church life, mission, and identity that would see Neuhaus turning his ways of ecclesial and personal conciliation in an ever more Rome-ward direction. But first he got fired from his day job.[22]

CHAPTER EIGHTEEN

The Raid

10:45 A.M., Friday, May 5, 1989: Richard John Neuhaus was standing in the rain on Madison Avenue, holding a garbage bag. Beside him were Paul Stallsworth and Davida Goldman, longtime staffers at the Center on Religion and Society, and also two newer hires, Maria McFadden, a young conservative writer who had become managing editor of *This World,* and James Nuechterlein, an American studies professor from Valparaiso University whom Neuhaus had lately recruited to New York to become the editor of *This World.* Eventually, they hailed cabs, dropped off their garbage-bagged belongings at 338 East 19th Street, and then went to lunch at a nearby Italian restaurant. After a good amount of food and drink, Neuhaus directed Stallsworth to find new office space and went back to 338 with Davida, who handed him the Rolodex. Then he got on the phone. Within a year, Neuhaus was directing the newly founded Institute on Religion and Public Life and presiding over its flagship enterprise, *First Things* magazine. Working with him throughout the intervening months and in the years thereafter were the four other people who had found themselves all but literally kicked to the Madison Avenue curb that May 5.[1]

Twenty-four hours earlier, all of them had been gainfully

employed by the Rockford Institute. As of that Friday morning, this was no longer the case. At 9 A.M., representatives from Rockford's main offices in Illinois showed up at the New York office. Leading the way was Rockford president Allan Carlson, who'd taken over from John Howard, the man who had first brought Neuhaus into the organization as the director of its East Coast operation. Carlson was accompanied by a locksmith; two men from Santini Movers; Michael Warder, another member of the Rockford Institute board; and, randomly, Warder's girlfriend—and also by two others whose presence wasn't so random. They were big guys and they didn't talk much. They just stood around, thick arms folded, while Carlson summarily fired everyone, handed out severance checks, and took possession of the office, of the equipment, of everything save personal effects, which the stunned, suddenly ex-employees were allowed to take with them in garbage bags. Before he went into a closed room to talk to Carlson about the situation, an exchange that involved Neuhaus harshly telling Carlson, "You don't want to do this, you don't want to do this," Neuhaus quietly gave Davida Goldman one instruction: take the Rolodex. She did, and when one of the toughs asked to inspect her belongings to see if she was taking anything that belonged to Rockford, she refused. This meant he would have to manhandle a visibly upset fifty-something woman if he wanted to inspect her stuff. He decided not to. And so she got out the door with a very valuable set of contacts, on a Rolodex that technically might have belonged to Rockford but anyway was what it was because of Neuhaus.[2]

It wasn't what happened but how it happened that turned "the Rockford Raid" into a national media story. The office shutdown drama, allegations of financial impropriety, a swirl of personal conflicts intensified by charges of anti-Semitism, racism, and xenophobia—all of this embodied and exposed finally mortal divides between two competing forms of American conservatism by the late 1980s. One model proposed and defended the natural integration of higher order, religiously informed values and principles with sensibilities and ways of life generally associated with rooted, small-town life, cultural homogeneity, and demographic continuities between past and present. The other model advanced that same integration, only with sensibilities and ways of life generally associated with vibrant urban experience, the heterogeneous energies of cosmopolitanism, and demographic dynamism. In their collaboration, Rockford and Neuhaus had tried to combine these models, and they certainly enjoyed some success before both realized that a parting of the ways had become necessary. Over the half decade prior to 1989, the Illinois think tank's interest in developing a national profile by establishing a prominent East Coast presence had aligned very well with Neuhaus' ever-rising profile. This was a profile continually developed through his prodigious writing, his recurring presence in national media, and his distinctively religio-intellectual shuttle diplomacy between New York, Washington, and various points in between and beyond, not least Rome.[3]

But midwestern conservatism and Manhattan conservatism were never going to be one and the same thing, and initially Neuhaus tried to approach this inescapable fact in positive terms. In 1985, he wrote his colleagues at Rockford to complain about an editorial on religious liberty that ran in *Chronicles,* the institute's flagship magazine, and ran counter to his own formulations on the matter. He emphasized that "differences are an important part of the effectiveness and joy of our collaboration," insofar as both parties to that collaboration understood their work as springing from a shared sense of what the renewal of American life would involve. By 1989, however, and specifically because of the arguments and ideas that *Chronicles* was advancing—with the implication that these ideas and arguments were condoned by Rockford itself—Neuhaus could no longer find any effectiveness, never mind joy, in their collaboration. In late February 1989, he wrote a detailed, confidential letter to Allan Carlson, at Carlson's suggestion, "to put into writing some of the concerns that have been raised about the direction of the Rockford Institute." After he expressed gratitude "for the cordial and entirely supportive relationship the Center [on Religion and Society] and I have had with you and John Howard over the past five years," and hopes for only more of the same "for years to come," Neuhaus made a case for why that likely wouldn't happen, unless Rockford made some significant changes. Using the latest issue of *Chronicles* as only the most recent and clear evidence of his concerns, Neuhaus described three areas of signal worry: first, anti-Semitic materials in the magazine's pages; second, nativist sentiments; and third, sectarian attacks on other conservatives, namely conservatives associated with Neuhaus.[4]

Of these, Neuhaus considered anti-Semitism the most worrisome: "morally odious and absolutely intolerable" in and of itself, but also "a direct and potentially lethal attack on [the] purpose" of the Center on Religion and Society, given "the critical role of Christian-Jewish collaboration" in its formal statement of purpose and ongoing effort at "advancing a religiously informed public philosophy for a free society." While Neuhaus noted that he could find evidence for this concern in prior issues of *Chronicles,* he decided to focus his prosecution on its latest, which was dedicated to exploring the current and future implications of America's perennial self-understanding as "a nation of immigrants." Neuhaus particularly attacked the magazine for its positive treatment of Gore Vidal in not one but two articles that credited him as "an authentic champion of a peculiarly American conservatism," as Neuhaus quoted from one of the pieces. In his strongly dissenting reading, Vidal's was an unreconstructed paleo-conservatism marked by what Neuhaus diagnosed as "the logic and language of classic anti-Semitism," which the profile uncritically permitted because, Neuhaus scoffed, apparently "among gentlemen of a certain conservative stripe, a little anti-Semitism is no big deal." Even worse, he continued, Vidal "has written prolifically against . . . traditional values, the family, the influence of religion (especially Christianity), and American 'imperialism,' while enthusiastically supporting abortion, the feminist agenda, and homosexuality." To celebrate such a person, and such positions, as conservative, was simply "grotesque," Neuhaus insisted.[5]

Meanwhile, "fatuous reason," "inflammatory intent," and "sophomoric posturings laced with nastiness" made up *Chronicles* editor Tom Fleming's lead piece for the issue, which called for "the reestablishment of national quotas" for immigrants, quotas that Fleming argued "should give first priority to the population base of the nation," which was hard not to read as code for the defense of white, European claims to American-ness over and against others. Fleming assembled his evidence in support of this case while simultaneously arguing that the very right to make this case was threatened by leftist thought police, who would level charges of racism and xenophobia. He was willing to do so regardless, given the dire stakes: "If the notion of aliens' rights really takes hold, we are in danger of losing the entire concept of American citizenship," and so "we have to quit lying to ourselves about who we are, and what we face." Neuhaus pushed back, hard: "It makes no sense for people to say that they should not be 'stigmatized as xenophobes and racists' when they seem to be endorsing the views of xenophobes and racists, just as it makes no sense for people to say that they are not anti-Semitic when they excuse anti-Semitism and celebrate anti-Semites." Having thoroughly established his rationale for rejecting the ideas and arguments to which *Chronicles* seemed committed, Neuhaus made his primary request to Carlson, a request for assurance "that in the future the Rockford Institute will have nothing to do with views that fair-minded and intelligent persons might reasonably understand to be xenophobic, racist, and nativist."

He wasn't finished in airing his grievances. Neuhaus next took issue with *Chronicles* for its ongoing campaign to run down other conservatives and wondered if this was Fleming's private battle turned public or a different direction [for] the Rockford Institute: "The current issue, like others, is filled with sneering references to neo-conservatives, global democrats, the New York–Washington axis of self-serving pseudo conservatives, ad nauseum. Among those who fall into *Chronicles'* definition of the enemy," Neuhaus pointed out, were people involved directly with Rockford's own New York operation and likewise those "closely associated with it," including Peter Berger, William F. Buckley, Jr., and also *Commentary* editor Norman Podhoretz. The last of these had likely intensified Neuhaus' reaction to *Chronicles* by writing to him in February 1989 about the issue in question with similar concerns that boiled down to his declaration, "I know an enemy when I see one, and *Chronicles* has become just that so far as I am personally concerned—and I would hope, so far as any decent conservative of any stripe is concerned."[6]

Neuhaus included a copy of Podhoretz's letter and a detailed critique of the issue in question from George Weigel along with his own, which ended by stressing, "This memo should not be construed as an ultimatum, yet I would be less than candid if I did not say that, unless these concerns are effectively addressed, some of us would be forced to reconsider our relationship to the Rockford Institute. None of us wants that." Carlson didn't respond well, at least judging from Neuhaus' subsequent correspondence with him. By Neuhaus' construal, based on a March 1989 letter he wrote to Carlson, Rockford's president took the first letter as a personal attack and didn't address Neuhaus' criticisms of *Chronicles* or questions of where Rockford's own sympathies lay. And so Neuhaus pointed out the inevitable, which he noted was underscored by phone conversations he had had with Carlson and Howard both during this period: "both there and here the conclusion is being reached that we should begin the process of amicable separation between the Rockford Institute and the Center on Religion and Society." These plans involved a formal break effective August 1, 1989, pending ratification of the decision by Rockford's board of directors at a May 8, 1989, meeting, according to a March 31 letter Neuhaus sent to William J. Lehrfeld, a Washington-based attorney whom he asked for counsel on the legal aspects of the Center's becoming an independent entity. In this same letter, Neuhaus made it clear that "between the Center and the Rockford Institute, it is intended that this separation be entirely amicable."[7]

So what led Carlson to make an early, harsh, and surprise move against Neuhaus and his Center, just three days before the Rockford board was to meet and ratify the plan? The answer came to light after the May 5 raid. More accurately, multiple and conflicting answers came to light, as an "entirely amicable" separation turned into a months-long feud that played out in the national media and more broadly within American conservatism. It began with "Magazine Dispute Reflects Rift on U.S. Right," a front-page, above-the-fold story in the May 16, 1989, issue of the *New York Times.* The *Times* had obtained Neuhaus' confidential memo to Carlson, quoted its criticisms and accusations, and then interviewed both men. Neuhaus rehearsed the same points he'd made in the memo, while Carlson argued that the closing of the Center had been brought about by "a shortage of money and by a widespread suspicion among the Rockford directors that Pastor Neuhaus was ignoring the parent organization's policies." Two weeks later, David Frum wrote about the "Cultural Clash on the Right" for the *Wall Street Journal.* In broader terms, Frum explained, "many conservatives view the Rockford-Neuhaus fight as symbolic of a permanent split in the intellectual coalition [that was] formed in the 1970s" by different conservative movements, who were united by their concern about the state of a nation governed too much by the dictates of leftist liberalism and secular progressivism.[8]

But Frum also pointed to a less intellectual source for the suddenness of the break: money. "The New York center had been promised in February a $200,000 grant from the Bradley Foundation of Wisconsin," the delivery of which was held up, according to Frum, over "whether the money had been granted against past expenses" and therefore belonged to Rockford, or "against future expenses," in which case the majority would go to Neuhaus' new, independent entity. Carlson disputed Frum's account in a letter to the editor, noting that Bradley had in fact decided not to give any of the actually $280,000 grant to Rockford in April of that year, which in turn made the continued operation of the New York center through to the end of July unfeasible. Carlson further alleged that the reasons for the break included Neuhaus' persistently working around, if not against,

Rockford to secure funding for his own work from various organizations; his threatening to resign and start up a competitor center; and the fact that he "repeatedly made damaging allegations concerning his employer to important outside parties." Whether these "important outside parties" were the likes of Podhoretz and Buckley or funders like the Bradley Foundation, Carlson didn't explain.

Nevertheless, these players and many others weighed in variously on the controversy; in addition to pieces in the *Times* and the *Journal,* there were stories and columns (that displayed conflicting sympathies) in dailies from across the country, including the *Washington Post* and the *Washington Times,* the *Chicago Tribune,* the *Arizona Republic,* the *Dallas Times Herald,* the *Milwaukee Journal,* and the *Indianapolis Star.* Religious publications—*New Oxford Review,* the *Lutheran,* the *National Catholic Register*—also took note, the latter reporting, if not crowing, that "the Cream of the religious right suffered a blow" that left "an influential theologian . . . unceremoniously fired." *National Review* was far more sympathetic to its religion editor in its own editorial on the matter, characterizing Rockford's May 5 move as something "much as Don Corleone would have done," before more substantially observing that within conservatism itself "there will always be strains, this way and that . . . and when efforts to maintain quarreling factions under the same roof fail, it is sometimes necessary to excrete unwholesome bodies, as in the past was done, e.g., to the John Birchers and the Ayn Randians." Hoping this wouldn't prove necessary with "Rockford conservatism," a troubling species based on its recent actions and publications, the editors of *National Review* made it clear that their own commitments were squarely with Neuhaus, who "is better off removed from any formal affiliation with Rockford, and Rockford certainly made that easy for him and his colleagues."[9]

In retrospect, the Rockford Raid might have been Richard John Neuhaus' best possible catalyst for the culminating project of his public ministry: *First Things* magazine. If for years now he had been making a case for why the religiously informed conservatism that he espoused and embodied should be welcomed into the public square, the details that emerged about *Chronicles* and Rockford's conservatism during coverage of the break significantly helped that case along: compared to the rearguard and resenting sensibilities that were emerging from Rockford and its magazine, Neuhaus and his arguments were far more persuasively positioned to contribute to American public life in ways that were forward-looking, integrative, and reasonable. His well-placed and sympathetic friends certainly thought so and encouraged him on to a new project. Peter Berger suggested a magazine that combined the conservative-minded, religiously informed articles, reviews, and essays that featured in the quarterly issues of *This World* with the *Religion and Society Report,* Neuhaus' monthly set of reliably incisive, pithy, caustic, funny, and gossipy observations about religion and public life. He also suggested that if Neuhaus really wanted to make an impact on broader conversation, the new magazine should run as a monthly, not a quarterly. Neuhaus was (of course) open to the idea of writing even more than he already was, but if the new magazine was indeed going to have a presence in an already crowded landscape of opinion journals, it would have to offer something distinctive, something potential readers couldn't find, say, in magazines about religion and American life like the liberal-minded *Commonweal* and the *Christian Century*; or in an ideologically conservative, policy-driven intellectual publication that was friendly enough to religious matters, like *Commentary*; or in a more politically engaged, conservative opinion-making publication like *National Review.*[10]

The potential distinctiveness of the new magazine was evidenced by the people Neuhaus turned to in search of this answer. Beyond Berger and Nuechterlein, Neuhaus brought together people like David Novak, Michael Novak, Stanley Hauerwas, and George Weigel for meetings about the new venture, which often took place in his living room at 338 East 19th Street: he brought them together not simply because they were like-minded friends and colleagues, of which he had found and cultivated many by 1989. They were certainly as much, and indeed among his closest and most respected. But independent of this personal connection, these were writers, scholars, and intellectuals who weren't persuaded by secular liberalism's proposals, nor were they attracted to rearguard or brimstone conservatisms. Instead, each of them self-consciously began from religious first principles and theological concerns in purposefully engaging dimensions of American culture, society, and politics. Their interests and work were meaningfully differentiated—Nuechterlein, a Lutheran historian and political thinker; Berger, a contrarian sociologist and Lutheran; Weigel and Michael Novak, Catholic neoconservative public intellectuals; Hauerwas, a pacifist Methodist theologian; and David Novak, a rabbi and moral philosopher interested in Jewish-Christian dialogue—but they were united by their alignment with Neuhaus' own intellectual mission and public ministry.

All of which meant that a clear way to continue and indeed enhance that mission and ministry would be to offer a recurring public platform for work by this group and others like them, with hopes of discovering a readership that was waiting for just such work. In short, Neuhaus predicted, correctly, that his writings and those of some of his closest friends and colleagues collectively formed a theologically ordered intellectual community and movement that others would want to join, support, and read, based on shared interests and priorities that were embodied in the new magazine's title: *First Things: A Journal of Religion and Public Life.*[11]

Later that same summer, Neuhaus left New York for his annual summer vacation at the family cottage in Pembroke, where he could visit with his mother, his few cousins in town, his brother living across the river in Quebec, and also host friends and visitors like the rabbi David Novak, who would show up with cabbage rolls and fail to keep up with Neuhaus as they sipped whiskey on the riverfront porch. By then, Neuhaus already had his staff in place, brought forward from the now dead Center on Religion and Society to work instead for the newly founded Institute on Religion and Public Life. It would purpose a similar program of activities as had its predecessor, and could count on funding commitments secured from Bradley and from the other conservative donors—Scaife, Olin, Smith-Richardson—who had initially supported Neuhaus in the mid-1980s when he began his association with Rockford, and who were more than willing to continue that association now. He also had the practicalities of a magazine launch and distribution plan in place thanks to Richard Vaughan, who ran a publishing management firm that had previously worked with Rockford publications but decided to work with Neuhaus instead. In correspondence with Vaughan, Neuhaus made it clear how crucial the magazine's success was to him: "We have to be thinking about how we can keep *First Things* going, no matter what happens."

Of course, this would be a shared effort. Through his summer meetings and Rolodex spinning, he had identified some of the leading figures who would serve on the board of the institute and likewise help develop the new magazine from early ideas to a fully realized publication. George Weigel was especially influential in this effort and in other important developments in Neuhaus' life during this period, and not simply in intellectual or religious terms. For Neuhaus, a bachelor pastor who lived at a great distance from his siblings and their families, and in a religious community with other single people, Weigel offered a thriving young family life to enjoy amid professional matters. This was evident that summer, when Weigel, his wife, Joan, and their children went to Pembroke and stayed with Neuhaus at the nearby cottage, a yearly trip that had started a few years earlier and would continue through to Neuhaus' final years. When he wasn't handing out Royal Canadian Air Force wings to the Weigel children for successful swimming feats, Neuhaus planned out the particular elements of the magazine with Weigel over hours of conversation in the simple rooms of the cottage and on the deck overlooking the Ottawa River.[12]

That fall, back in New York, plans continued apace for the new magazine, with Neuhaus and Davida working out of the basement at 338 and Nuechterlein set up in borrowed space at the Committee for the Free World's offices, space provided by its executive director Midge Decter, a longtime Neuhaus friend and supporter. This arrangement held until the operation moved into its permanent home at 156 Fifth Avenue, a onetime home of the National Council of Churches. This unexpected coincidence led Neuhaus later to quip, "We did not choose the building for its historic associations, and when we moved in we were undecided whether rites of exorcism or of rededication, or some combination of the two, were in order. While we did not choose it for those associations, and while we certainly don't want to make a big deal of it, there is the intriguing possibility that Hegel's 'cunning of history' is at work. Now that it is so manifestly obvious that the National Council of Churches of late failed to bring a measure of coherence to issues of religion and public life, it is perhaps fitting that the task should be started afresh from 156 Fifth."[13]

That task, as paramount as it was for him, was far from Neuhaus' singular focus in the final months of 1989 and the first half of 1990. In fall 1989, he continued to put out the *Lutheran Forum Letter* and the *Religion and Society Report*—the subscription list of which would be germinal for *First Things*—and wrote a series of columns for *National Review*, an essay for the *Christian Century*, a review for *Commentary*, another for the UK-based *Times Literary Supplement*, an essay for a book about John Courtney Murray, and a paper on the secular philosopher Richard Rorty for a January conference in California on the ongoing legacies of the Enlightenment, hosted by the conservative Claremont Institute. Also on his fall agenda was early work toward a June 1990 conference about the present circumstances and future course of Lutheranism, more immediately pressing work for a January 1990 conference about the present circumstances and future course of conservatism, and, not least, a speech for a major international audience.

In November 1989, with the fall of the Berlin Wall dramatically punctuating a series of democratic revolutions in formerly Communist countries from across Eastern Europe and pointing to the inexorable collapse of Communism, intellectuals and politicians at home and abroad turned their attention to world affairs beyond the Cold War. In this context, Neuhaus was invited to speak at the 1990 World Economic Forum, in Davos, Switzerland, specifically on "Religion and Democratic Revolution." Before Davos, Neuhaus went to Washington at the end of January, for a conference of some twenty leading conservative intellectuals, with William F. Buckley, Jr., as the titular host and presider while, as the *Washington Times* reported in its coverage, Neuhaus was in fact the prime mover behind the event. But reporting aside, Neuhaus' decisive influence was evidenced by the invitation list—which notably excluded Rockford people and like-minded allies, who were now dismissed as "paleoconservatives" by comparison to the neoconservatives in attendance at the conference—and by the most prominent piece of swag the attendees received, an advance copy of *First Things* 1.1.[14]

That first issue—copies of which Neuhaus also shared at Davos with attendees like the Agha Khan—featured contributions by longstanding and future members of Neuhaus' circle—Weigel, Hauerwas, Michael Novak, and David Novak—and also from Lutheran scholar Robert Benne, the Catholic theologian Russell Hittinger, Catholic legal scholar and Harvard law professor Mary Ann Glendon, and prominent, simpatico conservatives like the British writer Paul Johnson. The issue's heavy-stock beige pages also debuted "The Public Square," Neuhaus' own monthly survey of "Religion, Culture, and Public Life." Among other items in that first offering, Neuhaus thoroughly savaged Rockford's kind of conservatism as outmoded, distasteful, even dangerous: if Carlson and Rockford kicked Neuhaus out of his office, he responded by kicking them out of late-twentieth-century American conservatism. The magazine's first issue also featured a founding manifesto, entitled "Putting First Things First," that explained its focus and concerns—religion and public life as per Neuhaus' established formulations, which would consider all aspects of the ongoing story of a civilization defined by the interplay of beliefs, systems, and structures originating in Athens, Rome, and Jerusalem, a civilization that had lately neglected Jerusalem to its own detriment. The following statement also made a governing promise to its readers:

> *In these pages the reader will find items that report, analyze, instruct, warn, exhort, and sometimes entertain. But the key word is conversation. A real conversation, as distinct from intellectual chatter, is marked by discipline and continuity. Gilbert Keith Chesterton observed that "tradition is the democracy of the dead." Agreeing with that, we intend to take on the questions of today and tomorrow, but always in conversation with the best that has been thought and said in the past. At every historical moment, the contemporary is afflicted by the crippling conceit of its utter novelty. We hope* First Things *will be an antidote to that intellectual and moral disease. When in the course of human events something new is launched, a decent respect for the opinion of others calls for a word of explanation. Of course this brief statement of what we're up to will be vindicated or falsified by this and subsequent issues of* First Things. *We very much hope that you will be part of the continuing conversation, and we invite you to hold us to our word.*

The early evidence was very promising: hopeful of securing five thousand subscribers and distributing another two thousand issues via newsstands and complimentary copies, *First Things* had six thousand subscribers in three months and a circulation of ten thousand after a year. The magazine had twenty thousand subscribers after three years, and thirty-thousand by the mid-1990s, a number that would remain constant thereafter and triumphantly exceed Neuhaus' initial prediction that "the reading public for a serious journal is 20,000."[15]

When he wasn't writing, reviewing, lecturing, or working on *First Things* during this period, Neuhaus was also, of course, preaching. By late 1989, he was living out his church ministry as an associate pastor at Immanuel Lutheran on East 88th, on the Upper East Side, a few blocks away from Central Park, a congregation with a joint Missouri-ECLA affiliation that Neuhaus became associated with after his time at St. Peter's and at Trinity Lutheran on the Lower East Side. Little is known about Neuhaus' contributions to Immanuel Lutheran or to the other Lutheran congregations he was involved with in the period between his departure from St. John the Evangelist and his conversion to Catholicism, and that's likely because there's comparatively little to be said about them. Across these three affiliations, he had associate pastor status and preached and led a regular Sunday service, but the calls he secured for himself from his ecclesial superiors throughout—to be a "pastor on assignment" focused on "urban ministries" as he defined these—enabled him largely to be exempt from any further local congregation involvements. As a result, he lost any sense of active involvement or deep investment in the lives and struggles of ordinary churchgoers comparable to what he had experienced, indeed cherished, for years in Brooklyn.

Avoiding such connections wasn't Neuhaus' motivation, and indeed when he was called on as a pastor rather than as a public intellectual by colleagues, he responded as such, as when David Brooks, then working at the editorial pages of the *Wall Street Journal,* asked Neuhaus to write a get-well card to William J. Eddy, a minister friend of Brooks' who was "a great admirer" of Neuhaus and in the final stages of brain cancer. Neuhaus fulfilled the request immediately and wrote a moving note to Eddy, which began, "The usual thing to be said in such circumstances is that there is not much to be said, but you and I know that is not the case. Between Christians there is a great deal to be said." Such ministrations took the place of regular pastoral work within a congregation during this period and thereafter, alongside a broader and consistent array of vocational mentoring and personal counseling, for Community of Christ residents, for friends and colleagues, for friends of friends, readers, and assorted young people who sought him out or were encouraged by others to enter his orbit. To all of this he devoted a great deal of time and energy, alongside the commitments he made to his writings and to his various intellectual, political, and religious involvements in national and international contexts.[16]

And never mind remarks for Davos or D.C. conservatives or the various demands of starting up *First Things*—in late 1989 and early 1990, Neuhaus was trying to make sense of whether there was still a viable place for himself in Lutheranism. To that end, from November onward, he was in correspondence with a series of influential Lutherans—Carl Braaten, Paul Hinlicky, Robert Jenson, Leonard Klein, George Lindbeck, and his own bishop, William Lazareth—about plans for a June 1990 conference at St. Olaf College in Minnesota. The conference was set to consider the state of contemporary American Lutheranism and particularly to discuss the growing and divisive liberalism taking root in ELCA (the church that broke away from Missouri in the aftermath of the Seminex crisis and had since merged with two other Lutheran churches) over matters of sexuality, gender, abortion, and ecumenism. As Carl Braaten matter-of-factly captured the situation at the time, "Not everyone was mad about the same things, but neither was everybody happy with everything." Neuhaus' own hopes were for a "confessional renewal," which for him meant a return to what he regarded as the core self-understanding and purpose of Lutheranism itself, as a reform movement internal to the universal Catholic Church that was working toward a healing of the breach of the sixteenth century. At the conference itself, divisions between what Braaten terms "evangelical Catholic" Lutherans and "denominational" Lutherans, over ecumenism, ministry, and ecclesiology, were more pronounced than evidence of shared doctrinal concerns. And while Neuhaus was one of the main speakers, no doubt pressing for "confessional renewal" by his decades-long construal, and despite his outsized profile compared to many of the other participants, his was but one proposal for Lutheranism's future, and account of its past. Unlike his proposals for the future of conservatism, or for a distinctive new magazine, his proposal for a Lutheranism renewed by catholic-framed and catholic-focused ecclesiology was not to be the victor.[17]

Neuhaus' formal involvement at St. Olaf was as editor of the *Lutheran Forum Letter,* one of the conference sponsors, even though he had tendered his resignation from editing the journal to his ELCA bishop, William Lazareth, in March 1990, the same month that *First Things* came out. That timing was logical enough, and Neuhaus promised Lazareth he would stay on past the June conference, through to the end of July. He went to Pembroke in August, the same month the *Christian Century* reported that "rumors have been flying for weeks that a prominent Lutheran clergyman is about to leave the 'encircling gloom' of Protestantism and 'go over to Rome.'" The article wittily predicted that "if this Catholic moment does arrive, we anticipate that it will be announced at a press conference—nakedly, in the public square." Neuhaus was interviewed for the piece, and did nothing to dispel the rumor: "That such a move has been under active consideration for years is no secret. I have written about it and spoken about it. That it is under active consideration now is not news."[18]

It was news to Orlen Lapp, Clem Neuhaus' successor as pastor of St. John's in Pembroke. Over the years, Neuhaus would preach at St. John's while staying at the cottage for August and often catch up with Lapp at his farm, whether over a beer or while bringing the Weigel children along to see the pastor's horses. These were for leisurely riding through the lovely country now; they were no longer necessary for the snowy treks to the mission church that the old St. John's pastor used to make in the 1930s. And so, meeting outside the horse barn some fifty-four years after he was born in Pembroke and baptized in the kitchen sink of the family home beside his father's church, Neuhaus came to see his father's successor. He shared his plan to convert to Catholicism that September. Lapp was stunned and tried to argue, reminding Neuhaus that as a cradle Lutheran he knew full well why he didn't want to be a Catholic.

But Neuhaus was settled on this, and it felt good and right, though he knew his father would be turning over in his grave, and he was worried about what his mother would think when she found out. But those weren't worries enough. And so, later that August, after preaching a final time in his father's church, on the hymn "The Church's One Foundation," and posing for a picture with his mother before its dark wood altar, Neuhaus left Pembroke for New York, and Missouri for Rome.[19]

Part IV

FIRST THINGS FIRST: A CATHOLIC PRIEST IN THE PUBLIC SQUARE, 1990–2009

"There is now a great peace, but I know it will not always be peaceful. I ask you, of your goodness, to pray for me."

Richard John Neuhaus, letter announcing his conversion to Catholicism (1990)

CHAPTER NINETEEN

Neuhaus Becomes a Catholic . . . Neuhaus Named Catholic of the Year

September 10, 1990

Dear friends,

On September 8, 1990, the Nativity of Mary, I was received into full communion with the Roman Catholic Church. In the months ahead, I will be preparing to enter the priesthood of the Catholic Church. With the full support of my bishop, John Cardinal O'Connor, I will continue to serve as director of the Institute on Religion and Public Life and as a member of the Community of Christ.

This decision is the result of years of prayer, reflection, study, conversation, and, I firmly believe, the leading of the Holy Spirit. Especially over the last five years, I have resisted with great difficulty the recognition that I could no longer give an answer convincing to others or to me as to why I was not a Roman Catholic.

Over the last 20 years and more, I have repeatedly and publicly urged that the separated ecclesial existence of Lutheranism, if it was once necessary, is no longer necessary; and if no longer necessary, such separated existence is no longer justified. Therefore, co-operating with other evangelical catholics who shared my understanding of the Lutheran destiny and duty according to the Augsburg Confession, I devoted myself to the healing of the breach of the sixteenth century between Rome and the Reformation. This meant and means ecclesial reconciliation and the restoration of full communion with the Bishop of Rome and the Churches in communion with the Bishop of Rome. That is a consummation for which I continue to pray, and to which I earnestly hope my present decision will contribute.

At the same time, I have been brought, reluctantly but surely, to the recognition that this understanding of the Augsburg Confession and of the Reformation has been rejected—in institutional fact, and frequently in theological principle—by the several jurisdictions of the Lutheran Communion. With respect to the Evangelical Lutheran Church in America of which I was a pastor, the evidence compelled me to the conclusion that its operative understanding of the Church is informed not by the ecclesiology of the New Testament, nor by that of the Fathers, nor by that of the Augsburg Confession, but by American denominationalism. I can no longer persuade myself that Lutheranism is an evangelical catholic movement of Gospel reform within and for the one Church of Christ. It now seems to me that Lutheranism is a Protestant denomination among Protestant denominations, and is determined to remain so.

I have always understood that, as I was baptized into one Christ, so was I baptized into his one, holy, catholic, and apostolic Church. It was therefore my desire and duty, as a Western Christian formed by the Reformation tradition, to be in full communion with the fullest and mostly rightly ordered reality of that Church through time. I am persuaded that that reality subsists in the Roman Catholic Church. I can readily attest that, in the words of the Second Vatican Council, "many elements of sanctification and of truth can be found outside the Church's visible structure." *Lumen Gentium* continues, "These elements, however, as gifts properly belonging to the Church of Christ, possess an inner dynamic toward Catholic unity." The inner dynamic of the catholic substance I knew in Lutheranism has compelled me to become a Roman Catholic.

I know well the claim of some Lutherans that separated ecclesial existence is necessary for the sake of the Gospel—as the Gospel is understood in terms of justification by grace through faith because of Christ. I beg such Lutherans to consider that the Gospel can be proclaimed today in the Roman Catholic Church, and in fact is so proclaimed. Moreover, it is by no means evident that the Lutheran denomination of our time does, as a matter of fact, bear witness to that Gospel.

The Reformers rightly insisted that the Church lives from the Gospel. Lutheranism, however, has not understood that the Church is an integral part of the Gospel. The Church is neither an abstract idea nor merely a voluntary association of believers, but a divinely commissioned and ordered community of apostolic faith, worship, and discipleship through time. "I delivered to you what I also received," said St. Paul (I Cor. 15). Under the guidance of the Spirit promised to the Church, apostolic Scripture is joined to apostolic order in the faithful transmission and interpretation of revealed truth. The Gospel is the proclamation of God's grace in Christ and his body in the Church. It is for the sake of that Gospel, and the unity of the Church gathered by that Gospel, that I am today a Roman Catholic.

I cannot begin to express adequately my gratitude for all the goodness I have known in the Lutheran Communion. There I was baptized, there I learned my prayers, there I was introduced to Scripture and creed, there I was nurtured by Christ on Christ, there I came to know the utterly gratuitous love of God by which we live astonished. For my theological formation, for friendships beyond numbering, for great battles fought, for mutual consolations in defeat, for companionship in ministry—for all this I give thanks and know that I will forever be in debt to the Church called Lutheran. Most especially I am grateful for my 30 years as a pastor. There is nothing in that ministry that I would repudiate, except my many sins and shortcomings. My becoming a priest in the Roman Catholic Church will be the completion and right ordering of what was begun 30 years ago. Nothing that was good is rejected, all is fulfilled.

I have been left in no doubt that many Lutherans, and perhaps others, will be grievously disappointed and even angered by this decision. I cannot ask them to try to understand. As God permits, I will at some future time give a fuller explanation of why I have done what I had to do. Those who know my writings know that I am aware of the problems to be encountered also in the Roman Catholic Church. But for now it is enough, it is beyond all deserving, that I have been brought this far. To those of you with whom I have travelled in the past, know that we travel together still. In the mystery of Christ and his Church, nothing is lost, and the broken will be mended. If as I do believe, my communion with Christ's Church is now the fuller, then it needs be that my unity with all who are in Christ is the stronger.

I do not presume to think that I could ever repay those who, over the months and years, have borne with me through the studies, conversations, arguments, and doubts of this decision's making. I am most grateful to my former bishop, William Lazareth, and my new bishop, John Cardinal O'Connor, for their friendship, understanding, counsel, and constant support.

There is now a great peace, but I know it will not always be peaceful. I ask you, of your goodness, to pray for me.—Richard[1]

In Rome, a delighted John Paul II heard of Neuhaus' decision while at lunch with Australian archbishop George Pell; in Missouri, a vindicated Herman Otten all but declared *good riddance* and *I told you so*. Meanwhile, Neuhaus' sisters were driving to Pembroke. Richard had given them a few days' advance notice, and admitted he hadn't told Ella. He didn't seem inclined to either. With other siblings worried about how the aging matriarch, a lifelong Lutheran and wife and mother to Lutheran pastors, would take the news, Johanna and Mim decided they would fly to Ottawa, rent a car, and go be with her when she found out. They were too late. The *Ottawa Citizen* broke the news the very day Johanna and Mim arrived. "So Richard's going to turn Catholic," Ella said. That was all she said.[2]

In the months following Neuhaus' conversion—he was formally received into the Catholic Church on September 8, 1990, at a Mass celebrated by John O'Connor in his private chapel beside

St. Patrick's Cathedral, with Avery Dulles and George Weigel serving as his confirmation sponsors—few others would prove as tersely accepting and matter-of-fact in their response. Lutherans, particularly those who understood themselves as evangelical catholics along the lines of Neuhaus' self-understanding before he converted, variously lamented the decision. Robert Wilken told the *New York Times* he disagreed with his best friend's rationale and remained convinced that Lutheranism retained capacities and resources for ecclesial renewal beyond its present difficulties. Many other Lutherans debated the implications for the state and prospects of the broader church, while most everyone (save Herman Otten) at least wished their former brother well. And despite his requests not to let his conversion encourage Catholic triumphalism, conservative Catholics already attuned to Neuhaus' understanding of the faith celebrated the news. For instance, based on overwhelming reader preference, *Catholic Twin Circle* magazine named him "Catholic of the Year" after just four months. Meanwhile, others wondered how much the currents of public life itself—politics, ideology, and the culture wars—had factored in the decision. Rejecting such interpretations, Neuhaus was adamant in framing the decision in theological and ecclesial terms. This higher-order, more exclusively religious framing was undoubtedly the case, but by his own efforts for years if not decades, Neuhaus had consistently proposed to the world at large that matters of theology and ecclesiology couldn't be artificially divided from matters of public life, from politics, ideology, and the culture wars. In other words, his own conversion was at once a deeply personal decision and an act informed by decades of change in Western Christianity, American church life, and political-intellectual realignments dating from the sixties through to the end of the Cold War.[3]

During his first year as a Catholic, Neuhaus received a personal course of instruction and preparation for his ordination as a priest from his good friend the Jesuit priest and theologian Avery Dulles, at John O'Connor's direction. In the meantime, he attended

Mass at Epiphany Church, a few blocks from 338 East 19th Street, and sported a necktie while at the *First Things* office. He also wasted little time making his presence felt in broader Catholic circles, only now as a fellow Catholic rather than as an exceedingly interested observer. He focused particularly on the intersection of Catholicism, U.S. foreign policy, and world affairs following Saddam Hussein's invasion of Kuwait in August 1990, which served as the catalyst for the first Gulf War. This conflict followed fast upon the fall of Communism and opened up a domestic debate about the United States' strategic interests in the Persian Gulf, its moral responsibilities to the people of Kuwait, and the nature and significance of its leading role in post–Cold War global affairs, affairs that were especially focused in late 1990 and early 1991 on deliberations over whether to take decisive action against Iraq. Religious leaders offered strong and concerned views. In his Christmas 1990 *Urbi et Orbi* address, John Paul II declared "*The light of Christ is with the tormented Nations of the Middle East.* For the areas of the Gulf, we await with trepidation for the threat of the conflict to disappear. May leaders be convinced that *war is an adventure with no return!*" With Hussein defying UN ultimatums to withdraw his forces from Kuwait, a U.S.-led full-scale military operation commenced on January 17, 1991. The pope then turned his efforts to helping secure a swift resolution to the conflict, through public statements and personal communications with President Bush, Hussein, and the UN secretary-general.[4]

Meanwhile, in the United States, discussion and debate over the war amounted to a "great and confusedly democratic deliberation" to which "significant sectors of the country's religious leadership contributed little," as far as Neuhaus was concerned. He offered this blunt estimation in a major essay for the *Wall Street Journal*, entitled "Just War and This War," which ran twelve days after U.S. and allied forces began an air campaign against Hussein's forces. The piece accomplished three aims: first, it contextualized Bush's January 28 declaration that "Operation Desert Storm" was a "just war" by providing a historical context for just war doctrine, citing the works of Augustine, Aquinas, and seventeenth-century Dutch philosopher Hugo Grotius, and detailing the principles and criteria that guide just war deliberations. Second, it surveyed the roles of American religious leaders in "the great moral debate leading up to our action in the Gulf," and found that the majority "did not so much inform and elevate [that] moral discourse as promote their own policy prescriptions"—which were predominantly in opposition to the U.S.-led campaign. In particular (as ever), Neuhaus criticized the National Council of Churches for what he regarded as a blinkered pro-peace campaign that had more to do with nostalgia for the 1960s antiwar movement than with prudential judgments about the situation in the Persian Gulf. In more involved terms, he also took the National Conference of Catholic Bishops to task over November 1990 statements calling for political leaders to consider the ethical (as well as military and geopolitical) implications of the war, and calling in turn for the U.S. government "to continue to pursue the course of peaceful pressure and not resort to war."

Having quoted the bishops, Neuhaus chastised them for the "patronizing" presumption "that religious leaders have a corner on moral concern and wisdom, while politicians and generals are interested in 'simply military and geopolitical considerations.'" He further identified "dissonance between at least the tone of the bishops' statements and other statements of the church," specifically formulations from the Vatican II document *Gaudium et Spes,* about the legitimacy of differing opinions on specific matters, and the Church's own respect for the authority of experts on these matters. Finally, he openly, sarcastically questioned the bishops' competency in making judgments about the situation in the Gulf: "One wonders whether the bishops really want the faithful to have to choose between their comprehension of the military and geopolitical realities and that of, say, George Bush, [National Security Advisor] Lee Aspin and [Chairman of the Joint Chiefs of Staff] Colin Powell."[5]

An inveterate citer of John Paul II's words since the late 1970s, Neuhaus didn't once mention the pope or any of his statements about

Iraq in his two thousand words published in the *Wall Street Journal* about the contributions of religious leaders to deliberations over a major international war. Moreover, Neuhaus' criticisms come across as selective, if not contradictory: generally convinced that religiously informed propositions were crucial to the healthy functioning of a pluralist democracy, he faulted such propositions and deemed them effectively unwelcome when he clearly disagreed with them. Charges of selective citing and criticizing would follow Neuhaus for the rest of his life and work, particularly over his positions on questions of war and U.S. foreign policy and his assessments of other religious leaders and intellectuals, usually those on the Left. He always disputed such charges, putting his considerable rhetorical and argumentative skills to work. This pattern was evident from the start of his life as a publicly engaged Catholic intellectual, when prominent left-leaning priest George Higgins wrote a column for *Catholic New York* accusing Neuhaus (and also Michael Novak and George Weigel, in their own just war arguments) of working to a rather obvious double standard: "Why is it deemed appropriate to criticize the bishops for opposing the war while remaining completely silent about the pope's statements?" Higgins hazarded a guess: "The polemical tone of the criticism of the bishops, coupled with complete silence about papal statements about the war, raises the suspicion that the critics delight in bishop bashing." Neuhaus responded with a letter to the editor in which he insisted there was "a qualitative difference between publicly criticizing the NCCB and publicly criticizing the Holy Father," and then cited Catholic doctrine's privileging of the teaching office of the latter over the former, and also noted the narrow gauge of his focus (just war theory in an American context about the situation in the Gulf, about which John Paul II had said nothing, for his pronouncements addressed war and peace in the Middle East).[6]

Neuhaus was absolutely in the right, technically, but he came across in this exchange as either blissfully or purposefully ignorant of how his high profile and extensive effort to "respectfully note several problems" (as he put it) with the bishops' statements could be perceived as a concerted effort to undermine their efforts. Regardless, he pressed on in his effort, if more discreetly. A month after he wrote about the bishops and not about the pope for the *Wall Street Journal,* Neuhaus took a premium back-channel approach to exerting his influence on the Church's response to the question of war against Iraq. He wrote to Ratzinger. After noting, "It pains me to be critical of our bishops' conference, and I hope my comments are appropriately restrained," Neuhaus did in private what he wouldn't do in public: "Some of the public statements of the Holy Father in the last two weeks have caused considerable consternation here," he wrote, because "at least in what we have seen, he has not lifted up traditional just war criteria" in making these statements. Moreover, the effect of John Paul's words, which Neuhaus summarized to be that "the allied response in the Middle East is a morally unjustified resort to military force," would, he warned, "have momentous implications for Catholic thinking about the military aspect of the world order in the years ahead." Along with this letter, Neuhaus included a copy of a March 1991 *First Things* article by George Weigel that offered an extended and more detailed version of the same critique and argument Neuhaus had made in the *Wall Street Journal.* He did as much, it would seem, in extraordinarily presumptuous hopes of informing the pope's thinking and statements on the matter from a position much closer to his own than that of the American bishops, who would always remain closer to John Paul than Neuhaus was to either, at least over questions of war.[7]

These public and private efforts to shape American thinking from a conservative Catholic position, and shape papal thinking from a conservative American Catholic position, became even more pronounced and controversial a few months later, when Neuhaus published another essay on Catholic matters for the *Wall Street Journal.* In this instance, he discussed John Paul's latest encyclical, *Centesimus Annus,* and specifically the pope's articulation of an economic system and related individual modes of action and self-understanding that would reflect human dignity, promote equality and justice, and extend economic opportunities in the post–Cold War era. By Neuhaus' reading, the encyclical offered "a ringing endorsement of the market economy" framed by important qualifications and warnings about the dangers of raw capitalism unchecked by any higher-order ethical concerns. In sum, Neuhaus was convinced the encyclical affirmed a position that, at least as he was construing it, was dramatically at odds with earlier Catholic teachings on economics, and specifically the U.S. bishops' formal position on the matter: "Capitalism is the economic corollary of the Christian understanding of man's nature and destiny," he declared, in his one-phrase distillation of the encyclical. He then argued that the pope's document effectively outflanked and outmoded the U.S. bishops' 1986 statement on economic matters, *And Justice for All,* insofar as that statement's more leftward "controlling assumptions" on the subject "must now be recognized as unrepresentative of the church's teaching." Bolder still was the essay's title: "The Pope Affirms the 'New Capitalism.' "[8]

The essay got Neuhaus into two kinds of trouble. First, he was reprimanded by the general secretary of the National Conference of Catholic Bishops, who wrote Neuhaus to share "a most serious objection to your violation of the embargo for the encyclical letter of Pope John Paul II." It turns out Neuhaus broke the embargo by publishing his piece in the *Journal* on May 2, a day before the encyclical was formally released in the United States. He pushed back, insisting he didn't know about the embargo, blamed the bishops for not alerting him when they gave him the copy,[9] and absolved himself of responsibility for the timing: "You will no doubt appreciate that I do not control the publishing schedule of the *Wall Street Journal,*" he wrote. But here Neuhaus protested too much. Even if he was once again technically correct in his pleas of innocence, the most effective possible timing of the essay's appearance—meaning, in effect, a preemptive appearance—was something he would have been intent upon, knowing full well how important it was to set the terms for the encyclical's American reception. Moreover, this reception represented the fulfillment of long-standing interests on his part. Dating at least from his anticommunist turn in the early 1980s, Neuhaus was a proponent of a religiously informed understanding of capitalism as the economic structure of a pluralist democracy. He had also long been an admirer of Michael Novak's 1983 book *The Spirit of Democratic Capitalism,* where this proposal received its fullest elaboration, and with *Centesimus Annus,* Neuhaus, together with Novak and Weigel's respective writings on it, had an opportunity to establish a public Catholic position that they could argue was in fidelity with the latest papal teaching and superseded the American bishops' own position on the subject. With that prospect before him, a public reprimand from some Bishops Conference bureaucrat was well worth it.[10]

The second kind of trouble for Neuhaus came from the substance rather than the timing of his writing about the new encyclical, and once more it was George Higgins who took him to task. In a lengthy letter to the *Journal,* Higgins persuasively criticized Neuhaus for "hasty theologizing on a matter of considerable consequence," which, he argued, "makes for careless and, in this case, suspiciously partisan rhetoric." In turn, he picked apart Neuhaus' convoluted and negative formulations about the American bishops' own statements on economic matters in light of *Centesimus,* before concluding, "This is not the first time Mr. Neuhaus and others who share his views have tried to play the pope off against the bishops, to the disadvantage of the latter. . . . There simply has to be a better way than that for people of varying points of view and differing ideological leanings to carry on a reasoned dialogue about the precise meaning and import of the new encyclical. In short, the encyclical is too important a document to be used selectively for polemical purposes." As a sometimes dispassionate and thoughtful observer of the complex interplay of religion and public life, Neuhaus would no doubt readily agree with Higgins' closing statement, but in this particular instance, Neuhaus was far more a partisan player seeking advantage for his position against that of his opponents. And while critics might argue that this was in fact Neuhaus' (hypocritical) modus operandi throughout his public life and especially as an anticommunist, neoconservative, and culture-warring right-wing American Catholic, he would often reasonably mitigate his own efforts by framing them as correctives to public discussions that were already imbalanced in favor of exclusively secular and leftward Christian contributions. Not so, however, with *Centesimus,* where Neuhaus was the clear victor in the news-cycle and spin games.[11]

This victory was not without its drawbacks, as Neuhaus would learn a year later in the lead-up to the publication of *Doing Well and Doing Good: The Challenge to the Christian Capitalist* (1992), a book he wrote by and large as an expansion of the arguments he had advanced in the *Journal* piece about *Centesimus.* In August 1992, while vacationing at his cottage near Pembroke, Neuhaus learned of the jacket copy that his publisher, Doubleday, was planning to use for the book, which began, "Richard John Neuhaus has been called a man with an instinct for the new things of the spirit. And the spirit, he believes, is calling for a very new thing: to make money, even lots of it." From there it got worse: "There is nothing bad about hustling to make a buck, Neuhaus says," and to help this along, the copy enthused, he "has written a groundbreaking work that unashamedly seeks to bestow a blessing on business." In other words, with his latest book Neuhaus wasn't trying to understand the rights and responsibilities of human freedom in a modern economic context by drawing on recent papal teachings. Instead, he was a well-spoken Prosperity Gospel huckster sporting a Roman collar. Calling this an "outrageous offense," he dictated a letter of protest to Davida by phone from Pembroke, demanding the publisher change the copy before the book was distributed, or else he'd disassociate himself from it.

Copies with the offending jacket blurb were nonetheless distributed, and they only encouraged the critical reaction initially encouraged by his *Journal* essay on *Centesimus,* which was that Neuhaus was more than willing to bring religion to bear on conservative positions, not as a leaven or brace, but instead, in essence, to bless them. Indeed, the book generated extensive review coverage that lined up along obvious ideological lines. Those already predisposed to Neuhaus' extended reading of *Centesimus Annus* as conducive to positive formulations about the relationship of Christianity and capitalism were admiring and affirming of his effort—Father Robert Sirico, writing in the *Wall Street Journal,* and Paul Johnson, writing in *Commentary,* for instance. Those predisposed to a more skeptical construal of Christianity and capitalism's alignment—Jesuit priest Paul McNelis, writing in *America,* and Milwaukee archbishop Rembert Weakland, writing in *Commonweal,* for example—were decidedly more critical of Neuhaus for offering, in Weakland's words, "a discontinuous and selective reading" of *Centesimus* that was captured by the caustic title of the review, "Pontifex Maximus Abridged." In a subsequent letter to the editor, disputing the review's criticisms, Neuhaus pushed back with tart respectfulness for Weakland, one of the more prominently left-leaning members of the U.S. Catholic episcopacy. Neuhaus admitted that he was surprised to learn that Weakland was critical of Neuhaus' initial call, in the *Journal* essay, for "a careful and perhaps painful, rethinking" of *And Justice for All,* which, incidentally, Weakland had presided over. He was surprised, he wrote, because "I have always understood him to be a proponent of careful, indeed painful, rethinking with respect to so many aspects of Catholic faith and life."[12]

By the time *Doing Well and Doing Good* came out in fall 1992, the book's putative blessings and apologies for capitalism were coming not simply from a neoconservative Catholic intellectual, but from an ordained Catholic priest. Neuhaus' ordination took place a year after his conversion, on September 7, at St. Joseph's Seminary in Dunwoodie, New York, about fifteen miles from midtown Manhattan. Robert Wilken and Mary Ann Glendon gave the readings, and Michael and Karen Novak brought up the gifts. Flanked by a fellow cardinal, and also archbishops, auxiliary bishops, and priests from New York and from across the country—there were some sixty concelebrants in total, including Neuhaus' formation guide, Avery Dulles—John O'Connor presided and also preached the homily. It was, from him, a typical combination of joyful sincerity and pointed joke-making—he emphasized the great gift of the priesthood and Neuhaus' unworthiness to receive it, and his own unworthiness to preside over its bestowal. More than once, O'Connor reminded Neuhaus that while he was now a priest, O'Connor was still the bishop, that he was now Richard's bishop, that he was now, and always, in charge. Indeed, among the invited guests, which included Neuhaus' sisters and his various Catholic, Lutheran, and Jewish friends and colleagues from a public life that was becoming increasingly synonymous with *First Things,* Norman Podhoretz might have had the best line, when he explained why he wanted to be there for the ordination. "Just once, I want to see Richard prostrated before somebody."[13]

Easily the most offending line spoken during the ordination itself, at least for the Lutheran pastors in attendance, came from O'Connor. Reading from the *Rituale Romanum*'s "Rite for ordination of priests," he prayed over Neuhaus, "Almighty Father, grant to this servant of yours the dignity of the priesthood." To John Heinemeier, Neuhaus' longtime brother pastor at St. John the Evangelist in Brooklyn, the line effectively invalidated Neuhaus' Lutheran pastorhood—and by extension, the validity and fullness of his own and those of the other Lutheran pastors present, because only now upon his Catholic ordination did God grant Neuhaus "the dignity of the priesthood." Heinemeier and some of the other Lutherans there, who obviously did not subscribe to the Catholic Church's understanding of the priesthood, discussed this afterward while others lined up, as is customary, to receive a first blessing from the newly ordained priest. One notable Lutheran in the blessings queue was Johanna, Neuhaus' baby sister. Fifty years before, she had been her big brother's first and only parishioner while the two of them played church around the house on Miller Street. Back then, in a Lutheran pastorage in small-town Canada, neither could have ever imagined the scene they played out together five decades later, at dusk light in

Neuhaus meeting with President Ronald Reagan, mid-1980s. Among other accomplishments, Neuhaus credited Reagan with helping along book sales for *The Naked Public Square* with his 1984 reelection campaign.

Neuhaus Estate/Institute on Religion and Public Life (provided with permission to use by George Weigel and Robert Wilken)

Neuhaus in conversation with William F. Buckley, Jr. on PBS's *Firing Line*, mid-1980s. Affectionate allies for many years, Neuhaus and Buckley were never more generous than when each let the other man speak.

Neuhaus Estate/Institute on Religion and Public Life (provided with permission to use by George Weigel and Robert Wilken)

Neuhaus attending a Rockford Institute conference, mid-1980s. With tensions increasing between the New York and Illinois offices thereafter, Neuhaus wouldn't be so comfortable in such company for much longer.

Neuhaus Estate/Institute on Religion and Public Life (provided with permission to use by George Weigel and Robert Wilken)

Neuhaus hosting a seminar with Cardinal Josef Ratzinger, the future Pope Benedict XVI, in New York, January 1988. Neuhaus had originally proposed a discussion of his book *The Catholic Moment,* but Ratzinger decided the seminar would concern modern scholarship and the Bible. Despite the sober subject, Ratzinger's public address in New York was disrupted by protestors.

Neuhaus Estate/Institute on Religion and Public Life (provided with permission to use by George Weigel and Robert Wilken)

Neuhaus ordained a Roman Catholic priest by Cardinal John O'Connor, Dunwoodie, New York, September 7, 1991. A deep admiration and affection held between Neuhaus and O'Connor. The cardinal preached the homily at the ordination Mass and reminded his newest diocesan priest that he, O'Connor, was the bishop, which meant O'Connor, not Neuhaus, was in charge.

Neuhaus Estate/Institute on Religion and Public Life (provided with permission to use by George Weigel and Robert Wilken)

Early planning for *First Things* at 338 East 19th Street, New York, Spring 1989. Among the magazine's founding figures, here meeting in Neuhaus' living room shortly after the infamous "Raid" on Rockford's New York office, are (left to right) Maria McFadden, James Nuechterlein, George Weigel, Stanley Hauerwas, David Novak, and Peter Berger.

Neuhaus Estate/Institute on Religion and Public Life (provided with permission to use by George Weigel and Robert Wilken)

The original staff of *First Things* at its offices at 156 Fifth Avenue, in the lead-up to the magazine's March 1990 launch. Pictured (left to right) are Paul Stallsworth, Nuechterlein, Neuhaus, Neuhaus' longtime personal assistant Davida Goldman, and McFadden.

Neuhaus Estate/Institute on Religion and Public Life (provided with permission to use by George Weigel and Robert Wilken)

Neuhaus with Pope John Paul II, mid-1990s. Neuhaus was a keen follower of John Paul's papacy and, together with George Weigel and Michael Novak, met with much success and controversy in establishing themselves as the leading American interpreters of John Paul's encyclicals.

Neuhaus Estate/Institute on Religion and Public Life (provided with permission to use by George Weigel and Robert Wilken)

Neuhaus meeting with President George W. Bush in the Oval Office, January 2004 (also pictured, left to right, are close friend George Weigel and colleague Mary Ann Glendon). Neuhaus first met Bush in 1998, when the then-governor of Texas was considering a presidential run. The two corresponded and met on multiple occasions thereafter and, as *Time* magazine reported, Bush famously credited Neuhaus with helping him "articulate these [religious] things."

Neuhaus Estate/Institute on Religion and Public Life (provided with permission to use by George Weigel and Robert Wilken)

Fr. Neuhaus setting the terms for the conversation (as usual).

Neuhaus family (provided with permission to use by Johanna Speckhard and Mildred Schwich)

Neuhaus with his oldest friend, Robert Wilken, New York, October 13, 2008. Wilken delivered the annual Erasmus lecture that evening, weeks before illness would hasten Neuhaus' decline and eventual death.

Neuhaus Estate/Institute on Religion and Public Life (provided with permission to use by George Weigel and Robert Wilken)

Fr. Richard John Neuhaus: May 14, 1936–January 8, 2009.

Neuhaus Estate/Institute on Religion and Public Life (provided with permission to use by George Weigel and Robert Wilken)

a Catholic seminary courtyard thirty minutes from Times Square, the Lutheran sister kneeling before her now Catholic brother, who laid his hands on her to bestow the gift of a priestly blessing.[14]

The next day, on the first anniversary of his conversion, Neuhaus celebrated his first Mass, at Epiphany, where he'd been attending Mass the prior year. With twenty priests concelebrating, the readings done by William F. Buckley, Jr., and Mary Ellen Bork, wife of Justice Robert Bork, and prayers of the faithful and offertory presentation by George Weigel and his family, this was a Mass that made clear the robustly conservative community Neuhaus had joined within American Catholicism. In his homily, Neuhaus singled out one person in particular, Avery Dulles, who had vested him in his priestly robes beforehand, guided him through a year of modified seminary studies, and been a dialogist and collaborator on theological matters since the 1960s. Neuhaus called him "a mentor, a colleague, a friend," in this case first among many other Catholics who had figured in his life for decades. Not that he entirely forsook his Lutheran life: the closing hymn at the first Catholic Mass he celebrated was "A Mighty Fortress Is Our God," one of the most beloved hymns in Lutheranism and one composed by Martin Luther himself. After the Mass, guests went to lunch at a Gramercy Park restaurant, where Buckley, no doubt speaking for all in attendance, gave remarks that celebrated Neuhaus' new life and ministry as a Catholic priest. There was, to be sure, an important continuity in his ministry, from Lutheran pastor through Catholic priest: O'Connor assigned him to Immaculate Conception Parish, on East 14th, a few blocks south of 338 East 19th Street, as an associate pastor, with the clear understanding that beyond presiding at a Sunday Mass and weekday Masses when he was in town, he was to continue on in his public ministry, presiding over *First Things* and the Institute on Religion and Public Life.[15]

In 1991 and into 1992, this ministry also involved work on his next books, *Doing Well and Doing Good* and also *America Against Itself: Moral Vision and the Public Order,* which was essentially a reworking of his *Naked Public Square* arguments beyond the context of ascendant Moral Majoritarians. These arguments were situated now in the midst of full-on culture wars between America's religious and secular-minded ranks. Intending the work as a diagnosis of that culture war and proposal for its just resolution—as ever, through the acceptance of thoughtful, religiously informed contributions to public life—the book inevitably reads as a formidable religious conservative's latest foray into the culture wars. It generated little public interest beyond a few reviews and a "Critic's Choice" award from *Christianity Today,* the conservative evangelical magazine. In the meantime, Neuhaus was generating more than enough public interest through *First Things,* through a constant schedule of talks—at the University of Tulsa, at a Wisconsin think tank, at Princeton, and also preaching the annual September "Red Mass" for New York's public leaders—and through writings for other venues. The latter included a blistering essay for the *Wall Street Journal* on the *Planned Parenthood v. Casey* Supreme Court decision, which upheld and expanded abortion rights and led Neuhaus to declare it "The Dred Scott of Our Time."[16]

That essay came out in July 1992, while Neuhaus was in Europe with Weigel and Michael Novak, at the inaugural meeting of what would eventually be called "the Tertio Millennio Seminar." This was an annual summer program for graduate students from North America and Europe who came together to study Church social teaching, and specifically John Paul II's works, in hopes of developing a faith-informed mode of cultural and societal engagement in the post–Cold War era. Neuhaus, Weigel, and Novak gave classes, as did the seminar's European organizers, Polish priest Maciej Zieba and Italian academic Rocco Buttiglione, whose scholarly interest was in the works of the former Karol Wojtyla. This was an interest that in turn positioned him to become a confidant of the pope and one of John Paul II's most prominent European interpreters. Buttiglione followed the American scene more closely than most European Catholic intellectuals. With John O'Connor's encouragement, he took note of

Neuhaus, Weigel, and Novak's all but open competition with liberal Catholics, and especially the U.S. bishops, to establish themselves and their arguments as John Paul II's preeminent American interpreters and interpretations. Informed of their efforts, the pope was not displeased, according to Buttiglione, and indeed he encouraged Buttiglione to forge connections with them. The Tertio Millennio Seminar was one notable outcome, and another was a series of meetings and lunches in Rome that in turn led to the three Americans forging more direct connections with John Paul II. Indeed, the papal household subscribed to *First Things,* and Stanislaw Dziwisz, the pope's longtime personal secretary, close friend, and the eventual cardinal-archbishop of Kraków, told Weigel and Neuhaus on multiple occasions that he read the magazine with great interest, and that he always opened *First Things* to the back pages to read Father Neuhaus first.[17]

Rome, New York, Washington; books, magazines, talks; a new and immediately prominent sacred office—all in all, by fall 1992, Richard John Neuhaus was exactly where he discerned he should be in his life and ministry. But four months later, his health would take a dramatic turn, threatening his thriving ministry and his very life.

CHAPTER TWENTY

As He Lay Dying

It had come to this. George Weigel was threatening to hit Richard John Neuhaus over the head with a bottle of Scotch. They weren't arguing about papal matters or about the potential meanings and consequences of Bill Clinton's recent election win. This was a few days before Clinton's inauguration, and Weigel was making his annual post-Christmas visit to 338. He was shocked by Neuhaus' state. Weigel was shocked still more by his refusal to admit how sick he was, even though Neuhaus would later admit the pain was so intense, it felt like his stomach was exploding. And so, with caustic humor Weigel had resorted to threats of blunt head trauma because he could think of no other way to get his friend to agree with what was obvious to him and also to Larry Bailey, who was also standing in Neuhaus' apartment, early evening, January 10, 1993, surrounding a man who desperately needed to get to the hospital. Eventually, they persuaded Richard to get into a cab and go over to Cabrini Medical, a couple blocks away. They showed up at a crowded emergency room, and the nurse at the admissions desk wasn't especially interested in Neuhaus' situation. Crumpling up the admission form, Weigel insisted his friend needed to be admitted immediately. Doubled over in pain, Neuhaus fell to the floor and passed out. Then the nurse decided this was an emergency, and he was lifted onto a gurney and sped away for treatment. And so began a four-month medical odyssey that was variously near-tragic, tragicomic, and mystical. This was an odyssey that attested in personal rather than public terms to the strength of Richard John Neuhaus' will, a strength that could be stubborn, demanding, and entirely beside the point during a life-threatening illness that also led to what had to have been the strangest and most wondrous religious experience of his life.[1]

By Neuhaus' own later account of his nearly mortal bout of cancer in early 1993, things should have never become as bad as they were before he finally got to the hospital. At the time, Neuhaus was seeing an esteemed Park Avenue doctor whose colleague gave Neuhaus regular colonoscopies, in keeping with standard guidelines for early detection of colorectal cancer in men aged fifty and higher. Nothing had shown up, even in a test a few days before Neuhaus went into the hospital. Making matters worse on January 9, when Neuhaus had called his doctor before they went to the hospital and described his symptoms, the covering physician prescribed a powerful laxative. In and of itself, this could have proven fatal, other doctors would later suggest, because of what the emergency room surgeon at Cabrini discovered in an X-ray of Neuhaus' colon: a tumor the size of an apple. Before the operation, Weigel called Monsignor Harry Byrne, who had been Neuhaus' parish priest during his necktie year at Epiphany. Byrne administered the last rites, and Neuhaus went in for surgery. Overnight, the doctors successfully removed the tumor and sewed him up, but then he began hemorrhaging and his vital signs started to fail. The doctors went back in and discovered the cause of Neuhaus' sudden and terrible turn: his spleen had been nicked during the operation to remove the tumor. They removed the spleen, he stabilized, and off he went to the intensive care unit. The hospital called Weigel at the apartment to report that Neuhaus had survived the operations. In turn, he called Mim Schwich, then living in Pensacola, Florida, and herself now a widow after her husband had died a few years earlier, of colon cancer no less. Mim got on the phone with her siblings, and they debated whether to tell Ella, now ninety and in a retirement home in Pembroke. Regardless, it was decided a family member had to be there, and Mim agreed to go.

As for the patient himself, the next thing he remembered in all of this was the frustrating experience of disappointing the doctors and nurses gathered around his bed, the morning after the operation. They were deliberating over his situation and were worried that he wasn't responding to their efforts to elicit a response from him that would confirm he had fully come through. Wiggle your toes, your fingers, your thumb—he could hear their requests but was incapable of responding. According to his later account of the experience, nothing was working until Neuhaus heard someone say, "The cardinal is here." O'Connor bent down beside Neuhaus and called him by name, then told him to wiggle his nose: "It was a plea and a command," Neuhaus recalled in his candid account of this near-death experience, which first appeared as an essay in a 2000 issue of *First Things* and then formed the center of his 2002 book *As I Lay Dying*. "I wanted to do it more urgently than anything I have ever wanted to do in my life. The trying, the sheer exercise of will to wiggle my nose—to order my nose to wiggle itself—seemed to go on and on, and then I felt a twinge." O'Connor saw and celebrated, the surgeon didn't see and remained skeptical, and so O'Connor told Richard to do it again. Neuhaus did it again, and then "the cardinal and the doctors and the technicians all began to exclaim what a wonderful thing it was, as though one had risen from the dead." Unsurprisingly, he dedicated *As I Lay Dying* to John O'Connor, "who called me back." He subtitled the book "Meditations upon Returning, on Facing Death and Living Again."[2]

This return led next to his being transferred to a regular patient's room, and his primary care was taken over by a new doctor that Weigel arranged after consulting with Leon Kass, the noted ethicist and MD who had given the 1991 Erasmus lecture, the major annual talk sponsored by the Institute on Religion and Public Life, and had since become yet another of Neuhaus' well-placed and like-minded friends, colleagues, and collaborators, notably on an ongoing series of essay collections that the two of them would co-edit between 1994 and 2000 under the rubric "The Ethics of Everyday Life." Before that began, of course, Neuhaus had to recover from major back-to-back surgeries—"It was as though you had been hit twice by a Mack truck going sixty miles an hour," one doctor told him afterward. In the early days, Mim was his constant companion. She read to him from Willa Cather novels and served as gatekeeper, admitting and denying visitors (including another reading companion, Midge Decter) based on Neuhaus' preferences and moods. Now living out the inherent and difficult dignity of suffering rather than only writing about it, Neuhaus wasn't one for the sort of machismo tactics to be expected from an alpha male of his generation who was self-evidently in a weakened state for all to see, even if they themselves didn't want to. He would write about an unnamed young admirer who visited: "He would not look at me, at this ghastly pallor, this blasted body. . . . He was embarrassed for one he had looked up to, and I was embarrassed," Neuhaus admitted, but then he accepted his weakened, humiliated situation, and he asked his visitor to look at him, to join him in not being afraid of human frailty and suffering. Accepting this didn't mean accepting the surrounding culture's ways of dealing with frailty and suffering: along with instructions for the colostomy bag he would have to use during his recovery, Neuhaus was invited to join "Colostomates," a support group. He declined the invitation.[3]

Neuhaus wrote about all of this in *As I Lay Dying,* and also offered an extended and loving paean to Mim for watching over him, but he didn't mention their only quarrel. It happened on January 20, 1993. Mim, who'd voted for Clinton, wanted to watch the presidential inauguration. Neuhaus, who didn't vote for Clinton, didn't want to watch. But when she offered to go watch it in a lounge, he relented: if having to watch Bill Clinton on television for a little while was the price of having his big sister stay with him, fine. He began complaining shortly into the proceedings and told Mim to mark his words, you heard it from him first: this was the beginning of what could only ever be a failed presidency. Neuhaus would make similar predictions at later intervals in Clinton's terms, but in early 1993 he was more focused on getting through long days in the hospital, which were relieved eventually by his return to writing pieces for *First Things, National Review,* and other venues. At night, Mim would go sleep in his apartment, and it was during one of his nights alone that Neuhaus suddenly discerned he was not, in fact, alone. Later, he would describe an out-of-body experience that involved an encounter with two "'presences.' I saw them and yet did not seem them, and I cannot explain that. But there they were." After a few moments they spoke to him:

> *This I heard clearly. Not in an ordinary way, for I cannot remember anything about the voice. But the message was beyond mistaking. "Everything is ready now." That was it. They waited for a while, maybe for a minute, maybe longer. . . . Then they were gone, and I was again flat on my back with my mind racing wildly. . . . Had I been dreaming? In no way. I was . . . as lucid and wide awake as I had ever been in my life.*[4]

In making sense of what he described as a "near-life experience" in the pages of *As I Lay Dying,* Neuhaus acknowledged, indeed shared in, the skepticism that such an account of encountering Divine presences would create, while insisting on its truthfulness. Perhaps in part, this insistence accounts for why Neuhaus took the otherwise unusual step of securing formal Church declarations—the *Nihil Obstat* and *Imprimatur*—that appear on the book's publication information page, affirming that it has been deemed "free of doctrinal or moral error." If he was exceedingly careful in this respect, he was entirely reckless in another, near the end of his treatments. In Lent 1993, Neuhaus called Mim, then visiting with their brother Tom and his family in Quebec, requesting that she once again be with him in the hospital, because the doctors were to perform a final operation before releasing him. She agreed, the operation went fine, and Neuhaus entered a final period of recuperation. But he was sick of recuperating. And now it was Easter. He wanted out. He wanted to be back at 338 for the Community's annual Easter feast. No one at the hospital thought this was a good idea, and neither did Mim, but she was woken up early Easter Sunday morning by her brother calling from the hospital and demanding that she come now and bring him home. Mim approached Harry Byrne, who agreed to drive, and so Neuhaus was able to be at home for Easter, with his sister and the Community of Christ in the City.

He looked awful. He couldn't walk very well, and he was exhausted. But he insisted on being there for the party, and in his bathrobe was set up in his reading chair in the living room. He casually asked for a cigar. Everyone thought he was joking. He wasn't. No one would give him a cigar, so instead he demanded dessert. Every Easter, Larry Bailey made Paskha, a traditional Russian pudding loaded with eggs and sugar and cream and sweet cheese. This was a rich treat, and for a man who'd recently been in hospital with colon cancer and a ruptured, now removed spleen, a very bad idea. But he insisted. He had to prove he was back and life as it always had been had now resumed. On Easter Sunday, this meant Paskha! He had one, two spoonfuls, and the point was made. Then he got up, went to the bathroom, and threw up violently. He retched beneath all the many pictures he'd framed and put in there over the years: Richard with Ronald Reagan, Richard with Martin Luther King, Richard with Joseph Ratzinger, and so on. He emerged from the bathroom and decided he was done for the night. No one at that Easter dinner party disagreed.

By May 1993, Neuhaus was back to work. Photos from this period, accompanying various interviews and profiles in mostly Catholic publications, mostly about pro-life matters, register the "Mack truck effect" his illness had had on him. His face was lined and drawn, unlike in pictures from just a year before, and his eyes—usually bright and lively—were sunken, dark. But his energy was back. 7:30 A.M., in Omaha, Nebraska, midsummer 1993, Neuhaus "hastily gobbled several favorite targets along with scrambled eggs, toast, and coffee," as one typically admiring profile ran. Neuhaus was in town to give a talk on his usual subject, religion and public life, this time occasioned by the twenty-fifth anniversary of *Humanae Vitae,* Pope Paul VI's encyclical on human sexuality and family life. By the mid-1990s, Neuhaus had become intensely focused on exposing what he described as "the truly dangerous and lethal logic" of the *Roe v. Wade* Supreme Court decision in 1972, which had been affirmed and even amplified by the *Casey v. Planned Parenthood* decision in 1992. And to make the strongest possible case against abortion was to make a case that drew on a religiously informed understanding of the human person and the sacred value of human life, Neuhaus argued. The problem, as ever, as far as he was concerned, was that making a case against abortion on those terms wasn't acceptable to "certain sectors of [America's] cultural leadership," by which he meant "people in the world of the *New York Times,*" a phrase he shared with his receptive Omaha interviewer in "an exaggerated conspiratorial whisper." Here, Neuhaus was very much playing to his immediate audience, both sincerely encouraging them in their shared pro-life commitments and validating their sense of feeling like cultural outsiders because of those commitments and the religious convictions at their core.[5]

This combination characterized much of Neuhaus' efforts during this period, whether in interviews with reliably admiring Catholic newspapers and other religious publications or in the university lectures, commencement speeches, and conference talks he gave. And while for the first time in years he wasn't at work on a full book, he kept up his prodigious writing—ten thousand monthly words for *First Things,* his reviews and opinions, his public speeches—which he habitually pursued for the better part of the morning in his basement office at 338 on whatever was the latest Apple computer. He wrote before heading over to the *First Things* offices on Park Avenue closer to lunch, greeting everyone loudly and jovially, and then going to his own office to begin dealing with magazine and Institute matters and his endless personal correspondence, all of which kept him at the office until it was time to return to 338 for evening prayer, around 7 P.M. Neuhaus' office work included dealing with advertisers, pitches and submissions, and accepted pieces already circulating through the staff for comment and critique, and preparing for upcoming talks and conferences. His correspondence included fan mail, angry mail, matters that readers hoped he would address in future columns, invitations to assorted events and speaking engagements, responses to things he'd written from strangers and from colleagues, random requests for his prudential judgment of distant parish politics, and confidential counsel for spiritual crises. He made a point of replying to most everything—out of pastoral responsibility in some cases, out of gratitude and affection and plain good manners in others. His capacity to write so much, so regularly, when it came to correspondence alone, was nothing compared to his monthly "Public Square" essays and "While We're At It" items in *First Things*. These writings were joined during the three years following his bout of cancer with regular pieces for the *Wall Street Journal*—which notably included essays on the significance of John Paul II's ideas in an American context, pegged to successive encyclicals and papal statements—and also columns for *National Review* and the *National Catholic Register* and extensive review essays for *Commentary,* all among other publications.[6]

Throughout, a consistent focus was his vehement opposition to the abortion license and euthanasia, alongside similarly critical estimations of emerging advances in biotechnology that were indifferent to religiously grounded understandings of human life. He likewise targeted the institutions that were supportive of these developments and in his opinion exercised undue influence on public perceptions and actual laws. In Neuhaus' estimation, the *New York Times* was the principal villain in the perception game—"The sleazy old lady of American journalism," went a typical jab, from a 1995 issue of *First Things.* As for the laws of the land, Neuhaus began to level increasingly intense criticisms against the judiciary, which he characterized as an unchecked, overreaching power rendering conclusive decisions on cases involving abortion and euthanasia, and thereby preventing the deliberation of these matters from taking place as it should, by democratically elected representatives of the people. A looming consequence, he warned, was the alienation of religiously committed citizens, so much so that secular-progressive judicial activism was forcing them to "think long and painful thoughts about their allegiance to this political and legal regime," as a May 1996 *First Things* editorial ran, criticizing a Ninth Circuit decision that identified, in the court's language, "a liberty right" to assisted suicide.[7]

Before this rhetoric and logic would lead *First Things* to become the center of a months-long controversy beginning in fall 1996, the magazine was thriving by doing exactly what it proposed: advancing religiously ordered arguments, reviews, and articles about all dimensions of public life, unmatched by both conservative-intellectual and religiously focused publications for the range, vitality, and firepower in evidence.[8] Beyond the usual suspects, the magazine was attracting high-profile contributors like Czech president and Cold War dissident playwright Václav Havel, calling for a rediscovery of the religious sources of modern democracy; accomplished Hebrew scholar Robert Alter, reviewing a new translation of the Psalter; and renowned conservative Middle East and Islamic studies scholar Bernard Lewis, writing about an Oxford Encyclopedia of Modern Islam in the same issue that Jonathan Sacks, chief rabbi of Great Britain, advocated for the civilizational importance of maintaining religious traditions in a nonreligious time. The journal was also successful in engaging unexpected interlocutors and subjects. Building out of the ongoing symposium on "The Ethics of Everyday Life" that Neuhaus was running with Leon Kass under the auspices of a research institute at the University of Notre Dame, *First Things* devoted part of its January 1995 issue to thoughtful, playful meditations on the moral meanings of Shel Silverstein's classic children's book *The Giving Tree,* which the magazine reprinted in its pages along with the meditations themselves.

The magazine also pursued mission-focused investigative journalism during this period, which led to a major May 1995 article by Dean M. Kelley on the antireligious elements that figured in the 1993 federal government siege of the Branch Davidian religious cult compound in Waco, Texas. That same year, through parallel essays and responses, Neuhaus mixed it up with contrarian literary scholar and intellectual Stanley Fish on the question of whether religious persons could be accommodated in public life through the premises and dictates of contemporary secular liberalism, or if they posed too great a demand, indeed risk, to the liberal order. Neuhaus called his essay "Why We Can Get Along," and called for accommodation for religious citizens, in the best interests of all. Fish countered, "Why We Can't All Just Get Along," remained skeptical of the accommodation argument, and had the last word in the exchange. Of course, Fish didn't have the last word in Neuhaus' own magazine; in its back pages, that same issue, Neuhaus disputed Fish's skepticism and once more stated his own case, and so enjoyed the true last word.[9]

That *First Things* was very much Neuhaus' publication was never in question. This was obvious in the ultimate veto he exercised with respect to what the magazine published, and in turn the kinds of materials that were published—"The Catholic Luther," an article by Lutheran theologian David Yeago, appeared in the March 1996 issue, and on the facing page ran a quotation describing abortion as murder, from a German theologian whom Neuhaus greatly admired, Nazi resister Dietrich Bonhoeffer. That this was his magazine was likewise obvious in Neuhaus' capacity to make use of his direct connections to the Vatican to lend unrivaled credence to his own positions. For instance, in the October 1995 issue, Neuhaus addressed the ongoing debate in U.S. circles over the status of Church teaching on the death penalty in light of John Paul II's latest encyclical, *Evangelium Vitae,* which offered strong arguments against the need for capital punishment in an increasingly modernized age. Upon the encyclical's publication, Joseph Ratzinger made remarks that were interpreted by some as suggesting that the encyclical could lead to a change in Church teaching, as codified in the *Catechism,* from not excluding the death penalty (albeit in highly circumscribed circumstances), toward a total opposition to the death penalty, in more perfect consonance with its total opposition to abortion. U.S. conservative Catholics, who were generally more supportive of the death penalty, resisted this interpretation, while liberal Catholics encouraged it and (for once) were invoking Ratzinger as support for their particular position.

But what had Ratzinger meant to say about the encyclical's impact on the Church's teaching about capital punishment, and more importantly, about the perception that centuries of Church teaching could be changed from one encyclical to another? Neuhaus settled the matter as really only he could: "We asked Cardinal Ratzinger for a clarification and are pleased to publish, with his permission, his response." Ratzinger wrote that the encyclical had deepened the Church's understanding of why the death penalty was increasingly unnecessary, but it had not abrogated or even altered the basic position as stated in the *Catechism.* In turn, Neuhaus all but crowed,

> *The above clarification should be welcomed by Catholics who may in good faith disagree over whether the death penalty is necessary for the defense of society, and by the many other people who depend upon the constancy of the Church's teaching. We expect it will not be so very welcome among those who have triumphantly declared that* Evangelium Vitae *condemns capital punishment, while they have at the same time largely ignored the encyclical's forceful and unambiguous condemnation of abortion, euthanasia, and other crimes that characterize "the culture of death."*

In this particular case, Neuhaus' touch was relatively light. That he could ask Ratzinger directly for a clarification, publish it in his own journal, and meanwhile position the clarification in support of his particular arguments and interests meant he did not need to point out (at least not this time) how well placed he was, between Rome and America, thanks in part to a long-standing personal connection to the cardinal.[10]

Indeed, one other strong indicator of Neuhaus' proprietary presence in *First Things* was his penchant for expansive, at times excessive, self-reference. When this penchant led to writings about his personal life and experiences, the result was usually meaningful, amusing, and featured unexpected anecdotes about various people and periods of his life, whether involving Clem Neuhaus, Daniel Berrigan, or even the Dalai Lama—as he would note now and then when the "Free Tibet" movement made news, in the late 1970s and early 1980s, Neuhaus became his self-described "man in New York" by way of his work at CRIA and his religious liberty and anticommunist activism. But when this penchant led to writings about his own ongoing projects and ministry, the result wasn't nearly as winning. In March 1994, he wrote about Patrick Allitt's book on post–World War II Catholic intellectuals and American conservatism, and complained playfully but pointedly that he wasn't written about: "It is a pity that Allitt stops at 1985, before 'the Catholic moment' was promulgated by a definitely non-authoritative source." A few issues later, Neuhaus wrote about a George Weigel essay about Neuhaus' work, which he had decided against publishing in *First Things* because this seemed "too self-referential," though this didn't stop him from quoting its most admiring portions anyway.

As cheering personal correspondence sent to Neuhaus during this period suggests, his fans and the supporters of his work enjoyed all of this, and likewise his frequent, frequently acidic attacks on opponents[11]—the *National Catholic Reporter* was "the floundering flagscow of the Catholic Left"; the National Council of Churches was "our sick friend"; the *New Yorker* under new editor Tina Brown had become "specious, spurious, meretricious, and dishonest," and also just "plain vulgar." Neuhaus also began reporting on attacks leveled at him, which he seemed to enjoy even more than attacking others. He ended the December 1995 issue with a note about *Free Inquiry*, a publication sponsored by the Council for Democratic and Secular Humanism, whose promotional material explained that part of its mission of "preserving our freethought heritage" was to monitor "the rise of Richard John Neuhaus" and explain to concerned readers "why he bears close watching." To which Neuhaus replied: "I've been wondering about those people going through my garbage pails. Imagine, sneaky Humanists disguising themselves as the homeless. I can't wait until tomorrow. 'Good morning, Professor Kurtz. Looking for free thoughts?' "[12]

In fact, Neuhaus received much harsher criticism during these years from the Right than from the Left. Leading the charge from 1992 through 1996 was Joseph Sobran, a former associate of William F. Buckley, Jr.'s at *National Review,* who had been pushed out in 1993 because of the anti-Semitic propensities he displayed in columns for the magazine. Sobran became a willing scourge of cosmopolitan conservatives and of the neoconservative movement, and Neuhaus was one of his prime targets. In October 1994, Neuhaus wrote a lamenting, stinging criticism of Sobran for his writing about "the sinister influence of Jews in American life, and the alleged captivity of U.S. foreign policy to the 'Jewish lobby' working on behalf of Israel," which amounted to "a considerable talent wasted," as far as Neuhaus was concerned. Sobran came back at him, hard. In one of his columns for the conservative Catholic newspaper the *Wanderer,* Sobran described Neuhaus as an opportunistic church-jumper capable of "suave theological hustle, perfectly tailored to the New York neoconservative crowd he [runs] with." Sobran then rehearsed the Rockford controversy from a Rockford-friendly vantage, noting, autobiographically, that "adroitly hinting to his New York friends that his former employers were anti-Semitic [was] a standard Neuhaus ploy." He then melodramatically confessed, "My heart sank when I heard this operator was going to become a Catholic priest," cited other criticisms of Neuhaus' selective citation and advocacy with recent papal encyclicals, and concluded this first in a series of Neuhaus attacks, "You almost have to admire the smooth effrontery of a guy who explains, in tones of exquisite condescension, what the Pope *meant* to say. We're lucky he didn't get his hands on the Sermon on the Mount before it went to press."[13]

If Sobran was sharp-tongued and sarcastic about Neuhaus—in future columns, he would describe him as a craven purveyor of "disingenuous mush" about the necessity of strong Christian-Jewish relations, and as a "one-man magisterium of the neoconservative crowd [who] has come into the Church for the purpose of throwing others out"—Herman Otten bordered on a pathological obsession with his old Lutheran adversary. He started up a dedicated column in his monthly newsletter, *Christian News,* that he titled "Neuhaus Watch" and reported on Neuhaus' endless dark deeds on behalf of Rome and New York City neoconservatism. The alarmist and overheated attention turned especially ugly in November 1995, when Otten ran a cartoon in his paper that featured side-by-side illustrations of Neuhaus under the heading "Young Liberal, Old Romanist." The first, dated circa 1960, showed a young man in clerics, a finger raised to the heavens, as he declared, "We reject an infallible Bible! No slavery to a 'Paper Pope'!" This was harmless enough, even silly. The second illustration, dated circa 1995, was harsh: it showed Neuhaus hunched over a bowl of dog food, eagerly kissing the pope's foot while gushing, "Thank you your infallible holiness for inviting me to dinner!" while the pope himself asks one of his cardinals to get Neuhaus to stop with all the foot-kissing. The immediate catalyst for this, Otten's latest attack, wasn't simply reports of Neuhaus' friendliness with John Paul II,[14] but his discussing the concept of *sola fide* with the *National Catholic Register* in a November 1995 interview that was more broadly focused on evangelical Christian beliefs about faith and salvation versus Catholic beliefs about the same.[15]

By November 1995, in fact, evangelical-Catholic relations had become a major focus for Neuhaus, and the source both of new influence and controversy. In October 1995, during a trip to the United States, John Paul II met with a series of prominent American evangelicals among a larger group of Christian leaders, at an event hosted by John O'Connor and shaped in no small part by Neuhaus. The most controversial person at the event was Pat Robertson, the Southern Baptist minister and televangelist turned 1988 Republican presidential primary candidate and thereafter a reliable source of unsophisticated, Bible-covered jeremiads about godless, decadent American life. He was, in other words, exactly the kind of unsophisticated advocate for religion's place in public life that Neuhaus would criticize as unhelpful to religion and public life both (certainly by comparison to the sophisticated and cosmopolitan contributions he could make instead).

But if Robertson was invited to a meeting with the pope in Manhattan, at John O'Connor's place—a turn of events only imaginable with Neuhaus playing a role in it—what had changed? The *National Catholic Reporter* (that "floundering flagscow of the Catholic left," as he once described it with especial vim) considered Robertson's invitation nothing less than "scandalous" because, argued editorial writer Tom Roberts, "any mainstream Catholic leader would have enormous problems with Pat Robertson's theology—his 'prosperity gospel'; his nervous, frightening end-times speculation; his thinly disguised anti-Semitism, and his exaggerated statements about other mainline [*sic*] Protestants." He further insisted that "there are evangelicals and fundamentalists who find it offensive to have Pat Robertson identified as the spokesperson and leader of that segment of American Christianity." So what got him in the room? According to Roberts, and plausibly so, it was Robertson's involvement with Evangelicals and Catholics Together, an ecumenical theological initiative with strong political elements that was the brainchild of Richard John Neuhaus and his friend, Charles Colson.[16]

Colson was the Nixon aide who had been imprisoned for his part in the Watergate scandal, converted to evangelical Christianity, and become a leading figure in the movement thanks to his pastoral outreach to prisoners, his writings, and his public initiatives as an evangelical. He and Neuhaus first met in 1985, when Colson invited him to give a talk in Washington on *The Naked Public Square*. They stayed in regular contact thereafter; in September 1992, Neuhaus invited Colson to a meeting sponsored by the Institute on Religion and Public Life, along with a group of fellow evangelical leaders and theologians and an equal number of Catholics. The meeting's focus wasn't the United States, in fact, but Latin and South America, where the competing proselytization efforts of evangelicals and Catholics were threatening to turn into sectarian conflict. Neuhaus had arranged for the group to hear a presentation from a husband-and-wife team of English scholars who had been studying the situation in Brazil and Chile. During a break in the session, Colson approached Neuhaus, proposing that an information session wasn't enough—Catholics and evangelicals had to do something together, in hopes of counteracting what they were doing to each other, and simultaneously to the faith.

Colson had a distinct sense that Neuhaus was already thinking this way, and with his long-standing ecumenical interests and penchant for coalition and statement-making, Neuhaus ran with it. His 1993 illness put the project on hold, but in early winter 1994, Neuhaus brought together some fifteen Catholics and evangelicals at the Union League Club. The list included conservative Catholics like Archbishop J. Francis Stafford, Bishop Francis George, Father Avery Dulles, and George Weigel, and prominent evangelicals like Richard Land and Larry Lewis. During this meeting, they agreed to a declaration that was marked by a clear effort to identify points of common belief and attesting actions, while also acknowledging points of continued division. According to Colson, Neuhaus was responsible for the initial draft of the statement, which is unsurprising based on the end result, which endorses, among other elements, the importance of "mediating structures" to a healthy public policy, and also the natural and necessary place of religion, specifically Judeo-Christianity, in American public life. These were formulations Neuhaus had, of course, long worked with in other contexts.[17]

In theological terms, the declaration emphasizes a shared affirmation of Christ as Lord and Savior, and quotes the Apostles'

Creed as "an accurate statement of scriptural truth" for both groups. The declaration lists areas of clear disagreement—which include Scripture's stand-alone authority versus an authority based on the Church's interpretations; priesthood understood as open to all or to those in apostolic succession; the status and significance of Mary and the saints; and the symbolic versus efficacious power of sacraments—and also provides a complex account (originating in the 1992 meeting on Latin and South America) of the competing goods of religious liberty, proselytization, and mutual respect between two faiths seeking converts from each other's ranks. At the beginning of the declaration, the signatories make it clear that they know "this statement cannot speak officially for our communities," and that they intend the document only to address each community and draw attention to "the distinctive circumstances and opportunities of Evangelicals and Catholics living together in North America." By and large, in this first declaration, the opportunities beyond ecumenism were undeniably political in focus. If the Hartford Appeal was very much about ecclesial politics between liberal and conservative branches of American Christianity, the founding declaration of Evangelicals and Catholics Together (ECT) was more straightforwardly about politics itself.

In addition to devoting attention to theological and ecclesiological points held in common and apart, the declaration lists a veritable social conservative and neoconservative wish list for political action. Robust opposition to abortion, "the leading edge of an encroaching culture of death," is foremost; more broadly, the signatories promise, "We will do all in our power to resist proposals for euthanasia, eugenics, and population control that exploit the vulnerable, corrupt the integrity of medicine, deprave our culture, and betray the moral truths of our constitutional order." Beyond these topmost social issues, the statement also advocates for school choice, for "a renewed appreciation of Western culture," and "a vibrant market economy" as defining features of a free and morally serious society, and the firm belief that "U.S. foreign policy should reflect a concern for the defense of democracy and, wherever prudent and possible, the protection and advancement of human rights, including religious freedom."[18]

The declaration, signed by the participants in the first ECT formal meeting at the Union League Club, was in turn endorsed by another two dozen prominent Catholics and evangelicals (including John O'Connor and Pat Robertson). According to Colson, upon its spring 1994 release and publication in *First Things,* the ECT declaration met with significant resistance, particularly from evangelicals who lacked a significant ecumenical tradition and were critical of their brethren for allegedly undermining if not abandoning core tenets like the singular salvific powers of Scripture and of faith, propositions that historically had been developed and sustained in self-conscious opposition to Catholicism. Meanwhile, liberal Catholics like Tom Roberts regarded ECT as an instrumentalist move on the part of its leading Catholic participants, who were effectively subordinating universal Catholic tenets to American conservative political gain. Neuhaus attempted to mitigate these characterizations by telling the *New York Times* that he'd pursued the declaration with the encouragement of unnamed Vatican officials. Nevertheless, he also told the *Times* that he regarded ECT as a means of encouraging "grass-roots" cooperation between evangelicals and Catholics, cooperation that had clear political implications. Certainly others saw it this way: in an interview, Ralph Reed, then executive director of Pat Robertson's Christian Coalition organization, in many respects a 1990s successor to Falwell's Moral Majority, credited Neuhaus and the ECT with providing a higher-order articulation of the shared concerns of the Catholic swing voters that the Republican Party sought to consolidate with its evangelical base in the 1994 and 1996 elections.

Neuhaus certainly spoke at the Coalition's "Road to Victory" conventions, though his remarks were more critical than commendatory, and the overall experience caused him to worry about a too-easy limning together of conservative faith and right-wing politics, as he would remark in a May 1996 reflection in *First Things*. As for ECT itself, though direct partisan gain wasn't Neuhaus' primary intention with the initiative, exerting influence on American politics was an obvious result that played out as partisan gain. In his characterization of this outcome, Baptist theologian Timothy George minted a phrase for what Neuhaus and Colson achieved by founding Evangelicals and Catholics Together: "ecumenism of the trenches."[19]

That this likely impacted electoral politics to conservative advantage is something Neuhaus never successfully squared away with his reliable outrage at liberal Christian leaders directing their support to Democrats, beyond arguing that his effort was more faithful to theological orthodoxy and Church teaching than theirs. Of course, they would insist likewise. But by the mid-1990s, Neuhaus was clearly winning out against his old Mainline opponents. He was wielding an unprecedented amount of power and influence within the trenches of the culture wars and likewise from the helm of *First Things*. And then, in late 1996, convinced that the judicial licensing of abortion was threatening to imperil American democracy, he would take himself and his magazine into the culture wars as he'd never done before, and in the process lose old friends and win many new subscribers.

CHAPTER TWENTY-ONE

The End of Democracy? The Beginnings of Greater Influence

Among his thousands of publications, none generated greater controversy or got him into more personal trouble than the unsigned editorial Neuhaus wrote for the November 1996 issue of *First Things*. This trouble and controversy came not just from the usual suspects, his longtime opponents on the secular and religious Left, or from his established opponents on the far hard Right for that matter, but also, to his great surprise and frustration, from among his closest, oldest friends and colleagues and collaborators. The overall effects, while lacking the immediate kicked-to-the-curb dramatics of the Rockford Raid, would prove just as significant in demonstrating Neuhaus' unrivaled capacity for impacting the course of American conservatism in ways that transformed what otherwise would have seemed like self-enclosed intellectual magazine skirmishing into national news. The editorial that accomplished all of this introduced the main section of the issue and appeared in the weeks leading up to the 1996 presidential election day. The main section was comprised of a symposium set of papers by Robert Bork, Russell Hittinger, Hadley Arkes, Charles Colson, and Robert P. George, who variously considered the implications of recent judicial decisions on life matters, for the health of public life and the continued viability of democracy itself. This exercise took place under a provocative, if not alarmist, even incendiary title: "The End of Democracy? The Judicial Usurpation of Politics."[1]

The idea for the issue developed soon after the Federal Court of Appeals Ninth Circuit's April 1996 decision identifying a right to doctor-assisted suicide in the liberty protections of individual citizens housed within the Fourteenth Amendment. At the magazine's annual editorial board conference in May, Neuhaus openly wondered if "the jig was up," as James Nuechterlein recalls. Had the courts finally gone so far that democracy itself had become imperiled? At the very least, was this not a question the magazine should take up? The proposal received much support around the table, while Nuechterlein's was the notable dissenting voice. You could raise such concerns in conversation, but to put them in print was a whole other matter, he warned his editor in chief, not least because some of their more notable friends and allies in the conservative world were unlikely to welcome the effort. Nuechterlein would be proven right, but he had little sway with Neuhaus before an editorial board whose members, at least those present for this meeting, were intent on considering the greatest and gravest implications of rising judicial activism, particularly in the areas of abortion and euthanasia. None of the actual essays commissioned to take up this question attracted as much attention as the editorial that introduced them, which provided this frame for the matter the authors were considering: "The question here explored, in full awareness of its far-reaching consequences, is whether we have reached or are reaching the point where conscientious citizens can no longer give moral assent to the existing regime." Similarly dramatic sentences followed, not least one that came out of a commendation of Princeton constitutional scholar Robert George's contribution to the symposium, which was a critical reading of U.S. court decisions on abortion and assisted suicide in the context of John Paul II's encyclical on the dignity and sanctity of life, *Evangelium Vitae.* After noting that the encyclical invoked earlier "papal statements condemning the crimes of Nazi Germany," the editorial declares,

> *America is not and, please God, never will become Nazi Germany, but it is only blind hubris that denies it can happen here and, in peculiarly American ways, may be happening here.*

Hedging, qualified, halting, but nevertheless insistent: Neuhaus here avowed that what took place under the Nazis could someday take place—no, might already be taking place—in an America unjustly governed by an overreaching federal judiciary. The authors contributing essays on this situation, the editorial continues, "examine possible responses to laws that cannot be obeyed by conscientious citizens—ranging from non-compliance to morally justified revolution." In this same section, the editorial self-consciously declares, "We are prepared for the charge that publishing this symposium is irresponsibly provocative and even alarmist." In fact, Neuhaus was not nearly as prepared for such charges as he should have been.[2]

Peter Berger resigned from the editorial board when he read the issue. Having missed the May editorial board meeting, he had no idea what had been planned, and he was steadfastly against what he regarded as the magazine's counterproductive, even contradictory effort to radicalize conservatism. As he would later lament, this break created a deeper and more permanent break between himself and Neuhaus, after decades of great friendship and close, fruitful collaboration. Once the "End of Democracy?" controversy eventually died down, the two would resume their connection, but for years thereafter it was only old friends reminiscing, rather than two industrious and enterprising intellectuals cooking up new ideas for books and statements and conferences over late-night drinks. The "End of Democracy?" issue, and what he similarly regarded as Neuhaus' growing focus on abortion to the exclusion of other concerns in public life, suggested to Berger that theirs was no longer a shared vision and mission. Berger's departure may have been the most painful for Neuhaus personally, but similarly damaging to the magazine's standing among the intellectual elites of the Right were historian Gertrude

Himmelfarb's and constitutional scholar Walter Berns' resignations from the board. Meanwhile, Midge Decter, likewise absent from the May meeting, wrote to the editors, to Neuhaus specifically, whom she had first edited in the early 1970s at Doubleday, to chastise him for trafficking in "the kind of careless radicalism you and I not all that long ago prayed for our country to have put behind it." Like Berger, Himmelfarb, Berns, and others, as they variously explained their decisions to resign in both *First Things* and in a later, related issue of *Commentary,* Decter was particularly upset by the editorial's "profoundly morally offensive" willingness even to entertain questions of the government's legitimacy and to invoke the possibility that a case for morally justified revolution could be made in and about 1990s America.[3]

Over at *Commentary,* Norman Podhoretz was less lamenting than plainly outraged, and bluntly at odds with his erstwhile friend and collaborator. To push back against the doomsday noise coming out of *First Things,* Podhoretz took to the pages of his magazine to declare the 1996 elections "a victory for conservatism." After all, the Republicans had maintained control over both houses of Congress, consolidating the advances made under the Newt Gingrich–led GOP rise in the '94 midterms, while Clinton's reelection was made possible, Podhoretz argued, by his tacking to the center, if not to the right, on much domestic policy—on balanced budgets, welfare reform, law and order policies, even signing a bill defending traditional marriage (DOMA). To be sure, Podhoretz continued, Clinton remained steadfastly liberal on affirmative action and also on abortion, the latter signaled by his vetoing legislation that banned partial-birth abortions, but nevertheless, Podhoretz insisted, "conservatism [has] showed itself alive and well in the 1996 elections," and as a result, "the splits in conservatism have become very troubling indeed." While noting fissures and worse on foreign policy and between fiscal and social conservatives, Podhoretz assigned blame for this division squarely to Neuhaus and *First Things* for running its "End of Democracy?" issue. Podhoretz charged that in its channeling sixties-era "anti-Americanism" into 1990s domestic policy debates, the magazine effectively provided "aid and comfort . . . to the bomb-throwers among us" just as it "has served to undermine and besmirch" the late conservative project to resist and roll back the ongoing excesses of sixties-era liberalism in government and culture both. All of which led Podhoretz to demand "nothing less than a frank and forthright recognition of error (or should I say act of contrition?)," matched to a request: that his "old friend Richard Neuhaus . . . once more undergo a process of deradicalization and re-emerge as a born-again neoconservative."[4]

Podhoretz's published comments on "The End of Democracy?" appeared in the February 1997 issue of *Commentary*, following equally pointed personal correspondence with Neuhaus immediately after the controversial issue came out, with both men copying a select group of well-positioned common friends and colleagues—Peter Berger, William F. Buckley, Jr., Gertrude Himmelfarb, Michael Novak, James Nuechterlein, and George Weigel. In one exchange of private letters, Neuhaus weakly attempted to disavow the dramatic implications of the issue's title by pointing out that it was a question, not a declaration, but Podhoretz would have none of it: "As George Will once put it in an analogous context," he shot back, "one does not hold a conference on the theme 'Wither Incest?' in order to reaffirm the prohibition against incest."[5]

Podhoretz was arguably Neuhaus' most vociferous critic from the neoconservative Right, going so far as to devote the February issue of *Commentary* to debating "the Future of Conservatism" as a response to the November *First Things* issue. In fact, he published supportive and critical views both, a spectrum of responses that reflected coverage of the magazine issue, and of reactions to it, in broader conservative and mainstream media from fall 1996 through spring 1997. The conservative press variously took up the question of whether *First Things* had gone too far. *Commentary*'s editor certainly thought so, but Podhoretz's was far from the only view. On the farther side of the Right, Neuhaus' relentless scourge Joseph Sobran published a more sympathetic opinion that "Distrust of Government Isn't Anti-American" in *Conservative Chronicles,* while longstanding traditional conservative leader William Rusher also wrote a sympathetic piece, declaring, "It's Time to Rein in the Courts" in *Viewpoint.* Neuhaus found other allies elsewhere in the neoconservative world, notably the editors of the *Weekly Standard,* who likewise issued a call that it was "Time to Take on the Judges." But as an indicator of how divisive the "End of Democracy?" issue had become, David Brooks, also writing in the *Weekly Standard,* argued that *First Things* was encouraging observers to wonder, "Is the Right About to Go Anti-American?" Brooks sharpened this point by quoting Neuhaus against himself, specifically his warning from two years earlier, in commenting on the racial controversies surrounding Charles Murray's 1994 book *The Bell Curve,* about the irresponsibility of intellectuals and academics engaging matters of grave public implication without consideration for the felt consequences of their "utterly dispassionate and socially disengaged" efforts.[6]

National Review's editors published two editorials on the issue, both reading the "End of Democracy?" symposium in the most generous light. In the second of these pieces, a December editorial rather dramatically entitled "The War of the Roses," the editors further took it upon themselves to play mediator among the opposed camps. As with their initial November 1996 piece, "First Things First," the editors framed the *First Things* symposium as a serious-minded intellectual effort to make sense of the nature and demands of loyalty in "a democratic society whose laws are no longer set by the people." Although the December *National Review* editorial made it clear that the symposium wasn't in fact issuing a call "for revolutionary defiance," it also recognized that it could be (and was being) taken this way, and steadfastly distanced itself from this outcome, noting that *National Review* had "never condoned protests in any other form than political and intellectual." But its driving concern was to avoid a civil war on the intellectual Right: "Most conservatives will acknowledge the usefulness of sharpening the discriminating faculties that allocate loyalties; but they will decline a war against our political regime, and most emphatically decline a war against our brethren, the neocons."[7]

That same month, Jacob Heilbrunn wrote an extensive analysis of this war for the *New Republic,* noting that a late November meeting of conservative leaders—Neuhaus, William Kristol, and William F. Buckley, Jr.—failed to end the conflict, which Heilbrunn only intensified by introducing the term "theocon" into public discourse as a way of explaining the uproar over the "End of Democracy?" According to Heilbrunn, this uproar exposed a deep division on the intellectual Right, with Neuhaus and the *First Things* project on one side, and Podhoretz and the neoconservatives associated with *Commentary* on the other. The distinction, according to Heilbrunn, who would also later write a book on the subject, was that "the neoconservatives believe that America is special because it was founded on an idea—a commitment to the rights of man embodied in the Declaration of Independence—not in ethnic or religious affiliations. The theocons argue, too, that America is rooted in an idea, but they believe that idea is Christianity. In their view, the United States is first and foremost a Christian nation, governed ultimately by natural law," and best directed by Catholic teachings from the likes of Aquinas and John Paul II. Neuhaus would have a hard time recognizing his long-standing vision for a public philosophy in Heilbrunn's assignment of an essentially Erastian, if not neo-medieval agenda to him and his colleagues and their magazine—not least because he subscribed to the main neoconservative view of American exceptionalism and saw his distinctive role as advocating for its Judeo-Christian elements for both demographic and intellectual reasons. Regardless, by the end of 1996, the divisions and terms were set, and the war was joined.[8]

Observers from the mainstream media and intellectual Left paid much attention to the "End of Democracy?" issue and the infighting it was generating on the Right, which continued to debate the matter for months in columns and letters in various intellectual, political, and religious conservative publications. In fact, as early as October 9, *New York Times* columnist Frank Rich (whom Neuhaus elsewhere dismissed as a "toy Doberman" for his shrunken and vicious writings about religious conservatives) predicted that a "bitter culture war" was in the making that had implications and consequences well beyond the current presidential election campaign. Rich read the "End of Democracy?" issue as a strong indicator of the "escalating passions" and even apocalyptic rhetoric emerging in conservative America. And in perhaps the only instance where Frank Rich and Norman Podhoretz would be in total agreement, Rich suggested its intellectual leaders "sound as angry and bellicose as the very '60s radicals they despise," a theme Rich would take up again with an updated version of the piece, now caustically entitled "The New New Left," in a March column for the *Times.*

Broader coverage and responses from across the country were in full swing throughout these months and beyond, in *Newsday,* the *Wall Street Journal,* the *Detroit News,* the *Washington Post,* the *Boston Herald, U.S. News and World Report,* the *Seattle Times,* the *Chicago Tribune,* and other outlets, and the controversy attracted international coverage as well: Christopher Hitchens wrote about the "Civil War" on the Right that the issue had started, for the London *Sunday Times* in late December, and a month later Ambrose Evans-Pritchard took a view more sympathetic to Neuhaus and the issue in the London *Sunday-Telegraph.* All told, *First Things'* most famous, and to many, infamous, issue inspired more than two hundred articles, providing the magazine with unprecedented media attention. It also had a measurable effect on the magazine's circulation: the issue itself sold 20 percent more copies at newsstands than its November 1995 predecessor; it generated noticeably more subscription orders via the offer insertions in its pages compared to other fall 1996 issues; there were some six hundred direct requests for copies of the issue, compared to the one hundred or so requests usually made; and finally, while the overall active paid circulation for *First Things* made an annual increase of one thousand in November 1996, to 27,000 subscribers, the circulation had jumped to 31,500 by November 1997.[9]

What was Neuhaus doing, during weeks and then months of intellectual firestorm and personal conflict, media blitz and magazine growth? Unsurprisingly, he was doing many things, though not fully in control of any one of them, as is signaled by a December 31, 1996, handwritten note he faxed to Gary Bauer, then president of the Family Research Council:

> Dear Gary, Please let me beg off for January 9 [a luncheon in Washington]. I'm still recovering from surgery, my mother died this past weekend, and things are in a general state of disarray. Richard.

This is an unaccustomedly un-positive note from Neuhaus—particularly the candid admission of "a general state of disarray" around him, and with obvious good cause. First, he would have been grieving and paining, and not simply about losing friends over a magazine issue and some bad press. Pain came from having his gall bladder removed in late fall 1996, a procedure that was needed to deal with the ongoing aftereffects of his cancer bout. Grief came from Ella dying, aged ninety-two. Joining his siblings for the funeral, Neuhaus went home to Pembroke, where Ella had returned many years earlier from the small town of Simcoe, Ontario, following Clem's death. He did not preside, of course, at the Lutheran service, but he stepped forward at the burial site to offer a blessing to his mother, a small and quietly determined, devout Lutheran wife and mother who kept her counsel close throughout her life and could always surprise people, including her own children, as with her nonchalant response to news of her son's conversion to Catholicism, or with her remark years before, when she was in Valparaiso to visit Johanna and also hear Richard give a lecture. At the reception afterward, crocheting in the corner while Neuhaus enjoyed kudos for his remarks from a room packed with admirers and university officials, Ella eventually spoke up, offering a mother's review of a son's work. She declared, "Well Richard, all I can say is you sure write better than you speak," and brought the house down.

In far graver terms, in conservative intellectual terms in late 1996 and early 1997, bringing the house down was effectively what Neuhaus was being accused of doing with his writing, and of course he inevitably wrote more in response to these charges as the "End of Democracy?" controversy kept on. In addition to his semiprivate correspondence with Podhoretz, Neuhaus wrote Peter Berger a dense, four-page personal note expressing his great disappointment at Berger's resignation, adamantly defending the symposium nevertheless, and sadly acknowledging the personal rupture this had clearly created. Likewise in letter form, he turned for solace to William F. Buckley, Jr., expressing his gratitude for Buckley's support from *National Review* along with his disappointment that some of their colleagues "continued to take the bait" and hook themselves onto a mischaracterization of the issue's purposes and in turn contribute more to the problem, for evidence of which he cited *Commentary*'s February 1997 counter-symposium on the future of conservatism, to which Neuhaus was conspicuously not invited to contribute.[10]

Of course, Neuhaus had his own platform for addressing the matter, and in the January 1997 issue of *First Things,* he published yet another strident editorial. "To Reclaim Our Democratic Heritage" acknowledged the November issue had "generated intense debate about many things," and while he offered deeply felt "regret" about the resignations from the editorial board, nevertheless Neuhaus insisted that "neither the editorial introduction nor the essays in the symposium asserted that the government of the United States is illegitimate. We thought that was made clear, but apparently not." What becomes clear, in the remainder of the piece, is Neuhaus' emphatic position that he and the magazine did not bear primary responsibility for the situation they and others were now dealing with: "We did not choose this controversy. It was started by a judiciary, and most particularly by a Supreme Court, that has increasingly arrogated to itself the legislative and executive functions of the government." Careful this time not to set off any rhetorical trip wires with Nazi Germany analogies, Neuhaus nevertheless doubled down: "The problem before us is precisely one of judicial *usurpation*," and the "End of Democracy?" issue was, its presider argued, "part of a very long tradition of moral and political thought about legitimate responses to illegitimate government. As explained above, we do not believe that the government of the United States is illegitimate. Ours is not a revolutionary situation, and, please God, never will become that." And so, out of a "devotion to this constitutional order and the rule of law . . . we therefore call for the vigorous pursuit of every peaceful and constitutional means to return our country to its democratic heritage," a pursuit that required the reawakening and reapplication of morally informed public reasoning to the great questions of the day, which was precisely the mission of *First Things* itself. All of which was rhetorically more sober than the earlier issue's statements on this problem and solution, yet Neuhaus could not resist a subtly threatening kicker: "If, as we hope, we are not on the way to the end of democracy, the judiciary will restrain itself, or it will be restrained."[11]

Unbowed in print, Neuhaus was far more conflicted in private. Late nights in his apartment at 338 during the months of the controversy, he sought relief from the stress of the daily intensities at the magazine's office, from all the letters and phone calls, and likewise from the need to appear before his staff and the public world as still in strong command of the situation. He sought this relief in the company of his editor, which was mostly too bad for James Nuechterlein, as he later recalled: after a few drinks, and a few soliloquies questioning why people like Norman and Midge could not understand that Neuhaus was doing, at least trying to do, the good and necessary thing, he refocused his frustration on Nuechterlein directly, "screaming" at him for not supporting and defending him from his opponents. Of course, Nuechterlein had been the one warning all along that the issue was going to create serious problems for Neuhaus and the magazine with their long-standing allies, but rather than admit as much now that it was clearly the case, Neuhaus blamed and raged at him. A discreet, prudent, and impeccably professional man, Nuechterlein was a safe outlet-cum-target for Neuhaus, because Neuhaus knew none of the screaming and lamentations would leave the apartment. Only eight years later, when Nuechterlein retired from his editorship, did Neuhaus quietly acknowledge that he may have had a point, years before: "I could count on the fingers of one hand the number of articles we published that he opposed . . . and in retrospect, he was mostly right (I suspect he has been waiting a long time for that admission)."[12]

If Neuhaus was the controversial center of ongoing attention in American conservative life from fall 1996 through spring 1997, he found himself in a decidedly opposite position in late 1997, when he went to Rome for a month to serve as a comparatively lowly delegate at the Special Assembly for America of the Synod of Bishops. Upon arrival, he discovered that on the published list of the three hundred attendees, or "Synod fathers," his name was "dead last." This led to a candid self-discovery of sorts, as he would recount: "I am not accustomed to that back in my little world among the many worlds of New York City. But this is Rome." Despite the undeniable privileges of access and even influence Neuhaus may have enjoyed during the John Paul II pontificate by comparison to other U.S. clerics, at a conference in Rome he was just another bored-looking American priest who could not speak Italian, a priest who incidentally published an intellectual magazine back home. This assembly was part of John Paul II's broader call, in his apostolic letter *Tertio Millennio Adveniente* (1994), for the Church to conduct a series of extended meetings, organized by continent (or, with the Americas, by hemisphere), to discuss geographically and culturally shared exigencies and aspirations at the turn of the millennium. Neuhaus was directly appointed to the gathering by John Paul II and was not, he noted, "indifferent to the honor," but that having been said, "not since that year in the fourth grade have I experienced such tedium," he would later write.

Worse was tedium experienced vicariously, as George Weigel discovered. In evening sessions over bourbon, Neuhaus complained to Weigel about the seeming pointlessness of the assembly. The whole affair struck him as little more than an elaborate pretext for three hundred men to enjoy the sound of their own voices, one by one, hour after hour, and he was last on that list. Weigel was himself in Rome because by this point he was well into his work on the biography of John Paul II, a project for which he had secured the encouragement and personal cooperation of the pope via a 1995 dinner in the papal apartment, where Neuhaus was also at the table and serving as a willing advocate for his friend. In other words, while Weigel could sympathize with his friend's frustrations about Rome, he had more pressing matters to attend to than listening to Richard go on about all these other people, higher on the assembly list, going on and on. Knowing his friend all too well, Weigel likewise knew that the best way to get Richard to stop talking about something was to get him to start writing about it instead. "Why don't you do a book about this?" Weigel suggested.[13]

Appointment in Rome was published two years later, as "a *very* unofficial report on what happened at the Synod for America," as Neuhaus noted in the preface. What happened, for Neuhaus, was that he discovered just how dramatically different U.S. and Roman religious and intellectual culture could be. Back home, a few provocative sentences in a journal lost him friendships and editorial board members while winning him new readers and months of media coverage. Here, hour upon hour of reports and interventions bore little relation to the lived-out challenges and opportunities of the Church in the Americas at the end of the twentieth century. Instead, these amount to "an argumentative muddle" of an affair, typified by displays of personal power by Church leaders and showy name-dropping by lesser players who sought to advance themselves through the Vatican's baroque bureaucracies. But John Paul II was present for the proceedings, and so, Neuhaus reasoned, there had to be some higher purpose to them, even if Neuhaus caught sight of the pope occasionally "reading a book kept discreetly beneath his desk" while the speeches went on. Neuhaus' impatience with the assembly turned to "humbling" frustration, when he realized how little influence his own work, advocating "that the Church can or should seize the initiative in transforming the culture," enjoyed: what he personally regarded as his "much-discussed book, *The Catholic Moment*," he discovered, had been little discussed beyond his immediate orbit.[14]

Yet the pope wanted Neuhaus in Rome for this, and not without reason. Neuhaus certainly made a strong impression with his formal contribution to the assembly, a report he delivered on the work of Evangelicals and Catholics Together, which argued that millennial evangelization in the Church of Americas would best contribute to Christian unity if, he told his Roman audience, "in the next century, evangelical Protestants and Roman Catholics can evangelize and re-evangelize *with* one another rather than against one another." Having already complained about his seeming smallness in the affair, Neuhaus had little compunction about noting all the warm words and congratulations he received for his report, "including a smile and a wave from the Holy Father which I chose to interpret as encouragement." Still more encouraging was the personal note Neuhaus received from John Paul II—brief, cordial, positive, signed in spidery script, and identifying the book as a welcome contribution to the Church's effort to take its mission into the third millennium and further into the Americas. This came after Neuhaus sent him a copy of the published book, which otherwise generated little public attention beyond reliably positive reviews from U.S. conservative Catholic journals. When the book's Italian edition came out, Neuhaus was reprimanded in writing by Brazilian cardinal Eugenio de Araújo Sales, who had presided over the assembly, for allegedly breaking "the obligation of secrecy" that covered the comments made at the synod, as Neuhaus ironically describes this very expectation in the book itself. He countered by sending Sales a copy of John Paul II's note, suggesting with tart respect that here was a reviewer with a different view.

He did the very same with Orlen Lapp, the longtime pastor at St. John's Pembroke. After reading a copy of *Appointment in Rome* that Neuhaus had sent along, Lapp wrote a friendly but also critical response, arguing that Neuhaus' calls for ecumenical integration between Catholics and Protestants were unpersuasive by Lapp's Lutheran lights because Neuhaus' vision of ecumenism, and of Christianity itself, struck him as so strongly Catholic in its emphases, notably on the significance of Mary, as to make it difficult for a Protestant to find meaningful commonality with this proposal. And so Neuhaus sent Lapp another copy of John Paul II's note, suggesting with tart affection this time that here was a reviewer with a different view. This clear evidence of Neuhaus' personal connection to the pope himself greatly impressed the small-town pastor; starstruck, he later asked Neuhaus what it was like to meet the pope, to get to visit him in the papal apartment and have lunch with him and all. "Well Orlen," Neuhaus airily replied, "it's not like going to McDonald's, you know." Obviously Orlen Lapp knew this, as he pressed Neuhaus for details about an encounter he could not otherwise imagine happening for the Pembroke-born son of the longtime Lutheran pastor he had succeeded. Neuhaus knew as much and enjoyed the wowed attention he received back home for his successes in the great world: he sent copies of every book and magazine issue he published to his relatives in Pembroke; few read them cover-to-cover, but they were proudly displayed and talked about around town.[15]

By the time *Appointment in Rome* was published and read in Rome and Pembroke both, Neuhaus had spanned a similar gap between his comparatively minor origins and his current influence and prominence, this time in a Texas context. In early May 1998, five months after he returned to New York from his month in Rome, Neuhaus accepted successive invitations for two Texan engagements. The first was from Concordia-Austin, which proudly had one of its most illustrious graduates come back to give a talk as part of its Distinguished Alumni Series. Presumably, Neuhaus chose not to scandalize the audience this time by swearing up a storm as part of his performance, as he'd done decades before in going off the wholesomely censored script for the Concordia Drama Society's rendition of *Stalag 17*. The second Texas invitation came from Karl Rove, for Neuhaus to have breakfast at the governor's mansion with George W. Bush, who was then considering a run for the presidency in 2000. Rove's invitation was a clear signal of Neuhaus' unparalleled status as a Catholic intellectual leader among America's social and cultural conservatives, who was likewise known for his ecumenical work with evangelicals and regularly commanded national media attention. With this kind of crossover profile, Neuhaus would have been of signal interest and value to Rove, who, as part of his work as Bush's personal advisor for a presidential run, was intent on identifying and creating a coalition of religious conservatives, primarily made up of Catholics and evangelicals, that could translate into a substantial electoral advantage. In no small part, this meant ensuring that his candidate understood their concerns and could speak to them with persuasive sympathy. Neuhaus was at once the perfect tutor and guarantor for these plans and needs, a position helped along by his recurring reproaches of the Clinton presidency on both personal terms and in terms of the administration's policies.

He leveled his many criticisms in the back pages of *First Things* throughout the 1990s and also, in spring 1998, shortly before meeting Bush in Austin, with a more dramatically staged criticism of Clinton: at the conclusion of a prayer breakfast with the president, Neuhaus was one of the leaders in a successful effort to have the five thousand religious figures present stand in silence, rather than applaud, and in this way bear pointed witness to Clinton's besmirching of the office of the presidency with his personal moral failings. Neuhaus' cutting assessments of Clinton culminated in a bravura piece he wrote in the wake of the Monica Lewinsky scandal, entitled

"Bill Clinton and the American Character," in which he argued that Clinton was more than a serial liar or even compartmentalizer of his personal and political activities: he was, in fact, endowed with "a species of autism" that explained his otherwise inexplicably self-involved behavior, behavior that for too long had been enabled by an increasingly crude national culture and a citizenry that was at times little more than a bunch of "slobs." All of which meant that "for the next little while we are stuck with a President who, beyond reasonable doubt, is guilty of perjury, tampering with witnesses, and obstruction of justice, and who probably is a rapist."[16]

Neuhaus wrote this about a year after meeting the man he was confident would be a very different kind of president, in personal morality and public policy both, a confidence that came not least because Bush was so clearly open to Neuhaus' counsel, which Neuhaus was so clearly willing to give. Immediately upon returning to New York from Austin, after their May 1998 meeting, Neuhaus wrote Bush to tell him that "our wide-ranging conversation gave me abundant reason to hope that you will seek the opportunity to be of still greater service to our country." But Neuhaus had more business here than friendly flattery: he commended Bush's ambition to propose a "politics of hope" to the American people rather than any superficial optimism. He emphasized that what was "absolutely indispensable" to that effort would be, "as we discussed, the strong support of the 'social conservatives' who yearn, above all, for a revival of moral responsibility. And absolutely indispensable to the support of that constituency," Neuhaus continued, "is unmistakable public clarity on abortion and related 'life issues.'" Acknowledging Bush's pragmatic reluctance to "'lead' with the abortion question" because it was so politically divisive, Neuhaus pushed back: "The only way of preventing it from becoming the lead question is to settle it securely with your supporters to whom it matters most." Here Neuhaus turned openly strategic: "Let me urge you as strongly as I can to view the pro-life position not only as a moral imperative but as a big political plus," which he detailed by citing polling data that pointed to ultimately limited and soft support for hard-line abortion policies, which in turn would provide "a great advantage to any leader firmly and articulately supportive of the goal: 'Every unborn child protected in law and welcomed in life.'" Having underlined this statement in his letter to Bush—who would use it repeatedly in his future presidency to articulate his pro-life policy goal—Neuhaus concluded by offering his prayers, and an offer of further assistance should Bush seek it. He also threw in the latest issue of *First Things*.[17]

Bush immediately wrote back, expressing his gratitude to Neuhaus for providing "enlightenment on the main issue that matters in the long run of our country, the need for a cultural shift" toward what Bush called "the responsibility era," which would help bring about a healthier "civil society that respects life and liberty and allows for people to pursue happiness." To emphasize their already common vision on life matters, Bush "enclosed a few documents and a letter regarding my public positions on the abortion issue." He concluded with a subtle but telling request to Neuhaus that suggested Bush's regard for his connections: "Perhaps, someday you can introduce me to your friends up north," Bush suggested, before making a promise that suggested the two of them got along at their breakfast beyond policy and politics: "In the meantime, should I make it to Cisco, I will give them all your best." Bush closed his note, "I look forward to seeing you again"—and he would, in the Oval Office no less, in the early years of a tumultuous new period in American life and world affairs.[18]

CHAPTER TWENTY-TWO

A Time of Triumph, a Time of War, a Time of Scandal

On August 7, 2000, the kitchen phone rang at the Neuhaus family cottage in Pembroke. Neuhaus answered and spoke for a while. The call concluded, he turned to his immediate audience—his big sister Mim, and also Mary and Erwin Prange, elderly relatives from Ella's side—and casually noted, "Well, that was the *New York Times.* Five minutes ago, Al Gore just announced Joe Lieberman as his running mate and so their reporter called me to see what I thought about it." "And what did you say?" Uncle Erwin asked on behalf of the others, who were all starstruck enough by this clear signal of their little brother and nephew's standing in the great world that they took a picture with him afterward to commemorate the occasion. His mouth curling a wry grin, Neuhaus told his captive kitchen audience, "I told her, we can handle him." In fact, Neuhaus was more objective and encouraging than sharp-tongued and partisan in talking to the *Times* about Lieberman's selection; at least he was published as such. "For a lot of serious Christians," Neuhaus was quoted in the article that ran the next day, "the fact that he's an observant Jew would be viewed very positively. America is incorrigibly and confusedly a religious nation, and the fact that a person is viewed as religiously devout, someone who lives what he believes, is clearly a plus."[1]

That Neuhaus was tracked down in the Ottawa Valley to offer his views indicates that by August 2000, he had become perhaps the nation's leading commentator and, on the neoconservative Right, its prime influencer on how religion was figuring in day-to-day electoral politics. In fact, two months before *Times* reporter Laurie Goodstein sought his opinion on the significance of Lieberman joining Gore on the Democratic ticket, Andrew Sullivan, an often critical and provocative observer of the American scene, especially of the overlapping worlds of intellectualism, politics, and religion, wrote more directly about Neuhaus' growing influence in the electoral race, for the *Sunday Times* of London. Sullivan credited Neuhaus and also Michael Novak with providing "intellectual fiber" to Republican candidate George W. Bush's program of "compassionate conservatism." More specifically, Sullivan argued that Neuhaus and Novak had already laid the groundwork for Bush's success with Catholic voters in aligning Catholic social teachings with U.S. conservative emphases through their writings in the 1980s and 1990s, efforts that were now enjoying campaign year currency as evidenced by Bush's stump speech references to "solidarity" and "the common good," not to mention (unreported by Sullivan but noted elsewhere) his use of a hallmark John Paul II phrase, "the culture of life," as a shorthand to signal his proposed plans in social policy.[2]

Two years before establishing Neuhaus' importance to U.S. politics for a British audience, Sullivan did some groundwork of his own with a *New York Times Magazine* profile of the "deeply influential" new forces in American conservative culture, namely William Kristol and the magazine he edited, the *Weekly Standard,* and Neuhaus and *First Things,* the latter duo credited by Sullivan as together sustaining nothing less than a "neoreligious revival" within conservatism, attesting to the magazine's status (and its editor in chief by extension) as "the spiritual nerve center of the new conservatism." This was phrasing that would feature in *First Things* advertising for years after Sullivan's October 1998 piece for the *Times Magazine*, which came a few months after Neuhaus had first breakfasted with Bush at the governor's mansion as he was considering a run for the presidency. Two years later, Neuhaus was being called upon and cited by journalists and campaigning politicians alike, largely for his distinctive capacity to explain to multiple audiences what it meant, what it took, and what it made possible, in higher-order religious and pragmatic political terms, when a person of faith sought public office. And how was Neuhaus himself demonstrating what it meant to "live what he believes," during an intensely political season in American life? Given his natural inclinations toward both media and political engagement, and the great standing he was enjoying in these overlapping contexts, he certainly ran the risk of becoming little more than a pundit with a Roman collar, and critical observers tracking only his campaign-related activities could find reason to regard him as such. But this was far from a full account of Richard John Neuhaus' sense of himself and his religious vocation, as was made powerfully clear by the book he published in the midst of a presidential election campaign.[3]

> *Our lives are measured by who we are created and called to be, and the measuring is done by the One who creates and calls. Finally, the judgment that matters is not ours. The judgment that matters is the judgment of God, who alone judges justly. In the cross we see the rendering of the verdict on the gravity of our sin. We have come to our senses. None of our sins are small or of little account. To belittle our sins is to belittle ourselves . . . to belittle their forgiveness, to belittle the love of the Father who welcomes us home.*

This stark, eloquent challenge to the Christian to understand himself in the context of God's super-abundant love—nowhere more apparent than in Christ's hanging upon the cross for each and all—comes not from a pundit reliable for punchy copy. Rather, it comes from a priest leading his parishioners to a greater reckoning with the central event of Christianity itself: that God loved the world so much, He sent His only son to die for our sins and be resurrected from the dead; that through this redemptive expiation, we may come to know God fully and perfectly in eternal life. The passage comes from early on in Neuhaus' *Death on a Friday Afternoon: Meditations on the Last Words of Jesus from the Cross,* a contemplative book that began as a three-hour meditation that he preached at the Church of St. John the Evangelist, on First Avenue at 55th, in the mid-1990s. Upon the book's March 2000 release, John Cardinal O'Connor hosted a reception at his residence, though he was too ill to attend himself. Neuhaus delivered remarks at the reception, and mindful that the cardinal was failing, he focused less on his latest book than on the man to whom he owed a "debt beyond calculation." This debt reached back to their first meeting in 1984, when O'Connor was announced as New York's new archbishop, and went from there to Neuhaus' entry into the Church and ordination, and thereafter to the "Richard, wiggle your nose" moment in the intensive care unit. At the end of his remarks, Neuhaus spoke of O'Connor's having metaphorically followed the example of his father, who had worked as a gold-leaf craftsman, but "It is a different kind of gold. . . . The gold of kindness, of generosity, of uncompromised witness to the truth, of devoted service to the end." Neuhaus very much regarded O'Connor as his own spiritual father, and in fact, following O'Connor's death that May, this devotion to him could bring Neuhaus to tears late nights at 338 when he discussed the great man, the great New Yorker, the great priest, the great example for himself and his own ongoing vocation to bear witness to the truth.[4]

In the preface to *Death on a Friday Afternoon,* Neuhaus also acknowledged the others who were crucial to his efforts in this respect, not least the support of his longtime assistant Davida Goldman, to whom he dedicated the book, along with Jim Nuechterlein and Matthew Berke, another longtime editor at *First Things.* He glossed this trio as "loyal companions on the way from strength to strength, with detours," an affectionate and self-critical account of what it meant to work with Neuhaus day-to-day for years on end that likely no one else could appreciate such as they did. *Death on a Friday Afternoon* would remind its dedicatees, its broader readership, and indeed likely its very author that opining about presidential politics, advising would-be presidents, even putting out a magazine, were all ultimately lesser endeavors compared to the sacred responsibilities to which Neuhaus was consecrated, as a priest, of leading people into the "world of worship, prayer and contemplative exploration into the mystery of Christ's presence."

He fulfilled the first and second imperatives through his daily and Sunday celebrations of the Mass at Immaculate Conception, a few blocks south of 338; he fulfilled that third imperative movingly with this book, divided into seven chapters that correspond to the seven words—or distinct phrases—that Christ speaks from the cross on Good Friday, which demand and reward close, sustained attention. For, Neuhaus observed, "in the derelict who cries from the cross is, or so Christians say, the Alpha and the Omega, the beginning and the end. The life of all on this day died." And so, he proposes, "stay a while with that dying." Thereafter, in relating a symptomatic experience of his, he makes clear the personal challenge he faced in achieving this kind of higher-order patience because of the nature of his public profile. A few years before, Neuhaus was giving a talk to a large group of clergy in the Midwest. They had for two days been studying sacramental and liturgical theology, "and it came time for the bishop to introduce me. 'It has been a rewarding two days,' he said, 'as we have been thinking about worship and the sacramental life, but now we have Father Neuhaus to return us to the real world as he addresses the subject of the Church and social responsibility.' Really? The real world?" Neuhaus was clearly disappointed in the irony that his seeming accomplishment with *First Things* was an elevation of mere "social responsibility" matters over worship and sacrament, the absolute first things for all Christians, public square–bestriding priests included.[5]

Certainly, *Death on a Friday Afternoon* emphasizes these absolutes, with its rich, chapter-by-chapter meditations on Christ's last seven words, and from spring through fall 2000, the book was warmly and positively reviewed on just these terms. It was often written about alongside *The Eternal Pity,* an anthology Neuhaus edited of writing from across centuries and cultures about the difficulties and greater dignities of end-of-life experiences. The anthology formed the latest installment in the "Ethics of Everyday Life" seminar-cum-book series, and its selections ranged from Tolstoy, John Donne, and the Qur'an to Ralph Abernathy and writings from *First Things* itself, by Gilbert Meilaender and Jody Bottum. In fact, alongside his sister Mim—"for her loving presence through the long watches of death's vigil"—Neuhaus dedicated the book to Bottum, a literary-minded Catholic intellectual then serving as the poetry editor of *First Things,* who, out of great admiration and devotion, would take on an increasingly significant role in Neuhaus' overlapping personal and professional lives in the years to come, culminating in his attending closely to Neuhaus in his own final days and taking over *First Things* upon its founder's death.[6]

By fall 2000, even with two new books having come out in the preceding months that attested to the profundity of his commitment and attentiveness to the higher-order demands of his priesthood and of human life itself, Neuhaus was, nevertheless, like much of America, intensely focused on the presidential race. In October, he attended a Claremont Institute dinner honoring William F. Buckley, Jr., at the Waldorf Astoria; he delivered the invocation and after dinner repaired to a private suite at the hotel, alongside Buckley and others, to watch that night's presidential debate. On election night itself, as Neuhaus would later admit, "I paid the price of relying on inside information from the Bush camp," which led him, wrongly, to expect a clear victory. Instead, Gore won the popular vote while Bush prevailed in the electoral college, the latter a constitutionally decisive victory itself disputed because of the vote count in Florida. Days and then weeks of legal maneuvering came to an end in

December 2000, when the Supreme Court intervened and stopped a state court–ordered recount, a decision Gore accepted, which conclusively affirmed Bush's victory. In his February 2001 *First Things* reflection on the election and its complicated and controversial denouement, Neuhaus crowed about a triumph he had some hand in, at least after deprecating his skills as an election-night political prognosticator. Parsing exit polls, he noted Bush's advantage among voters who cited "moral/ethical values" as their primary concern, and likewise among Catholics who self-identified as weekly attendees at Mass, which he took as confirmation "that a pro-life position is an election plus" and that the Bush campaign's (Neuhaus-formed) "message, especially on abortion and [also] parental choice in education, is getting through to Catholics within hearing range." Those "within hearing range" were those given to regular Mass attendance, which had emerged in this election as a reliable indicator of Republican voting preferences.[7]

If sanguinely pleased in that respect, Neuhaus was oddly triumphant in another. He noted the ways in which the Florida court battle over the state's vote count resulted in "sundry pundits recalling what we have been saying about the judicial usurpation of politics and suggesting that this journal is owed apologies. Apologies, I should note, are accepted graciously and without even a hint of smug self-congratulation." In fact, Neuhaus' post–2000 election analysis is overdetermined by just this ungracious quality, both in terms of his reading of the socially conservative voter preferences that figured notably in Bush's victory, and even more so in terms of his reading of the judicial steps that led to Bush's eventually being declared victor. On the latter point, having declared himself and *First Things* vindicated by commentary from "both left and right" about "the tyranny of judicial usurpation" at play in the Florida recount drama, Neuhaus then criticizes partisan pundits who credited the Supreme Court with intervening to halt the recount and thus "spar[ing] us the awful prospect of self-government through the constitutional means of representative democracy."

He then immediately turns partisan pundit himself: "Having said that, I do think the decision of the Supreme Court was the right one. It was a sharp and dramatic rebuke of the Florida court's usurpation of legislative authority in attempting to change election laws after the election. A more effective challenge to the regime of judicial usurpation, however, awaits an occasion where a wayward court is set right not by another court, but by those who are elected to represent the sovereign people." That final sentence notwithstanding, Neuhaus is clearly satisfied here with a judicial intervention that advanced his own political and policy preferences, and it's difficult not to read the accompanying account as little more than a victor's too easily assured self-justification, all the more so because in this particular case, the victor finds a double kind of vindication: yes, as this editor and magazine warned four years earlier, judicial intervention can be dangerous to American democracy, and yes, in this particular case, it's altogether welcome because, Neuhaus concluded, he was confident that now the nation had a president willing to "restore the difficult but necessary dialectic between the politics of rights and laws and the politics of rights and wrongs."[8]

"This changes everything," Neuhaus said, standing in his living room. He was watching television, the evening of September 11, 2001. The door to his apartment was open, and members of the community and *First Things* staffers were coming in and out to discuss the shocking events of earlier that day, including Vincent Druding, a new intern who was supposed to have reported for his first day of work at the magazine that morning. As for Neuhaus himself, that sun-bright, clear blue morning of the Al Qaeda terrorist attacks on the World Trade Center, he had been walking down First Avenue to Fourteenth to celebrate Mass at Immaculate Conception and looking south into the financial district, when for a moment he thought he'd just seen a plane fly into one of the WTC towers. Of course that couldn't be, so he went on to the church. Mass completed, Neuhaus stepped out of the church into a suddenly wrecked city.

Dust- and ash-covered workers streamed up First Avenue, smoke was rising from the south, sirens were everywhere. Neuhaus answered a local hospital call for priests, only to arrive and be told he wasn't needed: the hospital had miscalculated; there were comparatively few injured in need of emergency care or priestly ministrations; if someone was caught in the towers when the planes hit, that person was no more. The *First Things* office was a shocked and tense place. Located at Fifth Avenue and 21st, by mid-morning, September 11, its south-facing windows offered a clear and terrible view where scant hours before the towers had stood, a view of black smoke thick like "applesauce," as Davida Goldman recalled. Inside the office itself, a recent addition to the magazine, associate editor Damon Linker, a political science scholar and former Rudolph Giuliani speechwriter, was especially worried: his brother had been in the financial district that morning. Eventually they were able to make contact, and planned to meet. By mid-afternoon, Goldman went home as well, and the office was shuttered on September 12—in compliance with the mayor's request that no workers come into Lower Manhattan the day after the attacks, so as to avoid taxing the transportation grid or complicating the recovery efforts. By September 13, Neuhaus and his staff were back at *First Things* and the magazine resumed its daily operations, now with a new focus: the destruction in New York, Washington, and rural Pennsylvania forced an immediate and fundamental reorientation of U.S. national interests, and Neuhaus was keen to influence this reorientation.[9]

"Know that I stand ready to help in any way I can," Neuhaus wrote to Pete Wehner, White House deputy director of speechwriting, the week after the attacks. This help began, in the same letter, with an emphasis on defending the right-ordered construal of religion's natural and necessary place in American life: "Especially in the current situation, it is important that we not downplay the Judeo-Christian grounding of our culture. Contra the conventional secularist view, it is not DESPITE the fact that we are an overwhelmingly Christian country but BECAUSE we are an overwhelmingly Christian country that we are tolerant of others—especially Muslims." After emphasizing that America's pluralism would endure, provided its Judeo-Christian foundation was recognized and valued as such, Neuhaus then commended the President through Wehner for the remarks Bush gave at the National Cathedral in Washington on September 14. He wasn't offering flattery for its own sake: "In the magnificent reflection at National Cathedral," Neuhaus observed, indeed instructed the President's speechwriter, "it should have been 'answer these attacks and rid the world of *this* evil.' . . . Ridding the world of evil is a little like 'infinite justice.'" His comments, as always, were well received by the Bush White House.[10] Wehner answered his letter to let him know that in offering such suggestions, "in many ways, you're pushing on an open door," and that White House officials were grateful and mindful that Neuhaus was "keeping a careful eye out for us," in terms of the administration's own formulations of message and meaning in the early days after 9/11.[11]

In the public square, Neuhaus pursued his own formulations directly, of course, and had ample opportunity to do so. In fact, later that September, he wrote Joseph Zwilling, the director of communications for the Archdiocese of New York, to say that he was overwhelmed with media requests to comment on the attacks. He asked for "a list of priests, with phone numbers, who you know are *good at this kind of thing*," he emphasized—meaning at once fast, cogent, and up-to-speed on the latest developments and eloquently faithful to Church teachings—even if it was obvious that few were as good at "this kind of thing" as Neuhaus was. Beyond tutoring the White House and taking reporters' calls in the days and weeks following 9/11, Neuhaus put his talents to particular work in a lead editorial for the December issue of *First Things,* the magazine's first opportunity to address the attacks. "This is war," the editorial begins, and "not, as some claim, a metaphorical war. Metaphorical airplanes flown by metaphorical hijackers did not crash into metaphorical buildings leaving thousands of metaphorical corpses."

After emphasizing the events of 9/11 as indeed conscious acts of war waged against the United States by Osama bin Laden and Al Qaeda—rather than as crimes in need of policing—the editorial commends the President for invoking God's wisdom and watchfulness over America as it responds to the attacks: "In a time of grave testing, America [through Bush's September 14 remarks at National Cathedral] has once again given public expression to the belief that we are 'one nation under God.' . . . This is not national hubris. Confidence that we are under His judgment is humility. This relationship with God is not established by our being Americans, but by the fact that He is Father of the common humanity of which we are part." The editorial is clear in its reading of America's rights and responsibilities in a time of war, which, by December 2001, primarily involved American-led forces fighting in Afghanistan against Al Qaeda and sympathetic forces based there, and likewise dismantling the Taliban-led state that hosted and sponsored terrorist activities: "The present war is just in its cause and, we may reasonably hope, will be just in its conduct. . . . It seems likely that unjust acts will be committed, also by our side, and when they are known they must be condemned. Known or unknown, they are wrong."[12]

In other words, Neuhaus was making it clear that *First Things* would not serve as an uncritical mouthpiece for an aggressive U.S. military campaign against global terrorism, even though, as the War on Terror developed and led to the March 2003 invasion of Iraq, this would often seem the case to the magazine's (and the administration's) critics on the secular and religious Left. In fact, these very critics were another focus of the December 2001 editorial, which made a pointed distinction between "pacifists, real and fraudulent," with the distinction clear in the degree to which a pacifist consciously participates in "a long and venerable history in the Christian tradition" of nonviolent resistance, as opposed to living in "an unreal utopian fantasy world that has no basis in Christian faith" and idealistically ignores the very real demands and threats of the present moment. The editorial was far harsher in its treatment of intellectually driven dissenters from the war effort, namely members of "our morally debilitated professoriate . . . going on endlessly about how violence breeds violence and how we must address the root causes of resentment, etc., etc. They are inveterate complexifiers, offering detailed analyses of the seven sides of four-sided questions. . . . They test the patience of ordinary Americans who view reality from the moral pinnacle of common sense." Less useless but still wrong, the editorial charged, were "American pundits and editorialists" who accounted for the motivating hatreds behind the attacks by citing envy and resentment of America's wealth and power and freedoms. Allowing that "there is something in that," Neuhaus countered that it was still too mundane and self-regarding a diagnosis, and moreover one that failed to reckon with the religiously ordered concerns and religiously derived imperatives driving radicalized Islam:

> *They hate us because they believe that the West, now indisputably led by America, has marginalized, exploited, and oppressed them for centuries. They hate us for the cultural decadence that we export and that many of them hate themselves for enjoying. They hate us because we have troops on their sacred soil, and they hate us because we support what they view as the alien State of Israel on their land. Intertwined with all of the reasons they hate us, they hate us because we are the infidel who has for years beyond numbering in ways beyond numbering humiliated the chosen people of God.*

The editorial closes by focusing on the ultimate source of conflict in an era of fundamentally reconfigured and war-framed geopolitics. This source was the long-standing conflict internal to Islam itself, over which iteration of the faith was its most accurate rendering and, simultaneously, over the relationship of that rendering to its competitors, and their collective relationship to modernity and to the Judeo-Christian West. More sober than jingoistic, and prescient rather than ominous, the editorial concludes, "We are at war.

Pray that our cause will prevail. Pray that those other traditions will in time prevail. Pray that the one outcome does not preclude the other."[13]

The War on Terror, and thereafter the Iraq War, would become a recurring focus in *First Things* for years, with George Weigel taking the most prominent and robust role as a proponent of just war thinking that articulated a morally coherent account for U.S. foreign policy—or reliably apologized for it out of overriding partisan loyalties, according to the harsher critics of the effort. The most prominent critic on this subject was also the first and most respected: Stanley Hauerwas, the Methodist theologian who had been collaborating with Neuhaus since the Hartford Appeal in the mid-1970s and who had been a founding member of the *First Things* editorial board. He wrote an extensive and plaintive critique of the "In a Time of War" editorial that appeared in the February 2002 issue, explaining that his effort had been demanded by the "gross and distorted characterization of pacifism, as well as the defense of the American (military) response to September 11" in the December editorial. Hauerwas was especially troubled that "the Editors of FIRST THINGS, captured by their enthusiasm for destroying what they consider an unambiguous evil, are sublimely untroubled" by questioning just how well-fitted was their just war thinking to the situation at hand, rather than prima facie presuming as much and proceeding to defend it. "These are serious matters that are not just about a magazine," he continued, "but about friendship": he notes that he has long maintained his association with a neoconservative (or even theoconservative) publication because it "has been a venue for some of the best theological journalism available," the achievement of which Hauerwas emphatically ascribes to Neuhaus himself.

That said, Hauerwas was skeptical that genuine friendship could withstand the deep rifts in considered judgment that were evident between the December 2001 editorial and his response to it. With this statement, Hauerwas resigned from the *First Things* editorial board, despite a friendly phone call from Neuhaus asking him to reconsider, reminding him of the other times over the years when Hauerwas had objected to a particularly muscular foreign policy formulation in the pages but remained on the masthead. In the past, the tensions were diffused by their mutual affection and by higher-order ribbing. Neuhaus would chide the pacifist Hauerwas, "Oh, Stan, one of these days you're going to have to take responsibility for the world in which you find yourself," and Hauerwas would come back with the sincere if wry compliment that if Richard "had to choose between Jesus and Washington, he'd always choose Jesus, even though Richard thought that that choice could be put off a great deal longer than I did," as he would later recall. As far as Hauerwas was concerned, however, in the months following 9/11, Neuhaus had committed himself and his magazine too much to Washington and to advocating for the muscular, defensive-cum-expansive U.S foreign policy that was taking shape as the War on Terror.[14]

As significant as these geopolitical events and accompanying domestic developments were, and as much as Neuhaus engaged them in correspondence with the Bush administration and in media interviews and in his own journal, by early 2002 another major and troubling development was demanding his attention. In January 2002, the *Boston Globe* began to publish a series of disturbing, even shocking reports on allegations of sexual abuse against teenagers and children perpetrated by dozens of priests of the Boston Archdiocese, over the course of decades.[15] In far too many cases, priests accused of misconduct were simply reassigned, while the leadership of the archdiocese itself seemed more concerned with avoiding public scandal than dealing with the accused priests or attending to those who had been so profoundly harmed by them. With the *Globe*'s revelations, the archdiocese and the greater Church in America were soon engulfed in a public scandal that turned into an ongoing national news story, as more instances of alleged abuse and seeming, even systematic cover-up broke in Boston, wider New England, and around the country. The gravity of the situation became all the more evident when John Paul II summoned the U.S. cardinals to Rome in April 2002 to discuss the situation. From this period onward, Neuhaus wrote repeatedly about the clergy abuse scandal in *First Things,* analyzing the events themselves and likewise their framing and reception in ecclesial and public contexts. From early on, he was convinced that there was more to the matter than simply the latest round of Church bashing, which is how one reader attempted to dismiss it in a note to him that he discussed in the May 2002 issue of the magazine. The reader complained that *First Things* was "'pandering to anti-Catholic hysteria' by even paying attention to priestly scandals. 'Remember the maxim that the Church thinks in centuries. Ignore it and it will go away,'" ran the note's counsel. Neuhaus countered, "No, I don't think it will go away anytime soon. And the questions now raised should not go away anytime soon."

These questions, as far as Neuhaus was concerned, were primarily about the U.S. clerical cultures that contributed to the abuse and to its cover-up; and about the just and prudent responses demanded of Church leadership, to victims and to guilty and wrongfully accused priests, and to the greater Catholic faithful. All of which he wrote about across many issues of *First Things,* at least when he wasn't discussing it all with reporters: by his own measure, from January through the summer months of 2002, he spent some thirty hours per week in media interviews about the scandal, as he noted in an extended June 2002 treatment pointedly titled "Scandal Time (Continued)." It was also in this piece that Neuhaus first delivered the resonant liturgical metaphor that captured his sense of the ongoing, variously awful story:

> *One day the present scandals will be yesterday's news. The lawyers, prosecutors, therapists, and spin masters will leave the stage. The reporters will go chasing after other disasters. The Church will remain. About that there is no doubt. Please God, the Church will*

remain renewed. I do believe that will happen. Whether and how it happens depends upon the bishops who are primarily responsible for the shame and humiliation of the Long Lent of 2002.

While he was clearly never shy about attacking the media for unjustly and ignorantly attacking the Church, Neuhaus knew that the clergy abuse scandal was far more than a sensationalized news story, that it pointed to fundamental failures of vocation at the levels of priest and bishop both, and that it demanded, particularly from the American bishops, an extended journey of Lenten renewal, marked by "self-examination, confession, repentance, and publicly credible resolve to exemplify, by the grace of God, amendment of life in rediscovering, and calling others to rediscover, the vocation to fidelity."[16]

From 2002 through 2004, the Long Lent of the clergy abuse scandal, the War on Terror—particularly the divisive lead-up to the March 2003 invasion of Iraq and then the too hasty proclamations of victory thereafter[17]—and Bush's successful reelection campaign against Democratic challenger John Kerry were the most significant public concerns that Neuhaus engaged. During this period, he also published one of his most accessible and personally felt books, *As I Lay Dying: Meditations upon Returning,* his extended account of his 1993 near-mortal illness. The book earned strong if limited reviews—in scandal-ridden spring 2002, Neuhaus was of constant interest to the media, but not to talk about himself—and also occasioned the most personally revealing interview he ever gave, to Brian Lamb, the host of the C-SPAN program *Booknotes.* Over the course of a languorous-feeling hour, Neuhaus explored his personal life with much humor and self-effacement and frankness. The main focus was the book itself, and of course Lamb also asked Neuhaus to comment on the clergy abuse scandal, and he was assured and effective in both contexts, but the greater warmth and vitality came into his rolling deep voice when Lamb asked him about his early life, and about the people, places, and events that had brought him to the present. Neuhaus effectively surveyed his entire life, from growing up in Pembroke and making his rocky way through Nebraska and Texas ("And so, well, I knocked about"); into seminary in St. Louis; and from there, as a "starry-eyed kid" keen for urban ministry, to upstate New York and then Brooklyn and then Manhattan; from admiring the Church of Rome during John XXIII's days to joining it in John Paul II's era; from nearly dying in 1993 to bringing out a book about nearly dying in 2002.[18]

By 2003 and 2004, further book engagements had to compete for space amid his regular array of far-flung talks and lectures, and one-off writings and personal contributions, and continued attention to and from the Bush White House. That, in particular, was nowhere more apparent than in January 2004, when Neuhaus met with Bush in the Oval Office to discuss the Federal Marriage Amendment that would enshrine traditional marriage at the federal level over and against same-sex initiatives then emerging at the state level. George Weigel, Harvard law professor and *First Things* editorial board member Mary Ann Glendon, and conservative writer Maggie Gallagher were also present for the meeting, but the photographic evidence suggests Neuhaus' particular prominence. With the others seated on couches and facing both men, Bush and Neuhaus occupied chairs beside each other, just in front of the Oval Office fireplace. The particular moment captured by the White House photographer has Neuhaus mid-disquisition, his hand thoughtfully stroking his chin, with Bush, hands clasped on his lap, listening on. Bush's regard for Neuhaus was more publicly apparent in late April 2004, during an interview the President gave to a group of religious journalists, Neuhaus among them. Bush singled him out on two occasions in his comments. First, in policy terms, he noted, "Father Richard helped me craft what is still the integral part of my position on abortion, which is: Every child welcomed to life and protected by law." Second, in more affectionate and off-the-cuff terms when he was trying to explain the power of prayer to his ongoing presidency, he commented, "When I'm walking the rope line people say things different than they did four years ago. The thing they say different now than four years ago is, 'Mr. President, we pray for you.' That happens a lot. . . . And that is an incredibly sustaining part of the job of president. And people say—that's why I need Father Richard around more, he helps me articulate these things—I say, 'It helps a lot.' "[19]

In the time to come, Bush's interjected reference to Neuhaus would be parsed to fuel speculation about how much significant influence Neuhaus actually wielded over the President. Before such speculation began in earnest, Neuhaus kept at his usual hectic pace of writing and speaking and preaching. In the latter months of 2004, he wrote the preface to a Vintage Spiritual Classics edition of Kierkegaard's *Training in Christianity* and delivered the homily at the wedding Mass of George Weigel's oldest daughter, before flying to Sydney, Australia, to speak at St. Mary's Cathedral about the (future) legacy of John Paul II; back in the United States, in October he delivered remarks to the National Press Club in Washington about changes in U.S. Catholicism that he thought could be evident, a few weeks before Election Day, in a sizeable number of Catholic voters choosing a Methodist Republican over a Catholic Democrat. The following month, Bush was reelected. Neuhaus would later parse the exit polls with less victor's pride than in 2000, but still drew attention to the fact that voters who cited the religious faith of the President as a primary factor in their choice opted for Bush over Kerry 91 percent to 9 percent, and the fact that 61 percent of weekly churchgoers voted the same way.

In other words, religion and culture continued to matter significantly to the dynamics of American public life, a reality that *First Things* chose to observe by dedicating part of its November 2004 issue to a symposium on *The Naked Public Square,* the book published twenty years earlier that had so successfully described this reality. Stanley Hauerwas, Mary Ann Glendon, Harvey Cox, David Novak, Wilfred McClay, and others each wrote about their personal estimations of the book's significance and continued relevance. Neuhaus had the last word, of course. He argued with points that a few of his colleagues made, but saw little reason to go on at any length. "Were I to claim more space, [the other contributors] might accuse me of being unfair, even undemocratic," he said in closing. By late 2004, far be it from Neuhaus to preside over the end of democracy when he was perhaps at the height of his public influence in that democracy. This was an influence that others were now keen to credit in admiring ways, or expose in darker terms.[20]

CHAPTER TWENTY-THREE

"The Most Influential Clergyman in America," AKA the "Theocon-in-Chief"

Neuhaus liked to describe the United States as an "incorrigibly and confusedly religious nation." Over the course of his life and work he was proved right again and again, if never with as much personal implication as in early February 2005, when the latest issue of *Time* magazine came out. After all, what other nation but America could be so incorrigibly religious that its most prominent newsmagazine would run a feature on "The 25 Most Influential Evangelicals" in the country? And what other nation but America could be so confusedly religious that a former Lutheran pastor turned Catholic priest would show up as number nineteen on that list of evangelicals? As its accompanying citation demonstrates, *Time* was not concerned with the ecclesial, theological, and historical distinctions that made its commendation so patently ridiculous and patently American. What mattered more was how this publicly engaged Christian was playing a part in shaping American public life in avowedly Christian ways:

"Bushism Made Catholic"

When Bush met with journalists from religious publications last year, the living authority he cited most often was not a

> *fellow Evangelical but a man he calls Father Richard, who, he explained, "helps me articulate these [religious] things." A senior Administration official confirms that Neuhaus "does have a fair amount of under-the-radar influence" on such policies as abortion, stem-cell research, cloning and the defense-of-marriage amendment. Neuhaus, 68, is well-prepared for that role. As founder of the religion-and-policy journal* First Things, *he has for years articulated toughly conservative yet nuanced positions on a wide range of civic issues. A Lutheran turned Catholic priest, he can translate conservative Protestant arguments couched tightly in Scripture into Catholicism's broader language of moral reasoning, more accessible to a general public that does not regard chapter and verse as final proof. And there is one last reason for Bush to cherish Neuhaus, who has worked tirelessly to persuade conservative Catholics and Evangelicals to make common cause. It's called the conservative Catholic vote, and it played a key role last November.*

Even if the denominational premise for pointing out Neuhaus' significance was dubious, *Time*'s account of its defining features was exactly right: namely, his command at *First Things,* his contributions to the President's work, which Bush himself had warmly and publicly affirmed; his work with Evangelicals and Catholics Together; and, more comprehensively, his longstanding ability to offer a religiously informed account of public goods. That said, one item in particular from *Time*'s brief write-up would take on particular importance: the unnamed "senior administration official" confirming that he had, in fact, " 'a fair amount of under-the-radar influence' " in the White House on an array of policy issues. Interviewed about the extent of Neuhaus' influence on him personally and on his administration, George W. Bush made it clear that this influence was on the level of "policy and ideas," and that it came from the fact that "his recommendations on issues were based on strong theology and moral conviction." Finally, Bush explained that he was drawn to

Neuhaus because that moral conviction was matched to a great self-confidence: "He never seemed intimidated," Bush recalled, when the two men were together in the Oval Office, which made him "easy to talk to." That said, Bush also pointed out, "Mainly, I listened." "Policy and ideas" based on "strong theology and moral conviction" are all-but-synonymous with a religiously informed public philosophy for the right ordering of American life. In other words, Bush was willing to listen because he was a receptive audience for exactly what Richard John Neuhaus had spent a lifetime developing. But aside from photo opportunities and passing references in the back pages of *First Things,* the fact of Neuhaus' notable standing with the President wasn't especially well known as the second term began, at least until *Time* magazine put it very much on the radar of Neuhaus' most entrenched opponents in American intellectual and religious life—including an opponent, as it turned out, at his own magazine.[1]

In the April 2005 issue of *First Things,* Neuhaus drew his readers' early attention to what would eventually become the most significant public attack he would receive, even as he elsewhere addressed his appearance on the *Time* list. "It's not even a flirtation with false modesty to say that the story greatly exaggerates my influence," Neuhaus commented with great self-effacement on that matter, only then to remark, with considerably less self-effacement, "When *The Naked Public Square* appeared, Clare Boothe Luce, the widow of Henry Luce, sent multiple copies to friends and told me that, 'if only Harry were alive,' she would have arranged for me to be on the cover of *Time* the way she had arranged it for Father John Courtney Murray."[2] He ended this item, with playful vanity, "It's nice to have made it at last, even if I did have to share space with twenty-four others." Of course, Neuhaus had "made it" into *Time* on multiple occasions over the years, beginning with a 1965 article about Clergy Concerned, which he passed over (or artfully forgot) as he recounted his latest achievement to his 2005 readers. In this same issue of *First Things,* Neuhaus informed his readers that they would soon be reading more about him from a close and now departing source: Damon Linker, Neuhaus reported, "is resigning to write a book about the people involved with FT and their effort to advance a vibrant religious presence in the public square."

Linker had joined as associate editor in 2001 and succeeded Nuechterlein as editor in 2004. His was a short term in that position and was characterized by growing tensions and marked differences between himself and his editor in chief, tensions that were little evident in the fifteen-year working relationship between Neuhaus and Nuechterlein, or in Neuhaus' impeccably professional send-off for Linker: "Damon has been a conscientious, loyal, and exceedingly competent colleague, and I will miss him." "Exceedingly competent" is an exceedingly limited sort of compliment, likely inspired by two factors: first, by Neuhaus' happiness that Linker's departure meant the return as the new editor of *First Things* of Jody Bottum, for whom he had great personal affection. Second and more significantly, Neuhaus was guarded in his good-bye to Linker because he was concerned about what Linker was now going to write.[3]

As early as January 2005, Neuhaus was confiding to Jody Bottum that "I really don't know what Damon intends to do with the book, although there is cause for some concern." That cause could have been juicy rumors circulating in Manhattan publishing circles in fall 2004, that the editor of the "deeply influential" magazine that had become the "spiritual nerve-center of the new conservatism," as the *Times* Sunday magazine put it, was now shopping around a seventy-page book proposal that amounted to a critical insider's account about the editor in chief of that magazine. This was an account that promised to expose the concerted effort of a small group of religiously motivated intellectuals to entrench theoconservative principles in American politics and governance, an effort that was well positioned to succeed with a receptive Republican-controlled White House. According to Linker, there had been a long lead-up to his making the decision to write a book that would at once provide the money to let him exit *First Things* and also a platform from which to decry what he regarded as the dangerous work coming out of the magazine. In a few short years, Neuhaus had gone from working with an editor he trusted on most everything (save the subject of one 1996 issue) to an editor who, by Linker's own admission, found himself consciously and explicitly in growing disagreement with the magazine's overall direction by 2004 and with its publishing an array of articles that amounted to comprehensive editorial support for the Bush administration's domestic and foreign policies. Linker claims he attempted to draw Neuhaus' attention to these differences on multiple occasions, even visiting him at 338 one evening before Nuechterlein's successor was named, back in 2003, to withdraw from the running. He told Neuhaus that the two of them had ideological differences that had become too pronounced to sustain a viable relationship together at the helm of the magazine. The next morning, when they met at the office, to Linker's great surprise, Neuhaus offered him the job.[4]

Perhaps Neuhaus did so out of the belief that because he had come to work for *First Things,* Linker was and remained—ultimately, and despite many secondary disagreements—committed to the magazine's mission and worldview and indeed, as a recent Catholic convert and new member of *First Things,* to the robustly intellectual and conservative Catholicism associated with the magazine and its founder. Perhaps Neuhaus did so because he knew his long-trusted friend and colleague Jim Nuechterlein had initially encouraged Linker to apply for the editorship, had encouraged Neuhaus to appoint him, and would be in a position to mentor his successor toward a fuller investment in the magazine's mission in the months between his announced retirement and departure; perhaps he did so because there was simply no stronger candidate and Linker was, by all accounts, very good at running the day-to-day operation of putting out a magazine. Whatever the reason, it was a mistaken job offer and even more mistaken acceptance that led to months of tense and brittle cooperation capped by an awkward and acrimonious exit. On his last day at the magazine, Linker went to lunch with Neuhaus at the Greek restaurant where, four years before, they'd first met to discuss his joining the operation. Neuhaus pointed out that he had yet to see the book proposal Linker had written despite Linker's prior offers to share it, and that this naturally caused him to wonder just what kind of book he was writing. Linker admitted that it would be critical, and then, signaling just how critical, he let loose.

Not only did he air his disagreements with Neuhaus in extended detail, he also detailed his frustration that Neuhaus had not more candidly recognized these disagreements earlier, when, at least as far as Linker was concerned, Neuhaus kept dismissing the differences after tense editorial meetings, out of the unbending conviction that someone this close to him and his magazine could not but ultimately agree with him about these matters. Whether out of sheer surprise or sudden prudence, Neuhaus made little response at the time, and they finished their meal together with awkward chitchat, before heading back to the office for Linker's send-off party. There, at least one *First Things* staffer, Erik Ross, recalls Neuhaus seeming atypically downcast while everyone had cake and wine. By April 2005, Linker was gone, and while it would be some months before Neuhaus and his friends and supporters would discover just how negative his erstwhile "conscientious, loyal" editor would be about Neuhaus and his work, at that time they—indeed much of the world—were far more focused on events in Rome that signaled the end of a historic papacy.[5]

John Paul II died on April 4, 2005. Neuhaus flew to Rome two days later. After dropping his bags at the Hotel Michelangelo, near St. Peter's, he met Raymond Arroyo, a prominent Catholic broadcaster associated with the Catholic media channel EWTN. In the coming days, as a papal funeral gave way to a papal conclave and then the election of a new pope, the two men would spend many, many televised hours together manning the broadcast desk of an outdoor studio set up on the roof of the North American College, which overlooked St. Peter's. But before commenting on events in Rome for ETWN's audience, they first went to St. Peter's itself: Arroyo had arranged for them to bypass the queued thousands, all waiting to pray before the catafalque upon which lay John Paul's body. They went directly to the space near the body reserved for dignitaries, and in turn proceeded to the prie-dieu. Neuhaus was soon overcome with emotion and admiration and gratitude, as he would later write in a diary entry that would be excerpted in *First Things* and then published in a future book, *Catholic Matters:* "Through my tears, I tried to see again the years of his vitality, his charm, his challenge, his triumphs; the historic moments when I admired him from a distance; and the personal encounters when I was surprised by the gift of an older brother who was the Holy Father."[6]

Neuhaus' filial claim to a giant of world history might seem rather too much, or altogether one-sided, and, either way, self-aggrandizing. And given John Paul II's famed magnetism and the great numbers of people he directly engaged as pope, Neuhaus' was but one among many, many claims of intensely felt personal connection, in his case based on the dozen or so private audiences and shared meals he had had with the pontiff dating back to the late 1970s. But according to Rocco Buttiglione, the Italian philosopher and scholar of John Paul II's works who helped bring Neuhaus (and also Novak and Weigel) into John Paul's personal orbit in the 1980s, the feelings were far from one-sided. Based on his direct, personal knowledge, Buttiglione confirms that "the Holy Father knew the work of Father Neuhaus" and that Neuhaus "was in the circle of friends of John Paul II." As to why Neuhaus enjoyed this standing, Buttiglione believes it had less to do with their many doctrinal alignments or with Neuhaus' endless willingness to advocate on behalf of these doctrines in American circles—as welcome as these were in the papal apartment—but instead with a particular capacity, indeed charisma, that they shared: "John Paul II and Neuhaus were similar, as they were both centers of great communities of friends." And when the two men came together, Buttiglione explains, "these communities intersected," a convergence that both men sought—between Rome and the Holy See, and New York and Washington, as it were—

just as each man appreciated that this was best made possible because of the other.[7]

So as Neuhaus half-whispered, half-sobbed his gratitude to John Paul before his body, he would have been moved, no doubt, by the conviction that he had been a valued member of a rarified circle of people who had been personal witnesses, indeed contributors, to the most consequential religious life of the twentieth century. This personal connection aside, Neuhaus' feelings would have been interwoven with his decades of closely following John Paul's papacy from New York and writing and commenting extensively about the significance of his works and indeed his person in an American context. Neuhaus' interests and capacities in this respect were apparent not least in the weeks leading up to John Paul's death. With the pope's condition significantly deteriorating, reporters were questioning his capacity to continue leading the Church, just as another end-of-life situation—that of Terri Schiavo, a Florida woman put into a vegetative state by significant brain damage whose husband and parents were in an extended legal dispute over ending life support—was commanding extensive national attention: "As the pope, he's the father of a family, not the director of a corporation," Neuhaus told the *Philadelphia Inquirer,* before once again crisply reframing an American dilemma through John Paul's example: "As we are reminded by the Schiavo situation, you don't get rid of people when they no longer seem useful." Leaving St. Peter's after praying good-bye to John Paul, Arroyo and Neuhaus talked about the person they had just witnessed for a final time. Shaken, Arroyo remarked of the body upon the catafalque, "That wasn't him, he isn't there," but Neuhaus disagreed. "No, I said, he is there. These are the remains, what is left behind of a life such as we are not likely to see again, waiting with all of us for the resurrection of the dead, the final vindication of the hope he proclaimed."[8]

With the days of solemn witness and prayer marking John Paul II's death and funeral past and a conclave called to elect his successor, the conversation in Rome naturally and robustly turned to the question of the next pope. When he wasn't discussing this over dinner with George Weigel and others at favorite places like Taverna Giulia, just over the Tiber from St. Peter's, or at Armando's, off the Borgo Pio, just beyond the Leonine Wall, Neuhaus was discussing it for assorted television audiences, offering essentially the same five to seven minutes of commentary, on both the potential legacies of John Paul II and his potential successors, in response to the same questions from various reporters. Neuhaus admitted he was growing tired of the repetitiveness of the experience, not least of having to hear himself issue the same canned remarks again and again, but then he remembered a timely admonition from Abraham Joshua Heschel, back in their CALCAV days. It seems that on one occasion, to his own displeasure, Neuhaus was about to go to Chicago to say the same things he had just been saying in Kansas City and elsewhere. "Nuh, Richard, so you think in Chicago they know what you said in Kansas City?" Heschel chided him, before commanding, "Go to Chicago, Richard. Go to Chicago." In his Rome diary, Neuhaus explained that "when on airplanes going I know not where or why, I have over the years often heard the voice of Heschel, 'Go to Chicago, Richard. Go to Chicago.'" Asked the same questions in Rome—"What's John Paul II's legacy?" "Who's going to be the next pope?"—Neuhaus roused himself to go to Chicago, again and again and again.[9]

As did many other close observers of Church affairs, Neuhaus offered his predictions as to *papabile* (potential candidates) from the College of Cardinals, including the Jesuit archbishop of Buenos Aires, Jorge Bergolio, who would, in the next conclave, become Pope Francis. While noting that he was "high on every list" because of his reputation for a holy and austere life, Neuhaus was skeptical of Bergolio's chances in 2005, he wrote, because it had been more than a century since a member of a religious order had been elected. After citing other favorites and, in each case, his personal connection to them—George Pell of Sydney, Francis Arinze of Nigeria, Christoph Schönborn of Vienna—Neuhaus turned his attention to

Joseph Ratzinger, the cardinal he felt the strongest personal connection to, who was also the cardinal he was convinced was the rightfully leading candidate. Ratzinger was a renowned theologian and the longtime prefect of the Congregation for the Doctrine of the Faith (CDF), but also, Neuhaus attested autobiographically, a man of "great personal charm and profound holiness." And on April 19, 2005, a mere day after the conclave convened, Ratzinger was indeed elected; in broad strokes, conservatives were far more joyful over his succeeding John Paul II as Benedict XVI than liberals were, Neuhaus very much included. In his own immediate media commentary on the election, however, Neuhaus worked to counteract the presumption that, based on his putative track record, Ratzinger would be a steel-fisted enforcer of rigidly conservative Catholic doctrine.

To that end, shortly after the election, Neuhaus went on ABC News' *Nightline* with Ted Koppel to discuss Ratzinger's long-standing commitment to both a Christocentric theology for its own sake and interreligious dialogue ordered by and to it; he also informed publications like the *Toronto Star* that Ratzinger's work at CDF as "chief of the doctrinal patrol of the church" wasn't well suited to making friends, even while he was himself identified in the same article as a personal friend of the new pope for more than twenty years. Indeed, Neuhaus regarded Benedict's election as a victory for theological orthodoxy within the universal Church and for marked lines of continuity with John Paul II's papacy, given the men's years of close collaboration. Neuhaus also regarded the election as something of a personal victory, in no small part because his long-standing connection to Ratzinger—whom he had met on various occasions in Rome over the years, and whom he had also hosted for the infamously raucous 1988 Erasmus lecture—suggested that he was well positioned to continue enjoying direct access to the pope. While their personal correspondence over the years suggested a sense of mutual respect, interest, and affection, Neuhaus would not in fact enjoy nearly the same relationship with the shy and courtly Pope Benedict as he had with the more socially freewheeling and gregarious John Paul II. Nevertheless, Neuhaus' critics certainly presumed he would enjoy such access and influence.[10]

This much became clear in early October, when the *New York Review of Books* ran a exposé-style piece entitled "Fringe Government," by Garry Wills, who was in some ways Neuhaus' parallel on the Left in American public life: a onetime seminarian and *National Review* writer turned prominently and aggressively liberal Catholic intellectual, a contrarian (if generally liberal) observer of American culture and politics, and a prodigious writer. His article focused on a quartet of conservative American Catholic intellectuals who wielded an extraordinary amount of influence in Rome and Washington and were in fact committed to advancing an agenda that would only intensify Vatican-U.S. ideological and political collaborations along an aggressively rightist axis. Michael Novak and George Weigel, and also Joseph Fessio, the Jesuit priest who led Ave Maria University and the Catholic publishing house Ignatius Press, were each cited and their writings and activities discussed in some critical detail, but Neuhaus was far and away the article's main focus, beginning with a smirking cameo shot on the front cover and, accompanying the piece itself, a cartoon sketch by the *New York Review*'s legendary staff artist, David Levine. Bedecked in black clerics, arms crossed, there was Neuhaus with a smug, stern smile on his face. And in the article accompanying the caricature, Wills alleged that Neuhaus had good reason to be smug in his sternness. After all, he was the leading member of the quartet "situated at the contact points between the similar ruling systems of the Vatican and the White House," given his great personal standing with John Paul II and Pope Benedict XVI, and likewise, by way of the *Time* profile, with George W. Bush (and Karl Rove).[11]

Wills then rehearsed notable elements in Neuhaus' career—*The Naked Public Square,* ECT, the "End of Democracy?" issue—which, he argued, had given articulate voice to a minority group of extremist religious conservatives, Protestant and Catholic both, who had a "shared anxiety" about the cultural decadence of American life, and likewise about the malingering effects of Vatican II liberalism in contemporary Catholicism. "No one is better at fostering the sense of shared anxiety than 'Father Richard,'" Wills noted. "He does so with a quiet air of reasonableness which just makes his extremism more effective." Wills argued that this was an extremism that dovetailed perfectly with *both* Karl Rove's strategy for governing America *and* Benedict XVI's strategy for governing the Catholic Church, insofar as both preferred to advance ideological agendas that emerged from the "activist fringes of morality" and benefited from the imperative that Neuhaus and his colleagues were so successfully executing, whether regarding an apostate nation or an apostate Church: "A collection of aggrieved minorities must seize the levers of power in every way possible." Having done so with great success, Neuhaus, Novak, Weigel, and Fessio were nothing less than "perfectly able to serve as both the Pope's men and Rove's men; for reciprocally strengthening reasons," Wills concluded. "They are at the interface between two systems of power exercised from the fringes."[12]

While *Harper's* and the *Times* Sunday magazine had both run articles in prior years noting Neuhaus' significant—and, from a Left-liberal vantage, significantly negative—influence upon American public life, neither had ascribed such backroom preeminence or globe-spanning diabolical control as Wills did with his *New York Review* piece, which, for all its intellectual élan and cerebral brawn, had much in common with Herman Otten's foaming anti-Neuhaus diatribes and Joseph Sobran's acidic attacks. In all three cases, an entrenched critic—who might understand himself as meriting, under different ideological, political, and ecclesial climates and regimes, the very position of influence Neuhaus meanwhile enjoyed—ascribed a remarkable amount of power to Neuhaus. This was power little appreciated by a myopic public, a situation providing each Neuhaus critic with the self-valorizing pretext to present himself as the clearer-eyed exposer of that (nefarious) power. About a year after Wills' "Fringe Government" article was published, Damon Linker would publish a steroidal version of the same thesis and generate a great deal of public attention for the effort, if more for the melodramatic and conspiracy-freighted allure of the thesis itself: a onetime Lutheran leftist radical turned Catholic rightist radical was leading a Republican-aided and Republican-aiding crusade for the transformation of the United States into a latter-day medieval vassal state of the papacy, and here's an insider's story of how he's doing it!

These claims certainly attracted other journalists to Neuhaus' work, including Damian Thompson, a British writer who profiled Neuhaus for the conservative *Daily Telegraph* a few weeks after the *New York Review* piece ran, introducing him to British readers as a personal friend to popes and presidents, indeed, as nothing less than "the most influential clergyman in America." Cigar and quips at hand, Neuhaus sat for an interview with Thompson in his *First Things* office. He spoke in admiring, personally framed terms about Bush and Benedict as both fine individuals and impressive leaders, contrary to widely held views, and also addressed the ever-worsening situation in Iraq, the ongoing clergy abuse scandal in the United States, the place of religion in public life and of faith in public policy, and the worldview rise of militant and radical Islam. He said little that differed from his ongoing commentary in *First Things* on these matters, but he also made a point of speaking more specifically to his British audience, which, given the newspaper profiling him, would be largely conservative. He expressed his dismay at Tony Blair's views of abortion—"It's disappointing that someone who is impressive in many ways exhibits this glaring inconsistency on questions relating to the value of human life"—and was too readily sympathetic to what otherwise would seem like a xenophobic case for UK immigration restrictions: "You are right to be concerned about radical Islam," he told Thompson. "The concept of a people, a culture and a language has moral legitimacy, and if that faces an imminent threat, then a moral case can be made for saying we have to stop immigration for a time." Thompson pointed out that some of Neuhaus' statements readily led his critics to "caricature [him] as a mouthpiece for reactionary doctrines"—as with his tersely triumphant declaration elsewhere in his interview with Thompson that with Benedict XVI's succeeding John Paul II, liberal Catholics seeking "revolution" in Church doctrine about women's ordination and the like "now know that is not to be." But then Thompson pushed against this portrayal by praising Neuhaus as a writer: "His books reveal a nuanced conservative—he opposes an automatic ban on gay seminarians, for example—and a theologian who writes with great originality about 'the work of dying.'"[13]

In late 2005 and again in the early months of 2006, death began to exert its presence in increasingly proximate terms for Neuhaus. In December, his older brother Fred died, and Neuhaus flew to California for the funeral and delivered the eulogy. Years before, Fred, a California policeman and staunch Missouri Synod conservative who was far more attuned to Clem's Lutheranism than to Richard's, had been an occasional source for Herman Otten when he went after Neuhaus, and likewise had offered *Harper's* magazine a potted Freudian analysis of his little brother's 1960s radical activities as amounting to nothing more than an extended rebellion against his father. Presumably, Neuhaus chose not to invoke those elements in his funeral remembrance of his big brother. Based on interviews with Neuhaus' surviving siblings—the twins, Tom and George, and his sisters Mim and Johanna—each of them seems to have worked out a similar modus vivendi with their brother as they all grew older. They might see him every few years, either by passing through New York, or hosting him at one of their homes when he was nearby to give a talk, or when their visits to the cottage overlapped. In all cases, ecclesial and electoral and intellectual politics were by and large passed over for less volatile conversations about family life, past and present.

Of course, for Richard John Neuhaus, volatile conversations about ecclesial and electoral and intellectual politics were by and large the only conversations worth having. But he knew and came to accept that his siblings and their spouses and children had comparatively less time for and interest in such matters than the *First Things* crowd, or the assorted conservative friends who would gather in his apartment on Friday nights for cocktails, or the Community of Christ in the City members who would dine together on Saturday night, or the group of Lutheran pastors dating back to his St. John–Brooklyn days he'd still see for drinks and cigars every now and then, or the Weigel family, whom he'd invite up to the cottage near Pembroke every August. And so, when he saw his only family in later years, he was a milder and more affectionate presence, at least by comparison to his earlier self. He was still prone to habits that were endearing only in retrospect: he openly cheated at golf; he smoked his smelly cigars in other people's living rooms; he complained, "What's with the chintzy drinks?" when someone gave him a Scotch with not nearly enough Scotch in the glass.[14]

Having come to California to observe the passing of one of his brothers, in all likelihood Neuhaus would have invoked childhood memories of Fred and likewise told anodyne stories of their encounters in later years, and also no doubt spoken in eloquent, higher-order terms about Fred's journey beyond this earthly life, drawing on his abiding and great interest and capacity and vocational commitment, as a priest and writer both, to consider "the work of dying" in personally felt theological terms. He had cause to do so again, in more public terms, in April 2006, when William Sloane Coffin, Jr., died. Neuhaus wrote an extended remembrance that appeared in the summer issue of *First Things,* warmly invoking their working together in CALCAV in the 1960s and their late-night piano-playing at St. John the Evangelist, and then less warmly noting their 1975 debate against Harvey Cox at Riverside Church over the Hartford Appeal, a debate during which Coffin distanced himself from the Appeal and from Neuhaus. "We saw each other from time to time after that, but it was not the same," Neuhaus remarked in his remembrance, but this did not stop him from emphasizing that "the story of Bill Coffin is in significant part the story of a once dominant sector of religion in public life," a sector—the Mainline Protestant establishment—in a long decline and retreat that Neuhaus had himself worked for, through a constant barrage of criticisms of its doctrinal softness and leftist sympathies, dating from the mid-1970s.[15] He chose not to mention this fact in otherwise autobiographically observing Coffin's April 2006 death: "I loved him like a brother," Neuhaus concluded, "and pray that choirs of angels welcome him on the far side of the Jordan."[16]

In this same issue of *First Things,* Neuhaus also addressed recent reports of his role in establishing a newly dominant sector of religion in public life, the theoconservatives. He noticeably omitted one report—a nine-thousand-word essay by Damon Linker, which purported to review Neuhaus' latest book, *Catholic Matters,*[17] for the April 3, 2006, edition of the *New Republic* but was, in fact, a précis of the book Linker would publish that fall. With this piece, Linker put to rest any lingering doubts about what kind of book this was going to be, with no small help from the magazine itself, which commissioned cover art featuring a full-color cartoon drawing of a powerful and malevolent-looking Neuhaus branding a garish pink cross, under the title "Father Con." Neuhaus, front and center, was flanked by a veritable murderer's row of prominent conservatives—each likewise penned to look like some kind of right-wing supervillain—including Ann Coulter, Paul Wolfowitz, and Dick Cheney. Neuhaus made a brief reference to the piece in an April blog post for *First Things,* not even identifying Linker by name while reporting that the *New Republic* was "obsessing about me and my friends" and trafficking in "nonsense."[18] Otherwise he ignored Linker in print, and instead, in the summer issue of *First Things,* noted other reports on the dangerous rise of the theocons, like longtime political commentator Kevin Phillips' new book *American Theocracy: The Peril and Politics of Radical Religion, Oil, and Borrowed Money,* which hysterically compared the putative theoconservative agenda for American public life to Spanish life during the Inquisition, because "the fringe elements are very powerful at the present time" too.

For Neuhaus, the wording recalled Garry Wills' *New York Review* effort to expose "a vast conspiracy, in which your scribe plays a central role . . . in imposing on everybody the views of those who are, in fact, on the fringes of American public life." Neuhaus dismissed

Wills by caustically observing, "The charm of the paranoid style is that it is not vulnerable to inconvenient facts. . . . The fact that [I and my friends] are largely invisible only shows" paranoid cases like Wills "how devilishly devious [we] are." Combatting unwelcome characterizations from the Left, Neuhaus had to do rather the opposite on the Right. In a *Wall Street Journal* op-ed, Ross Douthat—a future *New York Times* columnist, author, and occasional contributor to *First Things,* who had been reading the magazine since the age of twelve, according to an admiring letter Douthat's father sent Neuhaus while his son was an undergraduate at Harvard—offered an enthusiastically sympathetic extension of Neuhaus' 1987 *Catholic Moment* argument. Entitling his piece "Theocon Moment," Douthat argued that "the closest thing to a credible public philosophy the GOP has to offer emanates from the once-unlikely alliance of evangelicals and Catholics, and their God-infused program of social reform." This alliance and program was made possible by Neuhaus himself, "the 'theocon-in-chief' to his enemies," remarked Douthat. He encouraged Neuhaus and others to embrace, "with a wink and a grin," the theocon moniker as a marker of their success in bringing about a religiously informed right ordering of American public life, which Douthat situated in the great tradition of Victorian-era social reformers and Civil Rights activists.[19]

Neuhaus would have nothing of it. In spite of Douthat's lionizing gloss on the term, "I don't think I'll go along with being called a theocon, not even accepting it with 'a wink and a grin,'" he remarked. "To too many, the term inevitably implies theocracy, which is the very opposite of what my friends and I have been contending for all these years." Their contending, he continued, had been "to renew the liberal democratic tradition by, among other things, opening the public square to the full and civil engagement of the convictions of all citizens, including their religiously-informed moral convictions . . . America is a nation *under* God, but not even at its best is it God's nation. And so," Neuhaus concluded, "while I appreciate Mr. Douthat's hopeful account of our influence . . . I protest being called a theocon." Come fall 2006, Neuhaus had greater reason to raise this protest: Damon Linker's book came out. Entitled, predictably, *The Theocons,* it sported an especially alarmist subtitle: *Secular America Under Siege.* While the book critically assessed the work of many of Neuhaus' long-standing collaborators and like-minded colleagues—namely Peter Berger, George Weigel, Michael Novak, Chuck Colson, Robert George, Mary Ann Glendon, David Novak, Gilbert Meilaender, Russell Hittinger, and Jim Nuechterlein—Neuhaus was the main focus. Indeed, Linker argued early on, setting the terms for the rest of the book, Neuhaus was the man primarily responsible for developing and advancing a "revolutionary religious ideology" that had gained a significant foothold in America during the Bush presidency and was thus positioned, unless stopped, to bring about "a cultural counterrevolution whose ultimate goal is nothing less than the end of secular politics in America." Linker warned that "such efforts, if successful, would not be fatal to the nation, but they would cripple it, effectively transforming the country into what would be recognized around the world as a Catholic-Christian republic. I hope," he said to conclude his dramatic preface, "that prospect is disquieting enough to inspire thoughtful Americans to educate themselves about the theocons, their ideology, and the very real threat they pose to the United States."[20]

Linker spent the rest of the book educating his readers about this threat, and offering along the way a brisk biography of Neuhaus informed by an interview with Jim Nuechterlein, who did not know, at the time, the altogether critical purposes to which his contribution would be put. Other than backhandedly crediting Neuhaus, early on, with being "a handsome, charismatic man who delights in public attention," Linker worked up a relentlessly negative account of Neuhaus' life and work. Seizing on Neuhaus' reckless rhetoric from the 1960s, Linker advanced readings of his writings and activities that emphasized their "characteristically prophetic and apocalyptic terms" and tracked his progress from positioning himself as a self-appointed "moral tutor to the American left" to his plan, by the mid-1970s, "to become America's Christian Marx, to author a comprehensive religious ideology that would enable the United States to break out of its spiritual crisis." Beyond the melodramatic frames, Linker's analyses here and throughout—of Neuhaus' turn toward conservatism in the 1980s, and his concomitant rise in prominence and influence, particularly in the 1990s and culminating in Bush's 2000 election—tend to be well contextualized and attentive to the relationship between Neuhaus' rise and political and cultural changes in American life.

That said, the book fails because it's so thoroughly mundane in its first principles: Linker could see only hard-packed ideology and partisan-political gains as Neuhaus' career-long motives. To be sure, Neuhaus trafficked in partisanship, politics, and ideology, at times to the detriment of his higher commitments to genuine theology and the development of a religiously informed philosophy for democratic public life, but Linker's account of his life and work was itself too rigidly ideological and partisan to admit this, or reckon with the accompanying tensions and complexities of Neuhaus' public vocation as at once a man of God, a man of ideas about religion and democracy, and a man of action in a "confusedly and incorrigibly religious nation." Instead, as far as Linker was concerned, Neuhaus was only and always a cross-wielding theocrat, occasionally dashing but usually dangerous. For the sake of nonbelievers, free-thinkers, and American democracy itself, Linker proclaimed, Neuhaus needed to be stopped.[21]

Neuhaus' friends and allies either dismissed the book out of hand—George Weigel told David Novak that the main fault of *The Theocons* was that "it was so boring"—or took to the review pages to dispute its tendentiousness and alarmist emphases: writing in *Commentary*, Joshua Muravchik noted that the book was far more revealing of dramatic political and ideological changes to Damon Linker than of theocrat-driven changes to America. As far as he was concerned, the book ultimately amounted to little more than the wearisome and overdone autobiography of an intellectual Benedict Arnold: "On the final page, he writes that 'I harbor no ill will toward the individual theocons, least of all my former boss, Richard John Neuhaus.' This is self-evidently true—in the sense that far from 'harboring' any ill will, he pours it forth in a torrent. A work of explanation and of self-examination might have been worth reading. This breathless and tedious traducing of former comrades is something else again." Leftward critics, obviously predisposed to Linker's view, were more welcoming: Alan Wolfe and Kevin Phillips offered encomiums, while the *Nation* cited the book as a source of straightforward insight and authority, in a larger article about religious conservatism's hold and reach in American life. Writing in the *New York Times Book Review,* Adrian Wooldridge was less concerned with the personal conflicts driving the book or with invoking it as some kind of clarion call to action for secular liberals. Instead, after granting Linker a few well-made points, he exposed its finally limited believability as an account of the threats Neuhaus et al. posed to the American public life:

> *In the end, the theocons are just too eccentric to exercise the sort of influence on America that Linker ascribes to them. Again and again—in their deference to papal authority, in their belief that American ideals and institutions derive from Catholic principles, in their willingness to sanction civil disobedience—the theocons come across not as harbingers of a conservative revolution but as a rather eccentric intellectual clique. Secular America has more potent enemies to worry about than the Rev. Richard John Neuhaus and his colleagues.*

Although more than "a rather eccentric intellectual clique," Neuhaus and his colleagues were certainly not the signal foes of secular America, as Wooldridge observed, and while Linker became as much in the world of *First Things,* Neuhaus himself never went after him. He made a few passing references to the book in later issues—"a recent and rather silly book attacking this magazine and me personally as dangerous proponents of theocracy," he termed it in a January 2008 essay—but wisely avoided the narcissistic dramatics of writing about it directly, or commissioning a review. According to Erik Ross, a member of the editorial staff during the *Theocons* moment who would later be ordained a Catholic priest of the Polish Dominican order, in no small part thanks to Neuhaus' mentorship and example, Neuhaus' reaction to Linker's book at the *First Things* office was all and only pastoral. When the book would come up, Neuhaus described it as cause only to be concerned for Damon, that he had decided to do this, rather than cause for the group to either lash out at an erstwhile colleague or indulge in hothouse gossip.[22]

Besides, they had a magazine to keep putting out. In late 2006 and early 2007, *First Things* debuted the first English translations of wintry meditations by Aleksandr Solzhenitsyn and published an essay advocating a new attentiveness to the example of the early Church Fathers as a stay against an age of "velvet barbarism," written by R. R. Reno, a Creighton University theologian, recent convert to Catholicism, and the future editor in chief of *First Things.* As for Neuhaus himself, in the November issue he offered a robust defense[23] of Pope Benedict's terribly received Regensburg address of that September, on faith and reason and the university. He emphasized Benedict's basic point—"To act against reason is to act against the nature of God. That is Benedict's argument"—over and against media and political portrayals of his remarks as a concerted attack on Islam.[24] Along the way, he also made a point of emphasizing why he felt an especial need to take on this task for American readers: in their own formal response to the address and ensuing controversy, the U.S. Bishops' Conference effectively threw Benedict under the bus, as far as Neuhaus was concerned. "The tone was condescending and patronizing, almost apologizing for the pope's inept disturbance of our wonderfully dialogical relationship with our Muslim brothers and sisters. We are assured that, despite his unfortunate statements, he really does want peaceful dialogue. I paraphrase, of course, but the statement was anything but a firm defense of the pope, never mind an effort to explain what he actually said."

Here, Neuhaus was in fine fighting form, and grateful that he was still going strong, but he was also moving toward a more reflective mood, as two brief but telling notes suggested, from the February 2007 issue. First, Neuhaus remarked that he'd been reading with great interest a new collection of stories about people preparing for good deaths, in the tradition of the *ars moriendi* manuals of the Middle Ages. He picked up the book, he explained, around January 10 of that year, which marked "fourteen years since I died" and returned, the experience that he had explored in *As I Lay Dying.* Neuhaus didn't observe this anniversary every year for his readers, but he felt the need to relate it this time, just as he felt a need, in another "While We're At it" item, to explain his name, Richard John. This led all the way back to the name-picking game that Clem had fixed up with Mim in Pembroke, in May 1936, and onward from there through the various variations of the names that he'd gone by over his life, and his choosing St. Richard of Chichester and St. John the Evangelist as his patrons. The one was far more important to Neuhaus' sense of himself than the other:

> *Richard was chancellor to Boniface, archbishop of Canterbury, who opposed Henry III's appointment of a bishop in Chichester and appointed Richard in his place. In the subsequent dispute, Rome came down on the side of Boniface and Richard, a decision that King Henry refused to accept until he was threatened with excommunication. St. Richard is, or so I fancy, the combative side of my patronal protection, especially when it comes to the rights of the Church. With no offense to St. Richard, St. John, the apostle and evangelist, is my premier patron. He is the disciple whom, as we are told in the Fourth Gospel, "Jesus loved." I take consolation from the conclusion of his gospel: "But there are also many other things which Jesus did; were every one of them to be written, I suppose that the world itself could not contain the books that would be written." After the millions of words I have written, and the millions I may yet write, I will have hardly begun to tell my story of his love.*

He would keep telling this story, for two more years.[25]

CHAPTER TWENTY-FOUR

Meeting God as an American

In late 1987, Richard John Neuhaus invited Saul Bellow to deliver the following year's Erasmus lecture. Bellow demurred; he was too busy working on his latest novel, but also because the premise of such a talk would seem to demand a more conclusive and definitive take on matters than he was ready to deliver in his early seventies: "Acceptance [of your invitation] would be a simple matter if I had arrived at the stage of Final Views," Bellow informed Neuhaus. "But for those, we might have to wait until the eighth decade." Neuhaus didn't miss a beat in answering Bellow. "So it is definite then: it is in the eighth decade that one arrives at the 'stage of Final Views.' What this obviously means is that we will have to come back to you when you have entered your final decade. . . . And I am serious in saying that we will be back in touch when your views are fully matured, even though God and a million readers know that they seem awfully well formed at present." By Bellow's standard, Neuhaus never arrived at the stage of Final Views: his last book and final writings for *First Things* were published in spring 2009, a couple of months following his death, which happened early on in his seventh decade. Of course, Neuhaus' views, ordered to and from a faith that matured and never seems to have been shaken or failed, were far more final far earlier in his life. Indeed, as much is evident in his final book, *American Babylon: Notes of a Christian Exile.* Here, Neuhaus delivers an extended autobiographical analysis of the inevitable and complex relationship between one's status as a citizen in this world and as a citizen in the next.

His effort has a decidedly self-referential cast: he quotes his own 1975 remarks to *Time* magazine, made in the context of its writing about his book *Time Toward Home,* that he expected to meet God as an American. Mindful of how easily this could be misconstrued, Neuhaus offered a thoughtful account of what he had meant:

> *And so we returned to the beginning. When I meet God, I expect to meet him as an American. Not mostly importantly as an American, to be sure, but as someone who tried to take seriously, and tried to encourage others to take seriously, the story of America within the story of the world. The argument, in short, is that God is not indifferent toward the American experiment, and therefore we who are called to think about God and his ways through time dare not be indifferent to the American experiment. America is not uniquely Babylon, but it is our time and place in Babylon. We seek its peace, in which, as Jeremiah said, we find our peace, as we yearn for and anticipate by faith and sacramental grace the New Jerusalem that is our pilgrim goal. It is time to think again—to think deeply, to think religiously—about the story of America within the story of the world.*

The passage encapsulates the premise and effort of the entire book, if not the premise and effort of Richard John Neuhaus' entire life's work in the public square.[1]

In 2007 and 2008, he continued on in that work on a variety of fronts, including a recurring engagement at Columbia University celebrating Mass on campus on Sunday afternoons, affording frequent contact with religiously and intellectually serious young people. That was an experience that Neuhaus always sought and enjoyed and approached with a sense of great responsibility, reaching back to his earliest days on Maujer Street with his collegiate Lutheran urban ministers, and from there through years of living and working with interns at *First Things* and in the religious community at 338, and teaching university students in the intensive Tertio Millennio annual summer seminars in Poland—all of which bore the fruit of many religious vocations. But beyond his unflagging commitment to forming young people in faith and mind, there were certainly dimensions of Neuhaus' life in its final years that he approached with noticeable fatigue and impatience. Davida Goldman recalls, for instance, the day an aging Neuhaus flew from New York to Boston to give yet another talk; he waited around at Logan for his host to pick him up—only a little while by most vantages, but far too long as far as Neuhaus was concerned: he boarded the same shuttle he'd just walked out of and flew right back to New York.

He showed a similar combination of fatigue and impatience in his writing during this period. In the April 2007 issue of *First Things*, he noted that "we occasionally—well, more than occasionally—receive letters from readers commending us for smiting the enemy hip and thigh. Thank you, I'm sure, but such encouragements sometimes prompt a wince." Neuhaus explained that while the "judicious use of polemic" could indeed be "helpful in gaining the attention of those who are not aware of the nonsense they are spouting," the effort of *First Things* itself was foremost to set out "paths of robustly constructive conversation" about public life. In other words, as he suggested in that same issue, he would much rather focus his readers on the higher order implications of Islam's enduring place in U.S. and world affairs, than issue yet another one of his blunderbuss reports, on, for instance, an "Episcopal priest in Seattle who says she is also a Muslim."[2]

Not that he was turning into a softy in his old age; as part of a larger piece on the importance of religious leaders engaging the secular media, Neuhaus pointedly contrasted New York archbishop Edward Cardinal Egan's position in public life with that of O'Connor, his outsized predecessor: "His public nonpresence has led some to suggest that New York is *sede vacante,* which of course it is not." And yet, ran the implication, though the prolepsis of the New Jerusalem might as well have been an empty-seated episcopate, "he is my bishop," Neuhaus concluded with a cool serving of clerical obedience, "and I would prefer to believe he knows what he's doing." He could still fire up his critical engines, to be sure. In November 2007, Neuhaus was invited to debate the place of religion in politics at an event sponsored by the *Economist* magazine, in New York. At the start of the debate, when the proposition was read out to the hundreds in attendance—"Religion and politics should always be kept separate"—it met with strong approval. Neuhaus' debating partner, *Economist* columnist and author Adrian Wooldridge, recalls that Neuhaus had relished the prospect of having to convince a crowd set in strong opposition against him, and indeed, his performance says as much, replayed as part of a CBC documentary that ran in December 2007, on the outsized American Catholic life and work of an Ottawa Valley Lutheran boy.

Seated at a table, using both hands to emphasize his points, and speaking in a cadenced rhythm more akin to a preacher's than a pundit's, Neuhaus briskly disavowed the position that many in the audience likely presumed a religious conservative might adopt. In other words, rather than insisting on a pristine and perfect vision of religion itself, Neuhaus observed that "religion, as a phenomenon, is as riddled through with human nonsense, and the capacity for evil, as any other aspect of human life." He paused a moment, looked around, and asked, "Do we think politics is more immune to evil?" The crowd broke up, and Neuhaus grinned and kept going, and, against long odds, won the debate. He was, in short, convinced, and likewise convincing, that the question was never whether religion and politics should come together, but instead, and always, how.[3]

This was the baseline premise that always featured in the pages of *First Things.* In the January 2008 issue, Neuhaus charged after intellectual historian Mark Lilla for arguing in his latest book that the achievement of contemporary democratic public life was, in fact, the exclusion of biblically formed proposals for human life and purpose. "After more than three hundred pages, he arrives at a conclusion that is, I believe, as wrongheaded as wrongheaded could be," Neuhaus declared. Elsewhere in *First Things* during this period, he was just as critical about secular-liberal apologies for the abortion license, the latest efforts of his antipodal Catholic counterparts Garry Wills and Notre Dame theologian Richard McBrien, and media malformations of both Benedict XVI's teachings and George W. Bush's policies. Indeed, with especial vim, Neuhaus diagnosed the *New York Times* coverage of the June 2007 meeting between Benedict and Bush as "a wondrous mix of fatuity and fiction" that emphasized Benedict's critical estimation of the situation in Iraq, and also Bush's indecorously referring to the pope as "sir" rather than "Your Holiness." Neuhaus explained that "in the mind of the journalistic herd, it is all Iraq, all the time. Spiced with the requisite sneer or two at Mr. Bush's putative verbal and social ineptitude." Neuhaus counteracted all of this, as only he could: "Sources in both the Vatican and the White House say that the meeting was exceedingly relaxed, cordial, and personally warm"; and contra the *Times* account, while the pope expressed concern about the plight of Christians in Iraq, "the rightness or wrongness of U.S. policy in Iraq was not raised in the conversation, according to sources in both the White House and the Vatican."

If he took a particular pleasure in correcting the paper of record on a story involving the topmost figures in U.S.-Vatican relations, this didn't stop him from elsewhere allowing that his own, ongoing construals of both Church and American political matters had their limits. In February 2008, *First Things* published an extended letter from Patrick Fleming, author of a book about the clergy abuse scandals. Fleming took issue with Neuhaus' "rather dismissive comments about the book" and in turn pointed out that Neuhaus' continual "explanation and rallying cry in regard to the scandal—'fidelity, fidelity, fidelity'—was fine and well but facile by comparison to systemic accounts of what had gone so terribly wrong and how to prevent its happening again. Neuhaus' response to Fleming's page-long statement was only a few lines, respectful and almost contrite, rather than (more usually the case when criticisms were published in the magazine) caustic and triumphant in having, as ever, the final word.[4]

Later on in that same issue, Neuhaus wrote an extended reflection on America's position in world affairs. By late 2007 and early 2008, the Bush administration was well into the "Surge" effort that saw thousands of U.S. troops added to the war effort in Iraq, in an attempt to turn back the ongoing chaos and sectarian slaughter that had been convulsing the country since the rapid defeat of Saddam Hussein's regime in 2003 and thereby exposing as wildly premature if not patently hollow the administration's early declarations of victory. Throughout this period, *First Things* was steadfast in its support of U.S. policy in Iraq, primarily through George Weigel's writings but also through Neuhaus' efforts. He was more likely to attack the administration's critics rather than defend the administration itself, largely by arguing that conducting the War on Terror was a necessary responsibility, among others, for the nation that singularly enjoyed "geopolitical primacy" in contemporary world affairs. But by February 2008, in a piece candidly entitled "American Preeminence, for Better and Worse," he acknowledged that "there are dramatically different views on how the Bush administration has handled, or mishandled, that primacy but—moments of crisis, tomorrow's polls, and this year's election campaign notwithstanding—American preeminence, with all the problems attending American preeminence, is a fact of life as far as anyone can see into the future."[5]

In 2007 and 2008 Neuhaus also took on a more reflective and personal frame in his writing, whether he was delivering a wistful paean to the Lionel train set of his attic days in Pembroke, recalling a chance and amusing dinner encounter with Jorge Borges, meditating on the experience of aging and dying, or indeed closely observing the passage of great and admired men, even in the midst of a new presidential campaign. William F. Buckley, Jr., died in late February 2008. Neuhaus last visited him at his Stamford, Connecticut, home the prior December, when the two men had lunch. They talked about the book on Ronald Reagan that Buckley was writing, and the health challenges that were preventing him from making much progress, namely emphysema, the result of years of smoking that Buckley told Neuhaus he was partly to blame for, because of all the very many postprandial cigar sessions the two men had shared. The visit had a valedictory cast to it; Buckley told a few old stories about Norman Mailer and others while touring Neuhaus around his famously paper-strewn study. There was also some business to discuss; Buckley suggested subjects to consider at the next meeting of "That Group," the conservative talking club the two of them had founded in the early 1990s, but, as Neuhaus recounted in an extended remembrance of Buckley in the May 2008 issue of *First Things,* "I do not really think that he expected to be there. I think we both knew that we were possibly, probably, meeting for the last time." Neuhaus left Buckley's in tears, and he was right: in lieu of seeing him again, Neuhaus wrote about Buckley instead, following his death. He wrote about Buckley's greatness on its own terms, and also detailed a fruitful friendship and professional collaboration that reached back to the early 1970s, marked by their shared interests in American conservatism, Catholicism, and making a winning case for both in public life.[6]

Of course, Neuhaus did more than write about him; he also prayed for his dear departed friend, concelebrating a memorial Mass for Buckley at St. Patrick's Cathedral on April 4, alongside fellow New York priest and author George Rutler, with eulogies from Buckley's son Christopher and from Henry Kissinger. This was the second time in three days that Neuhaus had said a memorial Mass at the cathedral; on April 2, he led hundreds of others in observing the third anniversary of John Paul II's death. As he would remark in a virtuoso piece for the summer issue of *First Things,* which would prove to be the last remarkable piece of sustained writing he did for the magazine, "April was a time of remembering, and of gratitude" for him, in recent and deep terms both. In addition to the commemoration of Buckley's and John Paul II's deaths in the early days of April 2008, Neuhaus was mindful of the much earlier deaths of two others whom he considered profoundly formative upon his sense of vocation. The first was of Dietrich Bonhoeffer, the great German Lutheran theologian who bravely embodied the most famous one-line statement of his theology—"When Christ calls a man, he bids him come and die"—when he was executed on April 9, 1945, in a concentration camp for his anti-Nazi activities. The second meaningful death anniversary was that of Martin Luther King, Jr., whose 1968 assassination fell on April 4. But in this reflection, Neuhaus didn't yet again defend a view of King's accomplishments as flowing from the primacy of his self-understanding as a Christian and a minister, or embroider his King commentary with autobiographical flourishes. Instead, Neuhaus situated King's efforts and hopes for race relations in America, far from fulfilled at the time of his death and thereafter, in the volatile here-and-now of a racially charged presidential primary campaign.[7]

In Spring 2008, Illinois senator Barack Obama's effort to secure the Democratic presidential nomination over New York senator and former first lady Hillary Clinton was mired in a controversy over Obama's ties to Jeremiah Wright, a minister whose church Obama was part of while living in Chicago. ABC News broke the story that Wright had preached vitriolic sermons over the years, notably calling for God's damnation of America because of its irredeemable racial legacies and, on the first Sunday following the attacks, describing 9/11 as fit recompense for a nation that supported state terrorism elsewhere: "America's chickens are coming home to roost," he proclaimed from the pulpit. Under extraordinary scrutiny because of his unwillingness to break with Wright fully, as opposed to simply repudiating his uglier statements, Obama instead delivered a major address in Philadelphia on America's ongoing arguments over race, which Neuhaus watched and then wrote about, with King very much on his mind, four decades after he died: "And now, forty years later, these arguments are being revisited. . . . Obama's Philadelphia speech was, of course, generated by the Reverend Jeremiah's preaching. Beyond the obvious purpose of damage control, it was a thoughtful reflection on questions that continue to vex our public life. . . . Is there any other national politician today capable of offering in public such a candid and personal reflection on an issue of such great moment? None comes readily to mind."[8]

Neuhaus wasn't about to endorse Obama, no matter how fine and credible a speech he gave on race—after all, this was also a speech marred by "the boilerplate leftisms of class warfare and what he depicts as a nation, black and white, of seething resentments," a speech that never mentioned abortion, which Neuhaus called, over race, "the single most polarizing question in our public life," and not simply because abortion wasn't relevant but because Obama's own position was "so extreme that he refuses to support even the 'born alive' legislation that would protect the lives of infants who survive the abortion procedure. His call [made elsewhere] for reconciliation [between pro-life and pro-choice camps], however rhetorically appealing, is more believably a call for capitulation by those who disagree." As for what he had to say about race itself, Neuhaus faulted Obama for declaring, "I can no more disown [Wright] than I can disown the black community," the parallelism of which implicitly and irresponsibly assigned Wright a representative status with respect to the black community itself, one that was wildly inaccurate and cause for further confusion and discouragement in the ongoing public debate about American race relations, never mind its potential effect on the Democratic primaries.

"In any event," Neuhaus concluded, Obama's was nothing less than a "remarkable reflection on race," an evaluation he based on the combined personal, political, and public stakes of the effort. The evaluation correlated to the contexts for observation and comment and critique that Neuhaus himself brought together beneath a religious frame in the pages of *First Things* at ten thousand words every month,[9] for nearly two hundred issues and twenty years, and never with greater vitality than when he could, indeed, integrate the personal, the political, and the public, as he did with his 2008 contemplation of "extraordinary April days. John Paul the Great, William F. Buckley, Martin Luther King, Dietrich Bonhoeffer. They were days of sorrow and gratitude. I count it as a gift beyond measure to have known three of them as friends. Each was great, albeit in different ways. The life of each awakens us to the possibilities of life lived greatly."[10]

Neuhaus' "Lives Lived Greatly" reflection was published in the summer issue of *First Things,* right around the time he paid an unexpected visit to his first best place in New York. Jonathan Priest, the pastor of St. John's, Brooklyn, walked out of a packed Sunday service to find a black town car idling on Maujer Street, in front of the church. "Father Neuhaus!" he exclaimed, when an old man in clerics climbed out of the back. Priest had heard of the congregation's famed former pastor but never met him before. "What are you doing here?" he asked. Neuhaus' answer surprised him. "Well, I was preaching at this tiny little Lutheran congregation," he explained, revealing a continued ministerial involvement in his Lutheran past: Neuhaus told Priest that he was part of a "pulpit supply" list and so had answered the call for a fill-in that particular Sunday at St. Mark's Evangelical Church, on Bushwick Avenue, which was near enough Maujer Street that he asked the driver to stop there on the ride back to Manhattan. Priest said that the visit was pleasant and consisted mostly of Neuhaus asking after old members of the congregation like June Braun, who happened to be there and was likewise surprised and happy to see the pastor who'd first brought her into urban ministry at St. John's, some forty-five years before. Before returning to the car and heading back to 338, Neuhaus stepped into the church itself, for the first time in many, many years. He looked around and observed, "We had a lot of good times here."[11]

That same summer, Neuhaus went to Krakow to participate once more in the Tertio Millennio Seminar with Weigel and the other members of the faculty. He returned from Europe and went to Ottawa Valley to spend August at the cottage. The Weigel family joined him, as usual, for part of the visit, which was spent as all of them were—with heady talk and strong drink flowing freely and ambitious leisure reading of the household's daily newspaper, a 1920 edition of the *Encyclopedia Britannica;* with visits to Orlen Lapp and also Timothy Moyle, a Catholic priest in Pembroke with whom Neuhaus became friendly in later years, and also with his various cousins and old friends in town. In late August, it was time to head back to work, back to New York, but because of a luggage mix-up with the Weigels, Neuhaus' passport accidentally ended up back in America before he did. And so, while he waited for its return, Neuhaus unexpectedly had a few days to himself in his boyhood home. These would prove a gift, of sorts: days to himself, time to himself, before returning to the ever-hectic demands of his work, not least commenting, once more, on the place of religion in a presidential election, demands that would be shunted aside by November because of mortal illness.

He spent these late summer days on his own attending, among other things, to his annual cottage habit of rereading great works—in past years these included Paul's epistles, Conrad, Dostoevsky, not to mention his all-time favorite novel, *Scoop,* Evelyn Waugh's crackling satire of the absurdities of the news business. This time, with Jody Bottum's encouragement, the focus was a selection of Charles Dickens novels, and while Neuhaus wasn't finally convinced to overcome his long-standing resistance to Dickens as an overly effusive writer, in sentiment and event both—he'd take Dostoevsky any day—he was glad to have been "reacquainted with Dickens" and his memorable characters, as he would write for the November 2008 issue of *First Things.* The summer reading report was part of a larger reflection on what would prove his final days in the little town "where I was born and reared." That reflection was warm and affectionate and, finally, melancholic, focused, from far away in New York, on imagining the cottage in the final months of the year, "now tightly closed against the fierce assaults of winter," assaults that his father Clem had pushed through with horse and cutter back in the 1930s, to preach the Gospel to the good Lutherans of the Ottawa Valley. Soon enough,

Neuhaus would be overcome by the fierce assaults of cancer, finding himself suddenly deep in the wintertime of his own life.[12]

By early October, people began to take notice of Neuhaus' declining health. On October 9, he flew to Salem, Virginia, to give a talk at the invitation of his longtime friend and interlocutor the Lutheran moral theologian Robert Benne. His topic, well fit to the closing months of a presidential election pitting Republican senator John McCain against Democrat senator Barack Obama, was "Moral Imperatives and Political Choices: A Christian Response." Benne was struck in three ways by Neuhaus' visit. First, by Neuhaus' physical situation: he moved slowly and seemed tired, and also in pain whenever he had to get in and out of a car, though he dismissed any talk of it when Benne asked him how he was feeling. Second, Benne was struck by Neuhaus' quiet social presence: glad to enjoy a cigar and sip a drink, he didn't dominate conversations and pontificate on the election and all else; rather, when he did speak, he was given to reminiscence. Third, at the event itself, which would prove Neuhaus' last public address, Benne was struck by its emphases, which were biblical and theological rather than "explicitly political stuff," which was what Benne and probably most of the audience would have been expecting from the likes of the famous Father Neuhaus, no less than four weeks before Election Day. Instead, early on in his remarks, Neuhaus observed that of late American public life always seemed to be in campaign mode, rendering a term like "the political season obsolete." And so he (mostly) stepped away from commenting on partisan politics or the immediate dramatics of the presidential race, and instead called his audience to focus their thoughts and plans on a great calling, to live out their shared and individual "responsibility for advancing a more just and free society."

Expanding on this, Neuhaus suggested that the quality and substance of justice and freedom were, in twenty-first-century America, in gravest dispute over the beginnings and endings of human life. But this didn't lead to a plea that his listeners simply vote Republican to put an end to abortion and euthanasia. He wanted his audience to know that justice and freedom were not so easily, so straightforwardly, achieved. Rather, he pointed out that questions of how to bring about that "more just and free society" led to an "endless and endlessly necessary conversation" and that "we must realize, that in this moment, we are never going to arrive at a satisfactory resolution, and that, by way of Augustine, even the best of aspirations can be twisted by 'by the work of evil . . . in our time and in every time.'" About this, Neuhaus concluded, "We are not naïve, we are not utopians. We are people filled with hope, we Christian people," and because of faith in the saving power and lordship of Christ, "we are vindicated, we know how the story turns out." And so, "for us, it is only this, that in our little moment—and all of us have but a little time—we are found faithful, found faithful in bearing witness to the truth, found faithful in living the truth. . . . No part of the Church has ever gotten it quite right, no, but we just have to keep on working at it, because that's what it means to respond to the invitation to follow Him."[13]

In public, at least in the years following the enflamed and righteous speech-making of his Movement days, Neuhaus was an unhurried speaker who liked to let the deep, mellow roll of his voice carry his public remarks at a measured, almost musical cadence. He spoke slowly at Roanoke as well, but in place of the twinkling eyes and sardonic grins that audiences had come to expect, there was a sense of a more concerted effort on his part, to get through his points and thank his listeners for their sustained applause with a little smile, and then take a long sip of water, and sit down. He returned to New York the next morning, and a few days later, on October 13, he hosted the 2008 Erasmus lecture at the Union League Club. This year, the subject was Christianity's encounter with Islam in the first millennium, and the distinguished lecturer was Neuhaus' oldest friend, Robert Wilken. They were photographed together to mark the occasion—two Lutheran junior college boys who had made their way into the great wide world and lived out their vocations to Christian life as neither could have imagined when they'd become friends in 1950s Austin. After that evening in Manhattan, Wilken wouldn't see Neuhaus again until just before Christmas. He would be shocked by his great friend's stark and grave decline.

Between October and December, Neuhaus' condition significantly worsened. On October 30, one of the young staffers at the magazine and residents at 338, Amanda Shaw, happened to be working late at the office, as was Neuhaus, as usual. He became sick to his stomach, blamed an ill-considered bowl of clam chowder, and, with Shaw's help, took a cab back to 338, where they watched an old Audrey Hepburn movie. He remained ill, and Shaw sensed there was more to this than iffy seafood. A day later, incapable of keeping anything down, Neuhaus went to the hospital with Shaw helping him. They spent Halloween night in the emergency ward of St. Vincent's, awaiting treatment alongside a guy dressed up in a cowboy costume, nursing a gunshot wound. By morning, Neuhaus had pulled out his IV, declared himself better, and gone home and written four thousand words for his next *First Things* column. This burst of productivity aside, he became increasingly infirm thereafter, with Shaw and a fellow young staffer and 338 resident, Nathaniel Peters, largely assisting him. Peters would take him to doctor's appointments for various tests—Neuhaus was convinced the issue was nothing more than a hernia, but in time the diagnosis would be cancer that was detected in his lymph nodes, near his neck and sternum—and Shaw would cook his meals and join him to listen to Bach and watch British miniseries.

Just before Thanksgiving, he became very sick and was hospitalized at St. Vincent's, where he had died and returned almost sixteen years before; former *First Things* staffer Matt Rose stayed with him, and kept up his spirits by reading Elvis' letter to Nixon, the Stalin reader, and other cerebral absurdities. Neuhaus was back at 338 in early December. During the day, Shaw and Peters would leave for work at *First Things,* where Jody Bottum began to take on a larger role in the magazine's operations because of Neuhaus' situation: other than occasionally coming by, he never returned to work at the office, but instead would go down to the basement when he was on his own and keep at his writing, whether for *First Things* or to look at the manuscript for *American Babylon.* After a final few journeys over to Immaculate Conception, daily Mass by later November exclusively happened in the apartment, at the dining room table where he sat and celebrated, his young attendants his impromptu parishioners. After the Gospel one time, as Shaw recalls, Peters began preparing the table for the Eucharist, and Neuhaus stopped him and said, "Aren't you going to sit? I'm going to preach to you."[14]

Neuhaus never preached publicly again, and the last time before his death that he was in church was a week before Christmas, for the funeral of the heralded Jesuit theologian Avery Dulles, his longtime friend, collaborator, fellow convert to Catholicism, and the man who had prepared him for his ordination as a priest. Neuhaus stood out among the 150 priests, bishops, and cardinals who concelebrated, not because of his well-known closeness to Dulles, which dated back decades, but because of his dramatic deterioration. Seated in a front pew, Robert Wilken watched as Neuhaus passed by in the opening procession. He recalls knowing then that his friend was dying, as he watched him struggle to keep up with the other priests making their way to the sanctuary. The whole way, Neuhaus was holding on to the arm of Raymond de Souza, the Canadian priest, newspaper columnist, and magazine editor who had begun a close friendship and mentorship with him in the 1990s, and discerned the priesthood in large part with Neuhaus' encouragement and guidance, and who would preach at his funeral Mass a few weeks later. De Souza sat beside Neuhaus for Dulles' funeral Mass, and recalls the constant suffering Neuhaus went through, all but steeling his body, his will, for each part of the Mass. Afterward, de Souza helped him to a seat in the sacristy, where several people lined up to say hello to him, all of them sensing they were likely saying good-bye. That night, back at the apartment, de Souza asked Neuhaus to autograph a photograph of de Souza's ordination, given his important role in that event. Neuhaus gave him a look that suggested to de Souza that he could tell why de Souza was making this request just now. "I'll sign it," he declared. In strong clear script, he wrote one line and asked de Souza if he remembered its origins. Of course he did: the line came from the homily Neuhaus had preached at de Souza's first Mass, six years before, and it served as Neuhaus' final message to him, indeed to all the men and women he had directed into religious vocations: "May ages see through you—Christ."[15]

The day after Christmas, Neuhaus was admitted to Sloan Kettering cancer hospital. According to Jody Bottum, who had essentially moved into Neuhaus' apartment in the days before Christmas, by which point Neuhaus was largely bedridden and incapable of keeping much down, he had resisted Bottum's requests that he seek early admission, because he wanted to die at home. Eventually Bottum called George and Joan Weigel; they came up from Washington and were able to persuade him to leave the apartment for the hospital. In turn, Neuhaus' sisters were called and came to be with their brother in his final days, joining a constant prayer- and hymn-filled vigil comprised of Catholics and Lutherans from throughout Neuhaus' life and work, including Joan Weigel and her daughter Monica, former *First Things* staffer Mary McFadden, Davida Goldman, de Souza's sister Marissa and Amanda Shaw, the former already, and the latter a future woman religious. By early January, the cancer had spread beyond treatment. Neuhaus could no longer speak, only hold others' hands while they prayed for him, or when Johanna softly sang him a children's hymn from the Pembroke days, "I am Jesus' little lamb, ever glad at heart I am." One time, when Johanna was keeping watch by herself, an elderly couple came into Neuhaus' room. Black and white, they were members of St. John the Evangelist, in Brooklyn, and Neuhaus had married them decades before, when he was their pastor. Since then he had faithfully called them every year on their anniversary, but when no call had come this year, the couple knew something was wrong and eventually found their way to Sloan Kettering. Johanna told them they were welcome to say good-bye, but pointed out that Neuhaus was beyond responding.

The woman approached, leaned in close, and said, "Father Richard," and he opened his eyes and smiled. Soon thereafter, he fell into a deep and final sleep. George Rutler came in and administered the last rites. His loving beloveds stayed with him to the end.[16]

Neuhaus' next column for *First Things* came out a few weeks after his funeral. It featured an extended and autobiographical meditation on the law-gospel complex in Lutheran theology, a warm good-bye to Avery Dulles, and sundry sharp observations about media silliness, good books and bad books, good and bad theologians and thinkers and writers, bad bishops and worse bishops—the usual, but for a prayerful and prophetic last item:

> *At the time of this writing, I am contending with a cancer, presently of unknown origin. I am, I am given to believe, under the expert medical care of the Sloan-Kettering clinic here in New York. I am grateful beyond measure for your prayers storming the gates of heaven. Be assured that I neither fear to die nor refuse to live. If it is to die, all that has been is but a slight intimation of what is to be. If it is to live, there is much that I hope to do in the interim. After the last round with cancer fifteen years ago, I wrote a little book,* As I Lay Dying *(titled after William Faulkner after John Donne), in which I said much of what I had to say about the package deal that is mortality. I did not know that I had so much more to learn. And yes, the question has occurred to me that, if I have but a little time to live, should I be spending it writing this column. I have heard it attributed to figures as various as Brother Lawrence and Martin Luther—when asked what they would do if they knew they were going to die tomorrow, they answered that they would plant a tree and say their prayers. (Luther is supposed to have added that he would quaff his favored beer.) Maybe I have, at least metaphorically, planted a few trees, and certainly I am saying my prayers. Who knew that at this point in life I would be understanding, as if for the first time, the*

> *words of Paul, "When I am weak, then I am strong"? This is not a farewell. Please God, we will be pondering together the follies and splendors of the Church and the world for years to come. But maybe not. In any event, when there is an unidentified agent in your body aggressively attacking the good things your body is intended to do, it does concentrate the mind. The entirety of our prayer is "Your will be done"—not as a note of resignation but of desire beyond expression. To that end, I commend myself to your intercession, and that of all the saints and angels who accompany us each step through time toward home.*[17]

Richard John Neuhaus died on January 8, 2009, in New York City, leaving its prolepsis for the New Jerusalem itself.

Acknowledgments

Over the past five years, I've been frequently asked about my intentions in pursuing this book: was I writing a hatchet job or a hagiography? This biography is neither. Instead, it's a sympathetic, critical-minded effort to explore the life and work of someone who spent decades praying, preaching, speaking, organizing, and writing about American democracy and Western Christianity and, in the process, lived out his vocation as a thoroughgoing man of God in the public square.

During this same period, I've been repeatedly asked if I had a personal connection to Richard John Neuhaus. After all, a Sri Lankan–Canadian novelist and English professor living in Toronto isn't the most obvious choice to write about a Canadian-born Lutheran pastor turned Catholic priest and conservative New York intellectual. My personal connection is minor compared to the hundreds upon hundreds for whom Richard John Neuhaus was a significant element in their personal and professional lives. I met him once, in 2003, following a Mass he celebrated at Immaculate Conception parish, a few blocks from his apartment. A few months earlier I'd published an essay in *First Things*. When I told him this, he was very happy to hear it, and even more impressed that a mere graduate student had somehow made it into the discriminating pages of the magazine. Neuhaus' compliments about my writing rather rapidly turned into compliments for *First Things* itself. After a few moments of this, he shook my hand and then sent me on my way with a jovial, booming encouragement—"If you want to be a writer, write!" Thereafter, I wrote an occasional piece for the magazine and remained interested in questions of religion and public life while pursuing a career as a professor of American studies, a book critic, and a novelist.

Six years later, shortly after Neuhaus died, I wrote about his life and work for a Canadian magazine, the *Walrus*. A few months later, frankly underwhelmed by the prospect of writing another conventional academic monograph, I thought about writing a biography of Neuhaus. I sent a brief query to Neuhaus' close friend George Weigel, whom I'd met independently and by sheer coincidence—my wife went to college with one of his daughters. To my surprise, Weigel informed me that no one was pursuing it. I began this work in January 2010.

Along the way, there have been many who have proven unfailingly generous in providing various kinds of support for this effort. Many of these individuals sat for multi-hour interviews and are identified in the notes to the biography's chapters. I'd like to take this opportunity to identify those who were especially important to the work.

In addition to George Weigel, Peter Berger and Robert Wilken were unfailingly gracious with my many queries over the past few years. Neuhaus' sisters Mildred Schwich and Johanna Speckhard shared a great deal of personal history and family effects. Orlen Lapp was a fine and friendly guide to meeting Neuhaus' childhood buddies and family in Pembroke. In New York, the staff of *First Things*—particularly R. R. Reno, Davida Goldman, and Denise Vaccaro—were excellent hosts during multiple research forays into Neuhaus' sizeable and mostly catalogued personal papers; and Larry Bailey and the Community of Christ in the City welcomed my family and me for a stay at 338 East 19th during one of these research trips. As a great help to understanding Neuhaus as a parish priest, Maria McFadden Maffucci organized a meeting of his parishioners at Immaculate Conception for me.

At my home institution, Ryerson University, I have enjoyed timely and generous support from colleagues Alan Shephard, Mohamed Lachemi, Amy Casey, Jean-Paul Boudreau, and Dennis Denisoff, and also benefited from the efforts of research assistants Paul Mathew, Scott Dobbin, Heather Mercer, and Basit Iqbal. I also wish to acknowledge receiving research funding for this book from the Social Sciences and Humanities Research Council of Canada.

Throughout the time I've been working on Neuhaus' life story, I have been very fortunate to enjoy a regular dialogue with two fellow biographers who are interested in the life of the conservative mind, Sam Tanenhaus and Robert Sullivan. I was also fortunate to receive encouraging and challenging responses from a scholarly reading group in American Catholic studies at the University of Notre Dame that held a session on a selection from the work in progress.

From its earliest stages, my editor Gary Jansen has been a robust advocate for this biography and encouraged me to approach it in the highest possible religious, intellectual, and cultural terms. The book would not exist without him.

Partway through the writing of this book, I began working with Kimberly Witherspoon of InkWell Management, whose keen interest in my writing has been a source of great encouragement in both personal and professional terms.

Three people read early drafts of the manuscript and have made important suggestions that strengthened the telling of Neuhaus' story: T. H. Adamowski, Kevin Belgrave, and James Nuechterlein, whose editorial judgment Neuhaus relied on like no one else's—I understand why.

My wife Anna and our daughters Mira, Olive, Ever, and Imogen have been with me throughout this work, which has taken us from

Toronto to Texas and Indiana and Washington and New York and Rome and New York again. This work has also left them on their own for the hundreds upon hundreds of hours I have been in my office, working on what one of my young children refers to as the "Father Moo Cows" book. This biography, like all else in my life and work, is dedicated to them.

Notes

CHAPTER ONE. A PASTOR'S SON, BORN AND BAPTIZED ON "THE CANADIAN FRONTIER"

1. Epigraph: Neuhaus interview with James Finn for Finn's *Protest: Pacifism and Politics* (New York: Random House, 1967), p. 165; family details in paragraph one: Author interview with Mildred Schwich (June 2, 2011).
2. C. B. Pappin, *A Century in Christ, A Future in Faith: A History of St. John's Lutheran Church, Pembroke, 1891–1991* (Pembroke, ON: DFT Printing, 1991), pp. 7–18; Eric W. Gritsch, *A History of Lutheranism*, 2nd ed. (Minneapolis: Fortress Press, 2010), pp. 197–202.
3. Pappin, *Century in Christ*, pp. 7–18, 42; author interview with Mildred Schwich, June 1, 2011.
4. Author interviews with Johanna Speckhard (August 6, 2012) and Tom Neuhaus (August 31, 2011).
5. Richard John Neuhaus, *In Defense of People: Ecology and the Seduction of Radicalism* (New York: MacMillan, 1971), p. 247; Richard John Neuhaus, *First Things* 90 (February 1999), p. 73.
6. Author interview with Mildred Schwich (June 2, 2011); Lutheran Church Lectionary as posted at http://www.lcms.org/page.aspx?pid=448; Acts 5:42 (KJV); Richard John Neuhaus, *First Things* 45 (August/September 1994), p. 68.
7. Author interviews with Beverly Wishart (October 27, 2010) and Orlen Lapp (October 29, 2012); E. Clifford Nelson, ed., *The Lutherans in North America*

(Philadelphia: Fortress Press, 1980), p. 389; Richard John Neuhaus, *First Things* 45, p. 68.

8. Irwin E. Prange, "Fishers of Men," *First Things* 192 (April 2009), p. 46; author interview with Judy Stevenson (October 29, 2010).
9. Gritsch, *History of Lutheranism,* pp. 192–197; Sydney E. Ahlstrom, *A Religious History of the American People* (New Haven, CT: Yale University Press, 1972), pp. 750–755; family history and obituary notice provided to author by Johanna Speckhard and Mildred Schwich.
10. Author interview with Mildred Schwich (June 2, 2011).
11. Ibid.
12. Author interviews with Mildred Schwich (June 2, 2011) and Johanna Speckhard (August 6, 2012); Richard John Neuhaus, *First Things* 102 (April 2000), p. 86.

CHAPTER TWO. PEMBROKE'S MOST PATRIOTIC PASTOR, AND ITS YOUNGEST AND MOST NEWSWORTHY

1. Author interviews with Johanna Speckhard (August 6, 2012) and George Neuhaus (August 23, 2011).
2. Pappin, *Century in Christ,* pp. 25–50.
3. Author interview with Johanna Speckhard (August 6, 2012); Clemens Neuhaus quoted by Richard John Neuhaus in *First Things* 45 (August/September 1994), pp. 68–70.
4. Pappin, *Century in Christ,* pp. 48–49.
5. Nelson, *Lutherans in North America,* pp. 472–481.
6. Author interview with Johanna Speckhard (August 6, 2012).
7. Richard John Neuhaus, *As I Lay Dying: Meditations upon Returning* (New York: Basic Books, 2002), pp. 3–4.
8. Ibid, p. 3.
9. Author interviews with Beverly Wishart (October 27, 2010), Donald Stressman (October 29, 2011), and Johanna Speckhard (August 6, 2012); Richard John Neuhaus, *Death on a Friday Afternoon: Meditations on the Last Words of Jesus from the Cross* (New York: Basic Books, 2000), pp. 153–154.
10. Neuhaus, *Death on a Friday Afternoon,* p. 155; author interview with Johanna Speckhard (August 6, 2012).
11. Author interviews with Mildred Schwich (June 2, 2011) and Johanna Speckhard (August 6, 2012).
12. Ibid.; Richard John Neuhaus, "How I Became the Catholic I Was," *First Things* 122 (April 2002), pp. 14–15; Richard John Neuhaus, *Catholic Matters: Confusion, Controversy, and the Splendor of Truth* (New York: Basic Books, 2006), pp. 44–46.

CHAPTER THREE. AN "UNEDUCABLE" LITTLE LUTHERAN PROFESSOR ENLISTS IN A GRAND CAUSE

1. Richard Friedenthal, *Luther,* trans. John Nowell (London: Weidenfeld and Nicolson, 1970), pp. 127–294.
2. Author interview with Donald Stressman (October 29, 2011).
3. Author interviews with Mildred Schwich (June 2, 2011), Tom Neuhaus (August 31, 2011), and Nathaniel Peters (May 17, 2011).
4. Author interviews with Johanna Speckhard (August 6, 2012) and George Neuhaus (August 23, 2011).
5. Author interviews with Tom Neuhaus (August 31, 2011) and George Neuhaus (August 23, 2011).
6. Author interview with Donald Stressman (October 29, 2011).
7. Richard John Neuhaus, *America Against Itself: Moral Vision and the Public Order* (Notre Dame: University of Notre Dame Press, 1992), p. 1; author interview with Johanna Speckhard (August 6, 2012).
8. Author interview with Johanna Speckhard (August 6, 2012); Neuhaus, *As I Lay Dying,* pp. 34–35.

CHAPTER FOUR. BOARDING SCHOOL DAYS: PRAYER AND MISCHIEF WITHOUT CEASING

1. Richard John Neuhaus personal correspondence with Leroy E. Vogel: RJN-PP, 1990 files. (Author's note: Neuhaus' personal papers are predominantly housed in bankers' boxes at the Institute on Religion and Public Life, which publishes *First Things.* The papers are catalogued by decade and alphabetized within each series of years. While researching this book, I also came across unfiled personal papers at his apartment, and as well relied on event and publication notes kept and filed by Davida Goldman, his longtime personal assistant. In the notes, I have used the designation "PP," for personal papers, for these sources, with specific year or source designations thereafter, as per above.); History of Concordia Seward as found at the Concordia University, Nebraska, website (http://www.cune.edu/about/history-of-concordia/); author interview with Johanna Speckhard (August 6, 2012).
2. Neuhaus, *America Against Itself,* p. 2; author interview with Mildred Schwich (June 2, 2011).
3. Gritsch, *History of Lutheranism,* pp. 34–35; Neuhaus correspondence with Vogel, 1990.
4. Author interview with Mildred Schwich (June 2, 2011); Neuhaus correspondence with Vogel, 1990.

5. Author interview with Mildred Schwich (June 2, 2011); Richard John Neuhaus interview with Brian Lamb, *Booknotes,* May 26, 2002, video and transcript found at http://www.booknotes.org/Watch/169660-1/Richard+John+Neuhaus.aspx.
6. "Manners and Morals: Epidemic," *Time* magazine, June 2, 1952; author interview with Johanna Speckhard (August 6, 2012); *Golden Embers* 1952, Concordia-Seward yearbook.
7. Neuhaus, *Catholic Matters,* pp. 51–52.
8. This was a disparaging moniker that evoked both a fanatical spiritualism on the part of early anti-ritual Reformation Christians and also "a swarm of insects buzzing around Luther's head," as his biographer Richard Friedenthal explains (*Luther,* p. 314).
9. Neuhaus, *Catholic Matters,* p. 52; Friedenthal, *Luther,* p. 314.

CHAPTER FIVE. A JACKRABBIT-SHOOTING CISCO KID TURNS ARBITER ELEGANTARIUM

1. Author interviews with Keith Loomans (January 7, 2011), Mildred Schwich (June 2, 2011), and Johanna Speckhard (August 6, 2012); Neuhaus interview with Brian Lamb, *Booknotes.*
2. Author interviews with Keith Loomans (January 7, 2011) and Richard O. Ziehr (January 3, 2011); Richard John Neuhaus, "Under the Shadow," *First Things* 69 (January 1997), p. 56; Peter Bogdanovich, dir., *The Last Picture Show* (Columbia Pictures, 1971).
3. Author interviews with Keith Loomans (January 7, 2011) and Richard O. Ziehr (January 3, 2011); Neuhaus interview with Brian Lamb, *Booknotes.*
4. Neuhaus, "Under the Shadow."
5. Author interviews with Keith Loomans (January 7, 2011), Mildred Schwich (June 2, 2011), Johanna Speckhard (August 6, 2012); Neuhaus interview with Brian Lamb, *Booknotes;* Henry P. Studtman and Ray F. Martens, *From the Beginning: A History of Concordia Lutheran College of Texas* (Austin, TX: Concordia Lutheran College of Texas, 1977).
6. *The Concordian,* 1955, yearbook of Concordia College, Austin, personal edition of Robert Wilken.
7. Author interviews with Henry Biar (February 2, 2011), John Heinemeier (March 16, 2011), and Robert Wilken (October 3, 2011).
8. Ibid.; *The Concordian,* 1955; *New York Times,* July 2, 1953.
9. Richard John Neuhaus, "Santayana Lately Revisited," *First Things* 150 (February 2005), pp. 28–29.
10. Author interviews with Henry Biar (February 2, 2011), John Heinemeier (March 16, 2011), and Robert Wilken (October 11, 2011); Richard John

Neuhaus, "While We're At It," *First Things* 84 (June/July 1998), p. 67; Neuhaus, "Santayana Lately Revisited," p. 28.

11. Ibid.; Richard John Neuhaus, "While We're At It," *First Things* 158 (December 2005), p. 75.

CHAPTER SIX. GOAL, MALADY, MEANS: A SEMINARY FORMATION IN CHURCH AND CHURCH POLITICS

1. Author interviews with Robert Wilken (October 3, 2011), Henry Biar (February 2, 2011), and Orlen Lapp (October 29, 2010); *The Church: Selected Writings by Arthur C. Piepkorn,* Michael P. Plekon and William S. Weicher, eds. (Delhi, NY: American Lutheran Publicity Bureau Books, 1993), pp. 299–302.
2. Ibid. Neuhaus' account of Piepkorn's ecclesiology has been disputed by other Lutherans, including Philip Secker, another Concordia graduate. He debated Neuhaus in the pages of *First Things* and also in private correspondence about what Secker regarded as Neuhaus' downplaying Piepkorn's emphasis upon the priority of the Augsburg Confession in understanding the true identity and nature of the universal Catholic Church: author correspondence with Philip Secker (June 10, 2014); and see also "The Piepkornian Vision," *First Things* 122 (October 2002), p. 4.
3. Carl S. Meyer, *Log Cabin to Luther Tower: 125 Years Toward a More Excellent Ministry/Concordia Seminary 1839–1964* (St. Louis, MO: Concordia Publishing House, 1965), pp. 1–5, 144–205; Roosevelt quoted in Nelson, *Lutherans in North America*, p. 481; James C. Burkee, *Power, Politics, and the Missouri Synod* (Minneapolis: Fortress Press, 2011), p. 19; Richard John Neuhaus, *Freedom for Ministry* (San Francisco: Harper & Row, 1979), p. 173.
4. Author interviews with Robert Wilken (June 6, 2012) and John Heinemeier (March 16, 2011).
5. Author interviews with Tom Neuhaus (August 31, 2011), Beverly Wishart (October 27, 2010), Mildred Schwich (June 2, 2011), and Robert Wilken (June 6, 2012).
6. Biblical inerrancy is a defining element of Lutheranism that represents an elaboration of Luther's famous *Sola Scriptura* formulation. It was codified in the 1577 "Solid Declaration" of the confession's beliefs and tenets. Forming part of the Book of Concord, the Solid Declaration declares that "the prophetic and Apostolic scriptures of the Old and New Testaments are the pure, clear fountain of Israel. They are the only true standard and norm by which all teachers and doctrines are to be judged" (http://bookofconcord.org/sd-ruleandnorm.php).
7. This largely began with the influential and controversial work of the German scholar and theologian Friedrich Schleiermacher, who in the early

nineteenth century subjected the Bible to critical methods and historical contextualization that threatened to undermine its sanctity and integrity as the received Word of God.

8. Neuhaus, *America Against Itself*, p. 2.
9. Author interviews with Robert Wilken (June 6, 2012) and Herman Otten (October 5, 2012); Burkee, *Power, Politics and the Missouri Synod*, pp. 1–56.
10. Author interview with Robert Wilken (October 3, 2011); Richard John Neuhaus, "The Best and the Brightest," *First Things* 76 (October 1997), p. 79; Richard John Neuhaus, "The Death of a Pioneer," *First Things* 93 (May 1999), 85; Richard John Neuhaus and Leon Klenicki, *Jew and Christian in Conversation* (Grand Rapids, MI: William B. Eerdmans, 1989), pp. 6–7; Sol Bernard's obituary, *Jewish Daily Forward*, November 26, 2004.
11. Without explicitly naming the church, Neuhaus would share this memory while chatting with a fellow clergyman in South Africa in the early 1980s. In turn, he would recount it in the book that came of that work, *Dispensations: The Future of South Africa as South Africans See It* (Grand Rapids, MI: William B. Eerdmans, 1985), p. 163. Author interview with Robert Wilken (October 3, 2011); Zion Church and Runge history obtained from www.ziondetroit.org; "Trouble in Detroit," *New York Times*, July 27, 1943.
12. He wouldn't have received much sympathy or support back home for this: when a black pastor from Chicago came through Pembroke earlier in the 1950s, Clem and Ella had no choice but to put him up but took certain measures: Ella chose to eat in the kitchen the night he came to dinner, and after the pastor left the next morning, Clem ordered the bedsheets washed—immediately. Author interview with Mildred Schwich (June 2, 2011).
13. Author interviews with Mildred Schwich (June 2, 2011) and Robert Wilken (October 3, 2011).
14. Author interview with Robert Wilken (October 3, 2011).
15. Ibid; Jaroslav Pelikan, *The Riddle of Catholicism* (New York: Abingdon Press, 1959), pp. 232–234; Neuhaus, *Freedom for Ministry*, ix.
16. Author interview with Johanna Speckhard (August 6, 2012); Pembroke newspaper account provided by Mildred Schwich.

CHAPTER SEVEN. A YOUNG PASTOR DISCOVERS "THE GLORY AND TRAGEDY OF LIFE IN THIS CITY"

1. Details about Neuhaus' early years and experiences at St. John the Evangelist: RJN-PP-St. John the Evangelist file; more details about his years at St. John: Gilbert Meilaender, "Obituary," *Studies in Christian Ethics* 22, no. 4 (2009), pp. 496–503; background on Lutherans in Brooklyn: George Wenner, *The*

Lutherans of New York: Their Story and Their Problems 2005 [EBook #14638], http://www.gutenberg.org/dirs/1/4/6/3/14638/14638.txt; on Williamsburg projects: "La Guardia Hails Housing Advance," *New York Times,* April 15, 1936; on Williamsburg history: the Brooklyn Public Library site, http://www.bklynpubliclibrary.org/ourbrooklyn/williamsburg/; on the history of St. John the Evangelist: http://sjebrooklyn.org/about.html; installation details: "Letter to the Editor," Harvey W. Von Harten III, *First Things* 192 (April 2009), p. 9; further details about the congregation and Neuhaus: author interviews with June Braun (September 30, 2011) and John Heinemeier (March 16, 2011); sermon preached by Robert Louis Wilken, "An Anniversary," April 1971, at St. John the Evangelist, Brooklyn, posted digitally in January 2010 at http://www.firstthings.com/onthesquare/2010/01/an-anniversary.

2. Details about Neuhaus' visit to Concordia-Bronxville: author interview with June Braun (September 30, 2011).
3. Ibid; details about the neighborhood and changing demographics and "new people" quotation: Neuhaus, *In Defense of People*, pp. 11–16.
4. Details about the urban ministry and culture of worship at St. John the Evangelist: author interviews with June Braun (September 30, 2011) and John Heinemeier (March 16, 2011); "thigh-thumper" reference cited by Neuhaus in his personal papers describing in correspondence how his Brooklyn congregation used to praise good sermons: RJN-PP, 1987 files; specifics about the content and focus of Neuhaus' sermons: Wilken sermon "An Anniversary."
5. German service detail: author interview with John Heinemeier (March 16, 2011).
6. Details about chaplain work at King's County hospital: Neuhaus, *As I Lay Dying,* pp. 55–60.
7. Ibid.
8. Letter quoted in Wilken sermon "An Anniversary."

CHAPTER EIGHT. FROM BROOKLYN PASTOR TO NATIONAL NEWSMAKER

1. Quotations from Johnson and Neuhaus, and related context: "Clergymen Defend Right to Protest Vietnam Policy," *New York Times,* October 26, 1965, p. 4.
2. "Letter from Birmingham Jail" publication details: Taylor Branch, *Parting the Waters: America in the King Years, 1954–1963* (New York: Simon and Schuster, 1988), p. 804; letter itself reprinted in *Reporting Civil Rights Part One: American Journalism 1941–1963* (New York: Library of America, 2003), pp. 777–794; timeline of 1962/1963 Civil Rights events sourced from *Reporting Civil Rights*

Part One, pp. 908–911; Neuhaus on the "Letter": "Remembering Martin Luther King," *First Things* 126 (October 2002), p. 98; "Lives Lived Greatly" *First Things* 184 (June/July 2008), p. 61; "MLK Today" blog post, January 12, 2007, http://www.firstthings.com/onthesquare/2007/01/rjn-mlk-today.

3. Civil Rights as a subject of Neuhaus sermons: author interview with June Braun (September 30, 2011); details about Neuhaus and Wilken encounters during this period: author interview with Robert Wilken (October 3, 2011).
4. Details about the March on Washington: Branch, *Parting the Waters,* pp. 846–883; Justin Vaisse, *Neoconservatism: The Biography of a Movement,* trans. Arthur Goldhammer (Cambridge, MA: Harvard University Press, 2010), pp. 120–121.
5. Details about the LHRAA: Burkee, *Power, Politics, and the Missouri Synod,* p. 50; details about Neuhaus and his brothers: author interview with Tom Neuhaus (August 31, 2011).
6. Details about Neuhaus, college chaplaincy network, Atlantic District activities, and personal connections to future collaborators: author interviews with Leonard Klein (August 16, 2011) and James Nuechterlein (August 7, 2011); Michael Novak, "Talking 'bout My Generation," *First Things* 192 (April 2009), p. 39.
7. Further Atlantic District details: author interview with James Nuechterlein (August 7, 2011); Two Kingdoms theology references: Carl Braaten, *Because of Christ: Memoirs of a Lutheran Theologian* (Grand Rapids, MI: Wm. B. Eerdmans, 2010), pp. 151–166.
8. Forell quoted in Braaten, *Because of Christ,* pp. 151–166.
9. Correspondence with John Robert Hannah: RJN-PP, 1987 files; details about Piepkorn and army enlistments: author correspondence with Robert Wilken (February 20, 2013).
10. The larger public and political implications of Neuhaus' speech would have been evident for his audience, which would meantime have been hearing of the ongoing battles in Washington over proposed Civil Rights legislation. These battles yielded a dramatic legislative victory for Civil Rights proponents on July 2, 1964, when President Johnson signed the newly passed Civil Rights Act into law and thereby empowered the federal government to implement a nationwide desegregation of all public accommodations, including most notably freedoms and rights around voting, schooling, and employment.
11. Author interview with James Nuechterlein (August 7, 2012); Richard John Neuhaus, "Should We Save Brooklyn Lutheranism?": RJN-PP, Publications List.

CHAPTER NINE. MISSOURI'S MILITANT INSTRUMENT OF GOD'S PEACE

1. Details about Neuhaus at the 1965 LCMS Detroit convention: Burkee, *Power, Politics, and the Missouri Synod,* pp. 55–52; author interview with James Burkee (September 21, 2011).
2. Neuhaus' retrospective comments about his father: author interview with James Nuechterlein (August 7, 2012); details about the 1965 LCMS Detroit convention, Neuhaus' comments, and Otten's responses: Burkee, *Power, Politics, and the Missouri Synod,* pp. 58–59.
3. Neuhaus and Selma: author interview with Peter Berger (November 17, 2010); Heschel and Selma: Edward K. Kaplan, *Spiritual Radical: Abraham Joshua Heschel in America* (New Haven, CT: Yale University Press, 2007), p. 223; details about the March: "The Big Parade: On the Road to Montgomery," *New York Times,* March 22, 1965.
4. Details about the Chicago LHRAA conference: author interview with Karl Ludtze (August 2, 2012); Burkee, *Power, Politics, and the Missouri Synod,* pp. 59–60.
5. Lyndon B. Johnson State of the Union Address as published by Pennsylvania State University, available at http://www2.hn.psu.edu/faculty/jmanis/poldocs/uspressu/SUaddressLBJohnson.pdf; details about the 1964/1965 developments around the Vietnam War: Lien-Hang T. Nguyen, *Hanoi's War: An International History of the War for Peace in Vietnam* (Chapel Hill, NC: University of North Carolina Press, 2012), pp. 74–77; on the elements comprising the antiwar movement in its early stages: Adam Garfinkle, *Telltale Hearts: The Origins and Impact of the Vietnam Antiwar Movement* (New York: St. Martin's Press, 1995/1997), pp. 57–68; for a brief summary of antiwar activism by clergy prior to October 1965: Mitchell K. Hall, *Because of Their Faith: CALCAV and Religious Opposition to the Vietnam War* (New York: Columbia University Press, 1990), pp. 1–12.
6. Details about the events leading up to the founding of CALCAV: Hall, *Because of Their Faith,* pp. 13–19; "Clergymen Defend Right to Protest Vietnam Policy," *New York Times,* October 26, 1965, p. 4; Neuhaus on democratic legitimacy: Taylor Branch, *At Canaan's Edge: America During the King Years, 1965–68* (New York: Simon and Schuster, 2006), pp. 357–358; Pope John XXII, *Pacem in Terris* [Encyclical on Establishing Universal Peace in Truth, Justice, Charity, and Liberty], April 11, 1963, http://www.vatican.va/holy_father/john_xxiii/encyclicals/documents/hf_j-xxiii_enc_11041963_pacem_en.html; Neuhaus citing *Pacem in Terris:* among others, *Being Christian Today: An American Conversation* (Washington, D.C.: Ethics and Public Policy Center, 1992); see also "The Church's Love Letter to the World," UCCB pamphlet, 1996.
7. Details about the November 1965 conference: Hall, *Because of Their Faith,*

pp. 13–19; regarding Spellman's position on Vietnam: "Spellman Arrives for Five-Day Visit With Vietnam G.I.'s," *New York Times,* December 24, 1965.

8. Details about Neuhaus and Coffin's friendship: Richard John Neuhaus, "The Death of William Sloane Coffin, Jr.," *First Things* 164 (June/July 2006), pp. 58–61; details about Clergy Concerned's beginnings: Francine du Plessix Gray, *Divine Disobedience: Profiles in Catholic Radicalism* (New York: Random House, 1969), p. 101; Coffin's 1966 press conference remarks: quoted in Hall, *Because of Their Faith*, p. 1.
9. Details about CCAV and its early work and developments: Hall, *Because of Their Faith,* pp. 13–23; Gray, *Divine Disobedience,* p. 101.
10. Biographical details about Robert MacAfee Brown: obituary, *New York Times,* September 7, 2001.
11. Details about Clergy Concerned's early organizing: Hall, *Because of Their Faith,* pp. 13–25; du Plessix Gray on Neuhaus: Gray, *Divine Disobedience,* p. 91; on the 1966 peace march: "St. Patrick's Greets 62 Interfaith Peace Marchers with a Prayer Service," *New York Times,* March 30, 1966.
12. Details about Clergy Concerned's hiring Fernandez, etc.: Hall, *Because of Their Faith,* pp. 13–19; author interview with Harvey Cox (November 16, 2010); details about the peace fast: Hall, *Because of Their Faith*, pp. 29–30; "Three Clergymen Here Begin Protest Fast," *New York Times,* July 4, 1966; Neuhaus' situation at St. John the Evangelist, in 1966 and thereafter: author interview with John Heinemeier (March 16, 2011); Neuhaus preaching in Simcoe, 1966: author interview with Mildred Schwich (June 2, 2011); *Simcoe Reformer,* July 25, 1966; Clem Neuhaus letter found, un-catalogued, in Neuhaus' private papers (as opposed to the "personal papers" housed at the Institute for Religion and Public Life and cited in these notes as RJN-PP).

CHAPTER TEN. 1968: PASSIONATE DIATRIBES AND TUMULTUOUS RECEPTIONS

1. Details about Neuhaus after the 1968 Democratic National Convention: author interview with Peter and Brigitte Berger (November 17, 2010); on the situation at the convention and Norman Mailer on Dailey: Mailer, *Miami and the Siege of Chicago: An Informal History of the Republican and Democratic Conventions of 1968* (World Publishing Company, 1968); *New York Review of Books* 2008, p. 103 and elsewhere; details about Neuhaus at the convention, CALCAV, and in Chicago: Hall, *Because of Their Faith*, p. 72; obituary, *Washington Times,* January 8, 2009 (Paul Newman press conference); author interview with David Novak (March 2, 2011); on Neuhaus' forceful removal from the convention floor: "New York Delegate Dragged from Hall by Police," *New York Times,* August 29, 1969; Richard John Neuhaus, *First Things*

88 (December 1998), p. 75 (Mailer); Richard John Neuhaus, *First Things* 108 (December 2000), pp. 73–74 (jail); Richard John Neuhaus, *First Things* 157 (November 2005), p. 79 (Niebuhr); Neuhaus, *America Against Itself,* p. 60 (listening to Humphrey speech and drinking and talking with Kempton); details about the circumstances of his arrest: "13 Protestors Guilty in Chicago Disorder," *New York Times,* April 15, 1969.

2. Almost total: By 1967, Neuhaus had also started writing politically charged intellectual journalism for national outlets like the lay Catholic magazine *Commonweal,* notably about the emerging political controversy concerning abortion rights legislation. These efforts differentiated him from the main secular-progressive currents he had otherwise been moving in.
3. Details about Peter and Brigitte Berger and Neuhaus' experiences with them: author interview with Peter and Brigitte Berger (November 17, 2010); about the discussion at their first lunch: Peter Berger and Richard John Neuhaus, *Movement and Revolution: On American Radicalism* (New York: Doubleday, 1970), p. 7; about Neuhaus and Wilken, and also about Neuhaus and Dulles: author interview with Robert Louis Wilken (June 6, 2012); about Neuhaus and Heschel: Richard John Neuhaus, *First Things* 89 (January 1999), pp. 68–69; author interview with David Novak (March 2, 2011); dedication, *Time Toward Home: The American Experiment as Revelation* (Seabury Press, 1975), p. iv; about Heschel himself: Edward K. Kaplan, *Spiritual Radical,* parts 3–5, pp. 175–386.
4. Both Clem and Neuhaus' older brother Fred—a policeman in California who had a sympathetic line to Herman Otten—were upset with him for his antiwar work, which they regarded as a personal betrayal of sorts, Richard going against his brothers' risking their lives for their country. Neuhaus clearly thought otherwise. On one home-leave trip through New York during this period, Tom recalled, his brother Richard proudly introduced his uniformed big brother to his antiwar friends but also offered him $15,000 cash to desert and seek refuge in Sweden. Neuhaus' sister Mim recalls the very same offer. In "Remembering the Movement," from 1992's *America Against Itself,* Neuhaus himself would note that at the same time that he was engaging in his intense antiwar activities, he was thinking a great deal about his "two brothers who were fighting in Vietnam" and about his ongoing arguments with them about the war, which Neuhaus described as mutually respectful if sharply at odds "about the rights and wrongs of the war" itself. Neuhaus' Volkswagen bus and CALCAV/DC- related activities and McNamara meeting: William Sloane Coffin, Jr., *Once to Every Man: A Memoir* (New York: Atheneum, 1977), pp. 220–229.
5. Neuhaus preaching at Catholic Worker house: *America Against Itself,* pp. 54–55; more on McNamara and CALCAV activities: Hall, *Because of Their Faith,* pp. 30–40; Joan Baez references: Neuhaus mentioned this connection

repeatedly over the years, harmlessly playing up what was likely no more than a passing acquaintance, as registered via author interviews with Russell Saltzman (August 8, 2011), Mildred Schwich (June 2, 2011), James Nuechterlein (August 7, 2012), and others; Neuhaus also acknowledged Baez as one of his "friends and associates from those [1960s] days" in "Conservative Changes," *First Things* 88 (December 1998), p. 78; sanctuary reference: author interview with Richard Fernandez (August 2, 2011); accounts of draft card ceremony at St. John the Evangelist: Neuhaus, *In Defense of People*, p. 280; Neuhaus, *Time Towards Home*, p. 14; Neuhaus, *America Against Itself*, pp. 66–67 (including Heschel remarks); author interview with John Heinemeier (March 16, 2011); Susan Sontag on Vietnam: quoted by Adam Garfinkle in *Telltale Hearts: The Origins and Impact of the Vietnam Antiwar Movement* (New York: St. Martin's Press, 1995), p. 108; Norman Thomas quotation: from Richard John Neuhaus, "Second Thoughts," in *Second Thoughts: Former Radicals Look Back at the Sixties,* Peter Collier and David Horowitz, eds. (New York: Madison Books, 1989), p. 8; also "Clergy: Should Ministers Be Draft Exempt?" *Time,* April 7, 1967, and "9 in Chains Stage Draft Protest," *New York Times,* July 3, 1968; on family concerns related to his brothers in Vietnam as noted in endnote: author interviews with Mildred Schwich (June 2, 2011) and Tom Neuhaus (August 31, 2011); Neuhaus, *America Against Itself,* p. 66. For a comparative context that suggests how distinctive (if not contrarian) Neuhaus was in his combination of the religious and patriotic in his conception and carrying out of antiwar/anti-draft work, see the following sources: Penelope Adams Moon, "Loyal Sons and Daughters of God? American Catholics Debate Antiwar Protest," *Peace & Change* 33, no. 1 (2008), pp. 1–30, a scholarly analysis of protest and Catholic vs. American identity in the context of the contemporaneous Berrigan brothers' more dramatic and controversial anti-draft actions; and Nancy Zaroulis and Gerald Sullivan, *Who Spoke Up? American Protest Against the War in Vietnam, 1963–1975* (New York: Doubleday, 1984), pp. 134–135, where the authors extensively detail various religious and secular forms of antiwar/anti-draft protest, none of which resemble Neuhaus'. As for Neuhaus himself, he evoked and defended his particular understanding and practice of antiwar patriotism in various forms, in both his books and in the pages of *First Things,* but perhaps nowhere more explicitly and substantially than in the chapter "Remembering the Movement" in *America Against Itself.*

6. Neuhaus' lunch with King et al. and related quotations: "Remembering Martin Luther King, Jr.," *First Things* 126 (October 2002), pp. 94–100.
7. In response to a query from the author and based on his work on King, King biographer Taylor Branch notes that Neuhaus' relationship to King wasn't particularly notable but was instead "slight, relative to King's relationship to Rabbi Heschel": author query to Taylor Branch (August 27, 2011).

8. Neuhaus quotation about when he saw King: Neuhaus, "Remembering Martin Luther King, Jr."; on King's locations and involvements in 1968 and 1967: Branch, *At Canaan's Edge,* pp. 683–722; Hall, *Because of Their Faith,* pp. 40–45; photographs of Neuhaus with and near King: reprinted in *First Things* 192 (April 2009); Neuhaus quotations about working with King: *Freedom for Ministry,* p. 13; *America Against Itself,* p. 56; *Doing Well and Doing Good: The Challenge to the Christian Capitalist* (New York: Doubleday, 1992), p. 6; *Catholic Matters,* p. 155; on Cox's connection to King: Branch, *Parting the Waters,* p. 204; author interview with Harvey Cox (November 16, 2010); on Heschel's connection to King: Kaplan, *Spiritual Radical,* p. 217; author query to Taylor Branch (August 27, 2011); Christmas card from Coretta Scott King to Neuhaus: found by author, undocumented, in Neuhaus' personal effects at 338 East 19th Street apartment; details about Coretta Scott King and Ralph Abernathy speaking at St. John the Evangelist and about Heinemeier taking over as senior pastor for Neuhaus: author interview with John Heinemeier (March 16, 2011); Neuhaus' MLK sermon: quoted in *Christian News,* January 19, 2009, Neuhaus memorial edition (Otten is the founder and editor in chief); MLK prayer and related details of the service: author transcription of original document at St. John the Evangelist Church, Brooklyn.
9. Further details about the congregation's response to Neuhaus stepping down as senior pastor: author interview with John Heinemeier (March 16, 2011); Neuhaus in Paris: author interview with Harvey Cox (November 16, 2010); Hall, *Because of Their Faith,* p. 81; specifics about the events leading up to the Catonsville Nine trial: Moon, "Loyal Sons and Daughters of God?" pp. 4–5; details about the trial itself: Gray, *Divine Disobedience,* pp. 158–164; details about Neuhaus' February 1969 CALCAV activities: Hall, *Because of Their Faith,* p. 81 (with endnote 13, p. 193, detailing FBI surveillance); Neuhaus on the meeting with Kissinger: "The World According to Henry Kissinger," *First Things* 96 (October 1999), p. 80.
10. Neuhaus' conversations with Berger: author interview with Peter Berger (November 17, 2010).

CHAPTER ELEVEN. A THOROUGHLY RADICAL WRITER MAKES A RADICAL RUN FOR CONGRESS

1. Their formal biographies in the book's preliminary pages expand on these profiles. Berger's straightforwardly notes his various publications and academic appointment. Neuhaus' is, predictably, more wide-ranging: it identifies him as "senior pastor" at St. John the Evangelist, as editor of *Una Sancta,* and, in addition to his affiliation with CALCAV, as a member of two other left-wing organizations of the period, the Coalition for a Democratic

Alternative (CDA) (a New York–based pro-McCarthy concern) and the National Committee for a Sane Nuclear Policy (SANE) (a national organization also committed to civil rights and antiwar protest over Vietnam). Moreover, the short biography makes it clear that Neuhaus was more than a book-writing radical; it ends by noting that at the 1968 Democratic Convention in Chicago, "he was arrested in a protest against the denial of civil liberties."

2. Citations from the preface, author biographies, and dates from *Movement and Revolution,* pp. 1–9; publishing notice: "New Books," *New York Times,* February 14, 1970; endnoted reference to CDA: *American National Biography Supplement Two,* Mark Carnes, ed. (New York: Oxford University Press, 2005), p. 418; endnoted reference to SANE: Garfinkle, *Telltale Hearts,* p. 44; details about publishing circumstances and also about Neuhaus and Berger in Mexico, with Illich and at CIDOC: author interview with Peter and Brigitte Berger (November 17, 2010); Berger, *Adventures of an Accidental Sociologist* (New York: Prometheus Books, 2011), p. 117; further details about Illich and CIDOC: Gray, *Divine Disobedience,* pp. 251–253.
3. Berger, *Movement and Revolution,* pp. 14, 84–86.
4. Neuhaus, *Movement and Revolution,* pp. 89–90. All subsequent citations and references to matters from Neuhaus' part of *Movement and Revolution,* "The Thorough Revolutionary," come from throughout this text.
5. Neuhaus' selected 1970 journalism: "The Good Sense of Amnesty," *Nation,* February 9, 1970, pp. 145–148; "Martin Luther King's Second Assassination," *New York Review of Books,* October 8, 1970, pp. 45–49; "Slur of the Year," *Christian Century,* September 16, 1970 (pages unknown); assorted reviews and opinions for *Commonweal* (issues April 17, July 10, December 25, 1970); "I Ordain and Consecrate Thee," *Lutheran Forum,* July/August 1980 (pages unknown).
6. Years later, reminiscing about his Movement days in *America Against Itself* (1992), Neuhaus would frame his writings on revolution as an effort at "cautionary counsel, warnings against facile and faddish calls for revolution . . . But to my regret, many reviewers and readers tended to miss the cautionary counsel and took it as a theoretical legitimation of revolution. To my regret, I say, because I now see that the caution should have been much more emphatic." More accurately, Neuhaus' caution about revolution could have been at least as emphatic as his invocations of its temptations and exigencies.
7. Indeed, he was ridiculed for being too much of one from the Right, in a *National Review* assessment of the book, which offered qualified praise to Berger's portion but caustically dismissed Neuhaus as "a glorious cliché-revolutionary Lutheran parson" who was desperate to seem "relevant, man." Meanwhile, liberal-minded *Commonweal* was more sympathetic, but it faulted Neuhaus for being "too academic" in making his case for revolution,

and for articulating criteria in ways that discouraged revolutionary action even as he (too academically) argued for it.

8. Damon Linker, *The Theocons: Secular America Under Siege* (New York: Doubleday, 2006), pp. 20–22; on *Movement and Revolution:* Jeffrey Hart, "The Kids," *National Review,* April 7, 1970, p. 365; review by Gertrude Pax, *Commonweal,* August 21, 1970, p. 421; endnote quotation from Neuhaus, *America Against Itself,* pp. 62–63.
9. Details related to Neuhaus' run for Congress: "National Leader Lacking," *New York Times,* February 2, 1970; "Rooney Faces Challenge from Brooklyn Pastor," *New York Times,* February 6, 1970; Clayton Knowles, "Reform Leaders Give Plans to Prevent Rooney Nomination," *New York Times,* March 3, 1970; Neuhaus on the decision to run, Lowenstein, etc.: Richard John Neuhaus, "Life and Death in the Movement," *First Things* 39 (January 1994), pp. 58–60.
10. Details about Neuhaus and Eikenberry's campaigns: author interview with Peter Eikenberry (April 15, 2011); for formal primary campaign details as well: Peter Eikenberry, "Runnin': How a Junior Associate Became a Congressional Candidate," *Federal Bar Counsel Quarterly* 2–3 (2010); about the election outcome: "Democratic Coalition Picks Candidate in 14th District," *New York Times,* March 24, 1970.
11. Today, the installation of phone lines and related operational equipment on church property as part of Neuhaus' campaign could be cited as plausible evidence of inappropriate church involvement in electoral politics and would be subject to scrutiny and even censure, though that doesn't seem to have been the case then, with these church-based political activities focused on a primary-before-the-primary race in Brooklyn, circa 1970. Indeed, back then, Neuhaus wasn't the only cleric running for office; in Massachusetts, Jesuit priest Robert Drinan also ran as an antiwar/pro-peace Democrat, with Neuhaus' direct encouragement no less, as Neuhaus would later admit. Drinan won and would serve as congressional representative for Massachusetts' 3rd District until 1981, when Pope John Paul II required all clerics to remove themselves from elected office.
12. Reactions to Neuhaus' run for Congress: author interviews with Harvey Cox (November 16, 2010), John Heinemeier (March 16, 2011), and June Braun (September 30, 2011).

CHAPTER TWELVE. THE LONELY RADICAL LOOKS ELSEWHERE

1. The *New York Times* was more moderate in its assessment. While acknowledging that the book reads like "a torrential preachment" against the ecology movement, it also noted that Neuhaus raises important ethical concerns

about the situation of the poor in the context of an environmentalism that either ignores them or, worse still, regards the poor as a problem to be dealt with in the course of a primary focus on the planet's health and preservation.

2. Neuhaus, *In Defense of People;* related quality-of-life index quotation: Neuhaus, *America Against Itself,* pp. 125–126; *Kirkus* review, October 7, 1971; *New York Times* review, October 17, 1971.
3. On September 30 1969, Otten filed false doctrine charges against Neuhaus, submitting his findings to Pastor Rudolf Ressmeyer, president of the Missouri Synod's Atlantic District and, as such, the Brooklyn-based Neuhaus' ecclesial superior. Otten's accusations against his old seminary foe were comprehensive, bordering on the obsessive. For evidence, he offered detailed quotations from Neuhaus' writings, pictures of him at assorted events, and selective newspaper reports on his various activities. The charges themselves were fivefold: Neuhaus "adheres to and promulgates doctrines which are contrary to Holy Scripture"; he "does not accept the binding nature of the Lutheran Confessions"; he "publically worships with Jews, Religious Liberals, and others who do not accept historic Christianity"; he "perverts the true nature of the Christian Church"; and he "encourages civil disobedience even when the government does not command the Christian to sin." According to Wilken and another LCMS colleague from this period, Pastor David Lotz, Otten's claims never came forward formally and Neuhaus was never charged with heresy.
4. And one he was careful to protect. According to Robert Wilken, upon his 1991 ordination as a Catholic priest who would serve in the Archdiocese of New York, Neuhaus requested a letter from John Cardinal O'Connor, to be placed in his personnel file, establishing Neuhaus' status with respect to parish duties against his continued public ministry through his editorship of *First Things.* Neuhaus wanted to make sure that O'Connor's successor would likewise allow him to focus mainly on his public ministry, as he was able to until his death, through his assignment to Immaculate Conception on 14th near Stuyvesant Town. He was not responsible for the day-to-day operational responsibilities of a parish priest; as an associate pastor, Neuhaus celebrated a daily morning Mass and at least one Sunday Mass per week when in town.
5. Details of Neuhaus' trip to Africa: author interviews with Peter and also Brigitte Berger (November 17, 2010); Neuhaus, *In Defense of People,* p. 10 and p. 15; Richard John Neuhaus, "The Necessary Opposition," *First Things* 24 (June/July 1992), p. 69 (Nyere reference); Richard John Neuhaus, "While We're At It," *First Things* 136 (October 2003), p. 84 (Gorée Island reference); Air Africa anecdote: author interview with Davida Goldman (June 8, 2012); July 13 and

29, 1971, letters from Neuhaus in Nairobi and Jerusalem to Wilken: provided to the author by Robert Wilken; *Harper's* reference: Richard John Neuhaus, "Not Nature Alone," *Harper's,* October 1971; twenty-five countries visited: Richard John Neuhaus, "A Radical Proposal," *First Things* 35 (August/September 1993), p. 66; endnoted details about Otten's heresy charges: reprinted in *Christian News,* January 19, 2009, Neuhaus memorial edition (Otten is the founder and editor in chief); author interview with Robert Wilken (who provided the David Lotz information); Berger's anecdote about Neuhaus in Dakar: Berger, *Adventures of an Accidental Sociologist,* pp. 125–126.

6. Vietnamization involved training South Vietnamese troops to take over the otherwise American-dominated war effort while beginning to withdraw significant numbers of American troops from the theater. Vietnamization was a leading element in the Nixon administration's approach to the war. It began to take shape after a November 1969 speech by Nixon proposing how his administration would "win America's peace" in Vietnam while gradually ending American involvement in the conflict.
7. All details related to CALCAV developments in 1971, and Neuhaus' contributions and reactions: Hall, *Because of Their Faith,* pp. 114–123; endnoted details about Vietnamization: Nguyen, *Hanoi's War,* pp. 129–132; transcript of Nixon's November 1969 speech available at http://vietnam.vassar.edu/overview/doc14.html.
8. Details of Clemens Neuhaus' later life: Pappin, *Century in Christ,* p. 64; details about his death: author interviews with Mildred Schwich (June 2, 2011) and Johanna Speckhard (August 6, 2012); details about Neuhaus' later recollections of his father: author correspondence with James Nuechterlein (October 13, 2013); details about Neuhaus coming back to Pembroke, beginning in the early 1970s: author interview with Orlen Lapp (October 29, 2010).
9. Details of Heschel's death: Kaplan, *Spiritual Radical,* p. 377; details of Piepkorn's death, and the related struggles in the Missouri Synod: Burkee, *Power, Politics, and the Missouri Synod,* pp. 95–149; details about the 1974 CALC memorial: Hall, *Because of Their Faith,* p. 123; details about Neuhaus' effort to find support for a condemnation of the government in Hanoi for its human rights abuses and persecution of religious minorities: Neuhaus, "Second Thoughts," p. 9; Neuhaus, *America Against Itself,* p .61; for a broader context, see Jim Finn's "Fighting Among the Doves," *Worldview* magazine, April 1977.
10. Neuhaus, "The Loneliness of the Long-Distance Radical," *Christian Century,* April 26, 1972, pp. 477–481; Hillary Rodham, May 1969 Wellesley College commencement address available at http://www.sojust.net/speeches/hillary clinton_commencement.html.

CHAPTER THIRTEEN. APPEALING FOR RIGHT RELIGION, APPALLING THE LEFT

1. William F. Buckley's founding statement: "Our Mission Statement," *National Review,* November 19, 1955, http://www.nationalreview.com/node/223549.
2. Media coverage of the Hartford Appeal: "The Hartford Heresies," *Time,* February 10, 1975; *Newsweek* and various religious publications' coverage mentioned by Berger in *Adventures of an Accidental Sociologist,* p. 133; "Theologians Plead for Social Activism," *New York Times,* January 6, 1976 (also offers details about the Boston declaration); "To March or Not to March," *New York Times Magazine,* June 27, 1976; Neuhaus, "Calling a Halt to Retreat," in *Against the World for the World: The Hartford Appeal and the Future of American Religion,* Peter Berger and Richard John Neuhaus, eds. (New York: Seabury Press, 1976), p. 138.
3. Details about the origins of the Appeal in Neuhaus and Berger's conversations: Berger, *Adventures of an Accidental Sociologist,* pp. 131–133.
4. Peter Berger et al., "An Appeal for Theological Affirmation," reprinted in *Against the World for the World: The Hartford Appeal and the Future of American Religion,* Peter Berger and Richard John Neuhaus, eds., pp. 1–7.
5. For example, responding to Theme 12: "The struggle for a better humanity is essential to Christian faith and can be informed and inspired by the biblical promise of the Kingdom of God. But imperfect human beings cannot create a perfect society. The Kingdom of God surpasses any conceivable utopia. God has his own designs which confront ours, surprising us with judgment and redemption."
6. Wednesday night pastor meetings at Neuhaus' apartment: author interviews with John Heinemeier (March 16, 2011) and Leonard Klein (August 16, 2011); quotation from the Hartford Appeal: Berger et al., p. 3.
7. Neuhaus sharply criticized Cox's work early on in his 1975 *Time Toward Home,* citing it as part of a broader analysis and critique of American religion's "loss of confidence"—not because it was principally responsible for this loss "but because it so accurately represented and *legitimated* that loss."
8. Neuhaus article for the *Christian Century:* "A Pilgrim Piece of Time and Space," *Christian Century,* February 19, 1975.
9. Neither Coffin's biographer Warren Goldstein nor Coffin himself, in his 1977 memoir, *Once to Every Man,* discusses Hartford or this debate (while both note Neuhaus' connections to Coffin in the antiwar context).
10. Neuhaus on Coffin and the Hartford Appeal and also the broader radical-establishment dynamics in the American Church during his Movement days: "The Death of William Sloane Coffin, Jr.," *First Things* 164 (June/July

2006), pp. 59–61; Coffin letter to Neuhaus, dated January 28, 1975: RJN-PP, 1975 files; Riverside Church debate transcript: published in *Christianity and Crisis* 35, no. 12 (July 21, 1975).

11. Lutherans for Life: http://www.lutheransforlife.org/about/.
12. The interview took place in Neuhaus' office at St. John the Evangelist, where, "with one leg occasionally draped over the side of his chair," he held forth with a combination of blitheness and bluntness about the overweening behavior of an America "telling the rest of the world what's good for them and telling them that if they don't see it our way, that they have only our bombs to look forward to."
13. The history of *Worldview* magazine and its sponsor: "Introduction to Worldview Magazine, 1958–85," January 9, 2008, http://worldview.carnegiecouncil.org/archive/worldview/overview; Neuhaus on *Worldview* and James Finn: "While We're At It" item, *First Things* 125 (August/September 2002), p. 103.
14. This wouldn't stop them from writing about each other. In his 1975 book *Time Toward Home,* Neuhaus accused Novak of encouraging people to "abandon the habit of searching for rationality and universals" in public discourse about the American Experiment and instead "return to thinking with the blood of our Italian, [etc.] or whatever cultural-genetic heritage." Novak replied with a caustic review of the book in the November 22, 1975, issue of the *New Republic.*
15. All quotations from Neuhaus' pieces for *Worldview,* 1967–1983, taken from its online archive at http://worldview.carnegiecouncil.org/archive/worldview/search_out?argtypes=sa_RelevantDate%3Adaterange%3BStructure%3Atext%3Bparentid%3Bsa_Topics%3Bsa_Keywds%3Bsa_Subtitle&query=&sa_Subtitle=Neuhaus&Submit=Search&group_size=20; Neuhaus on Carter vs. Ford: Neuhaus, "Why I Am for Carter," *Commonweal,* October 22, 1976.
16. From Lyndon Baines Johnson through at least the candidacy of Barack Obama, Neuhaus engaged the person and policies of every American president, whether in print alone or as combined with direct encounters under various circumstances. One such occasion, however, from the early post-Watergate era, was unexpectedly denied, when Neuhaus was on vacation at the family cottage in Pembroke. His mother was staying with him, and he gave her strict orders not to disturb him under any circumstances while he took an afternoon nap. A call came while he was sleeping. Ella asked who it was. "It's the President, calling for Pastor Neuhaus." "The president of what?" she asked. "The President of the United States." "I'm very sorry," she informed the White House, "but I can't disturb him. You'll have to call back another time." When Ella told her son after he woke up, he "hit the roof," according to his sister Mim, who shared this story. "I just did what you told me," explained Ella, nonplussed.

17. Neuhaus on Psalm 146: "From the Northern Front," *First Things* 107 (November 2000), p. 70.

CHAPTER FOURTEEN. BOOKS TO EMPOWER PEOPLE AND PASTORS ALIKE

1. Neuhaus, *Time Toward Home,* pp. vii.
2. Gilbert Meilaender, "Obituary: Richard John Neuhaus (1936–2009)," *Studies in Christian Ethics* 22 (November 2009), pp. 496–503; *Time* profile: "Religion Again, God's Country," *Time,* October 20, 1975; Neuhaus, *Time Toward Home,* p. vii.
3. Neuhaus, *Time Toward Home,* pp. 205, 209.
4. Richard John Neuhaus, *Christian Faith and Public Policy: Thinking and Acting in the Courage of Uncertainty* (Minneapolis, MN: Augsburg Publishing House, 1977), pp. 8, 9, 34, 58, 169–170, 210.
5. The evidence Neuhaus supplied for an official embrace was Bush's "Thousand Points of Light" national volunteerism program, though he lamented its weak implementation.
6. Peter Berger and Richard John Neuhaus, *To Empower People: The Role of Mediating Structures in Public Policy* (Washington, D.C.: American Enterprise Institute, 1977). All quotations from the text are taken from this edition. Berger on details related to the book's origins and relationship to the American Enterprise Institute: Berger, *Adventures of an Accidental Sociologist,* pp. 149–154; Neuhaus on *To Empower People*: Richard John Neuhaus, *Doing Well and Doing Good: The Challenge to a Christian Capitalist* (New York: Doubleday, 1992), p. 244; Richard John Neuhaus, "Speaking for the Common Good," *First Things* 37 (November 1993), pp. 45–46; Richard John Neuhaus, "A Paradigm at Twenty," *First Things* 64 (June/July 1996), pp. 61–62.
7. Indeed, for at least a decade, skeptics were questioning the intellectuals, and policy makers had been hearing from skeptics of Big Benign Government, like the influential and controversial thinker and politician Daniel Patrick Moynihan, who as early as 1967 began calling for liberals to "divest themselves of the notion that the nation—and especially the cities of the nation—can be run from agencies in Washington." A typical agency in this respect was the Office of Economic Opportunity, which, in intellectual historian Justin Vaisse's crisp summary of its purpose and Moynihan's critique, sought "to involve the poor in the management of projects designed to assist them. Ultimately, however, they created a parasitic class of social workers and unrepresentative community leaders who, Moynihan argued, hijacked the program and rendered it ineffective." The novelist Saul Bellow had a more memorable way of diagnosing these unintentionally bad

and outsized outcomes: they were courtesy of the "Good Intentions Paving Company."

8. Berger, *Adventures of an Accidental Sociologist,* p. 149; endnoted Moynihan quotations and references: Vaisse, *Neoconservatism,* pp. 56–57; endnoted Bellow quotation: *Saul Bellow: Letters,* Benjamin Taylor, ed. (New York: Viking, 2010), p. 414; American Enterprise Institute history: Sidney Blumenthal, *The Rise of the Counter-Establishment: The Conservative Ascent to Political Power* (New York: Union Square Press), pp. 32–33; Berger and Neuhaus, *To Empower People,* pp. 1–2.
9. Berger and Neuhaus, *To Empower People,* pp. 2–4.
10. Berger and Neuhaus, *To Empower People,* p. 4; Pius XI, *Quadragesimo Anno,* 1931, http://www.vatican.va/holy_father/pius_xi/encyclicals/documents/hf_p-xi_enc_19310515_quadragesimo-anno_en.html; see also "Subsidiarity," *Encyclopedia of Catholic Social Thought, Social Science, and Social Policy,* Michael L. Coulter et al., eds. (Lanham, MD: Scarecrow Press), vol. 2, pp. 1040–1042.
11. Berger and Neuhaus, *To Empower People,* pp. 11, 15, 21–22.
12. Ibid., pp. 26–33.
13. *"And with Many Tears,"* printed in the Commencement Program for Fourth Academic Year, Concordia Seminary in Exile, St. Louis, MO, May 13, 1977.

CHAPTER FIFTEEN. SEEKING FREEDOM FOR HIS OWN KIND OF MINISTRY

1. Again suggesting a notably detached relationship to his father, Neuhaus dedicated the book to an admired uncle, Henry Karau, "a good and honorable man who lived his own life living for others," rather than to Clemens, as might be expected if he was going to dedicate it to family over a seminary teacher or pastor mentor. Clem rates only a cordial and brief mention, early on, as "my father and the first pastor I knew, who taught me what ministry is and can be, and the difference between the two"—a formulation that could be taken in ways other than straightforward admiration.
2. Richard John Neuhaus, *Freedom for Ministry* (San Francisco: Harper and Row, 1979), pp. xii, 255. This book didn't make much of an impact, as Neuhaus' editor at *Harper & Row* pointed out in a 1980 letter to his author, reporting that only 2,655 copies had been sold: RJN-PP, 1980 files.
3. Neuhaus, *Freedom for Ministry,* p. xii. Among the many occasions where Neuhaus referred to "St. John the Mundane" was his 2002 interview with Brian Lamb for C-SPAN's *Booknotes.*
4. Initially, Neuhaus and Bailey had a third partner in the venture: Tom Dorris, a religion reporter who soon afterward moved to Geneva and became

involved with its English Evangelical Lutheran Church and also with the World Council of Churches. According to Larry Bailey, he later died in a car accident in Europe. Details about his involvements in Geneva are available at the website of the Geneva Lutheran, "Green-Book, 1991: The English-Speaking Congregation," http://www.genevalutheran.ch/apps/joomla/index.php?option=com_content&view=article&id=24:greenbook1991elcgesc&catid=7:theelcg&Itemid=81.

5. Details about Neuhaus' departure from St. John's, assignment to Holy Trinity, living situation before moving into 338 East 19th Street, and plans for 338: author interviews with John Heinemeier (March 16, 2011) and Larry Bailey (September 29, 2011); the "Community of Christ in the City" file: RJN-PP, 1988 files.
6. Three years later, Neuhaus successfully requested a change in his call to an even more elastic designation, "Pastor on Assignment for the East Coast Synod": RJN-PP 1979 and 1982 files. This designation followed upon his leaving St. Peter's and Trinity in 1983 or 1984, and joining Immanuel Lutheran Church, a congregation that had dual alignments to ELCA and Missouri. Congregation affiliations reported in "Neuhaus Sees Continuity Between New Projects and Earlier Vision," by Willmar Thorkelson (story dated October 4, 1984; no further publication information available; a transcription or computer printout of the story is filed among RJN press clippings for this year).
7. Details related to Neuhaus' application for the presidency of CRIA come from a copy of his letter of application, kept in RJN-PP, 1979 files. Biographical details about Robert J. Myers are taken from the *Washington Post*'s obituary (October 12, 2011).
8. Details about Neuhaus' proposed "Lexington Center" are taken from correspondence between Neuhaus and colleagues in RJN-PP, 1979 files. Background information on St. Peter's comes from the church's own history: http://saintpeters.org/home/.
9. Details about Neuhaus' application for the senior pastor position at St. Peter's, the call committee's response, and his Yale application come from RJN-PP, 1981 and 1982 files. Information about his 1979 teaching at Princeton comes from Paul Stallsworth's letter of condolence upon Neuhaus' death, published in *First Things* 192 (April 2009).
10. Details about Neuhaus' writing activities and lectures during this period are taken from "Articles and Manuscripts of Richard John Neuhaus," a comprehensive list that was maintained by his longtime secretary at the Institute for Religion and Public Life, Davida Goldman. Neuhaus was interviewed by *Newsweek* for its October 15, 1979, issue.
11. This complaint is far more in keeping with Neuhaus' long-standing understanding of the family than were the allowances he and Berger made for

"liberated families," and so on, in *To Empower People,* as discussed in the previous chapter.

12. Neuhaus' involvement with the Conference: Richard John Neuhaus, *The Naked Public Square,* 2nd ed. (Grand Rapids, MI: Wm. B. Eerdmans, 1986), pp. 96–97; the letter from Cuomo is found in RJN-PP, 1979 files.
13. Details related to the founding of IRD come from Neuhaus' 2005 "Reflections" talk, which he gave at the institute in October of that year. Details regarding Neuhaus and Novak's rapprochement: author interview with George Weigel (June 3, 2013).
14. Jeane Kirkpatrick, "Dictatorships and Double Standards," *Commentary* magazine, November 1979; see Vaisse, *Neoconservatism,* pp. 183–187, for more on Kirkpatrick and her influence on and appointments within the first Reagan administration; details about IRD's funding: "New Clergy Group Assails Church Aid to Leftists," *New York Times,* February 16, 1983.
15. "Foes and Supporters of Reagan Policies Plan Rallies," *New York Times,* May 3, 1981. In *Neoconservatism,* Vaisse cites "support for the government of El Salvador, under threat from Communists" as an example of the foreign policy positions that neoconservatives supported and advocated during the first Reagan administration. He further points out that there was always a gap in Reagan's foreign policy between "support for democratic forces" around the world and support for regimes and fighters "of dubious democratic credentials," before noting that this was resolved by the administration's priority commitment to challenging the influence of the Soviet Union wherever necessary because, following Jeane Kirkpatrick's analyses, it was "the greatest obstacle to democracy in the world" (p. 191).
16. Rael Jean Isaac, "Do You Know Where Your Church Offerings Go?" *Reader's Digest* (January 1983); "The Gospel According to Whom?" *60 Minutes,* originally broadcast January 23, 1983; transcript of the program compiled by Institute on Religion and Democracy staff, and a copy filed among Neuhaus' 1983–1988 "Media Clippings," stored at the Institute for Religion and Public Life.
17. For a scholarly treatment of the Institute on Religion and Democracy's campaigns against the NCC and Mainline Protestantism, see Steven M. Tipton, *Public Pulpits: Methodists and Mainline Churches in the Moral Argument of Public Life* (Chicago: University of Chicago Press, 2008). The NCC's response to the *Reader's Digest* and *60 Minutes* treatments and to the Institute on Religion and Democracy itself: "New Clergy Group Assails Church Aid to Leftists," *New York Times,* February 16, 1983.
18. Lutherans weren't pleased either. David Preus, an LCMS bishop whom Neuhaus chided in conversation for being supportive of an NCC initiative, pushed back that Neuhaus went too far in his *60 Minutes* comments: RJN-PP, 1983 files. The Reverend Paul Wee, general secretary of Lutheran

World Ministries, was angrier, and accused Neuhaus of willful deception in an interview about him in Thorkelson, "Neuhaus Sees Continuity Between New Projects and Earlier Vision."

19. Prior to this, Neuhaus was able to integrate his IRD and CRIA work more successfully, as with a June 15, 1981, off-the-record meeting he led on "El Salvador and Moral Judgment" at CRIA's offices. Its purpose was "to be of help to significant actors in shaping the religious communities' responses to international questions," and it included speakers from IRD and elsewhere addressing journalists from the *Washington Post, Christianity and Crisis,* and other publications: RJN-PP, 1981 files.
20. Robert Myers correspondence with Neuhaus: RJN-PP, 1983 files; details regarding the origins of the Center on Religion and Society: author interview with John Howard, July 15, 2013; "New Center Aims to Be 'Freedom Zone' for Religious Combatants," *Religious News Service,* March 12, 1984; further details of proposed activities: March 1984 funding proposal to Smith-Richard Foundation, from Rockford Institute, for Center on Religion and Society: RJN-PP, 1984 files.
21. Robert Myers correspondence with Neuhaus: RJN-PP, 1983 files; Philip Weiss, "Going to Extremes," *Harper's,* November 1983. After the *Harper's* piece ran, Neuhaus wrote an angry letter to the magazine's editor, Lewis Lapham, not intended for publication but to let Lapham know that that he regarded the story as "unprofessional, unethical, and probably libelous." He then disputed it in almost surgical detail before parting with a caustic comparison between *Harper's* and a pulpy gossip rag, with this profile of him coming in "about two notches below [what's] expected from the *National Enquirer*": RJN-PP, 1983 files.

CHAPTER SIXTEEN. 1984: THE NAKED PUBLIC SQUARE CAMPAIGN

1. Eerdmans letter to Neuhaus and Neuhaus letter to Pannenberg: RJN-PP, 1984 files.
2. James Finn, *Protest: Pacifism and Politics: Some Passionate Views on War and Nonviolence* (New York: Random House, 1967), p. 165; Richard John Neuhaus, "Religion and Addressing the Naked Public Square," *Worldview* 25, no. 1 (January 1982).
3. Neuhaus, *The Naked Public Square,* pp. 37, 122–123.
4. Neuhaus, *The Naked Public Square,* pp. 37, 201; John Courtney Murray, *We Hold These Truths: Catholic Reflections on the American Proposition* (New York: Sheed and Ward, 1960), p. 57.
5. Neuhaus, *The Naked Public Square,* pp. 15–16, 176.

6. Ibid., pp. 164–165, 264.
7. "Political and Religious Shifts Re-Kindle Church-State Issue," *New York Times,* September 2, 1984; "Falwell Says Religion Has a Place in Politics," *New York Times,* October 9, 1984.
8. John H. Simpson, "Socio-Moral Issues and Recent Presidential Elections," *Review of Religious Research* 27, no. 2 (December 1985), p. 115; "'Extremist Right Wing' is Castigated by Ferraro," *New York Times,* October 2, 1984; Mondale quotation: "Falwell Says Religion Has a Place in Politics," *New York Times,* October 9, 1984.
9. *Firing Line* show transcript for "Church and State" episode, Hoover Institution and Library, Stanford University; "Voices of Reason, Voices of Faith," *Time,* September 17, 1984.
10. A simple Google search reveals tens of thousands of usages of Neuhaus' phrase, both in relation to his work and as a stand-alone term for describing public and political situations that exclude religious elements. The scholarly engagement with this book is extensive, and ongoing. A summer 2013 query into the JSTOR academic publishing database reports at least forty different books and more than one hundred academic articles that engage with the work and its author. Meanwhile, in a 1997 contribution to the journal *Policy Review,* the dean of American conservative thought, George H. Nash, cited *The Naked Public Square* as one of "the most important and influential works advancing conservative ideas in the past 20 years," alongside titles like Kirkpatrick's "Dictatorship and Double Standards," Michael Novak's *The Spirit of Democratic Capitalism,* and Charles Murray's *Losing Ground.* Nash, "Modern Tomes," *Policy Review* 84 (July 1997), http://www.hoover.org/publications/policy-review/article/7194.
11. George F. Will endorsement: cover matter, Neuhaus, *The Naked Public Square*; "Putting God Back in Politics," *New York Times Book Review,* August 26, 1984; "Notable Books of the Year," *New York Times Book Review,* December 2, 1984.
12. Reviews and notices in 1984 ran in the *National Christian Reporter, National Review,* the *Wall Street Journal, Christianity Today, Commonweal,* the *New York Review of Books,* the *Dallas Morning News,* the *New York Tribune,* the *American Spectator,* the *Roanoke Times,* and others. Reviews, profiles, and columns by and about Neuhaus and *The Naked Public Square* as book, proposition, and argument would continue to appear in newspapers and periodicals at a regular rate in 1985 and 1986, as evidenced by the thick file of clippings from this period that Neuhaus collected and eventually stored at the Institute for Religion and Public Life RJN-PP, "Reviews: *Naked Public Square*" files.
13. Grace Church event: RJN-PP, 1984 files; December 20 remarks at the White House: RJN-PP, 1985 files; background on Bohemian Grove: "Bohemian Grove: Where Big Shots Go to Camp," *New York Times,* August 14, 1977;

Neuhaus' invitation to Bohemian Grove from Howard: RJN-PP, 1984 files; Meese correspondence: RJN-PP, 1984 files.

14. Neuhaus attempted to counteract this evident partisanship himself in various ways over the years, in part by regularly invoking his ongoing formal party affiliation, as with this November 26, 2005, blog entry for *First Things:* "Although I am usually described as a conservative—or, as some prefer, a neoconservative—I am still a registered Democrat." http://www.firstthings.com/onthesquare/2005/11/rjn-112605-its-nothing-new.
15. Neuhaus' White House remarks were transcribed by the Office of Public Liaison at the White House, and he was given a copy by J. Douglas Holladay in January 1985: RJN-PP, 1985 files.
16. Neuhaus letter to Holladay: RJN-PP, 1984 files.
17. O'Connor letter to Neuhaus: RJN-PP, 1984 files. See John McGreevy's account of O'Connor's national news-making involvements in the 1984 campaign shortly after he was installed as archbishop of New York, specifically that he "publicly chastised two New York Democratic Catholic politicians, Governor Mario Cuomo and vice-presidential nominee Geraldine Ferraro, for their unwillingness to oppose legal abortion," in *Catholicism and American Freedom* (New York: W. W. Norton, 2003), pp. 287–289. The *New York Times* obituary of O'Connor, written by Peter Steinfels, describes the circumstances of his appointment and details of his biography cited elsewhere in this section. The obituary also draws attention to his rapid rise to prominence in the context of the 1984 election. "Death of a Cardinal," *New York Times,* May 4, 2000.
18. O'Connor's involvements in the Pastoral Letter were detailed in "New York's Controversial Archbishop," *New York Times,* October 14, 1984. The quotation from the letter itself is taken from http://old.usccb.org/sdwp/international/TheChallengeofPeace.pdf. Neuhaus explained the origins of his connection to O'Connor in a September 1984 letter to Rockford president John Howard, in the midst of Neuhaus' effort to introduce O'Connor to New York media and intellectual leaders under the auspices of the Center on Religion and Society: RJN-PP, 1984 files. Neuhaus' own commitment to a strong military position was evidenced in part by his contributing to the similarly themed Coalition for a Democratic Majority's 1984 "Proposals for the 1984 Democratic Party Platform on Foreign Policy and National Defense," which, as Justin Vaisse notes in *Neoconservatism,* "failed to influence the Democratic platform" that election year, even as its ideas found stronger hearing from the Republicans (p. 212).
19. O'Connor's abortion remarks: "New York's Controversial Archbishop," *New York Times,* October 14, 1984; O'Connor-Neuhaus correspondence: RJN-PP, 1984 files.

20. Neuhaus efforts to introduce O'Connor around New York: RJN-PP, 1984 files.

CHAPTER SEVENTEEN. MORE AND MORE CATHOLIC MOMENTS, AMONG MANY, MANY OTHERS

1. Ralph McInerney, "Random Memories of Richard," *Catholic Thing,* January 2009; Neuhaus, *Catholic Matters,* pp. 39–44; RJN-PP, 1985 files.
2. The result, "Recovery in Rome: What the Synod Wrought," appeared in the February 14, 1986, issue of *National Review* and in turn formed the major portion of Neuhaus' treatment of the 1985 Extraordinary Synod in *The Catholic Moment.*
3. Neuhaus seeing O'Connor in Rome in December 1985: noted in correspondence between them: RJN-PP, 1986 files; further details about RJN in Rome: author interview with George Weigel (June 3, 2013), and also Neuhaus, *Catholic Matters*, pp. 114–117.
4. Daneels quoted in George Weigel's *Witness to Hope: The Biography of John Paul II* (New York: HarperCollins, 1997), p. 504; Neuhaus, *Catholic Matters,* p. 116.
5. In this same letter to Pannenberg, Neuhaus fulfilled a promise made in Rome itself. While there, he met directly with Ratzinger, and during this meeting he let the German Catholic theologian know about his friendship with a German Lutheran theologian. In turn Ratzinger asked Neuhaus to pass along his best wishes to Pannenberg: this is exactly the kind of go-between effort that Neuhaus was particularly adept at, forging connections between others that simultaneously strengthened, or, with Ratzinger, established, ties for himself.
6. Details regarding *This World* magazine negotiations: RJN-PP, 1986 files; congressional statement on U.S. Institute of Peace: http://www.usip.org/about-us/our-history. Neuhaus' various activities during this period are taken from RJN-PP, 1986 files, and also RJN-PP, Publication List, 1986.
7. RJN-PP, Publications List, 1986.
8. Details about his advances for *The Naked Public Square* and *Dispensations* are taken from correspondence with his publisher, Eerdmans: RJN-PP, 1986 files. The monthly allowance amount is noted in the personal information documents Neuhaus submitted to the White House as part of his becoming a director on the board of the United States Peace Institute: RJN-PP, 1985 files. Thereafter, while the various numbers would change with time and circumstance, the same practice continued, with Neuhaus directing his income to the Community of Christ in the City and drawing from it in turn, often

asking his assistant Davida Goldman to prepare checks for various charities. By 2007 and 2008, Neuhaus was receiving a yearly income of $145,000 from the Institute on Religion and Public Life (which published *First Things*) for serving as its president. The Community retained a financial advisor who managed investments of the Community's funds, predominantly earned by Neuhaus. Details provided by Davida Goldman, correspondence with author (July 17, 2013).

9. Community of Christ in the City information: RJN-PP, 1987 files; State Department response to his South Africa remarks: correspondence in RJN-PP, 1986 files; sales figure for *The Naked Public Square* noted in Neuhaus' negotiations with Harper & Row for *The Catholic Moment*: RJN-PP, 1986 files; Neuhaus, *The Naked Public Square*, p. xi.
10. Neuhaus, *Dispensations*, pp. ix–xiii.
11. Ibid., pp. 2, 33–34.
12. Sales figures noted in RJN correspondence with his publisher: RJN-PP, 1987 files. Reviews also ran in the *Wall Street Journal*, the *Boston Sunday Globe*, *Commentary*, the *Christian Century*, *Christianity in Crisis*, and *Human Events*: RJN-PP, "Reviews" file for *Dispensations*. J. M. Coetzee, "Waiting for Mandela," *New York Review of Books*, May 8, 1986.
13. *This World* plans noted in related Neuhaus correspondence: RJN-PP, 1986 files. In 1986 and 1987 alone, these writings totaled more than fifty separate publications, for venues like the *Wall Street Journal*, *Commentary*, the *Lutheran Standard*, the *Public Interest*, the *Cresset*, the *Human Life Review*, and the *Journal of Law and Religion*, among others: RJN-PP, Publications List, 1986–1987.
14. RJN correspondence with publisher: RJN-PP, 1986 files; Neuhaus, *Catholic Matters*, pp. 61, 114, 168.
15. Easily the most substantial engagement of *The Catholic Moment* came from Catholic theologian David L. Schindler, who wrote an extensive analysis of the work for a scholarly journal. Crediting the book for its "eloquence and wit" in making a case "that Catholics should assume their rightful place in the task of forming a culture, and indeed shaping a public philosophy in and for a pluralistic, democratic society," Schindler nevertheless was conclusively critical of Neuhaus' effort. He argued that in the liberal versus conservative, heterodox versus orthodox, inauthentic versus authentic distinctions he makes within the Church itself, Neuhaus effectively replicated the rigid, inaccurate, and alienating divisions between the respective roles and place in public life of sacred and secular that he rightly rejected elsewhere in his writings. Schindler, "Catholicism, Public Theology, and Postmodernity: On Richard John Neuhaus's 'Catholic Moment,'" *Thomist* 53, no. 1 (January 1989), pp. 107–143.
16. Neuhaus, *Catholic Matters*, pp. 2–3, 133, 162.

17. Neuhaus correspondence with Richard Mouw: RJN-PP, 1987 files; review information comes from the RJN-PP "Reviews" file for *The Catholic Moment*; Walter Sundberg, "The Precarious Catholic Moment," *Reformation* (fall 1987); "Lutheran Minister Prodding Catholics to Lead Christian Revitalization," *New York Times*, January 27, 1988.
18. Coverage of the event at St. Peter's and related Ratzinger quotations: "Gay Protest Rocks Vatican Biggie," *New York Post*, January 28, 1988; Neuhaus requested added security from Koch in a 1987 letter: RJN-PP, 1987 files.
19. Neuhaus wrote about sharing this headline with Ratzinger in a February 1988 letter to O'Connor: RJN-PP, 1988 files. Details about planning for the conference: Neuhaus-Ratzinger correspondence: RJN-PP, 1986 and 1987 files. Details about the conference itself: RJN-PP, 1987, files; O'Connor quotation and further details about the conference: "Cardinal Is Seen as Kind, if Firm, Monitor of the Faith," *New York Times*, February 2, 1988. Other information taken from Neuhaus-O'Connor correspondence during this period: RJN-PP, 1987 and 1988 files.
20. Information about Neuhaus' activities during this period taken from RJN-PP, 1988, files; correspondence with LaHaye: RJN-PP, 1988 files.
21. Plans and meetings regarding the June 1988 trip to Rome are noted in his correspondence with those listed: RJN-PP, 1988 files. For more on Neuhaus as a letter writer, see Randy Boyagoda, "Cordially, Richard John Neuhaus," *First Things* 225 (August/September 2012).
22. Ibid.

CHAPTER EIGHTEEN. THE RAID

1. Based on author interviews with Davida Goldman (September 30, 2011), Maria (McFadden) Maffuci (October 2, 2011), and James Nuechterlein (August 7, 2012), with further details from "Magazine Dispute Reflects Rift on U.S. Right," *New York Times*, May 16, 1989.
2. Based on author interviews with Davida Goldman (September 30, 2011), Maria (McFadden) Maffuci (October 2, 2011), and James Nuechterlein (August 7, 2012).
3. In addition to the regular publication of the *Religion and Society Report, This World*, and various one-off seminars and lectures, this collaboration involved a series of conferences on a variety of subjects bearing significance to questions of religion and society, with the participants made up usually of Neuhaus' colleagues and targeted scholars from various places and fields as determined by the given subject. The conference proceedings formed a book series published by Eerdmans from 1985 through 1988, each volume edited and introduced by Neuhaus. Conference topics included "Virtue—Public

and Private," "The Bible, Politics, and Democracy," "The Believable Futures of American Protestantism," and "The Preferential Option for the Poor."

4. RJN-PP, 1985 files and 1989 files.
5. RJN-PP, 1985 files and 1989 files.
6. RJN-PP, 1985 files and 1989 files (including a copy of Podhoretz's correspondence); *Chronicles,* March 1989.
7. RJN-PP, 1989 files. In spring 1989, Neuhaus also published another book, coauthored with Leon Klenicki, a rabbi, entitled *Believing Today: Jew and Christian in Conversation* (1989). A slim volume of one hundred pages, the book is comprised of an extended discussion between Neuhaus and Klenicki about the shared and divergent points between Christianity and Judaism, with an emphasis on shared points, frank recognitions of difference, and a self-evident common commitment to necessary dialogue. From Neuhaus' vantage, this dialogue was important because "the question of the relationship between Judaism and Christianity holds momentous import for a proper biblical understanding of the Christian reality itself" (p. 7). Dedicated to Heschel (by Neuhaus) and Jacques Maritain (by Klenicki), the book was endorsed by John O'Connor and David Novak but garnered little attention, in part because it was published mere weeks before the Rockford Raid.
8. David Frum, "Cultural Clash on the Right," *Wall Street Journal,* June 2, 1989.
9. All of the media coverage cited concerning the Rockford Raid is collected in "Clippings of the Rockford Institute, February 1, 1989–July 31, 1989" (Rockford, IL: Rockford Institute).
10. Berger's suggestion cited by James Nuechterlein in author interview (August 2, 2012).
11. Author interviews with Peter Berger (November 17, 2010), David Novak (March 2, 2011), Michael Novak (September 21, 2012), Stanley Hauerwas (May 17, 2011), and George Weigel (June 3, 2013).
12. Foundation funding details: Neuhaus correspondence with representatives from these foundations: RJN-PP, 1989 files, and author interview with James Nuechterlein (August 2, 2012); Pembroke details: author interviews with David Novak (March 2, 2011), Tom Neuhaus (August 3, 2011), Judy Stevenson (October 29, 2010), and George Weigel (June 3, 2013).
13. Office set-up details: author interview with James Nuechterlein (August 2, 2012); Richard John Neuhaus, "Real Estate and the Cunning of History," *First Things* 1 (March 1990).
14. Details of fall 1989 and winter 1990 activities based on RJN-PP, Publications List, 1989–1990, and the 1989 and 1990 files. Details about the January 1990 conference also based on "Conservatives War Over Dinner," *Washington Times,* February 5, 1990.
15. Agha Khan and other Davos recipients of *First Things* 1: Neuhaus correspondence: RJN-PP, 1990 files; the Editors, "Putting First Things First," *First*

Things 1 (March 1990); subscription and circulation numbers: "New Journal Targets Vital Public Role of Religion," *Washington Times,* June 22, 1990; *First Things* circulation data, published in *First Things* 9 (December 1990), *First Things* 37 (November 1993), and *First Things* 77 (November 1997).

16. Details about David Brooks' friend William Eddy taken from Neuhaus' correspondence with both men: RJN-PP, 1989 files. Details about Neuhaus' mentoring and counseling based on correspondence from throughout his 1980s, 1990s, and 2000s personal papers, and also based on interviews with some of those whom he counseled, including Nathaniel Peters, Father Erik Ross, Sister Amanda Shaw, Father Raymond de Souza, Sister Mary John de Souza, and Father Vincent Druding. As this list makes clear, Neuhaus was instrumental in helping many young people discern religious vocations.
17. Details based on Neuhaus correspondence with the Lutherans listed here: RJN-PP, 1989 and 1990 files; Braaten, *Because of Christ*, p. 130.
18. "The Underground Ecumenist," *Christian Century,* August 22, 1990.
19. Author interviews with Orlen Lapp (October 29, 2010) and Mildred Schwich (June 2, 2011).

CHAPTER NINETEEN. NEUHAUS BECOMES A CATHOLIC . . . NEUHAUS NAMED CATHOLIC OF THE YEAR

1. Neuhaus distributed this statement to friends and colleagues after September 8, and throughout that fall it was reprinted in several religious publications, including the *Pilot* (September 28, 1990), the *Tablet* (September 29, 1990), and *Crisis* magazine (October 1990). The statement was usually entitled "I Can Do No Other."
2. George Cardinal Pell, "Letter of Condolence," *First Things* 192 (April 2009), pp. 12–13; author interviews with Johanna Speckhard (August 6, 2012) and Mildred Schwich (June 2, 2011).
3. Details about Neuhaus' formal reception in the Church: "Citing Luther, a Noted Theologian Leaves Lutheran Church for Catholicism," *New York Times,* September 9, 1990 (which also quoted Wilken); "Lutheran Scholar Plans to Become Catholic Priest," *Washington Post,* September 8, 1990; an interview Neuhaus gave to *Origins* for a report that ran on September 20, 1990; a selection of notable Lutheran responses to the news: Herman Otten editorial entitled "Neuhaus Belongs with the Pope," *Christian News* (September 17, 1990); Paul Hinlicky, "Our Troubled Ministry," *Lutheran Forum* (December 1990); George Lindbeck's open letter to Neuhaus, *Lutheran Forum* (December 1990); Catholic responses, beyond reporting in various Catholic dailies and weekly newspapers: Ralph McInerney's editorial for *Crisis* magazine, "Richard's New House" (October 1990); *Catholic Twin Circle* magazine's

1991 "Catholic of the Year" award and profile (February 1991). Neuhaus advocated against a triumphalist Catholic reading of his conversion and for its theological and ecclesiological priority over the political and ideological in a September 13, 1990, interview with *Catholic New York*. Without mentioning Neuhaus by name, the liberal Catholic theologian Richard McBrien wrote a piece entitled "Why Would a Protestant Become a Catholic?" for the *Progress* that was critical of conversion decisions potentially based on politics and ideology (September 13, 1990). Neuhaus argued against various political and other rationales for his conversion in an interview for *30 Days* magazine, entitled "In Newman's Footsteps" (November 1990).

4. Weigel, *Witness to Hope*, pp. 619–622.
5. Richard John Neuhaus, "Just War and This War," *Wall Street Journal*, January 29, 1991.
6. George Higgins, column, *Catholic New York*, February 21, 1991. Neuhaus' letter to the editor appeared in the March 7, 1991 issue.
7. RJN-PP, 1991 files.
8. Richard John Neuhaus, "The Pope Affirms the 'New Capitalism,'" *Wall Street Journal*, May 2, 1991.
9. Neuhaus, Novak, and Weigel were provided with an advance copy of the encyclical from Rome, which Neuhaus obviously chose not to divulge in his sparring with the NCCB over the embargo question (author interview with Michael Novak, September 21, 2012, and author correspondence with George Weigel, July 23, 2013).
10. "A Convert's Quarrel," *New York Times*, May 18, 1991.
11. Higgins, "Letter to the Editor," *Wall Street Journal*, May 24, 1991.
12. Neuhaus, *Doing Well and Doing Good*, jacket copy; RJN-PP, 1992 files; Robert Sirico, "God and Mammon," *Wall Street Journal*, December 3, 1992; Paul Johnson, "Blessing Capitalism," *Commentary*, May 1993; Paul D. McNelis, book review, *America*, March 13, 1993; Rembert Weakland, "Pontifex Maximus Abridged," *Commonweal*, November 6, 1992; Neuhaus letter about Weakland, *Commonweal*, December 18, 1992.
13. Details of Neuhaus' ordination taken from "Cardinal O'Connor Ordains Ex-Lutheran Scholar as Catholic Priest," *Catholic News Service*, September 9, 1991. The Podhoretz quotation, unnamed, is from *Catholic Matters* (New York: Basic Books, 2006), p. 66, and was confirmed as "likely Norman" by George Weigel (author interview, November 10, 2013).
14. Author interviews with John Heinemeier (March 16, 2011) and Johanna Speckhard (August 6, 2012).
15. Relatedly, and for the rest of his life, despite his conversion and the increasingly Catholic demographic around him, Neuhaus would continue to lead evening prayer at 338 East 19th Street out of the Lutheran Book of Worship.

Details of Neuhaus' first Mass and his parish assignment are taken from Tracy Early, "Cardinal O'Connor Ordains Ex-Lutheran Scholar As Catholic Priest," *Catholic News Service*, September 9, 1991; and also from the Mass program: RJN-PP, 1991 files.

16. Richard John Neuhaus, *America Against Itself: Moral Vision and the Public Order* (South Bend, IN: University of Notre Dame Press, 1992); *Christianity Today* citation: "Press Pass: News and Reviews from University of Notre Dame Press," fall 1993; Neuhaus talks and publications during this period: RJN-PP, Publications List, 1991–1992.
17. Author interviews with Rocco Buttiglione (June 24, 2011) and George Weigel (June 3, 2013).

CHAPTER TWENTY. AS HE LAY DYING

1. The account of Neuhaus' 1993 illness is based on author interviews with Larry Bailey (September 29, 2011), Mildred Schwich (June 2, 2011), and George Weigel (June 3, 2013), and also on Neuhaus' own writing about the experience in *As I Lay Dying: Meditations upon Returning, on Facing Death and Living Again* (New York: Basic Books, 2002), pp. 79–128. This book began as an essay Neuhaus published in *First Things,* entitled "Born Toward Dying," *First Things* 100 (February 2000).
2. Neuhaus, *As I Lay Dying*, pp. v, 84–85.
3. Ibid., pp. 83, 108–110.
4. RJN-PP, Publications List, 1993; Neuhaus, *As I Lay Dying*, pp. 112–113.
5. "Role of Religion Stirs Passion, Fire at Pulpit," *Omaha World-Herald*, July 31, 1993.
6. Neuhaus' writing habits and office routine based on author interviews with James Nuechterlein (August 7, 2012) and Davida Goldman (September 30, 2011), and with other *First Things* staffers. His publications during this period are listed in RJN-PP, "Publications, 1993–1996."
7. Richard John Neuhaus, *First Things* 50 (February 1995), p. 70; Richard John Neuhaus, *First Things* 64 (May 1996), p. 12.
8. One indication of its relatively broad appeal during this period was its range of advertisers, which included the archconservative Catholic journal *New Oxford Review* and also *Forbes* magazine.
9. Vaclav Havel, "Forgetting We Are Not God," *First Things* 51 (March 1995); Robert Alter, "Retuning the Psalms," *First Things* 58 (December 1995); Bernard Lewis, "Islam Partially Perceived" and Jonathan Sacks, "To Be a Prophet for the People," *First Things* 59 (January 1996); Fish-Neuhaus exchange, *First Things* 60 (February 1996).

10. Author interview with James Nuechterlein (August 2, 2012); David Yeago, "The Catholic Luther," *First Things* 61 (March 1996); Richard John Neuhaus, "A Clarification on Capital Punishment," *First Things* 56 (October 1995).
11. At the same time, every few issues or so, *First Things* would publish letters from readers who were offended and upset at Neuhaus' caustic and condescending assessments of opponents. This is a representative example, from the October 1994 issue:

    The general tone of First Things *tends to be outrage that anyone would have the audacity to disagree with a position taken by the hierarchy of the Roman Catholic Church, supplemented by snide sarcasm and ad hominem arguments directed towards those who have such temerity. There are many problems faced by our society that will depend on the good will and combined efforts of religious individuals of somewhat differing opinions on many issues. To denigrate those who differ in some respects from your own positions without acknowledging their sincerity or even the possibility (incredible to you, I am sure) that they could occasionally be correct hurts all of our efforts. E. Thomas Dowd. Akron, OH.*
12. Richard John Neuhaus, "Hollywood Notwithstanding, Free Tibet," *First Things* 74 (June/July 1997), p. 71; Richard John Neuhaus, "Champions of a Lost Cause," *First Things* 41 (March 1994), p. 63; Richard John Neuhaus, "Those Neocons," *First Things* 55 (August/September 1995), p. 70; Richard John Neuhaus, "While We're At It," *First Things* 50 (February 1995), p. 69; Richard John Neuhaus, "Visiting the Intensive Care Unit," *First Things* 37 (November 1993), p. 48; Richard John Neuhaus, "The Creativity of Tina Brown," *First Things* (August/September 1995), p. 69; Richard John Neuhaus, "While We're At It," *First Things* 58 (December 1995), p. 76. Evidence of Neuhaus fan mail for these writings is found throughout his personal papers during this period: RJN-PP, 1993–1996 files.
13. Richard John Neuhaus, "Jews, Christians, and the 'Great Fear,'" *First Things* 46 (October 1994), p. 75. Sobran's writings about Neuhaus, quoted here and in the following paragraph, are taken from columns dating between November 1994 and June 1996: RJN-Media Clippings, 1994–1996.
14. This was a friendliness that became profoundly important in December 1995, when in Rome Neuhaus was invited to join George Weigel for a private dinner with John Paul II and his personal secretary, Stanislaw Dziwisz. Before this meeting, Weigel had raised the possibility with papal counselors of writing the pope's biography, an interest that emerged from Weigel's writings about the Church and John Paul II's role in the defeat of Communism. At the dinner itself, according to Weigel, Neuhaus made a pitch on his friend's behalf. John Paul changed the subject. Later on in the same meal, the pope turned to Neuhaus and asked him to encourage Weigel to write the book, which clearly wasn't necessary. And while Neuhaus, Weigel,

and Novak were criticized in American Catholic circles for presumptuously positioning themselves as John Paul II's primary U.S. interpreters and advocates, the pope's encouragement to Weigel to write his life story and promise to cooperate with him on it suggests that Neuhaus and Weigel and Novak weren't in fact as presumptuous as their critics alleged. (Author interview with George Weigel, June 3, 2013; also Weigel, *Witness to Hope,* pp. 14–15.)

15. "Neuhaus Watch," *Christian News,* November 27, 1995.
16. "Top Evangelicals Confer with Pope," *National Catholic Reporter,* November 13, 1995.
17. Author interview, via correspondence, with Charles Colson (August 31, 2011).
18. "Evangelicals and Catholics Together: The Christian Mission in the Third Millennium," *First Things* 43 (May 1994).
19. "Catholic and Evangelical: Seeking a Middle Ground," *New York Times,* March 30, 1994; author interview with Ralph Reed (August 1, 2011); Neuhaus' involvements with the "Road to Victory" Conventions: Richard John Neuhaus, "Against Christian Politics," *First Things* 53 (May 1996), p. 72; for a report of his specific remarks at the conventions: "Coalition Seeks Diversity 'to Create Nightmare' for Liberals," *Washington Times,* September 17, 1994; Timothy George on ECT: Timothy George, "Charles Colson's 'Ecumenism of the Trenches,'" *National Catholic Register,* April 25, 2012.

CHAPTER TWENTY-ONE. THE END OF DEMOCRACY? THE BEGINNINGS OF GREATER INFLUENCE

1. Richard John Neuhaus, "Introduction," *First Things* 57 (November 1996), reprinted in *The End of Democracy? The Judicial Usurpation of Politics: The Celebrated* First Things *Debate,* Mitchell S. Muncy, ed. (Dallas: Spence Publishing, 1997), pp. 3–10 (all references from this issue and responses published elsewhere, unless noted, are taken from this edition and cited by its pages); confirmation that Neuhaus was the sole author of the lead editorial for the November 1996 *First Things* issue: author interview with James Nuechterlein (August 7, 2012).
2. Details about May 1996 editorial meeting: author interview with James Nuechterlein (August 7, 2012).
3. Author interview with Peter Berger (November 17, 2010); Berger's comments, originally published in *Commentary* (February 1997), are quoted from Muncy, *End of Democracy?* pp. 69–74; Decter's letter of resignation was originally published in *First Things* 69 (January 1997) and is quoted from Muncy, *End of Democracy?* pp. 78–80; Himmelfarb and Berns' letters were also originally published in *First Things* 69 (January 1997).

4. Norman Podhoretz, "On the Future of Conservatism: A Symposium," *Commentary* (February 1997), quoted from Muncy, *End of Democracy?* pp. 98–103.
5. Podhoretz correspondence with Neuhaus: RJN-PP, 1996 files.
6. Norman Podhoretz et al., "On the Future of Conservatism," *Commentary* (February 1997); Joseph Sobran, "Distrust of Government Isn't 'Anti-American,'" *Conservative Chronicles* (November 20, 1996); William A. Rusher, "It's Time to Rein in the Courts," *Viewpoint* (December 1, 1996); Editorial, "It's Time to Take on the Judges," *Weekly Standard* (December 16, 1996); David Brooks, "The Right's Anti-American Temptation," *Weekly Standard* (November 11, 1996). All quoted from Muncy, *End of Democracy?* pp. 129–133.
7. The Editors, "First Things First," *National Review* (November 11, 1996); "The War of the Roses," *National Review* (December 31, 1996), quoted from Muncy, *End of Democracy?* pp. 127–128.
8. Jacob Heilbrunn, "Neocon v. Theocon," *New Republic,* December 30, 1996, quoted from Muncy, *End of Democracy?* pp. 143–154.
9. Frank Rich, "The War in the Wings," *New York Times,* October 9, 1996, and "The New New Left," *New York Times,* March 27, 1997; Neuhaus on Rich: "While We're At It" item, *First Things* 68 (December 1996), p. 53; Christopher Hitchens, "By the Right, Fall in for a Civil War," *Sunday Times,* December 29, 1996; Ambrose Evans-Pritchard, "The Rot Has Reached the Point Where Society Is Failing . . . ," *London Sunday Telegraph,* January 19, 1997; circulation data related to the November 1996 issue: Richard Vaughan/Publishing Management Associates, Inc., "Report on the Impact of the November 1996 issue," February 24, 1997.
10. Neuhaus correspondence with Gary Bauer: RJN-PP, 1996 files. Details about Ella Neuhaus' funeral and remarks at Valparaiso event: author interview with Johanna Speckhard (August 6, 2012). Neuhaus correspondence with Berger and Buckley: RJN-PP, 1996 files.
11. Richard John Neuhaus, "To Reclaim Our Democratic Heritage," *First Things* 69 (January 1997), quoted from Muncy, *End of Democracy?* pp. 114–123; confirmation that Neuhaus was the sole author of this editorial: author correspondence with James Nuechterlein (October 4, 2013).
12. Details about Neuhaus' private reactions to the "End of Democracy?" controversy: author interview with James Nuechterlein (August 2, 2012); Neuhaus on Nuechterlein: Richard John Neuhaus, "The Nuechterlein Factor," *First Things* 140 (February 2004), pp. 64–65.
13. Details about Neuhaus' 1997 experiences in Rome: Richard John Neuhaus, *Appointment in Rome: The Church Awakening in America* (New York: Crossroad Publishing, 1999), pp. xi–3; author interview with George Weigel (June 3, 2013).
14. Neuhaus, *Appointment in Rome,* pp. xiii, 16, 26, 64–65.
15. Ibid., pp. 123–126; details about Italian edition, Sales' reprimand, and

Neuhaus' response: RJN-PP, 1998 and 1999 files; details about Orlen Lapp's response to the book, and Neuhaus' responses: RJN-PP, 1999 files; author interview with Orlen Lapp (October 29, 2010).

16. Neuhaus' activities in Texas: RJN-PP, 1998 list of speaking of engagements; author correspondence with Karl Rove (April 7, 2011); information about the spring 1998 prayer breakfast silent protest and Neuhaus' role: "Clinton Faces Challenge at Annual Prayer Breakfast Today," *Washington Post* (September 11, 1998); Richard John Neuhaus, "Bill Clinton and the American Character," *First Things* 94 (June/July 1999).
17. RJN-PP, 1998 files. Bush used the "welcomed in life" phrase in his January 24, 2005, remarks to the annual March for Life rally in Washington, D.C., for instance, and again in April 2007, in a statement he made after the Supreme Court upheld the Partial-Birth Abortion Ban Act. "Bush Praises Anti-Abortion Rally," *New York Times,* January 25, 2005; "Justices Back Ban on Method of Abortion," *New York Times,* April 17, 2007. Meanwhile, in April 2004, addressing the National Right to Life Committee at a Washington event, Vice President Dick Cheney likewise used the phrase to signal the administration's commitments: "President Bush has often expressed his conviction that in a compassionate society, every child must be welcomed in life and protected in law. . . . America still has some distance to travel before that hope is realized." "Cheney Addresses Anti-Abortion Group," *New York Times,* April 21, 2004.
18. RJN-PP, 1998 files.

CHAPTER TWENTY-TWO. A TIME OF TRIUMPH, A TIME OF WAR, A TIME OF SCANDAL

1. Author interview with Mildred Schwich (June 2, 2011); Laurie Goodstein, "To Many Social Conservatives, An Ally," *New York Times,* August 8, 2000.
2. Andrew Sullivan, "Bush Woos Catholic Conservatives," *Sunday Times* (London), January 25, 2000; "Culture of Life" references in Bush's campaign noted (negatively) by Francis Kessling in a letter to the editor of *Roll Call,* November 6, 2000.
3. Andrew Sullivan, "Going Down Screaming," *New York Times Magazine,* October 11, 1998.
4. Richard John Neuhaus, *Death on a Friday Afternoon: Meditations on the Last Words of Jesus on the Cross* (New York: Basic Books, 2000), p. 19 (for the 1990s circumstances that led to the book, see p. xiv); Neuhaus' remembrance of O'Connor: "Always a Priest, Always Present," *First Things* 103 (May 2000), pp. 69–70; anecdote about Neuhaus' ardent devotion to O'Connor: author correspondence with James Nuechterlein (October 13, 2013).

5. Neuhaus, *Death on a Friday Afternoon*, pp. 2, 6.
6. Richard John Neuhaus, ed., *The Eternal Pity: Reflections on Dying* (Notre Dame, IN: University of Notre Dame Press, 2000). For a strong review of *Death on a Friday Afternoon*, see, for instance, Michael Potemra's admiring and thoughtful review, in *National Review* (March 20, 2000); for a similarly positive assessment of *Death on a Friday Afternoon* and *The Eternal Pity* together, see John Wilson's review in the *Weekly Standard* (July 31, 2000).
7. Details about Neuhaus at the October dinner for Buckley and viewing the debate afterward: RJN-PP, 1999 files; Neuhaus on the implications of the 2000 election: "The Two Politics of Election 2000," *First Things* 110 (February 2001), pp. 57–60.
8. Richard John Neuhaus, "The Two Politics of Election 2000."
9. "This changes everything" comment: author interview with Vincent Druding (October 25, 2011); details about Neuhaus' initial witness of the attacks: author interview with Nathaniel Peters (May 17, 2011); remaining details about Neuhaus' activities on September 11, 2011, and about the situation at *First Things:* author interview with Davida Goldman (June 8, 2012).
10. This positive reception had been the case throughout the early period of the Bush presidency. In February 2001, Neuhaus wrote to Wehner with a pleasing anecdote: Michael Novak told him that presidential advisor Karl Rove and the President himself had read *To Empower People* "so often and so carefully that the pages were falling out," a problem Neuhaus gladly corrected by arranging for fresh copies to reach the White House. In April 2001, he was again in happy correspondence, this time with chief Bush speechwriter Michael Gerson, offering praise for his work. In June 2001, Neuhaus wrote Bush directly, and with greater import, to advocate over his decision about federal funding for embryonic stem cell research. After recalling their 1998 breakfast meeting, in which Bush assured Neuhaus of the strength and quality of his pro-life commitments, Neuhaus called it a decision that would "define the relationship of your Administration and of the Republican Party to the Catholics of America or at least to the great majority of those who are observant Catholics—and to prolife Americans more generally." Thereafter, he issued a blunt warning to Bush, that even if "Catholics and prolife Americans have nowhere else to go in national politics" than the Republican Party, as Neuhaus knew some of Bush's counselors were suggesting, "if you endorse the taking of innocent human lives, these people, and I with them, will lose their enthusiasm for your Administration and the Party." Karl Rove wrote back on behalf of the President in early July, thanking Neuhaus for his "thoughtful letter to the President." A month later, Bush announced he would restrict federal funding for stem cell research to work done on preexisting lines. Sources: RJN-PP, 2001 files;

"President Discusses Stem Cell Research," White House Press Release, August 9, 2001.

11. RJN-PP, 2001 files.
12. Ibid; Richard John Neuhaus et al., "In a Time of War," *First Things* 118 (December 2001), p. 11–17.
13. Neuhaus et al., "In a Time of War."
14. "Stanley Hauerwas and the Editors on 'In a Time of War,'" *First Things* 120 (February 2002), pp. 11–15; author interview with Stanley Hauerwas (May 17, 2011).
15. In an all-but-coincidence, in the March 2002 edition of *First Things,* Neuhaus offered a robust defense of Father Marcial Maciel, the founder of the Legionaries of Christ, against allegations of sexual abuse, and then restated the points in the following issue, in first significantly addressing the developing situation in Boston. Richard John Neuhaus, "Feathers of Scandal," *First Things* 121 (March 2002), pp. 74–78; Richard John Neuhaus, "Scandal Time," *First Things* 122 (April 2002), pp. 61–64. Regarding Maciel: when the Congregation for the Doctrine of the Faith ordered him removed from public ministry to a life of prayer and penitence in May 2006, it became evident that Neuhaus' earlier, "morally certain" contention that Maciel was innocent of the charges was wrong. He acknowledged as much, if with far too much convoluted self-justification for his earlier claim and rhetorical qualifications about the CDF's decision, in "Person, Charism, and the Legionaries of Christ," *First Things* 165 (August/September 2006), pp. 71–73.
16. *Boston Globe* reporting of the clergy abuse scandal sourced from "*Boston Globe* Spotlight: Abuse in the Catholic Church" online compendium of reportage: http://www.boston.com/globe/spotlight/abuse/; Neuhaus' comments on the scandal: "Homosexuality and Abuse," *First Things* 123 (May 2002); and "Scandal Time (Continued)," *First Things* 124 (June 2002).
17. Neuhaus was usually qualified in his steady defense of invading Iraq. For instance, in the May 2003 issue of *First Things,* after affirming his complete agreement with John Paul II's hope for a peaceful resolution to the conflict—contingent upon Saddam Hussein's willingly subjecting his nation to weapons inspections and disarmament—he proceeded to emphasize that he believed "the war is just" and that "war, if it is just, is not an option chosen but a duty imposed." In closing, however, he allowed, "Whether it turns out to have been wise depends upon contingencies that are known to none but God." In the June/July 2003 issue, however, which appeared a few weeks after President Bush's now-hubristic "Mission Accomplished" speech, Neuhaus was too sanguine, declaring, "After the military success in Iraq, articles and news reports multiplied telling us that the real difficulties were just beginning," which was a lead-in to a snark about a wing-nut fundamentalist

Christian conference in Tampa Bay, devoted to biblical prophecy's connections to the war in Iraq. Privately, Neuhaus was more concerned about the war's outcomes than his published commentary might suggest. He was persuaded in this respect by conversations with an even more skeptical William F. Buckley, Jr., according to George Weigel, who was a far more confident supporter of the need for the invasion than either of them. In fact, in a rare instance of Weigel and Neuhaus not operating in full agreement, Neuhaus told him at one point, "You are much more out in front on this than I am." See Richard John Neuhaus, "The Sounds of Religion in a Time of War," *First Things* 133 (May 2003), pp. 76–82; Richard John Neuhaus, "While We're At It" item, *First Things* 134 (June/July 2003), p. 71; details about his private misgivings: author interview with George Weigel (June 3, 2013).

18. Neuhaus, *As I Lay Dying*; Neuhaus May 2002 interview with Brian Lamb, Booknotes, http://www.booknotes.org/Watch/169660-1/Richard+John+Neuhaus.aspx.
19. Details about Neuhaus' 2004 Oval Office meeting with Bush: RJN-PP, Publications List, 2004; author correspondence with George Weigel (October 12, 2013); details of Bush's April 2004 meeting with religious journalists: "Bush Calls for 'Culture of Change,'" *Christianity Today,* May 1, 2004.
20. Details of Neuhaus' various engagements in the latter months of 2004: RJN-PP, Publications List, 2004; Neuhaus on the 2004 election: "One Little Word," *First Things* 149 (January 2005), pp. 60–63; *First Things*' commemoration of the twentieth anniversary of *The Naked Public Square:* Stanley Hauerwas, Mary Ann Glendon et al., "The Naked Public Square Now," *First Things* 147 (November 2004), pp. 11–26.

CHAPTER TWENTY-THREE. "THE MOST INFLUENTIAL CLERGYMAN IN AMERICA," AKA THE "THEOCON-IN-CHIEF"

1. Neuhaus on the United States as a religious nation: quoted, for instance, by the *New York Times* when it interviewed him for its August 8, 2000, article on Lieberman's vice presidential selection; "The Twenty-Five Most Influential Evangelicals in America," *Time,* February 7, 2005; author interview with George W. Bush (via e-mail, April 7, 2011).
2. Clare Boothe Luce was indeed a great admirer of Neuhaus' work. The two of them corresponded warmly in the 1980s, and in addition to her admiration for *The Naked Public Square,* as Neuhaus notes above, she was also a keen reader of his monthly "Religion and Society Report," the precursor of his back page writings in *First Things*: RJN-PP, 1985 files.
3. Richard John Neuhaus, "While We're At It" items, *First Things* 152 (April 2005), pp. 60–62.

4. Neuhaus-Bottum correspondence: RJN-PP, 2005 files; details related to Linker's book proposal and interactions with Neuhaus during this period: author interviews with Damon Linker (September 29, 2011) and Erik Ross (April 28, 2011).
5. Author interviews with Damon Linker (September 29, 2011), James Nuechterlein (August 7, 2012), and Erik Ross (April 28, 2011).
6. Details of Neuhaus' April 2005 time in Rome: author interview with Raymond Arroyo (February 9, 2011); Richard John Neuhaus, "Rome Diary," *First Things* (June/July 2005), pp. 58–63 (selections) reprinted in Richard John Neuhaus, *Catholic Matters: Confusion, Controversy, and the Splendor of Truth* (New York: Basic Books, 2006), pp. 203–248 (complete).
7. Author interview with Rocco Buttiglione (June 24, 2011).
8. "New Worry as Pope Struggles," *Philadelphia Inquirer* (March 31, 2005); Arroyo-Neuhaus exchange quoted in Neuhaus, "Rome Diary."
9. Details of Neuhaus' activities during the conclave: author correspondence with George Weigel (November 5, 2013); Neuhaus, "Rome Diary."
10. Neuhaus, "Rome Diary"; Neuhaus on Benedict XVI: " 'Give Him a Chance,' Friends Say," *Toronto Star,* April 23, 2005.
11. Garry Wills, "Fringe Government," *New York Review of Books,* October 6, 2005.
12. Ibid.
13. "Why Bush Confides in a Catholic Priest," *Daily Telegraph,* October 29, 2005.
14. Neuhaus' December 2005 eulogy for his brother Fred: RJN-PP, Publications List, 2005; details about Neuhaus' relationship to family in later years: author interviews with Mildred Schwich (June 2, 2011), Johanna Speckhard (August 6, 2012), George Neuhaus (August 23, 2011), and Tom Neuhaus (August 31, 2011); the detail about RJN complaining about "chintzy drinks": Robert Susil, George Weigel's late son-in-law, personal anecdote shared with author (undated).
15. In fact, a few pages after Neuhaus remembered Coffin, he roughed up the president of the United Church of Christ, "for his attacks on conservative Christians, and on the Institute on Religion and Democracy in particular, who, he says, are trying to take over the [Mainline] Protestant denominations." Neuhaus drew attention to television commercials that showed "racial minorities, homosexuals, and handicapped people being rocketed out of church pews in conservative churches by the use of 'ejector seats.' " Neuhaus then observed, "This is in contrast, of course, to the very inclusive United Church of Christ which welcomes everybody. In the last four decades, United Church of Christ membership has declined from 2.2 million to 1.2 million. And that's without the use of ejector seats."
16. Neuhaus, "The Death of William Sloane Coffin, Jr.," *First Things* 164 (June/July 2006), pp. 58–61.

17. Reviewed respectfully by *National Review* and the *New York Times Book Review* alike, more out of respect for the author's standing than for the material itself, *Catholic Matters* is one of Neuhaus' weakest books. It's little more than a 2006 restatement of many now standard and familiar Neuhaus positions about the significance of the Church to a right-ordered democratic world and public culture, and about the importance of sustaining doctrinal orthodoxy within the Church to make that mission possible, positions that are flabbily elaborated and matched to subtler and more engaging autobiographical writings about his own migration to Catholicism. Much of the material—and all of the arguments—had already appeared in similar shape and form in *First Things*.
18. Damon Linker, "Without a Doubt," *New Republic,* April 3, 2006; Neuhaus blog notice (April 6, 2006): http://www.firstthings.com/onthesquare/2006/04/rjn-41106-mondays-and-tuesdays.
19. Charles Douthat correspondence about Ross Douthat: RJN-PP, 2000 files. Richard John Neuhaus, "While We're At It" items on Phillips, Wills, and Douthat, *First Things* 164 (June/July 2006), pp. 66–68.
20. Richard John Neuhaus, "While We're At It," *First Things* 164 (June/July 2006), 66–88; Damon Linker, *The Theocons: Secular America Under Siege* (New York: Doubleday, 2006), pp. 4, 5, 13–14.
21. Linker, *The Theocons,*, pp. 7, 20, 31.
22. Author interview with David Novak (March 2, 2011); Joshua Muravchik, Book Review, *Commentary,* November 2006; Eyal Press, "In God's Country," *Nation,* November 2, 2006; Wolfe and Phillips quotations appear on paperback edition of *The Theocons* (New York: Doubleday, 2007); Adrian Wooldridge, "Church as State," *New York Times Book Review* (September 24, 2006); Neuhaus' referring to *The Theocons, First Things* 179 (January 2008), p. 59; author interview with Erik Ross (April 28, 2011).
23. This came a few months after a *First Things* item in which Neuhaus described the "palpable uneasiness" among Ratzinger admirers, clearly including himself, with some of the early major appointments of his papacy. Neuhaus cited Archbishop Adam Levada's move from San Francisco to succeed Ratzinger at CDF, and the subsequent appointment of George Niederauer to take over in San Francisco. As far as Neuhaus was concerned, Levada wasn't especially strong or effective in defending Church teachings on homosexuality during his ten years in the "gay capital of the world," and his successor had a reputation in Salt Lake City for being "as it is said, gay-friendly" (Richard John Neuhaus, "The Truce of 2005?" *First Things* 160, February 2006, pp. 59–60). Neuhaus' comments suggested an unexpected fissure in the U.S.-Rome conservative bloc, and were reported widely at the time as such. Neuhaus made a point of addressing this in the June/July 2006 issue of *First Things.* He didn't retract his comment, reiterated his longtime personal admiration

for Ratzinger as a man of God and his respect for him as "Peter among us," and thought the media was making far too much of it: "There is nonsense, and then there is nonsense on stilts" (Richard John Neuhaus, "While We're At It" item, *First Things* 164, [June/July 2006], p. 65).

24. This was a portrayal instigated by Benedict's brief citation of a fourteenth-century Byzantine emperor's critical remarks about Islam, which, no matter how qualifiedly they were invoked, were ill-suited to the early twenty-first century's combustible world affairs.
25. Aleksandr Solzhenitsyn, "Miniatures 1996–1999," translated by Ignat and Stephen Solzhenitsyn, *First Things* 168 (December 2006), pp. 5–6; R. R. Reno, "The Return of the Fathers," *First Things* 167 (November 2006), p. 20; Richard John Neuhaus, "The Regensburg Address," *First Things* 167 (November 2006), pp. 63, 65.

CHAPTER TWENTY-FOUR. MEETING GOD AS AN AMERICAN

1. Neuhaus-Bellow correspondence: RJN-PP (1987 files). Richard John Neuhaus, *American Babylon: Notes of a Christian Exile* (New York: Basic Books, 2009), p. 55.
2. Columbia Mass details: Neuhaus PP, Publications List, 2007–2008; Boston details: author interview with Davida Goldman (June 8, 2012); Richard John Neuhaus, "While We're At It" item, *First Things* 172 (April 2007), p. 72.
3. Richard John Neuhaus, "While We're At It" item, *First Things* 176 (October 2007), p. 75; Richard John Neuhaus, "As Long As They Spell Our Names Right," *First Things* 177 (November 2007), p. 67; details about November 2007 *Economist* debate: author interview with Adrian Wooldridge (November 30, 2013); CBC Television's 2008 documentary on Neuhaus: http://www.youtube.com/watch?v=VFwMZKtHiaE.
4. Richard John Neuhaus, "Religion and Politics, 'The Great Separation,'" *First Things* 179 (January 2008), p. 59; Richard John Neuhaus, "While We're At It" item, *First Things* 175 (August/September 2007), pp. 74–75; Richard John Neuhaus, reply to Letter to the Editor, *First Things* 180 (February 2008), p. 9.
5. Richard John Neuhaus, "American Preeminence, for Better and Worse," *First Things* 180 (February 2008), p. 60.
6. Richard John Neuhaus, "William F. Buckley, Jr. and the Possibilities of Life," *First Things* 183 (May 2008), pp. 65–66.
7. Richard John Neuhaus, "Lives Lived Greatly," *First Things* 184 (June/July, 2008), p. 57; Dietrich Bonhoeffer, *The Cost of Discipleship,* translated by R. H. Fuller (German edition, 1937; 1959; New York: Touchstone, 1995), p. 89.
8. Details about the Wright controversy: Brian Ross, "Obama's Pastor: God Damn America, U.S. to Blame for 9/11," *ABC News* (March 13, 2008), http://

abcnews.go.com/Blotter/story?id=4443788; Richard John Neuhaus, "Lives Lived Greatly," *First Things* 184 (June/July 2008), p. 59.

9. Neuhaus' "Public Square" and "While We're At It" writings attested to a productivity and range that inspired his erstwhile critic Andrew Sullivan to credit him as "the original blogger," as Neuhaus noted elsewhere in this same piece, with mixed feelings about the seeming compliment.
10. Neuhaus, "Lives Lived Greatly," pp. 59–61.
11. Author interview with Jonathan Priest (September 30, 2011).
12. Details about Neuhaus' August 2008 time in Pembroke: Richard John Neuhaus, "Causes Beyond Left and Right," *First Things* 187 (November 2008), p. 66; author correspondence with George and Joan Weigel (December 6, 2013).
13. Author interview with Robert Benne (November 14, 2013); video of Neuhaus' Roanoke address available online at http://vimeo.com/60743164.
14. Author interviews with Amanda Shaw (May 9, 2011) and Nathaniel Peters (May 17, 2011); author correspondence with Matthew Rose (December 12, 2013); additional details provided by Nathaniel Peters' personal diary of Neuhaus' final months, shared with the author.
15. Details about Dulles' funeral: "For a Modest Cardinal, a Farewell Filled with Majesty," *New York Times,* December 18, 2008; details about Neuhaus' condition: author interview with Robert Wilken (June 4, 2013); author interview with Raymond de Souza (May 3, 2013).
16. Author interviews with Jody Bottum (May 25, 2011), Mildred Schwich (June 2, 2011), Amanda Shaw (May 9, 2011), Johanna Speckhard (August 6, 2012).
17. Richard John Neuhaus, "While We're At It" item, *First Things* 190 (February 2009), pp. 71–72.

Index